CAMBRIDGE CLASSICAL TEXTS AND
COMMENTARIES

EDITORS

C. O. BRINK   D. W. LUCAS   F. H. SANDBACH

5

CICERO'S LETTERS TO ATTICUS

VOLUME III

CICERO'S LETTERS TO ATTICUS

EDITED BY

D. R. SHACKLETON BAILEY

VOLUME III

51–50 B.C.

94–132 (BOOKS V–VII. 9)

CAMBRIDGE

AT THE UNIVERSITY PRESS

1968

Published by the Syndics of the Cambridge University Press
Bentley House, 200 Euston Road, London, N.W.1
American Branch: 32 East 57th Street, New York, N.Y. 10022

© Cambridge University Press 1968

Library of Congress Catalogue Card Number: 65-18929

Standard Book Number: 521 06927 0

Printed in Great Britain by
Alden & Mowbray Ltd
at the Alden Press, Oxford

FOREWORD

The publication of this and the succeeding volume completes the series, apart from an index volume still to come. For the letters contained in Books V–VIII of the traditional arrangement I have been able to use Professor W. S. Watt's Oxford Text published in 1965. Books IX and X formed part of my own Oxford Text, published in 1961, and the remarks in the Foreword to Vol. V of the present edition apply.

In the two volumes now appearing I owe a number of additions and corrections to the Commentary to my friend Professor Glen Bowersock of Harvard. Professor Sandbach and Mr Lucas have continued the help in proof correction acknowledged in the foreword to my first volume, and I have also to thank Mr James Diggle, Fellow of Queen's College, for similar help in these two volumes and in Vol. VI, already published. I should add that Professor Brink performed the same valuable office for Vol. V as for Vols. I and II, but that other preoccupations prevented him from rendering it thereafter.

Ceibwr   D. R. S. B.
March 1968

CONTENTS

Foreword   *page* v

Abbreviations   ix

TEXT AND TRANSLATION   I

COMMENTARY   187

Appendices

   I   CICERO'S ITINERARY IN 51,
          ATHENS–TARSUS   313

  II   CALIDIUS, NOT HIRRUS   314

Addenda to the Commentary   316

Concordance   319

Indices

   I   INDEX NOMINVM   320

  II   INDEX VERBORVM   324

 III   INDEX RERVM   326

Maps

     Greece and the Balkans   317

     Asia Minor   318

     Southern Italy   *at end of volume*

ABBREVIATIONS

The following may be noted:

Broughton = T. R. S. Broughton, *The Magistrates of the Roman Republic* (New York, 1951–60). References unless otherwise stated are to Vol. II.

Drumann–Groebe = K. W. Drumann and P. Groebe, *Geschichte Roms*. 2nd edition (Leipzig, 1899–1929).

K.-S. = R. Kühner and C. Stegmann, *Ausführliche Grammatik der lateinischen Sprache*: Satzlehre. 3rd edition (Leverkusen, 1955).

Lehmann, *de Cic. ad Att.* = C. A. Lehmann, *De Ciceronis ad Atticum epistulis recensendis et emendandis* (Berlin, 1892).

Lehmann, *Quaest.* = C. A. Lehmann, *Quaestiones Tullianae* (Prague and Leipzig, 1886).

L.-S.-J. = Liddell–Scott–Jones, *Greek–English Lexicon*, 9th edition.

Mommsen, *St.* = Th. Mommsen, *Römisches Staatsrecht*, 3rd edition (Leipzig, 1887–8).

Mommsen, *Str.* = Th. Mommsen, *Römisches Strafrecht* (Leipzig, 1899).

Otto, *Sprichwörter* = A. Otto, *Die Sprichwörter und sprichwörtlichen Redensarten der Römer* (Leipzig, 1890).

Propertiana = D. R. Shackleton Bailey, *Propertiana* (Cambridge, 1956).

RE. = Pauly–Wissowa, *Realencyklopädie*.

Schmidt, *Briefwechsel* = O. E. Schmidt, *Der Briefwechsel des M. Tullius Cicero von seinem Prokonsulat in Cilicien bis zu Caesars Ermordung* (Leipzig, 1893).

Sjögren, *Comm. Tull.* = H. Sjögren, *Commentationes Tullianae* (Uppsala, 1910).

Thes. = *Thesaurus Linguae Latinae.*

Towards a Text = D. R. Shackleton Bailey, *Towards a Text of Cicero, ad Atticum* (Cambridge, 1960).

T.-P. = R. Y. Tyrrell and L. C. Purser, *The Correspondence of Cicero*, third and second editions (Dublin, 1904–1933).

The Letters to Quintus and to M. Brutus are cited from W. S. Watt's Oxford Text, Asconius by line and page from that of A. C. Clark.

TEXT AND TRANSLATION

94–132 (BOOKS V–VII. 9)

51–50 B.C.

INDEX SIGLORVM

E = Ambrosianus E 14 inf. (saec. XIV).

G = Parisinus 'Nouv. Fonds' 16248 (saec. XIV-XV).

H = Landianus 8 (saec. XIV-XV).

N = Laurentianus (ex Conv. Suppr.) 49 (saec. XIV-XV).

V = Palatinus Lat. 1510 (saec. XV).

O = Taurinensis Lat. 495 (saec. XV).

R = Parisinus Lat. 8538 (anno 1419 scriptus).

P = Parisinus Lat. 8536 (saec. XV).

Ant. = Antonianus a Malaespina citatus.

F = Faërni codex a Malaespina vel Vrsino citatus.

codd. Mal. = Malaespinae codices ab ipso generatim citati.

Σ = consensus codicis E cum codicibus GH (vel H deficiente G) NV (vel O deficiente V) R aut omnibus aut eis qui quoquo loco praesto sunt.

M = Mediceus 49. 18 (anno 1393 scriptus).

b = Berolinensis (ex bibl. Hamiltoniana) 168 (saec. XV).

d = Laurentianus (ex. bibl. aedilium) 217 (saec. XV).

m = Berolinensis (ex bibl. Hamiltoniana) 166 (anno 1408 scriptus).

s = Vrbinas 322 (saec. XV).

δ = consensus codicum *bdms*.

Δ = consensus codicis M cum codicibus *bdms* aut omnibus aut tribus.

Ω = consensus codicum Σ (quotquot praesto sunt) et M = archetypum omnium quos supra nominavi codicum.

C = lectiones margini editionis Cratandrinae (an. 1528) adscriptae.

c = lectiones in textu eiusdem editionis primum prolatae.

Z = Tornesianus (de Z^l, $Z^{(l)}$, Z^b, $Z^{(b)}$, Z^β, $Z^{(\beta)}$ vide tom. I, p. 93).

λ = lectiones in margine alterius editionis Lambinianae (an. 1572–3) veteri codici (v.c.) adtributae.

Lamb. (marg.) = lectiones ibidem quibus littera 'L.' praefixa est.

ς = lectiones ex codicibus deterioribus, ut videntur, hic illic citatae vel in editionibus ante Cratandrinam primum inventae.

M^2, O^2, etc. = codicum M, O, etc. secundae manus.

3

94 (V. 1)

Scr. Minturnis iii aut prid. Non. Mai. an. 51

CICERO ATTICO SAL.

1 Ego vero et tuum in discessu vidi animum et meo sum ipse
testis; quo magis erit tibi videndum ne quid novi decernatur,
ut hoc nostrum desiderium ne plus sit annuum.

2 De Annio Saturnino, curasti probe. de satis dando vero, te
rogo, quoad eris Romae, tu ut satis des; et sunt aliquot
satisdationes secundum mancipium, veluti Mennianorum
praediorum vel Atilianorum. de Oppio, factum est ⟨ut⟩
volui, et maxime quo⟨d de⟩ $\overline{DCCC}$ aperuisti; quae quidem 5
ego utique vel versura facta solvi volo, ne extrema exactio
nostrorum nominum exspectetur.

3 Nunc venio ad transversum illum extremae epistulae tuae
versiculum in quo me admones de sorore. quae res se sic
habet: ut veni in Arpinas, cum ad me frater venisset, in primis
nobis sermo isque multus de te fuit; ex quo ego veni ad ea
quae fueramus ego et tu inter nos de sorore in Tusculano 5
locuti. nihil tam vidi mite, nihil tam placatum quam tum
meus frater erat in sororem tuam, ut, etiam si qua fuerat ex
ratione sumpta offensio, non appareret. ille sic dies. postridie
ex Arpinati profecti sumus. ut in Arcano Quintus maneret
dies fecit; ego Aquini, sed prandimus in Arcano (nosti hunc 10
fundum). quo ut venimus, humanissime Quintus 'Pomponia'
inquit, 'tu invita mulieres, ego vero adscivero pueros'. nihil
potuit, mihi quidem ut visum est, dulcius, idque cum verbis
tum etiam animo ac vultu. at illa audientibus nobis 'ego ipsa
sum' inquit 'hic hospita'; id autem ex eo, ut opinor, quod 15

Ep. 94] 2, 3 veluti *s*: vel his tu Ω 4 (h)atilianorum *P*Δ: atti- *NVRm* ut *s*:
om. Ω 5 quod de *Tyrrell*: quod *s*: quo Ω $\overline{DCCC}$ *Boot*: dccc Ω 7 nominum
NVRC: omnium Δ **3,** 8 sumpta *V*Δ: -tus *ENOPC*: -tum *R*: supradicta *G*
ille Ω (*praeter GH*) *C*: illo *GHbd* dies *EVRC*: die *GN*Δ 12 accivero *ς*

94 (V. I)

Minturnae, 5 or 6 May, 50

CICERO TO ATTICUS

1 Yes indeed, I saw your feelings when we said good-bye and can testify to my own. All the more reason for you to see to it that they don't pass some new decree, so that we may not have to do without one another for more than one year.

2 With regard to Annius Saturninus, I approve of what you have done. But about guarantees, may I ask you to give them yourself as long as you are in Rome? And there are some guarantees in respect of sale, e.g. for the Mennius and Atilius properties. As for Oppius, the steps taken are what I wished, especially in that you have explained about the 800,000. I particularly want this paid, by borrowing if necessary so as not to have to wait for the last penny to come in from my debtors.

3 I come now to the line in the margin at the end of your letter in which you remind me about your sister. This is how the matter stands. When I got to Arpinum, my brother came over and we talked first and foremost about you, at considerable length. From that I passed to what you and I had said between us at Tusculum anent your sister. I have never seen anything more gentle and pacific than my brother's attitude towards her as I found it. Even if he had taken offence for any reason, there was no sign of it. So much for that day. Next morning we left Arpinum. On account of the holiday Quintus had to stay the night at Arcanum. I stayed at Aquinum, but we lunched at Arcanum—you know the farm. When we arrived there Quintus said in the kindest way 'Pomponia, will you ask the women in, and I'll get the boys?' Both what he said and his intention and manner were perfectly pleasant, at least it seemed so to me. Pomponia however answered in our hearing 'I am a guest myself here'. That, I imagine, was because Statius had

antecesserat Statius ut prandium nobis videret. tum Quintus
4 'en' inquit mihi, 'haec ego patior cottidie'. dices 'quid, quaeso,
istuc erat?' magnum; itaque me ipsum commoverat; sic
absurde et aspere verbis vultuque responderat. dissimulavi
dolens. discubuimus omnes praeter illam, cui tamen Quintus
de mensa misit; illa reiecit. quid multa? nihil meo fratre lenius, 5
nihil asperius tua sorore mihi visum est; et multa praetereo
quae tum mihi maiori stomacho quam ipsi Quinto fuerunt.
ego inde Aquinum. Quintus in Arcano remansit et Aquinum
ad me postridie mane venit mihique narravit nec secum illam
dormire voluisse et cum discessura esset fuisse eius modi 10
qualem ego vidissem. quid quaeris? vel ipsi hoc dicas licet,
humanitatem ei meo iudicio illo die defuisse. haec ad te scripsi,
fortasse pluribus quam necesse fuit, ut videres tuas quoque
esse partis instituendi et monendi.

5   Reliquum est ut ante quam proficiscare mandata nostra
exhaurias, scribas ad me omnia, Pomptinum extrudas, cum
profectus eris cures ut sciam, sic habeas, nihil mehercule te
mihi nec carius esse nec suavius.

A. Torquatum amantissime dimisi Minturnis, optimum 5
virum; cui me ad te scripsisse aliquid in sermone significes
velim.

95 (V. 2)

Scr. in Pompeiano vi Id. Mai. an. 51 (§1)

CICERO ATTICO SAL.

1 A. d. vi Id. Mai., cum has dabam litteras, ex Pompeiano
proficiscebar, ut eo die manerem in Trebulano apud Pontium;
deinde cogitabam sine ulla mora iusta itinera facere. in

4, 1 quaeso *Manutius*: quasi Ω   10 et *EVR*: *om. GN*Δ   12 ei *ERs*: et *GNV*Δ
5, 3 sic *P*: si Ω   6 scripsisse de se *Lambinus*
Ep. 95] 1, 1 ex *G*: et *NVR*Δ: e *bs*

gone ahead of us to see to our luncheon. Quintus said to me
'There! This is the sort of thing I have to put up with every
4 day'. You'll say 'What was there in that, pray?' A good deal.
I myself was quite shocked. Her words and manner were so
gratuitously rude. I concealed my feelings, painful as they were,
and we all took our places at table except the lady. Quintus
however had some food sent to her, which she refused. In a
word, I felt my brother could not have been more forbearing
nor your sister ruder. And I have left out a number of things
that annoyed me at the time more than they did Quintus. I then
left for Aquinum, while Quintus stayed behind at Arcanum
and came over to see me at Aquinum early the following day.
He told me that Pomponia had refused to spend the night with
him and that her attitude when she said good-bye was just as
I had seen it. Well, you may tell her to her face that in my
judgement her manners that day left something to be desired.
I have told you about this, perhaps at greater length than was
necessary, to show you that lessons and advice are called for
from your side as well as from mine.

5   For the rest, make sure you execute all my commissions
before you leave Rome, and write to me about everything, and
get behind Pomptinus, and when you have left let me know,
and don't ever doubt how much I love and like you.

I parted very amicably from A. Torquatus at Minturnae, an
excellent person. You might intimate to him in conversation
that I have written something to you.

95 (V. 2)
Pompeii, 10 May 51
CICERO TO ATTICUS

1 I am dispatching this letter on 10 May, just before leaving
Pompeii for the Trebula country, where I am to stay the night
with Pontius. After that I propose to travel by full normal

Cumano cum essem, venit ad me, quod mihi pergratum fuit,
noster Hortensius; cui deposcenti mea mandata cetera universe 5
mandavi, illud proprie, ne pateretur, quantum esset in ipso,
prorogari nobis provinciam; in quo eum tu velim confirmes
gratumque mihi fecisse dicas quod et venerit ad me et hoc
mihi praetereaque si quid opus esset promiserit. confirmavi
ad eam causam etiam Furnium nostrum, quem ad annum 10
tribunum pl. videbam fore.

2   Habuimus in Cumano quasi pusillam Romam; tanta erat
in iis locis multitudo; cum interim Rufio noster, quod se a
Vestorio observari videbat, στρατηγήματι hominem per-
cussit; nam ad me non accessit. 'itane? cum Hortensius veniret
et infirmus et tam longe et Hortensius, cum maxima praeterea 5
multitudo, ille non venit?' non, inquam. 'non vidisti igitur
hominem?' inquies. qui potui non videre cum per emporium
Puteolanorum iter facerem? in quo illum agentem aliquid
credo salutavi, post etiam iussi valere cum me exiens e sua
villa num quid vellem rogasset. hunc hominem parum gratum 10
quisquam putet, aut non in eo ipso laudandum, quod laudari
non laborarit?

3   Sed redeo ad illud. noli putare mihi aliam consolationem
esse huius ingentis molestiae nisi quod spero non longiorem
annua fore. hoc me ita velle multi non credunt ex consuetudine aliorum: tu, qui scis, omnem diligentiam adhibebis,
tum scilicet cum id agi debebit, cum ex Epiro redieris.   5

De re publica scribas ad me velim si quid erit quod op⟨us

---

6 mandavi ς: -asti ΩC   proprie *Manutius*: -pe Ω   7 provinciam *Pius*: -as Ω
10 Furnium *c*: tur- Ω   **2**, 2 me *Tyrrell–Purser*   3 videbat *M corr.*: -tur Ω
στρατηγήματι *Tyrrell–Purser* (strategemate *Victorius*): stragem alto Ω   5 et tam λ:
etiam Ω   et (*post* longe) *NVR*λ: *om.* Δ   6 venit *Vs*: lenit *vel* levit *NOR*Δ
9 post etiam *Manutius*: postea iam Ω   exiens e *Manutius*: expense Ω*Z*ᵇ
11 laudari *NVRC*: audiri Δ   **3**, 1 noli *V* (*silet O*): -im *GR*Δ: nolo *N*   6 opus
sit scire *Watt*: opere *GVR*: operare *N*Δ: odorere *Vrsinus*

stages without any delays. While I was at Cumae I was very much pleased to receive a visit from our friend Hortensius. When he asked if I had any commissions, I replied in general terms except on one point: I particularly requested him, so far as in him lay, not to let my term of office be extended. I should be grateful if you would drive this home, and tell him how much I appreciate his coming to see me and promising this and any other service that may be called for. I have confirmed our friend Furnius in the same cause; he is clearly going to be Tribune in a year's time.

2   My place at Cumae was a Rome in miniature—so many people about down here. Among them was our little Rufus, who, finding himself under observation by Vestorius, foiled him by a ruse—he came nowhere near or by me. Odd, you may think. Hortensius called—a sick man, such a long way, and Hortensius to boot—and a great multitude besides, but not Rufus? Not Rufus. Didn't I see him then? How could I help seeing him when I walked through Puteoli bazaar? I said good morning to him there (he had some business on hand no doubt), and on a later occasion good-bye—as he was coming out of his villa he took his leave of me. Who could accuse *him* of failing in gratitude? Or rather, mustn't we commend him for his indifference to such commendations?

3   But I come back to this: you must believe that my one consolation in this colossal bore is that I expect it will only last a year. Many people don't believe I am sincere about this, judging me by others. But you, who know, must spare no pains, I mean naturally when the time for action comes, after you get back from Epirus.

I should be grateful if you would write to me about the

sit sc⟩ire. nondum enim satis huc erat adlatum quo modo
Caesar ferret de auctoritate perscripta, eratque rumor de
Transpadanis, eos iussos IIII viros creare; quod si ita est,
magnos motus timeo. sed aliquid ex Pompeio sciam.   10

96 (v. 3)

Scr. in Trebulano Ponti v Id. Mai. an. 51 (§3)

CICERO ATTICO SAL.

1 A. d. v⟨I⟩ Id. Mai. veni in Trebulanum ad Pontium; ibi mihi
tuae litterae binae redditae sunt tertio abs te die. eodem
autem exiens e Pompeiano Philotimo dederam ad te litteras; nec
vero nunc erat sane quid scriberem. qui de re publica rumores
scribe, quaeso; in oppidis enim summum video timorem, sed 5
multa inania. quid de his ✳ ✳ ✳ cogites et quando scire velim.
2 Ad quas litteras tibi rescribi velis nescio. nullas enim adhuc
acceperam praeter quae mihi binae simul in Trebulano redditae sunt; quarum alterae edictum †publi mihi† habebant
(erant autem Non. Mai. datae), alterae rescriptae ad meas
Minturnensis. quam vereor ne quid fuerit σπουδαιότερον in 5
iis quas non accepi quibus rescribi vis!
3 ⟨Apud⟩ Lentulum ponam te in gratia. Dionysius nobis cordi
est. Nicanor tuus operam mihi dat egregiam. iam deest quid
scribam et lucet. Beneventi cogitabam hodie esse. nostra
continentia et diligentia satis faciemus. a Pontio ex Trebulano
a. d. v Id. Mai.   5

---

7 quo *VR*: quoquo *GNΔ*   8 perscripta *VP*: pr(a)es- *GNRΔ*   9 IIII *Victorius*: illi
GMms: illi(u)s *Pbd*: il *VR*
Ep. 96] 1, 1 VI *Victorius*: v *Ω*   3 exiens e *'libri manuscr.' ap. Lambinum*: expense
Ω   4 quod *F*   6 *post* his *aliquid excidisse mihi videtur, velut* existimes et de
itinere quid   2, 2 simul *ς*: semel *Ω*   3 publi(i) mihi *GNVR*: publili mihi
vel sim. Δ: P. Licinii *ς*   4 alter(a)e *NVR*: -ra *GΔ*   rescript(a)e *VP*: -ta *N*: -tas
GRΔ   5 quam *ς*: qu(a)e *Ω*   fuerit *VP*: -rat *GORΔ*   3, 1 apud *add. Victorius*
Lentulum] *anne* Laenium?   gratia *Ernesti*: -am *Ω*   2 egregiam *ς*: e grecia *Ω*
quod *Malaespina*   3 hodie *Manutius*: hoc de *Ω*   esse *hoc loco Watt*: ante satis
ΩZ⁽ᵇ⁾λ: *del. Manutius*   4 faciemus *NVR*: -mus satis *GΔZ⁽ᵇ⁾λ*   Pontio *ς*: ponto *Ω*

political situation if there is anything I ought to know. Not enough has so far reached us here about how Caesar is taking the recorded Opinion; and there is a rumour about the Transpadanes, that they have been told to set up Boards of Four. If that is true I fear grave trouble. However I shall learn something from Pompey.

96 (v. 3)
Near Trebula, 11 May 51
CICERO TO ATTICUS

1 On 10 May I arrived at Pontius' place near Trebula. There I got two letters from you the third day after dispatch. I gave Philotimus a letter for you as I left Pompeii for this destination, and now I have nothing really to write about. Pray tell me what political rumours are afloat; I find intense anxiety in the towns, but there is a lot of empty chatter. I'd like to know what you think about all this, and what you propose about your trip, and when.

2 I don't know which letter you want me to answer. I have not received any up to date except the two which were delivered to me here together, one of them containing P. Licinius' (?) edict (it was dispatched the Nones of May), the other in reply to mine from Minturnae. I am greatly concerned in case there was something of importance in the one I didn't get and to which you want an answer.

3 I shall put you in Lentulus' good books. Dionysius is a man after my own heart. Your Nicanor is a great help to me. Now I have nothing more to say and it is getting light. I mean to get to Beneventum today. I shall be disinterested and conscientious enough to satisfy expectations. From Pontius' house near Trebula, 11 May.

97 (v. 4)

Scr. Beneventi iv Id. Mai. an. 51

CICERO ATTICO SAL.

1 Beneventum veni a. d. v Id. Mai. ibi accepi eas litteras quas
tu superioribus litteris significaveras te dedisse, ad quas ego
eo ipso die dederam ex Trebulano ⟨a⟩ L. Pontio. ac binas
quidem tuas Beneventi accepi, quarum alteras Funisulanus
multo mane mihi dedit, alteras scriba Tullius. gratissima est 5
mihi tua cura de illo meo primo et maximo mandato; sed tua
profectio spem meam debilitat. ac †me ille illud quod labat†,
non quo—, sed inopia cogimur eo contenti esse. de illo altero
quem scribis tibi visum esse non alienum, vereor adduci ut
nostra possit, et tu ⟨a⟩is δυσδιάγνωστον esse. equidem sum 10
facilis, sed tu aberis et me absente res †habebis mirationem†.
nam posset aliquid, si utervis nostrum adesset, agente Servilia
Servio fieri probabile. nunc, si iam res placeat, agendi tamen
viam non video.

2 Nunc venio ad eam epistulam quam accepi a Tullio. de
Marcello fecisti diligenter. igitur senatus consultum si erit
factum, scribes ad me; si minus, rem tamen conficies. mihi
enim attribui oportebit, item Bibulo. sed non dubito quin
senatus consultum expeditum sit, in quo praesertim sit com- 5
pendium populi. de Torquato, probe. de Masone et Ligure,
cum venerint. de illo quod Chaerippus (quoniam hic quoque
πρόσνευσιν sustulisti), o provincia! etiamne hic mihi curandus est? curandus autem hactenus, ne quid ad senatum,

---

Ep. 97] **1**, 3 eo ipso ς: ipse eo *HNOR*: eo *G* (*om.* ego): ipse *V*: ipso *c*: ipso eo ς
a *add. Pius* (*pro* L. *Manutius*)　7 me ille illud *VRMmZ^b*: me illud *Nbds*: de illo:
illuc *Kayser*　quod labat *NVRZ^b*: quidem l- *bds*: *om. Mm*: quidem labor
Kayser　10 tu ais *Turnebus*: tuis Ω　esset quidem *Z^b*　11 habebit admirationem *Vs*　12 Servilia *Tunstall*: -lio Ω　14 viam ς: aliam Ω　**2**, 1 eam
GNVRc: illam Δ　4 Bibulo ς: -li Ω　6 probo *N*　9 *fort.* ne si quid

97 (V. 4)

Beneventum, 12 May 51

CICERO TO ATTICUS

1   I arrived at Beneventum on 11 May and there received the letter
to which you referred in your earlier letter as having been
dispatched—I replied to the latter on the same day, writing
from Pontius' place near Trebula. Indeed I have received two
letters from you at Beneventum, one brought by Funisulanus
very early in the morning, the other by Secretary Tullius. I am
most grateful for the trouble you are taking about my first and
most important commission; but your departure weakens my
hope of success. About my little girl (?), I am inclining that
way (?), not that—but *faute de mieux* we must make the best of
him. As for the other man, whom you say you think not
unsuitable, I doubt whether my girl could be brought to
consent, and you say there's not much to choose. For my part
I have no wish to be awkward, but you will be away and in my
absence the thing will ＊＊＊. If both of us were on the spot
something acceptable might be made of Servius through
Servilia. As it is, even if I were to approve in principle, I see
no way of going to work.

2   I now come to the letter I got from Tullius. Thank you for
your efforts in connexion with Marcellus. If then a decree is
passed, you'll let me know; if not, you'll get the thing through
all the same, as I shall be entitled to a payment from the
Treasury, Bibulus also. But I am sure the decree presents no
difficulty, particularly as it means a saving to the public. Thank
you about Torquatus. We'll see about Maso and Ligus when
they arrive. As for Chaerippus' request—since here too you
have put 'inclination' out of court—, oh, who would be a
governor? Must I really look after *him*? I suppose so, to the
extent of making sure that nothing comes up before the

'consule!' aut 'numera!' nam de ceteris—sed tamen commode, 10
quod cum Scrofa. de Pomptino recte scribis; est enim ita
ut, si ante Kal. Iun. Brundisi futurus sit, minus urgendi
3 fuerint M. Anneius et Tullius. quae de Sicinio audisti etiam
mihi probantur, modo ne illa exceptio in aliquem incurrat
bene de nobis meritum; sed considerabimus, rem enim probo.
de nostro itinere cum statuero, de quinque praefectis quid
Pompeius facturus sit cum ex ipso cognoro, faciam ut scias. 5
de Oppio, bene curasti quod ei de D̅C̅C̅C̅ exposuisti, idque,
quoniam Philotimum habes, perfice et cognosce rationem et,
ut ⟨ne tecum⟩ agam amplius, si me amas, prius quam profi-
ciscaris effice; magna me cura levaris.

4   Habes ad omnia. etsi paene praeterii chartam tibi deesse.
mea captio est, si quidem eius inopia minus multa ad me
scribis. tu vero aufer CC; etsi meam in eo parsimoniam huius
paginae contractio significat. dum ⟨ades et⟩ acta et rumores,
vel etiam si qua certa habes, de Caesare exspecto; litteras et 5
aliis ⟨et⟩ Pomptino de omnibus rebus diligenter dabis.

98 (v. 5)
Scr. Venusiae Id. Mai. an. 51 (§1)

CICERO ATTICO SAL.

1 Plane nil est quod scribam; nam nec quid mandem habeo
(nihil enim praetermissum est) nec quid narrem (novi enim
nihil est) nec iocandi locus est; ita me multa sollicitant.

---

11 Pomptino *Victorius*: -nio λ: pompeiano Ωι   3 Anneius *Manutius*: annius Ω   L.
Tullius *Boot*   **3,** 1 etiam *Watt*: em *M*: enim *VR*: ea *G*: et *Nδ*   4 cum *Wesenberg*:
quod Ω   8 ut ne tecum agam *scripsi*: ne angar *Pius*: ut ne angar *Malaespina*
4, 3 CC *Sjögren*: ducentos Ω: -tas *Wesenberg*   4 ades et *addidi* (ades *pro* acta et
Sternkopf)   5 vel etiam *Stinner*: vellet iam Ω   6 aliis et *Boot*: aliis *GNORM*:
alias *Vδ*   diligenter *GNbds*: -tes *VRMm*: -tis λ
Ep. 98] **1,** 1 nil est *Edms*: nihil est *Rb*: id est *GM*: adest *N*: est *V*: deest *Victorius*
nec quod *Ernesti*   2 ne(c) quid Ω: nec quod *Ernesti*   3 nihil est *EVR*: mi(c)hi
est *GN*: mihi Δ

Senate(?)—'Divide' or 'Count'. As for the rest—but I'm glad you had a word with Scrofa. You are right about Pomptinus. The position is that if he is going to be at Brundisium before the Kalends of June M. Anneius and Tullius won't need to
3 be hurried so much. What you heard from Sicinius has my approval also, provided that the proposed saving clause does not impinge upon anyone to whom I owe a good turn. But I'll think it over, for in principle I agree. I'll let you know about my itinerary when I have decided it, and about what Pompey is going to do over the five Prefects when I learn it from himself. About Oppius, you did well to explain to him with regard to the 800,000; and as you have Philotimus with you, please get it done and examine the account and, not to go on urging you, just get it settled before you leave like a good fellow. It will be a great load off my mind.

4   Well, I have answered all your points—no I almost forgot, there's your shortage of paper. That's my funeral, if it means that you write less to me for lack of it. Do take a couple of hundred sheets, though my own parsimony in the matter will be evident from the way I have cramped this page. While you are on the spot I expect both the official news and the rumours, or reliable information if you have any, about Caesar. Mind you send fully discursive letters by Pomptinus among others.

98 (V. 5)
Venusia, 15 May 51
CICERO TO ATTICUS

1 I have really nothing to write about—no commissions for you since nothing has been overlooked, no news to tell since there is none; and jokes are not in season, there are too many things

tantum tamen scito, Id. Mai. nos Venusia mane proficiscentis
has dedisse. eo autem die credo aliquid actum in senatu; 5
sequantur igitur nos tuae litterae quibus non modo res omnis
sed etiam rumores cognoscamus. eas accipiemus Brundisi;
ibi enim Pomptinum ad eam diem quam tu scripsisti exspectare consilium est.

2   Nos Tarenti quos cum Pompeio διαλόγους de re publica
habuerimus ad te perscribemus; etsi id ipsum scire cupio,
quod ad tempus recte ad te scribere possim, id est quam diu
Romae futurus sis, ut aut quo dem posthac litteras sciam aut
ne dem frustra. sed ante quam proficiscare, utique explicatum 5
sit illud HS $\overline{\text{xx}}$ et $\overline{\text{DCCC}}$; hoc velim in maximis rebus et
maxime necessariis habeas, ut quod auctore te velle coepi
adiutore adsequar.

99 (v. 6)

Scr. Tarenti xiv Kal. Iun., ut vid., an. 51

CICERO ATTICO SAL.

1 Tarentum veni a. d. xv Kal. Iun. quod Pomptinum statueram
exspectare, commodissimum duxi dies eos quoad ille veniret
cum Pompeio consumere, eoque magis quod ei gratum esse
id videbam, qui etiam a me petierit ut secum et apud se essem
cottidie. quod concessi libenter; multos enim eius praeclaros 5
de re publica sermones accipiam, instruar etiam consiliis
idoneis ad hoc nostrum negotium.

2   Sed ad te brevior iam in scribendo incipio fieri dubitans
Romaene sis an iam profectus; quod tamen quoad ignorabo,

---

4 venusia *EG*: -am *NVRΔ*   mane *om. E*   **2**, 3 possim *EVR*: -sem *GNΔ*
4 quo dem *Manutius*: cui dem *C*: quod est Ω   posthac *Victorius*: post has Ω
6 illud de *Ernesti*
Ep. 99] **1**, 2 duxi Σ*s*: duxi ex(s)pectare Δ   dies eos *GNRΔ*: eos dies *EV*   4 qui
Victorius: quin Ω

on my mind. However I can tell you this much, that the letter
you are reading was dispatched on the Ides of May from
Venusia early in the morning as I left. I imagine that something
will be done in the Senate today, so I hope to be followed by a
letter from you to tell me not only all the happenings but the
rumours too. I shall receive it at Brundisium, where it is my
plan to wait for Pomptinus up to the day you named.

2   At Tarentum I shall write you a full account of my Dia-
logues on the Republic with Pompey—though on this very
point I am anxious to know up till when it will be all right for
me to write to you, i.e. how long you are going to be in Rome,
so that I either know where to send letters in future or else don't
send them to no purpose. But before you leave do without fail
get that matter of the 20,000 and the 800,000 straightened out.
I should be grateful if you would look on it as something really
important and urgent, so that what I came to want with your
prompting I may achieve with your assistance.

99 (v. 6)

Tarentum, 19 May (?) 51

CICERO TO ATTICUS

1   I got to Tarentum on 18 May. Having decided to wait for
Pomptinus I think it best to spend the days before his arrival
with Pompey, especially as I see he would like it. Indeed he
has asked me to spend every day with him at his house. I agreed
willingly, for I shall have much fine discourse from him on
public affairs and at the same time get some useful advice on
this business of my own.

2   But I am now getting more laconic in my letters to you,
being uncertain whether you are in Rome or already gone.
However as long as my ignorance on that point continues I

scribam aliquid potius quam committam ut tibi cum possint
reddi a me litterae non reddantur. nec tamen iam habeo
quid aut mandem tibi aut narrem. mandavi omnia; quae 5
quidem tu, ut polliceris, exhauries. narrabo cum aliquid
habebo novi. illud tamen non desinam, dum adesse putabo,
de Caesaris nomine rogare ut confectum relinquas. avide
exspecto tuas litteras, et maxime ut norim tempus profectionis
tuae.   10

100 (v. 7)

Scr. Tarenti xi Kal. Iun. an. 51

CICERO ATTICO SAL.

Cottidie vel potius in dies singulos breviores litteras ad te
mitto; cottidie enim magis suspicor te in Epirum iam profectum. sed tamen ut mandatum scias me curasse quo de
ante, ait se Pompeius quinos praefectos delaturum novos
vacationis iudiciariae causa.   5

Ego cum triduum cum Pompeio et apud Pompeium fuissem,
proficiscebar Brundisium a. d. xi[iii] Kal. Iun. civem illum
egregium relinquebam et ad haec quae timentur propulsanda
paratissimum. tuas litteras exspectabo cum ut quid agas tum
⟨ut⟩ ubi sis sciam.   10

101 (v. 8)

Scr. Brundisi iv Non. Iun. an. 51

CICERO ATTICO SAL.

1 Me et incommoda valetudo, e qua iam emerseram utpote

2, 5 quod *HV*   7 adesse δ: abe- Ω: te ade- *Lambinus*
Ep. 100] 3 quo de *Francken*: quod Ω   4 ante ait *Victorius*: -ea id *C*: -e ad Ω
quinos *Pius*: qui nos Ω*C*   5 vacationis *cod. Rav.*: -nes Ω*C*   iudiciariae *Madvig*:
-riam Ω*C*   causa ς: -am Ω*C*   7 xi *Corradus*: xii *N*: xiiii *GVR*Δ   10 ut *bm*:
om. Ω
Ep. 101] 1, 1 e *c*: om. Ω

shall write something rather than run the risk of your not getting a letter from me when you might have got one. Not that I have any more commissions to give you or anything to tell you. I gave you all my commissions, and I am sure they will be faithfully discharged, as you promise. I shall tell you news when I have any to tell. One thing I shall persist in as long as I think you are in town, and that is in soliciting you about Caesar's loan, to leave it settled. I am eagerly expecting a letter from you, more especially to learn the date of your departure.

100 (v. 7)

Tarentum, 22 May 51

CICERO TO ATTICUS

Every day, or rather from day to day, my letters to you grow shorter, for every day I suspect more strongly that you have already left for Epirus. However, to let you know that I have not forgotten your commission about which I wrote the other day, Pompey says that he is going to appoint five new Prefects in either province to get them exemption from jury service.

As for me, after spending three days in Pompey's company and at Pompey's house I am setting out for Brundisium on 22 May. I leave him in the most patriotic dispositions, fully prepared to be a bulwark against the dangers threatening. I shall expect a letter to tell me how you are and also where you are.

101 (v. 8)

Brundisium, 2 June 51

CICERO TO ATTICUS

1 This is my twelfth day at Brundisium. An indisposition from which I have now recovered (there was no fever) and the

cum sine febri laborassem, et Pomptini exspectatio, de quo
adhuc ne rumor quidem venerat, tenebat duodecimum iam
diem Brundisi; sed cursum exspectabamus.

2　　Tu, si modo es Romae (vix enim puto), sin es, hoc vehementer animadvertas velim. Roma acceperam litteras Milonem
meum queri per litteras iniuriam meam quod Philotimus
socius esset in bonis suis. id ego ita fieri volui de C. Duroni
sententia, quem et amicissimum Miloni perspexeram et talem 5
virum qualem tu iudicas cognoram; eius autem consilium
meumque hoc fuerat, primum ut in potestate nostra esset
res, ne illum malus emptor alienus mancipiis quae permulta
secum habet spoliaret, deinde ut Faustae quod cautum ille
esse voluisset ratum esset; erat etiam illud, ut ipsi nos si 10
3　quid servari posset quam facillime servaremus. nunc rem
totam perspicias velim; nobis enim scribuntur saepe maiora.
si ille queritur, si scribit ad amicos, si idem Fausta vult,
Philotimus, ut ego ei coram dixeram mihique ille receperat,
ne sit invito Milone in bonis; nihil nobis fuerit tanti. sin 5
haec leviora sunt, tu iudicabis. loquere cum Duronio. scripsi
etiam ad Camillum, ⟨ad Caelium⟩, ad Lamiam, eoque magis
quod non confid⟨eb⟩am Romae te esse. summa erit haec:
statues ut ex fide, fama reque mea videbitur.

2, 1 sin es *H*: sin est Ω　　2 Roma *Manutius*: -(a)e Ω　　7 fuerat *Brunus* (*M*⁴): -rit
Ω: fuit *Pius*　　8 alienus *V*: -nis *NR*Δ　　9 secum *m*: -ura Ω*Z*ᵇλ　　quod *scripsi*: quoi
V: qui *NRM*: cui δ　　10 esset *Vdms*: esse *NRMb*　　11 posset *V*: -sit *NR*Δ　　3, 3 si
ille *Brunus* (*M*⁴): sed i- Ω　　scribit *VPs*: -bis *R*: -bet *N*Δ　　6 scripsi *s*: -sit Ω 7
ad Caelium *add. Schiche*　　8 confidebam *s*: -dam Ω

expectation of Pomptinus' arrival, of whom not so much as a rumour has yet reached me, has kept me here. But I am waiting for a passage.

2   If you are in Rome, which I hardly suppose, but *if* you are, I should be very grateful indeed if you would give your attention to the following: I am told in a letter from Rome that poor Milo writes complaining of my ill-usage because Philotimus joined in the purchase of his estate. Now I so arranged this in consultation with C. Duronius, whom I well knew to be a very good friend of Milo's and of whose character I had formed just the same opinion as yourself. His idea and mine was in the first place that the business should be under our control, in case some sharp-dealing purchaser who did not know Milo might take away his slaves, of whom he has a great many with him; and in the second place to ensure for Fausta the property which Milo wished reserved to her. There was the further point that in this way we should most easily salvage anything that could
3   be salvaged for Milo himself. I should like you now to go into the whole business, for things often reach me by letter in an exaggerated form. If Milo is complaining and writing to his friends and Fausta feels the same way, then Philotimus must not hold the property against Milo's wishes, and so I told him verbally and so he promised. I will not have that for the world. But if it is not so serious after all, then you must use your discretion. Talk to Duronius. I have also written to Camillus and Caelius and Lamia, especially as I have no assurance that you are in Rome. The long and the short of it must be this: you will decide as you think best, having regard to my honour, reputation, and interest.

102 (v. 9)

Scr. Acti xvii Kal. Quint. an. 51 (§1)

CICERO ATTICO SAL.

1 Actium venimus a. d. XVII Kal. Quint., cum quidem et
Corcyrae et Sybotis muneribus tuis, quae et Araus et meus
amicus Eutychides opipare et φιλοπροσηνέστατα nobis congesserant, epulati essemus Saliarem in modum. Actio
maluimus iter facere pedibus, qui commodissime navigas- 5
semus; sed Leucatam flectere molestum videbatur, actuariis
autem minutis Patras accedere sine impedimentis non satis
visum est decorum.

Ego, ut saepe tu me currentem hortatus es, cottidie meditor,
praecipio meis, facio denique ut summa modestia et summa 10
abstinentia munus hoc extraordinarium traducamus. Parthus
velim quiescat et fortuna nos iuvet: nostra praestabimus.

2 Tu, quaeso, quid agas, ubi quoque tempore futurus sis,
qualis res nostras Romae reliqueris, maxime de $\overline{\text{xx}}$ et de $\overline{\text{DCCC}}$
cura ut sciamus; id unis diligenter litteris datis, quae ad me
utique perferantur, consequere. illud tamen, quoniam nunc
abes cum id non agitur, aderis autem ad tempus, ut mihi 5
rescripsisti, memento curare per te et per omnis nostros, in
primis per Hortensium, ut annus noster maneat suo statu,
ne quid novi decernatur. hoc tibi ita mando ut dubitem an
etiam te rogem ut pugnes ne intercaletur. sed non audeo
tibi omnia onera imponere; annum quidem utique teneto. 10

3 Cicero meus, modestissimus et suavissimus puer, tibi

Ep. 102] 1, 1 XVI c 2 muneribus tuis *NO*: mune robustius Δ: muneribus *R*
3 opipare et δ: opirare et *vel sim.* Ω congesserant *Manutius*: conce- Ω 4 saliarem *C*: alia rem *vel sim.* Ω 5 qui commodissime *R*: quin c- *O*: qui inc- *N*δ:
quin inc- *M* 6 sed Ω: et *Victorius* 10 facio *GNORc*: -iam Δ 11 munus *NP*δ:
unus *GORM*: unius *H* extraordinarium *Pbds*: exor- Ω 2, 1 tempore
λ: hoc t- Ω 2 xx *Bosius*: cxxΩ de (*alt.*) *del. Hervagius* 5 abes *bds*: h-
G: abest *NRMm* 6 rescrips(is)ti Ω: recepisti *Lehmann fort. recte*

22

102 (V. 9)

Actium, 14 June 51

CICERO TO ATTICUS

1 We reached Actium on 14 June, after feasting like aldermen both at Corcyra and at Sybota on the fare provided by your bounty and assembled for us in most hospitable profusion by Araus and my good friend Eutychides. From Actium we preferred to go by land, though the voyage had been excellent; but rounding Cape Leucata seemed too tiresome. Also I felt it would not be quite *convenable* to land at Patrae from small cargo boats without our luggage.

Every day I think of how to fulfil your often-repeated exhortations (which fell on willing ears) to get through this abnormal duty with the strictest decency and propriety, and so I impress upon my companions and so in fact I do. Only let the Parthian keep quiet and luck be on my side, I'll answer for my part.

2 On your side, pray let me know how you are and where you are going to be, with dates, and in what condition you left my affairs in Rome, especially with reference to the 20,000 and the 800,000. You can do all that in a single letter, dispatched by careful arrangement so that it is certain to reach me. But remember one thing,—you are away now when it doesn't arise but will return in time, so you have written back to me— to see personally and through all our friends, Hortensius first and foremost, that my year stays as it is and that no new decree is passed. Indeed, while I am about it, I am half inclined to ask you to resist any intercalation as well. But I must not put everything on your shoulders. The year then, hold fast to that whatever happens.

3 My boy sends you his love. He is a model of good behaviour

salutem dicit. Dionysium semper equidem, ut scis, dilexi, sed cottidie pluris facio, et mehercule in primis quod te amat nec tui mentionem intermitti sinit.

103 (V. 10)

Scr. Athenis iv Kal. Quint., ut vid., an. 51

CICERO ATTICO SAL.

1 Vt Athenas a. d. vii Kal. Quint. veneram, exspectabam ibi iam quartum diem Pomptinum neque de eius adventu certi quicquam habebam. eram autem totus, crede mihi, tecum et, quamquam sine iis per me ipse, tamen acrius vestigiis tuis monitus de te cogitabam. quid quaeris? non mehercule 5 alius ullus sermo nisi de te.

2 Sed tu de ⟨me⟩ ipso aliquid scire fortasse mavis. haec sunt. adhuc sumptus nec in me aut publice aut privatim nec in quemquam comitum. nihil accipitur lege Iulia, nihil ab hospite. persuasum est omnibus meis serviendum esse famae meae. belle adhuc. hoc animadversum Graecorum laude et multo 5 sermone celebratur. quod superest, elaboratur in hoc a me, sicut tibi sensi placere. sed haec tum laudemus cum erunt perorata.

3 Reliqua sunt eius modi ut meum consilium saepe reprehendam quod non aliqua ratione ex hoc negotio emerserim. o rem minime aptam meis moribus! o illud verum 'ἔρδοι τις . . . '! dices 'quid adhuc? nondum enim in negotio versaris'. ⟨pla⟩ne scio, et puto molestiora restare. etsi haec ipsa fero 5

Ep. 103] 1, 1 vii *Corradus*: xvi *GNVR*λ: xv Δ   4 iis *vulg.*: hiis *N*: is *m*: his *GVR*Δ   **2,** 1 de me ipso aliquid *P*: de i- al- *GNVR*: al- de i- Δ   5 hoc *G*Δ: omnia *N*: *om.* VR   **3,** 3 illud *Victorius*: -um Ω   τις *Victorius*: HC *vel sim.* Ω   4 dices ς: dicis Ω   5 plane scio *scripsi*: nescio Ω: non nes- *Klotz*: sane s- *Kahnt*: ne ego s- *Tyrrell–Purser* et ς: ut Ω   etsi *Victorius*: sed si Ω

and engaging manners. For Dionysius I always had a regard
as you know, but I think more highly of him every day, not
least, let me add, because he is so fond of you and sees to it
that your name is continually cropping up.

103 (V. 10)

Athens, 27 June (?) 51

CICERO TO ATTICUS

1 After reaching Athens on 24 June I have been here four days
waiting for Pomptinus, and have still no definite news of his
coming. But my thoughts, believe me, are all with you, and
though I have no need of such admonitions the traces of your
presence here call you the more vividly to my mind. In fact you
are really our single topic of conversation.

2   But perhaps *you* prefer to hear something about myself.
Here is what I have. Up to date no private individual or public
body has been put to expense on my account or that of any
member of my staff. We take nothing under the lex Julia or as
private guests. All my people recognize that they must be
careful of my good name. So far, so good. This has not gone
unnoticed, and the Greeks are praising it and talking about it at
large. As for the future, I am taking great pains over this point,
as I saw you wished me to do. But let us save the applause till
the end of the speech.

3   The rest is of such a nature that I often blame my unwisdom
in not having found some way of escaping this job. It's so hope-
lessly uncongenial to me. Indeed and indeed 'let the cobbler
...'. Early days, you may say, and point out that I'm not yet
in harness. Too true, and I expect there is worse to come. But
even here and now—well, I put up with it, even, as I think and

equidem, etiam fronte, ut puto et volo, bellis⟨sime⟩, sed angor
intimis sensibus; ita multa vel iracunde vel insolenter vel
in omni genere stulte, insulse, adroganter et dicuntur et aguntur cottidie; quae non quo te celem non perscribo sed quia
δυσεκλάλητα sunt. itaque admirabere meam βαθύτητα cum 10
salvi redierimus; tanta mihi μελέτη huius virtutis datur.

4　　Ergo haec quoque hactenus; etsi mihi nihil erat proposi-
tum ad scribendum, quia quid ageres, ubi terrarum esses,
ne suspicabar quidem. nec hercule umquam tam diu ignarus
rerum mearum fui, quid de Caesaris, quid de Milonis nominibus actum sit; ac non modo nemo domo, ne Roma quidem 5
quisquam, ut sciremus in re publica quid ageretur. qua re si
quid erit quod scias de iis rebus quas putabis scire me velle,
per mihi gratum erit si id curaris ad me perferendum.

5　　Quid est praeterea? nihil sane nisi illud: valde me Athenae
delectarunt, urbe dumtaxat et urbis ornamento et hominum
amore in te, in nos quadam benevolentia; sed mu⟨tata mu⟩lta.
philosophia sursum deorsum. si quid est, est in Aristo, apud
quem eram; nam Xenonem tuum vel nostrum potius Quinto 5
concesseram, et tamen propter vicinitatem totos dies simul
eramus. tu velim cum primum poteris tua consilia ad me

---

6 etiam *Nbds*: etiam in *M*: leta *V*: *om. m*: *fort.* et *vel* et id　et voltu *s*　bellissime *Ascensius*: bellis Ω (*sed om. V*): belliss. λ (*cf. Lambini adnotationem:* 'ut puto et
volo, bellissime) non potui omnium librorum manuscr. consensum negligere, qui sic fere
habent, non ut vulgati, ut puto, et vultu bellissimis'): belle *Sjögren*　8 stulte *VRC*:
-titi(a)e *NΔ*　insulse *Ps*: -si Ω　arroganter *s*: -tur Ω　aguntur *noluit Ernesti, recepit
Watt*: tacentur Ω　9 non (*alt.*) *VRc*: *om.* Δ　10 δυσεκλάλητα *Victorius*: ΔYCCEKIΛ-
ΛHTA Ω　4, 1 ergo *Victorius*: ego Ω　5 domo *Kayser*: modo Ω (*om. Nb*)　ne
GNORΔ: sed ne *V*　5, 2 (t)urbe Ω: urbs *Psλ*　ornamento *V*: -tum
GNORΔλ　3 amore *C*: amores (m- *N*) Ω　te et *C* (*fort. errore*)　quadam
GNORΔC: quaedam *VF*　mutata multa *scripsi*: mult(a)e a (-ta a *N*) Ω: -tum
ea *C*: -ta in *Watt* (-ta in ea *iam Reid*)　4 sursum deorsum Ω*CZᵇ*: ἄνω καὶ κάτω *ς*:
ἄνω κάτω *Bosius*　quid est *Victorius*: quidem *GORΔ*: quid *NVC*　est in Aristo
Manutius: est in aris tu *M*: est maristu *R*: marsicum *P*: est aristo *V*: (a)estimaris
(ext-) *GNOδC*　7 tu velim *Boot*: iunctim *Zᵇ*: -ti *Nm*: invecim *M*: invicem
bds: vives tu *V*: vivas tu *R*: *om. G*　cum *GNΔ*: quam *VR*

26

hope, with an excellent grace, but in my heart of hearts I am on thorns. Irritability, rudeness, every sort of stupidity and bad manners and arrogance both in word and act—one secs examples every day. I won't give you details, not that I want to keep you in the dark but because they are hard to put into words. So you will admire my self-control when we get safely home again. I am getting plenty of practice in that virtue.

4   So much for this then too. Not that I have anything in mind to write about, for I have not so much as a notion as to what you are doing or where in the world you are. Indeed I have never in my life been so long without knowledge of my affairs, what for example has been done about the money matters relating to Caesar and to Milo. Not only has no one come to me from home, nobody from Rome even has come to tell me what is going on in the political world. So if you have any information on matters which you think would interest me I shall be most grateful if you will get it conveyed to me.

5   What else is there? Why nothing, except this. I have greatly enjoyed Athens, so far as the city is concerned and its embellishments and the affection the people have for you, the good will they seem to have for me. But many things have changed, and philosophy is all at sixes and sevens, anything of value being represented by Aristus, with whom I am staying. I left your friend Xeno (I should say 'our') for Quintus, though as he lives so near by we are together all day. I hope you will write me your plans as soon as you can, so that I know what you are

scribas, ut sciam quid agas, ubi quoque tempore, maxime
quando Romae futurus sis.

104 (v. 11)

Scr. Athenis prid. Non. Quint. an. 51 (§4)

CICERO ATTICO SAL.

1 Hui, totiensne me litteras dedisse Romam, cum ad te nullas
darem? at vero posthac frustra potius dabo quam, si recte
dari potuerint, committam ut non dem.

  Ne provincia nobis prorogetur, per fortunas, dum ades,
quicquid provideri ⟨poterit⟩ provide. non dici potest quam 5
flagrem desiderio urbis, quam vix harum rerum insulsitatem
feram.

2 Marcellus foede de Comensi. etsi ille magistratum non
gesserit, erat tamen Transpadanus; ita mihi videtur non
minus stomachi nostro ⟨quam⟩ Caesari fecisse. sed hoc ipse
viderit.

3 Pompeius mihi quoque videbatur, quod scribis Varronem
dicere, in Hispaniam certe iturus. id ego minime probabam;
qui quidem Theophani facile persuasi nihil esse melius quam
illud nusquam discedere. ergo Graecus incumbet; valet
autem auctoritas eius apud illum plurimum.   5

4 Ego has prid. Non. Quint. proficiscens Athenis dedi, cum
ibi decem ipsos fuissem dies. venerat Pomptinus, una Cn.
Volusius. aderat quaestor. tuus unus Tullius aberat. aphracta

---

8 tempore *c*: *om.* Ω   9 sis] *hic deficit V*
Ep. 104] 1, 1 hui Δ: huic *P*: hic *R*: *om. N*   dedisse *bms*: -em Ω   2 at vero ϛ:
advenero Ω   3 committam ϛ: -to Ωλ   5 poterit *Schiche*: potest *ms*: *om.* Ω
6 quam vix *ORs*: quamvis *P*Δ: quasi *N*   2, 1 foede in (de *Bosius*) Comensi
Sigonius: sedendi comes *OR*Δ   3 quam *add. Malaespina*   3, 3 persuasi *Victorius*: -it Ω   4 illud nusquam *NOR*: illud n- quam illum n- *Mbd*: illud illum
n- *m*: illum n- *s*   4, 2 una *Bosius*: nam Ω   Cn.] Q. *Corradus*   3 aphracta
Baiter: practa *vel sim.* Ω: ἄφρακτα ϛ (*item epp.* 105.1, 106.1)

doing and where you will be at any particular time, and above all when you are going to be in Rome.

104 (V. 11)

Athens, 6 July 51

CICERO TO ATTICUS

1   Oh dear! 'I have sent so many letters to Rome and never one to you!' In future I shall rather risk sending a letter to no purpose than fail to send one if there is a good opportunity.

For mercy's sake, take every means you can find, so long as you are in town, to guard against any extension of my tenure. I cannot tell you how passionately I long for Rome, how difficult I find it to endure the insipidity of my present existence.

2   That was an ugly gesture of Marcellus' over the man from Comum. He may not have been an ex-magistrate, but he was at any rate a Transpadane, and so I imagine Marcellus has irritated our friend as much as Caesar. But that's his affair.

3   I too think Pompey is determined to go to Spain, as you say Varro says. I am not at all in favour of his doing so, and indeed I had no difficulty in persuading Theophanes that the policy of staying put is as good as any. So the Greek will exert his influence, to which Pompey much defers.

4   I am sending this letter as I leave Athens, on 6 July, after a stay of ten clear days. Pomptinus has arrived and Cn. Volusius with him. My Quaestor is here. Your friend Tullius is the only

Rhodiorum et dicrota Mytilenaeorum habebam et aliquid
ἐπικώπων. de Parthis erat silentium. quod superest, di iuvent! 5
5 Nos adhuc iter per Graeciam summa cum admiratione
fecimus, nec mehercule habeo quod adhuc quem accusem
meorum. videntur mihi nosse [nos] nostram causam et con-
dicionem profectionis suae; plane serviunt existimationi
meae. quod superest, si verum illud est, 'οἷαπερ ἡ δέσποινα...', 5
certe permanebunt; nihil enim ⟨a⟩ me fieri ita videbunt ut sibi
sit delinquendi locus. sin id parum profuerit, fiet aliquid
a nobis severius; nam adhuc lenitate dulces sumus, et, ut
spero, proficimus aliquantum. sed ego hanc, ut Siculi dicunt,
†ανεзιαν† in unum annum meditatus sum; proinde pugna 10
ne, si quid prorogatum sit, turpis inveniar.
6 Nunc redeo ad ea quae mihi mandas. in praefectis excusatio
ne s⟨it⟩; iis quos voles deferto. non ero tam μετέωρος quam
in Appuleio fui. Xenonem tam diligo quam tu, quod ipsum
sentire certo scio. apud Patronem et reliquos barones te in
maxima gratia posui, et hercule merito tuo feci; nam mihi 5
is [ter] dixit te scripsisse ad se mihi ex illius litteris rem illam
curae fuisse, quod ei pergratum erat. sed cum Patron mecum
egisset ut peterem a vestro Ariopago ὑπομνηματισμὸν tollerent
quem Polycharmo praetore fecerant, commodius visum est et

---

4 dicrota Mytilenaeorum *Victorius*: -tum emituleorum Ω: δίκροτα Myt- *Baiter*
5 ἐπικώπων *Gronovius*: ΕΠΙΚΟΝΔΕΙ *OMmZ*[b]: ἐπιπόνδει λ: ΕΠΙΚΝΑΕΙ *R*
5, 3 nosse nos Ω: nosse *bds* 5 οἷαπερ *'antiquum exemplar' ap. Victorium*: ΟΙΑΤΑΝ
vel sim. RMm: οἷα τ'ἂν *C*: οἷα τὰν *Watt* 6 a Pδ: om. Ω 7 sin *Victorius*: in Ω
profuerit *Manutius*: quod f- Ω 8 severius ς: ser- Ω 9 Siculi *Gronovius*: singuli
Ω 10 ΑΝΕΖΙΑΝ *RMm*: ἀνεξίαν *O*: ἀνιξίαν temptavi (vide comm.) 6, 1 ea *NOR*
s: om. Δ mandasti. praefectos *Koch* excusatio ne sit *scripsi*: -onis *R Ant.*,
Constans: -ones *O*: -o *NΔ* 2 iis *vel* hiis *vel* his Ω: causa *Constans* μετέωρος
ς: meteorus Ω 3 tam *bms*: quam *Md*: quem *NR* 4 sentire *bms*: -ret Ω patronem *O*: -num *RMm*: -nos *Nbms* 6 is *scripsi*: (h)ister *vel* his ter Ω: iste *b*: is
te (*poster. te del.*) *Orelli* 7 patron *O*²: -onum Ω 8 ariopago *OPbds*: are(o)p-
NRMm (*cf. infra*) 9 praetore *Pius*: pr. *M*: po. ro. *R*: pridie Nδ

absentee. I have some Rhodian open vessels, some Mytilenian two-deckers and a few rowing craft. Of the Parthians there is no whisper. As for the future, heaven be my help!

5   So far my journey through Greece has been the admiration of the country, and I must say that I have no complaint to make so far of any of my party. I think they know my position and the understanding on which they come. They are really jealous for my good name. As for the future, if there is anything in the old saying 'like master . . .', they will certainly keep it up, for they will see nothing in my behaviour to give them any pretext for delinquency. Should that not answer however, I am prepared for sterner measures. So far I am gaining their hearts by gentleness, and I hope that this is not without effect. But it is only for one year that I have steeled myself in this 'disinterest' (?), as they say in Sicily. So do your utmost, for fear that if my term is extended I may turn out a rascal after all.

6   Now I come back to your commissions. In the matter of the Prefects, let there be no excuses. Promise anyone you like. I shall not be so absent-minded as I was about Appuleius. For Xeno I have as much regard as yourself, and I am sure he is aware of it. Thanks to me you are *persona gratissima* with Patro and the other dunderheads, and upon my word you deserve to be. He told me that you wrote to him saying I had taken care of that matter in accordance with his letter, for which he was very much obliged! Actually, after Patro requested me to ask your Areopagus to rescind the decree they passed when Polycharmus was General, it seemed best to Xeno (and later to Patro

Xenoni me et post ipsi Patroni ad Memmium scribere, qui 10
pridie quam ego Athenas veni Mytilenas profectus erat, ut
is ad suos scriberet posse id sua voluntate fieri; non enim
dubitabat Xeno quin ab Ariopagitis invito Memmio impetrari non posset. Memmius autem aedificandi consilium
abiecerat, sed erat Patroni iratus. itaque scripsi ad eum 15
accurate; cuius epistulae misi ad te exemplum.

7   Tu velim Piliam meis verbis consolere. indicabo enim tibi
(tu illi nihil dixeris): accepi fasciculum in quo erat epistula
Piliae ad ⟨Quintum; abs⟩tuli, aperui, legi; valde scripta est
συμπαθῶς. Brundisio quae tibi epistulae redditae sunt sine
mea tum videlicet datas cum ego me non belle haberem; 5
nam illam †νομαηαρια me† excusationem ne acceperis. cura
ut omnia sciam, sed maxime ut valeas.

105 (v. 12)

Scr. Deli med. m. Quint. an. 51

CICERO ATTICO SAL.

1 Negotium magnum est navigare atque id mense Quintili.
sexto die Delum Athenis venimus. prid. Non. Quint. a Piraeo
ad Zostera vento molesto, qui nos ibidem Nonis tenuit.
a. d. VIII Id. ad Ceo iucunde. inde Gyarum saevo vento, non
adverso. hinc Syrum, inde Delum, utroque citius quam 5
vellemus, cursum confecimus. iam nosti aphracta Rhodiorum:

---

10 me *post* Patroni *transpos. Pius*   qui δ: quid Ω   12 is ad suos *Corradus*: si ad
vos Ω   13 Memmio] *nova ep. in* Ω: *superiori coniunxit Aldus*   14 Memmius
Corradus: manius ΩC   7, 1 enim *om.* λ   2 accepi *cod. Bod.*: accipe Ω   3 ad
Quintum; abstuli *scripsi*: attuli Ω: abst- ς   4 ἐμπαθῶς *Boot*   5 datas Ωλ: date *P*:
datae sunt *Ernesti*   6 aliam *Schiche, Watt*   NOMAHAPIA *vel sim. GRM: ultimam*
litt. pro praepositione a habuit Watt, ceteras del.   me *GN*Δ: meam *OR*
Ep. 105] 1, 4 ad ς: ab Ω   iocunde inde *OR*: vicum deinde *N*Δ   5 Syrum
Moser: sc(h)yrum *O*Δ: sc(h)irum *NR*   6 nosti *P*δ: -tri Ω

himself) for me to write to Memmius, who had left for Mytilene the day before my arrival in Athens, asking him to let his friends know that he had no objection. Xeno, you see, was certain that the Areopagites would not agree against Memmius' wishes. Memmius had given up the idea of building, but he was annoyed with Patro. Accordingly I have written to him with some care, and I enclose a copy of my letter.

7   Would you please say a word of comfort to Pilia *de ma part*? For I'll tell you, but you must not say anything to her: I received a parcel of letters in which there was one from Pilia to Quintus. I took it, opened it, and read it. It was very sympathetically written. The letters which were brought to you from Brundisium without one from me must have been dispatched when I was not so well—don't accept the excuse of ※ . Take care you send me all the news, but take special care of your health.

105 (V. 12)
Delos, mid-July 51
CICERO TO ATTICUS

1 Travelling by sea is no light matter, even in July. We have taken six days to get from Athens to Delos. On 6 July we sailed from Piraeus to Zoster with a troublesome wind which kept us there over the Nones. On the 8th to Ceos, pleasantly enough. Thence to Gyaros, under a savage gale, not blowing against us however. From there we made our way to Syros, thence to Delos, and to both faster than we should have liked. You know these Rhodian open ships—nothing makes heavier weather. So

nihil quod minus fluctum ferre possit. itaque erat in animo nihil festinare, nec me Delo movere nisi omnia ἄκρα Γυρέων pura vidissem.

2   De Messalla autem statim ut audivi, de Gyaro dedi litteras et ad ipsum ⟨et erat⟩ consilium nostrum etiam ad Hortensium, cui quidem valde συνηγωνίων; sed tuas de eius iudici sermonibus et mehercule omni de rei publicae statu litteras exspecto, πολιτικώτερον quidem scriptas quoniam meos cum 5 †Thallumeto† nostro pervolutas libros, eius modi, inquam, litteras ex quibus ego non quid fiat (nam id vel Helonius, vir gravissimus, potest efficere, cliens tuus) sed quid futurum sit sciam. cum haec leges, habebimus consules; omnia perspicere poteris, de Caesare, de Pompeio, de ipsis iudiciis.   10

3   Nostra autem negotia, quoniam Romae commoraris, amabo te, explica. cui rei fugerat me rescribere, de strue laterum, plane rogo, de aqua si quid poterit fieri, eo sis animo quo soles esse de aqua; quam ego cum mea sponte tum tuis sermonibus aestimo plurimi. ergo tu id conficies. praeterea 5 si quid Philippus rogav⟨er⟩it, quod in tua re faceres, id velim facias.

Plura scribam ad te cum constitero; nunc eram plane in medio mari.

---

8 nec me Delo *Lambinus*: delo nec me Ω: nec Delo me *Sternkopf* ἄκρα Γυρέων *Schneidewin*: ΑΚΡΑΤΗΡΕΟΝ *vel sim. ORMm*   9 pura *Schneidewin*: iura Ω   **2,** 1 autem *Watt*: ad te Ω: a te *cod. Mus. Brit. Add.* 6793 gyaro O²: giar(i)o *vel sim.* Ω 2 ad ipsum *OR cod. Mus. Brit. Add.* 6793 (*de N silent auctores*): id i- Δ et erat *add. Watt* 8 gravissimus Cλ: grati- Ω: gnavi- *Stangl* 9 sciam *Manutius*: etiam Ω habebimus ς: habemus Ω   **3,** 2 explica *ms*: -ari Ω de strue λ: de strues Z⁽ᵇ⁾: dest- Ω laterum *noluit Malaespina*: alt- ΩZᵇ: salt- λ 3 de aqua *del. Manutius* 5 tu id *Klotz*: quid Ω: aliq- ς: *del. Watt* 6 rogaverit *Schiche* (-arit *Pius*): -avit Ω: -abit *Corradus* 8 constitero s: -tituero Ω

I don't intend to hurry or to leave Delos until I see all 'the peaks of Gyrae' plain.

2   As soon as I heard from you about Messalla I sent off a letter from Gyaros to him, and it is my intention to send another to Hortensius, in whose anxiety I strongly sympathized. But I am expecting a letter from you on what people are saying about the trial, indeed on the whole state of public affairs; it should be in good statesmanlike style since you are thumbing my book with our friend Thallumctus (?)—I mean the sort of letter which will tell me not what is actually happening (your weighty client Helonius can do that much), but what's going to happen. When you read this we shall have Consuls. You will be able to make it all out—Caesar, Pompey, even the trials.

3   Since you are staying on in Rome, be a good fellow and sort out my affairs. With regard to the matter about which I forgot to answer your query, the brick-pile—yes, if anything can be done about the water, do please show your usual spirit where water is concerned. After your talk I attach great importance to it, as indeed I should in any case. So please get that settled. Further if Philippus asks you to help, I should be grateful if you would do what you would in your own case.

I shall write more to you when I settle down. At present I am right on the high seas.

106 (v. 13)

Scr. Ephesi vii Kal. Sext. an. 51

CICERO ATTICO SAL.

1 Ephesum venimus a. d. XI Kal. Sext., sexagesimo et quingentesimo post pugnam Bovill⟨an⟩am. navigavimus sine
timore et sine nausea, sed tardius propter aphractorum
Rhodiorum imbecillitatem. de concursu legationum, priva-
torum et de incredibili multitudine quae mihi iam Sami sed 5
mirabilem in modum Ephesi praesto fuit aut audisse te puto
aut quid ad te attinet? verum tamen decumani ⟨quasi ad se⟩
venissem cum imperio, Graeci quasi Ephesio praetori, se
alacres obtulerunt. ex quo te intellegere certo scio multorum
annorum ostentationes meas nunc in discrimen esse adductas. 10
sed, ut spero, utemur ea palaestra quam a te didicimus
omnibusque satis faciemus, et eo facilius quod in nostra
provincia confectae sunt pactiones. sed hactenus, praesertim
cum cenanti mihi nuntiarit Cestius se de nocte proficisci.

2 Tua negotiola Ephesi curae mihi fuerunt, Thermoque,
tametsi ante adventum meum liberalissime erat pollicitus
tuis omnibus, tamen Philogenem et Seium tradidi, Apollonidensem Xenonem commendavi. omnia se facturum recepit. ego praeterea rationem Philogeni permutationis eius 5
quam tecum feci edidi. ergo haec quoque hactenus.

Ep. 106] 1, 1 quingentesimo *Bosius*: quinto Ω   2 Bovillanam *Lamb.* (*marg.*):
-lam *NORs*: ambo villam Δ   5 qu(a)e mihi *OR*: qui mi *vel sim. N*Δ   6 in
modum *NORs*: *om.* Δ   fuit *s*: fuisse Ω   7 te *Schütz*: me Ω   decumani *cod.*
Bod.: -is Ω   quasi ad se *addidi* (quasi *Gronovius*)   8 praetori se alacres ς: -ri
alacres se *N*: -ris alacres *OR*: -ris ea alacres Δ   13 haec hactenus *Ernesti*
14 nuntiarit *Corradus*: -ret Ω   2, 1 negotiola *C*: -tio *M*: -tia *NR*δ   cur(a)e
*P*δ: cura *RM*: cara *N*   3 tradidi *N*: tradi *R*Δ   Apollonidensem *Malaespina*:
ap(p)ol(l)inicense Ω   4 xenonem *P*: se- Ω: ze- *bds*   commendavi *OP*: -di *NR*Δ
omnia *NPb*: omnia omnia *ORMdm*: omnino omnia *s*(*?*)ς   5 praeterea Δ: -er
eam *NOR*

36

106 (V. 13)

Ephesus, 26 July 51

CICERO TO ATTICUS

1 We arrived at Ephesus on 22 July, 559 days after the Battle of Bovillae. Our voyage was free from danger and sea-sickness, but rather slow because of the unstalwart quality of the Rhodian open craft. As for the concourse of deputations and individuals and the huge crowds which welcomed me even at Samos and in quite astounding numbers at Ephesus, I expect you have already heard, or if not, why should you worry? However, the tithe-farmers were as eagerly to the fore as though I had come to *them* with full powers and the Greeks as though I had been governor of Asia. I am sure you see from this that my professions of these many years past are now put to the test. Still I trust I shall practise the lessons you have taught me and satisfy everybody, which should be all the easier because the taxation agreements in my province have already been made up. But that will do, especially as Cestius sent me word during dinner that he is leaving before daybreak.

2 I have attended to your little affairs at Ephesus. Although Thermus had made very handsome promises to all your friends before I arrived, I introduced Philogenes and Seius to him and recommended Xeno of Apollonia. He undertook to do all that was asked of him. I further gave Philogenes particulars of the bill of exchange which I negotiated with you. So that will do for this subject, too.

37

3 Redeo ad urbana. per fortunas, quoniam Romae manes,
primum illud praefulci atque praemuni, quae⟨s⟩o, ⟨ut⟩ simus
annui, ne intercaletur quidem. deinde exhauri mea mandata
maximeque si quid potest de illo domestico scrupulo quem
non ignoras, dein de Caesare; quam in cupiditatem te auctore 5
incubui nec me piget. et si intellegis quam meum sit scire et
curare quid in re publica fiat—fiat autem? immo vero etiam
quid futurum sit, perscribe ad me omnia, sed diligentissime
in primisque num quid iudiciorum status aut factorum aut
futurorum etiam laboret. de aqua sit curae; et si quid Philippus 10
aget animadvertes.

107 (v. 14)

Scr. Trallibus, ut vid., vi Kal. Sext. an. 51

CICERO ATTICO SAL.

1 Ante quam aliquo loco consedero, neque longas a me neque
semper mea manu litteras exspectabis; cum autem erit
spatium utrumque ⟨prae⟩stabo. nunc iter conficiebamus
aestuosa et pulverulenta via. dederam Epheso pridie; has
dedi Trallibus. in provincia mea fore me putabam Kal. 5
Sext. ex ea die, si me amas, παράπηγμα ἐνιαύσιον commoveto.
interea tamen haec [quae] mihi quae vellem adferebantur,

3, 2 praefulci ς: -ce Ω   praemuni ς: -itus Ω   qu(a)eso δ: queo *vel*
sim. Ω   ut *add.* ς   4 maximeque si *cod. Mus. Brit. Add. 6793, C*: -moque si *N*:
-me (*sed* -ma *O*) qu(a)eso *OPΔ*   potes *N*   scrupulo *Pius*: -lum Ω   5 quam
scripsi: cum Ω: cuius *Victorius*   te auctore *Victorius*: et au(c)torem Ω   9 numquid ς: nunc q- Ω (*sed* nunc *om. Mm*)   10 sit curae *scripsi*: si cur(a)e Δ: sciture
R: scitur *G*: si tui *N*   et *scripsi*: est Ω   11 eget *c*
Ep. 107] 1, 3 pr(a)estabo *O*: est(ē) dabo *RM Ant.*: dabo *GNδ*: stabo *Z¹*
6 ea *ΩZ¹*: eo *Boot*   me amas *Victorius*: meas *ΩZ¹*   παράπηγμα *Tunstall*:
παράγγελμα *Z¹* (*ut vid.*) *c*: ΠΑΓΓΕΓΜΑ *vel sim. RMm*   7 interea tamen *NORc*:
t- i- Δ   quae *del.* ς   adferebantur *Victorius*: adi(e)reb- (-rab-) Ω: adgereb- *Z¹*

3   To come back to the affairs of the town. For mercy's sake, as you are staying in Rome, do pray first and foremost build up a powerful defensive position to ensure that my term remains annual, without intercalation even. Secondly, mind you discharge all my commissions, in particular with regard to that domestic worry, you know what I mean, if anything can be done, and further about Caesar. It was at your prompting I became so keen on that, and I don't regret it. And if you appreciate how much it is in my character to know and care about what is happening in public life (I say 'is happening', but I should add 'what is going to happen'), give me full and comprehensive reports, really conscientious ones, and first whether the state of the trials, past or future too, is unsatisfactory. Please attend to the matter of the water, and if Philippus does anything keep an eye open.

107 (V. 14)
Tralles (?), 27 July 51
CICERO TO ATTICUS

1   Until I get settled somewhere you must not expect my letters to be long or always in my own hand, but when I have the leisure I shall guarantee both. At present we are *en route*, and it is a hot and dusty road. I sent off a letter from Ephesus yesterday and I am sending this from Tralles. I expect to be in my province on the Kalends of August. From that day, if you love me, start moving the calendar. Meanwhile certain welcome reports

primum otium Parthicum, dein confectae pactiones publicanorum, postremo seditio militum sedata ab Appio stipendiumque eis usque ad Id. Quint. persolutum.   10

2 Nos Asia accepit admirabiliter. adventus noster fuit nemini ne minimo quidem sumptui. spero meos omnis servire laudi meae; tamen magno timore sum, sed bene speramus. omnes iam nostri praeter Tullium tuum venerunt. erat mihi in animo recta proficisci ad exercitum, aestivos mensis reliquos 5 rei militari dare, hibernos iuris dictioni.

3 Tu velim, si me nihilo minus nosti curiosum in re publica quam te, scribas ad me omnia, quae sint, quae futura sint. nihil mihi gratius facere potes; nisi tamen id erit mihi gratissimum, si quae tibi mandavi confeceris in primisque illud ἐνδόμυχον, quo mihi scis nihil esse carius.   5

Habes epistulam plenam festinationis et pulveris; reliquae subtiliores erunt.

108 (v. 15)

Scr. Laodiceae iii Non. Sext. an. 51 (§ 3)

CICERO ATTICO SAL.

1 Laodiceam veni prid. Kal. Sext.; ex hoc die clavum anni movebis. nihil exoptatius adventu meo, nihil c⟨l⟩arius; sed est incredibile quam me negoti taedeat, ⟨cum⟩ non habeat satis magnum campum ille tibi non ignotus cursus animi et industriae meae, praeclara opera cesset. quippe ius Laodiceae 5

---

8 parthicum *s*: p(h)art(h)inum Ω   9 appio ς: op- Ω   **2**, 1 fuit *hoc loco NOR*: *ante* sumptui Δ   nemini ne *b*: nemini *ORMds*: ne *NPm*   2 spero meos *m*: per meos *ORM*: spero eos *Nbds*   3 speramus *P*: par- Ω   6 dictioni *NRms*: -is *GMbd*   **3**, 4 -que *Corradus*: quid Ω   5 ἐνδόμυχον *Victorius*: ΕΝΟΜΥΛΟΝ *vel sim.* Ω: ἐνόμιλον *C*   scis *P*: scies Ω

Ep. 108] 1, 1 anni movebis *Bosius*: animo verbis ΩZ^b   2 optatius *c* clarius scripsi: ca- Ω   3 cum *add. Müller*   habet *bms*   4 cursus *bms*: -um Ω   5 cesset ΩCZ¹: -sat *N*   ius ς: tus *NOR*: et iis Δ

are coming in, first of quiet from the Parthian quarter, second
of the conclusion of the tax-farmers' agreements, lastly of a
military mutiny pacified by Appius and arrears of pay discharged up to the Ides of July.

2   Asia has given me a marvellous reception. No one is a penny
the poorer for my coming. I think that all my company are
jealous for my good name. None the less I am very apprehen-
sive, but hope for the best. All my party has now arrived with
the exception of your friend Tullius. I propose to go straight
to the army and devote the remaining summer months to
campaigning, the winter ones to administering justice.

3   Knowing my curiosity about politics to be quite as keen as
your own, I hope you will tell me everything, what is going
on and what is to come. You can't do me a greater kindness, or
rather only one, the greatest of all, and that is to dispatch my
commissions, above all that 'domesticity' which you know lies
nearest my heart.

Here then is a letter fully of hurry and dust. Those to follow
will be more detailed.

108 (V. 15)

Laodicea, 3 August 51

CICERO TO ATTICUS

1 I reached Laodicea on 31 July. From this day you must start
your year's reckoning. My arrival was most eagerly awaited
and widely acclaimed. But you cannot conceive how weary
of the business I am, for it gives no adequate scope for the
intellectual drive and industry which I think you will concede
me, and has interrupted the work that is my pride. To think of
it—me sitting on the bench in Laodicea while A. Plotius sits in

me dicere, cum Romae A. Plotius dicat! et, cum exercitum
noster amicus habeat tantum, me nomen habere duarum
legionum exilium! denique haec non desidero: lucem, forum,
urbem, domum, vos desidero. sed feram ut potero, sit modo
annuum; si prorogatur, actum est. verum perfacile resisti 10
potest, tu modo Romae sis.

2 Quaeris quid hic agam. ita vivam ut maximos sumptus
facio. mirifice delector hoc instituto. admirabilis abstinentia
ex praeceptis tuis, ut verear ne illud quod tecum permutavi
versura mihi solvendum sit. Appi vulnera non refrico, sed
apparent nec occuli possunt.   5

3 Iter Laodicea faciebam a. d. III Non. Sext., cum has litteras
dabam, in castra in Lycaoniam. inde ad Taurum cogitabam,
ut cum Moeragene signis collatis, si possem, de servo tuo
deciderem. 'clitellae bovi sunt impositae; plane non est
nostrum onus'; sed feremus, modo, si me amas, sit annus, 5
adsis tu ad tempus ut senatum totum excites. mirifice sollicitus
sum quod iam diu mihi ignota sunt ista omnia. qua re, ut ad
te ante scripsi, cum cetera tum res publica cura ut mihi nota sit.

Plura scribam ⟨alias, has sciebam⟩ tarde tibi redditum iri,
sed dabam familiari homini ac domestico, C. Andronico 10
Puteolano. tu autem saepe dare tabellariis publicanorum poteris
per magistros scripturae et portus [et] nostrarum dioecesium.

---

10 annum *C*   2, 3 ut *NRs*: aut Δ   permutavi *bs*: -multavi (multa vi)
Ω   4 versura Δ: -am *NOR*   refrico ς: reficio Ω   3, 2 castra *ORs*: -ro
*GN*Δ   3 Moeragene *Corradus*: mofr- Ω*Z^bλ*   4 deciderem *Manutius*: decedere
Ω   plane *Amm. Marc. xvi. 5.* 10: illa ne (-ane) *GNRbdCZ^b*: illa *Mms*   5 sit Ω:
sim *Manutius*   annus Ω: annuus *s, codd. Mal., Manutius*: annuum *Corradus*
6 adsis tu ad ς: at si tu a(d) *vel sim.* Ω   7 mihi ignota sunt *GNORc*: i- s- m- Ω
9 plura . . . sciebam *ita Orelli*: p- scribam Ω*Z^(b)*: p- scribebam *bds*: epistulam
sciebam *Gronovius*   redditum iri *anon. ap. Lambinum*: -tu iri *Z*: red(d)itu
ire *G*: -ituro *N*Δ: -turus *OR*   12 et *del. Manutius*

Rome! And to think that while our friend has his huge army,
I have a nominal force of two skeleton legions! And when all's
said, it isn't this sort of thing I'm pining for, it's the world, the
Forum, Rome, my house, my friends. But I'll stick it out as
best I can so long as it's only for a year. If there is a prorogation,
I give up. But that can be resisted very easily if only you are in
Rome.

2   You ask what I am doing here. Spending the devil of a lot
of money. I quite revel in this system. My strictness according
to your precepts is so remarkable that I am afraid I may have to
raise a loan to meet the bill I negotiated with you. I don't
scratch Appius' sores, but they show and can't be hidden.

3   As I send off this letter, on 3 August, I am on my way from
Laodicea to the army in Lycaonia. From there I mean to move
to the Taurus to try for a settlement with Moeragenes (on the
battle-field) about your slave. 'Now the ox is fairly pannier'd!
No, 'tis not the load for me!' But I'll bear it, only if you love
me let it be for one year and you be on the spot at the crucial
time to rouse the whole Senate. I am terribly anxious because
for a long while now I have been in total ignorance of affairs in
Rome. Therefore, as I asked you before, see that I am kept
au fait with everything, particularly politics.

I shall write more another time. I know that this letter will
be a long while reaching you, but I am giving it to a man I
know well, one of our own people, C. Andronicus of Puteoli.
You will have plenty of opportunities to send letters by the
tax-farmers' couriers through the Directors of Land-Tax and
Customs for my Districts.

109 (v. 16)

Scr. in itinere inter Synnada et Philomelium xvii Kal. Sept., ut vid., an. 51

CICERO ATTICO SAL.

1 Etsi in ipso itinere et via discedebant publicanorum tabellarii et eramus in cursu, tamen surripiendum aliquid putavi spati, ne me immemorem mandati tui putares. itaque subsedi in ipsa via, dum haec, quae longiorem desiderant orationem, summatim tibi perscriberem. 5

2 Maxima exspectatione in perditam et plane eversam in perpetuum provinciam nos venisse scito prid. Kal. Sext., moratos triduum Laodiceae, triduum Apameae, totidem dies Synnade. audivimus nihil aliud nisi imperata ἐπικεφάλια solvere non posse, ὠνὰς omnium venditas, civitatum gemitus, 5 ploratus, monstra quaedam non hominis sed ferae nescio cuius immanis. quid quaeris? taedet omnino eos vitae.

3 levantur tamen miserae civitates quod nullus fit sumptus in nos neque in legatos neque in quaestorem neque in quemquam. scito non modo nos faenum aut quod e lege Iulia dari solet non accipere sed ne ligna quidem, nec praeter quattuor lectos et tectum quemquam accipere quicquam, multis locis ne 5 tectum quidem et in tabernaculo manere plerumque. itaque incredibilem in modum concursus fiunt ex agris, ex vicis, ex ⟨oppidis⟩ omnibus; et omnes mehercule etiam adventu nostro reviviscunt, iustitia, abstinentia, clementia tui Ciceronis ⟨cogn⟩ita, quae opiniones omnium superavit. 10

Ep. 109] 1, 4 desiderant *EORs*: se d- *m*: se deserant *NMbd*　　**2**, 2 venisse *EOPms*: inv- *NRMbd*: iam v- *Klotz*　3 moratos *s*: -tus Ω　biduum Laodiceae *Wesenberg*　apamee *m*: -mi(a)e Σ*b*: -me *Mds*　4 ἐπικεφάλια *Victorius* (-λαια *ς*): epicephalia Ω　5 ὠνὰς *Victorius*: onas Ω　6 hominis *EPm*: -nes *NORΔ* 7 omnino eos *Manutius*: omnium nos Ω　　**3**, 3 e Σ: ex *H*: de Δ: *om. Om* 5 ne *OR*: nec *EGNΔ*　8 oppidis omnibus *Ernesti*: nominibus Ω: domibus *ms* et omnes *Watt*: ex omnibus Ω　9 tui *EObds*: tua *GNRM*: tuai *m*　10 cognita quae *Watt*: itaque Ω

109 (V. 16)

En route, *between Synnada and Philomelium, 14 August (?) 51*

CICERO TO ATTICUS

1 The tax-farmers' couriers are leaving as we are actually on our road, in full travel, but I felt I must steal a few minutes so that you should not think I had forgotten your injunction. Accordingly I have sat myself down in the road to write this letter, a summary of matters which deserve a longer description.

2 I must tell you then that on 31 July I made my eagerly awaited entry into this forlorn and, without exaggeration, permanently ruined province, and that I stayed three days in Laodicea, three in Apamea, and as many at Synnada. I have heard of nothing but inability to pay the poll-taxes imposed, universal sales of taxes, groans and moans from the communities, appalling excesses as of some savage beast rather than a human being. In a phrase, these people are absolutely tired of their

3 lives. However it is some relief to the wretched communities that no expense is incurred on my account or that of my Legates or my Quaestor or anyone whosoever. I may tell you that besides hay or what is customarily given under the lex Julia we even decline wood; and except for four couches and a roof no one takes anything—in many places not even a roof; they usually sleep under canvas. So the way the people flock in from every country district, village, and town is hardly to be believed. Upon my word the mere fact of my arrival brings them back to life, knowing as they do the justice, the abstinence, and the clemency of your friend Cicero, which has surpassed all expectations.

45

4   Appius ut audivit nos venire, in ultimam provinciam se
coniecit Tarsum usque. ibi forum agit. de Partho silentium
est, sed tamen concisos equites nostros a barbaris nuntiabant
ii qui veniebant. Bibulus ne cogitabat quidem etiam nunc
in provinciam suam accedere; id autem facere ob eam causam 5
dicebant, quod tardius vellet decedere. nos in castra properabamus, quae aberant bidui.

110 (v. 17)

Scr. in itinere inter Synnada et Philomelium xvi Kal. Sept., ut
vid., an. 51

CICERO ATTICO SAL.

1   Accepi Roma sine epistula tua fasciculum litterarum; in
quo, si modo valuisti et Romae fuisti, Philotimi duco esse
culpam, non tuam. hanc epistulam dictavi sedens in raeda
cum in castra proficiscerer, a quibus aberam bidui. paucis
diebus habebam certos homines quibus darem litteras; itaque 5
eo me servavi.

2   Nos tamen (etsi hoc te ex aliis audire malo) sic in provincia
nos gerimus, quod ad abstinentiam attinet, ut nullus terruncius insumatur in quemquam. id fit etiam et legatorum
et tribunorum et praefectorum diligentia; nam omnes mirifice συμφιλοδοξοῦσιν gloriae meae. Lepta noster mirificus est. 5
sed nunc propero. perscribam ad te paucis diebus omnia.

3   Cicerones nostros Deiotarus filius, qui rex a senatu appel-
latus est, secum in regnum. dum in aestivis nos essemus, illum
pueris locum esse bellissimum duximus.

4   Sestius ad me scripsit quae tecum esset de mea domestica

4, 4 ne cogitabat *s*: negotiabat Ω (-tur G)   7 tridui *Schiche*
Ep. 110] 1, 1 roma *bs*: rom(a)e Ω   2, 2 nullus *NORms*: -lius *GMbd* ter-
uncius ς: ter(r)entius *vel sim.* Ω

4 When Appius heard I was coming he plunged into the furthest corner of the province, right to Tarsus, where he is holding an assize. Of the Parthian there is no whisper, but travellers say that some of our cavalry have been cut to pieces by the orientals. Bibulus is not so much as thinking of getting to his province even now; his motive is said to be that he wants to take his time about leaving it. I am hastening to join the army, which is two days' journey away.

110 (V. 17)
En route, *15 August* (?) *51*
CICERO TO ATTICUS

1 I have received a bundle of letters from Rome but none from you. The fault I take to be Philotimus', not yours, assuming you were well and in Rome. I am dictating this letter as I sit in my carriage on my way to join the army, which is two days' journey away. In a few days' time I have got reliable persons to take letters, so I am reserving myself till then.

2 However, my conduct in my province (though I'd sooner you heard of it from others) is such, so far as financial strictness goes, that not a penny piece is spent on anyone. This is partly due to the conscientiousness of my Legates and Tribunes and Prefects, who are all admirably ambitious for my credit. Our friend Lepta is admirable. But I'm in a hurry now. In a few days I shall give you the whole story.

3 Our boys have been taken by the younger Deiotarus, who has been granted the title of king by the Senate, into the kingdom. We thought that would be the best place for the children while we are campaigning.

4 Sestius has sent me an account of his conversation with you

47

et maxima cura locutus et quid tibi esset visum; amabo te, incumbe in eam rem et ad me scribe quid et possit et tu censeas.

5   Idem scripsit Hortensium de proroganda nostra provincia dixisse nescio quid. mihi in Cumano diligentissime se ut annui essemus defensurum receperat. si quicquam me amas, hunc locum muni. dici non potest quam invitus a vobis absim; et simul hanc gloriam iustitiae et abstinentiae fore 5 illustriorem spero si cito decesserimus, id quod Scaevolae contigit, qui solos novem mensis Asiae praefuit.

6   Appius noster cum me adventare videret, profectus est Tarsum usque Laodicea. ibi forum agit, cum ego sim in provincia. quam eius iniuriam non insector; satis enim habeo negoti in sanandis vulneribus quae sunt imposita provinciae, quod do operam ut faciam quam minima cum illius contumelia. 5 sed hoc Bruto nostro velim dicas, illum fecisse non belle qui adventu meo quam longissime potuerit discesserit.

III (v. 18)

Scr. in castris ad Cybistra xi Kal. Oct. an. 51

CICERO ATTICO SAL.

1   Quam vellem Romae esses, si forte non es! nihil enim certi habebamus nisi accepisse nos tuas litteras a. d. xiiii Kal. Sext. datas, in quibus scriptum esset te in Epirum iturum circiter Kal. Sext. sed sive Romae es sive in Epiro, Parthi Euphraten transierunt duce Pacoro, Orodis regis Parthorum filio, cunctis 5 fere copiis. Bibulus nondum audiebatur esse in Syria; Cassius

---

5, 2 dixisse *cod. Bod.*: dixit Ω   4 muni *CZ*ᵇ: ama Ω   6 illustriorem *Victorius*: iniusti- Ω   6, 2 Laodicea ⟨: -ce(a)e (-cie) Ω   3 iniuriam *OR*: -a *GN*Δ   5 minima cum *s*: inimicum Ω
Ep. III] 1, 3 esset] est *noluit Orelli*   4 euphraten, -em, eufr- *codd.*   5 transierunt *GNORm*: -iverunt Δ   6 fere *CZ*ᵇ: referto Ω

about the domestic concern which is so much in my mind, and of your opinion thereon. Do be a good soul and give it your best attention and write to me both the possibilities and your own opinion.

5   Sestius also wrote that Hortensius had said something about my term being extended. At Cumae he undertook to do his utmost to keep it to one year. If you care for me at all, fortify this position. It is inexpressibly irksome to me to be away from you all. Besides I think the fame I'm winning for justice and integrity is likely to shine all the brighter if I lay down my office quickly, as Scaevola was lucky enough to do—he was governor of Asia for only nine months.

6   When our friend Appius saw me coming he made off from Laodicea all the way to Tarsus. There he is holding an assize though I am in the province, a piece of discourtesy which I am not taking up because I have enough on my hands in healing the hurts inflicted on the province. This I try to do with as little reflexion on him as possible. But you might tell our friend Brutus that he has not behaved very politely in getting as far as possible out of the way when I arrived.

III (V. 18)

Camp outside Cybistra, 20 September 51

CICERO TO ATTICUS

1   How I wish you were in Rome, unless perhaps you are—I have no definite information except that I got your letter dispatched 19 July, in which you wrote you would be going to Epirus about the Kalends of August. However, whether you are in Rome or in Epirus, the Parthians have crossed the Euphrates under Pacorus, son of King Orodes of Parthia, with almost their entire force. There is no word so far of Bibulus being in

in oppido Antiochia est cum omni exercitu, nos in Cappadocia
ad Taurum cum exercitu ad Cybistra; hostis in Cyrrhestica,
quae Syriae pars proxima est provinciae meae. his de rebus
scripsi ad senatum; quas litteras, si es Romae videbis putesne 10
reddendas, et multa, immo omnia, quorum κεφάλαιον ne
quid inter caesa et porrecta, ut aiunt, oneris mihi addatur
aut temporis. nobis enim hac infirmitate exercitus, inopia
sociorum, praesertim fidelium, certissimum subsidium est
hiems. ea si venerit nec illi ante in meam provinciam tran- 15
sierint, unum vereor ne senatus propter urbanarum rerum
metum Pompeium nolit dimittere. quod si alium ad ver
mittit, non laboro, nobis modo temporis ne quid prorogetur.

2   Haec igitur, si es Romae; sin abes aut etiam si ades, haec
negotia sic se habent. stamus animis et, quia consiliis, ut
videmur, bonis utimur, speramus etiam manu. tuto con-
sedimus, copioso a frumento, Ciliciam prope conspiciente,
expedito ad mutandum loco, parvo exercitu sed, ut spero, 5
ad benevolentiam erga nos consentiente; quem nos Deiotari
adventu cum suis omnibus copiis duplicaturi eramus. sociis
multo fidelioribus utimur quam quisquam usus est; quibus
incredibilis videtur nostra et mansuetudo et abstinentia.
dilectus habetur civium Romanorum; frumentum ex agris 10
in loca tuta comportatur. si fuerit occasio, manu, si minus,
locis nos defendemus.

3   Qua re bono animo es; video enim te et, quasi coram adsis,
ita cerno συμπάθειαν amoris tui. sed te rogo, si ullo pacto
fieri poterit, si integra in senatu nostra causa ad Kal. Ian.

---

7 Antiochia est *Heraeus*: -c(h)i(a)e Ω: -chia *Manutius*   8 Cybistra ϛ: cib(r)ustra
vel sim. Ω   12 porrecta ϛ: proiecta ΩC   **2**, 1 es rom(a)e *NORMm*: rom(a)e
es *Gbds*   4 copioso *NRms*: quo piso Δ   a *NMbd*: *om.* O*Rms*   5 mutandum
ΩZᵇ: dimica- *Koch* loco Zᵇ: locum Ω   8 est *Faërnus*: esset Ω   9 videtur
GO*Rms*: videretur *HNMbd*   nostra et *Kayser*: et (*om.* N) n- Ω   10 dilectus
Lambinus: del- Ω   **3**, 3 senatu *GNOR*: -um Δ

Syria. Cassius is in the town of Antioch with his entire army. I am in Cappadocia in the Taurus region with my army near Cybistra. The enemy is in Cyrrhestica, the part of Syria nearest my province. I am writing to the Senate on these matters. Please see, if you are in Rome, whether you think my letter ought to be delivered—and to many other points, all other points in fact, but first and foremost that nothing is added to my responsibilities or my tenure 'twixt the cup and the lip, as they say. For with an army as feeble as mine and so little in the way of allies, loyal ones particularly, my best resource is winter. If that comes without the enemy invading my province first, my only fear is that the Senate will not want to let Pompey go in view of the dangers at home. But if they send someone else by the spring I shall not worry, as long as my own term is not extended.

2   So much then if you are in Rome. But if you are away—or for that matter if you are there—this is how things stand here. There is nothing amiss with our morale, nor I hope with our military effectiveness, because our plans are, I believe, sound. I have taken up a strong position, with plenty of corn available, almost in sight of Cilicia. I can easily change my ground, and the army, though small, is, I think, unanimously well-disposed towards me. When Deiotarus joins us with his full muster I shall double it. I have the loyalty of the provincials in far greater measure than any governor before me; my mildness and abstinence seems to them beyond belief. A levy of Roman citizens is in progress. Corn is being taken from the countryside to safe places. Come the occasion, we shall defend ourselves with our weapons; if not, by the strength of our positions.

3   So be of good cheer. I can see you and perceive your affectionate concern as though you were here beside me. But I do ask of you, if it can by any means be managed and if nothing

manserit, ut Romae sis mense Ianuario. profecto nihil accipiam
iniuriae, si tu aderis. amicos consules habemus, nostrum 5
tribunum pl. Furnium. verum tua est opus adsiduitate,
prudentia, gratia. tempus est necessarium. sed turpe est me
pluribus verbis agere tecum.

4   Cicerones nostri sunt apud Deiotarum, sed, si opus erit,
deducentur Rhodum. tu si es Romae, ut soles, diligentissime, si in Epiro, mitte tamen ad nos de tuis aliquem
tabellarium, et ut tu quid nos agamus et nos quid tu agas
quidque acturus sis scire possimus. ego tui Bruti rem sic ago 5
ut suam ipse non ageret. sed iam exhibeo pupillum neque
defendo; sunt enim negotia et lenta et inania. faciam tamen
satis, tibi quidem, cui difficilius est quam ipsi; sed certe satis
faciam utrique.

112 (v. 19)

Scr. in castris ad Cybistra x Kal. Oct. an. 51 (§1)

CICERO ATTICO SAL.

1 Obsignaram iam epistulam eam quam puto te modo per-
legisse scriptam mea manu, in qua omnia continentur, cum
subito Apellae tabellarius a. d. xi Kal. Oct. septimo quadragesimo die Roma celeriter (hui tam longe!) mihi tuas litteras
reddidit. ex quibus non dubito quin et Pompeium exspectaris 5
dum Arimino rediret et iam in Epirum profectus sis, magisque
vereor, ut scribis, ne in Epiro sollicitus sis non minus quam
nos hic sumus.

---

4 sis *Pius*: essent Ω   5 nostrum λ: -ros Ω   4, 4 et ut tu *GNOR*: et ut *Mbd*:
ut et *ms*   6 suam *NORs*: sic iam *G*: si iam Δ
Ep. 112] **1,** 1 eam *P* (*sed post* iam) λ: meam Ω   3 Apellae *Moll*: ap(p)elli Ω:
apellit *C*   4 Roma ς: -am Ω   hui *Victorius*: ivit *vel sim.* Ω   5 et *R*: ut *GNOΔ*:
tu *Pius*   6 et iam *OPs*: etiam *GN*Δ

happens in the Senate to prejudice my position before the New Year, to be in Rome in January. I am sure I shall take no harm if you are standing by. We have friendly Consuls and a Tribune, Furnius, on our side. But your assiduity and skill and influence are required. It is a crisis. But it would be indecent for me to urge *you* at greater length.

4   Our boys are with Deiotarus, but if necessary will be sent away to Rhodes. If you are in Rome, write to me with your usual admirable diligence; if in Epirus, all the same send me one of your people as courier so that you may hear of my doings and I of yours, present and future. I am looking after your friend Brutus' interests more zealously than he would himself. But I am now producing my ward in court and make no defence—they are a dilatory lot and as poor as charity. However, I shall satisfy expectations, including yours, which are harder to meet than Brutus' own. But rest assured I shall satisfy you both.

112 (V. 19)

Camp outside Cybistra, 21 September 51

CICERO TO ATTICUS

1   I had already sealed the letter which I expect you have just read, written in my own hand and containing all my news, when Apella's courier suddenly arrived with a letter from you—on 20 September, 46 days after setting out from Rome; a rapid journey, and oh, what a long one! The letter leaves me in no doubt both that you waited for Pompey's return from Ariminum and that you have now left for Epirus; rather I am afraid that, as you say, you will have as much on your mind in Epirus as I have here.

De Atiliano nomine scripsi ad Philotimum ne appellaret
2 Messallam. itineris nostri famam ad te pervenisse laetor
magisque laetabor si reliqua cognoris. filiolam tuam tibi
iam Romae iucundam esse gaudeo, eamque quam numquam
vidi tamen et amo et amabilem esse certo scio. etiam atque
etiam vale.   5
3 De Patrone et tuis condiscipulis, quae de parietinis in Melita
laboravi ea tibi grata esse gaudeo. quod scribis libente te
repulsam tulisse eum qui cum sororis tuae fili patruo certaret,
magni amoris signum. itaque me etiam admonuisti ut
gauderem; nam mihi in mentem non venerat. 'non credo' 5
inquis. ut libet; sed plane gaudeo, quoniam τὸ νεμεσᾶν interest
τοῦ φθονεῖν.

113 (v. 20)

Scr. in castris ad Pindenissum xii Kal. Ian. an. 51 (§5)

CICERO ATTICO SAL.

1 Saturnalibus mane se mihi Pindenissitae dediderunt, septimo
et quinquagesimo die postquam oppugnare eos coepimus.
'quid, malum? isti Pindenissitae qui sunt?' inquies; 'nomen
audivi numquam.' quid ego faciam? num potui Ciliciam
Aetoliam aut Macedoniam reddere? hoc iam sic habeto, 5
nunc hoc exercitu hic tanta negotia geri potuisse. quae
cognosce ἐν ἐπιτομῇ: sic enim mihi concedis proximis litteris.

---

9 atiliano G: at(t)el(l)iano RΔ   2, 3 iam rom(a)e Ω: tantopere *Orelli*: tam
caram ac *Koch*   5 vale. de *Victorius*: valde Ω   3, 1 parietinis *anon. ap.*
Victorium: tarent- Ω   Melite (*sic*) *Gassendus*: militia Ω 2 libente te *Lipsius*: -nter
Ω   3 filii *s*: -iis Ω   certarat *Lamb.* (*marg.*): -rit *Corradus* 6 διαφέρει *Boot*
Ep. 113] 1, 1 *et* 3 Pindenissitae *Lambinus*: -sae *Zᵇ*: pendentiss(a)e (*v.* 1) *et*
pendenti (*v.* 3) Ω   2 quadragesimo *Zᵇ*   3 quid *EOR*: qui *NΔ*   4 num Δ:
non *EOR*: unde *N*   6 nunc *scripsi*: nec Ω   nec hic *Wesenberg*   7 cognosce
s: -ere Ω   mihi concedis Σ: c- m- Δ

About the Atilius debt, I have written to Philotimus not to
2 call on Messalla. I am happy to know that the good report of
my journey has reached your ears and shall be still happier when
you learn the sequel. I am glad that your little daughter is now
a pleasure to you in Rome, and never having set eyes on her I
am very fond of her none the less and sure she deserves it. Once
again, good-bye.

3   With regard to Patro and your fellow-pupils, I am happy to
hear you are pleased with the trouble I took over the ruins in
Melita. It's a great sign of affection to say you are glad about
the defeat of your sister's son's uncle's rival. Indeed it's a
prompter to me to rejoice too—which hadn't occurred to me.
You don't believe me? Just as you like, but frankly I do rejoice,
since malice is one thing, righteous indignation another.

113 (V. 20)

Camp at Pindenissum, 19 December 51

CICERO TO ATTICUS

1 Pindenissum surrendered to me on the Saturnalia, eight weeks
after we began the siege. 'Pindenissum?' you'll say, 'And what
the deuce may that be? Never heard of it.' Well, that's no fault
of mine. I couldn't make Cilicia into Aetolia or Macedonia.
You can take it from me here and now: at this time, with this
army, and in this place, just so much could be done. Let me give
you a *résumé*, as you permit in your last letter.

E   55

Ephesum ut venerim nosti, qui etiam mihi gratulatus es illius diei celebritatem, qua nihil me umquam delectavit magis. inde oppidis iis quae erant mirabiliter accepti Laodiceam 10 prid. Kal Sext. venimus. ibi morati biduum perillustres fuimus honorificisque verbis omnis iniurias revellimus superiores; quod idem Apameae quinque dies morati et Synnadis triduum, Philomeli quinque dies, Iconi decem, fecimus. nihil ea iuris dictione aequabilius, nihil lenius, nihil 15 gravius.

2   Inde in castra veni a. d. vii Kal. Sept. a. d. iii exercitum lustravi apud Iconium. ex his castris, cum graves de Parthis †et ceris† nuntii venirent, perrexi in Ciliciam per Cappadociae partem eam quae Ciliciam attingit, eo consilio et ut Armenius Artavasdes et ipsi Parthi Cappadocia se excludi putarent. 5 cum dies quinque ad Cybistra Cappadociae castra habuissem, certior sum factus Parthos ab illo aditu Cappadociae longe abesse, Ciliciae magis imminere; itaque confestim iter in Ciliciam feci per Tauri pylas.

3   Tarsum veni a. d. iii Non. Oct. inde ad Amanum contendi, qui Syriam a Cilicia in aquarum divortio dividit; qui mons erat hostium plenus sempiternorum. hic a. d. iii Id. Oct. magnum numerum hostium occidimus; castella munitissima nocturno Pomptini adventu, nostro matutino cepimus, 5 incendimus; imperatores appellati sumus. castra paucos dies habuimus ea ipsa quae contra Darium habuerat apud Issum Alexander, imperator haud paulo melior quam aut tu aut

---

8 quin λ   9 celebritatem *codd. Ball. et Bod. FZ*[(b)]: -tate Ω   10 qu(a)e erant Ω: qua iter erat *Boot*: quae in itinere erant *Baiter*: quae erant in via *Watt*   accepti *ms*: -pi Ω   12 fuimus ς: fuerunt Ω   13 idem *NOR*: idem dein ΔZ[(b)]   14 Iconii ς: icon(a)e (yc-) Ω   **2**, 1 in *ms* λ: *om.* Ω   vii Δ: vi *N*: viii *OR*   2 iconium (yc-) *NRb*: -nicum *OP*Δ   3 et ceris *ENO*: ceteris *R*: *om.* Δ: et litterae et *vel* et crebri *Watt*   4 et ut *NOR*: ut et *E*: ut Δ   6 Cybistra ς: cibus- Ω   7 aditu *EPbms*: aud- *NORMd*   **3**, 2 a cilicia in *NΔZ*[b]: ac ciliciam *EOR*   3 erat *OP*: erit *ENR*Δ   7 issum *b*: ipsum Ω   8 haud *EOPms*: aut *R*Δ: hanc *N*

You know about my arrival in Ephesus, indeed you have congratulated me on the assemblage that day, one of the most flattering experiences of my life. From there, getting wonderful welcomes in such towns as there were, I reached Laodicea on 31 July. There I spent two days with great *réclame*, and by dint of courteous speeches effaced all earlier grievances. I did the same at Apamea, where I spent five days, and at Synnada (three days), at Philomelium (five days), at Iconium (ten). My administration of justice in these places lacked neither impartiality nor mildness nor responsibility.

2   Thence I arrived in camp on 24 August, and on the 28th reviewed the army near Iconium. As grave reports were coming in about the Parthians, I marched from camp there to Cilicia through that part of Cappadocia which borders Cilicia, so that Artavasdes of Armenia and the Parthians themselves would feel that their way to Cappadocia was blocked. After encamping for five days at Cybistra in Cappadocia I received intelligence that the Parthians were a long way away from that approach to Cappadocia and that the threat was rather to Cilicia. I therefore marched forthwith into Cilicia through the Gates of Taurus.

3   I reached Tarsus on 5 October and pressed on to the Amanus which separates Syria from Cilicia at the watershed, a mountain range full of enemies of Rome from time immemorial. Here on 13 October we made a great slaughter of the enemy, carrying and burning places of great strength, Pomptinus coming up at night and myself in the morning. I received the title of general from the army. For a few days we encamped near Issus in the very spot where Alexander, a considerably better general than either you or I, pitched his camp against Darius. There we

ego. ibi dies quinque morati direpto et vastato Amano inde discessimus. interim (scis enim dici quaedam πανικά, dici 10 item τὰ κενὰ τοῦ πολέμου) rumore adventus nostri et Cassio, qui Antiochia tenebatur, animus accessit et Parthis timor iniectus est; itaque eos cedentis ab oppido Cassius insecutus rem bene gessit; qua in fuga magna auctoritate Osaces dux Parthorum vulnus accepit eoque interiit paucis post diebus. 15 erat in Syria nostrum nomen in gratia.

4   Venit interim Bibulus. credo, voluit appellatione hac inani nobis esse par: in eodem Amano coepit loreolam in mustaceo quaerere. at ille cohortem primam totam perdidit centurio-nemque primi pili, nobilem sui generis, Asinium Dentonem et reliquos cohortis eiusdem et Sex. Lucilium, T. Gavi 5 Caepionis locupletis et splendidi hominis filium, tribunum militum; sane plagam odiosam acceperat cum re tum tempore.

5   Nos ad Pindenissum, quod oppidum munitissimum Eleutherocilicum omnium memoria in armis fuit; feri homines et acres et omnibus rebus ad defendendum parati. cinximus vallo et fossa; aggere maximo, vineis, turre altissima, magna tormentorum copia, multis sagittariis, magno labore, apparatu, 5 multis sauciis nostris, incolumi exercitu, negotium confecimus. hilara sane Saturnalia militibus quoque, quibus exceptis ⟨captivis⟩ reliquam praedam concessimus. mancipia venibant Saturnalibus tertiis; cum haec scribebam, in tribunali res erat ad HS c̄x̄x̄. hinc exercitum in hiberna agri male pacati de- 10 ducendum Quinto fratri dabam; ipse me Laodiceam recipiebam.

---

10 interim Σ: *om.* Δ   11 KENA (κενὰ) *ORΔC:* κοινὰ ς: καινὰ *Bill*
12 accessit Σ: ce- Δ   4, 2 loreolam (laur- *EO*) in mustaceo ΣC: -la minus t- Δ
5, 1 Pindenissum *Z^b*: pendeni- *vel sim.* Ω   2 omni *Lambinus*   4 aggere
*GN*Δ: et ag-*EOR*   7 quibus *NOR:* eq- *M:* equis δ   8 captivis *add. Wesenberg:*
mancipiis *Tyrrell–Purser* (*ambo ante* exceptis)   venibant ς: venieb- Ω   9 tertiis
Victorius: tertis *vel* terris Δ: fertis *N:* certis *OR*   10 ⌐c̄x̄x̄⌐ *Watt: num* ⌐x̄x̄⌐?

stayed five days, plundering and laying waste the Amanus, and then left. Meanwhile—you have heard tell of panics and of nerve-warfare[1]—the rumour of my advent encouraged Cassius, who was shut up in Antioch, and struck terror into the Parthians. Cassius pursued their retreat from the town and gained a success. Osaces, the celebrated Parthian general, died a few days later of a wound received in the flight. My name stood high in Syria.

4   Bibulus arrived meanwhile. I suppose he wanted to be even with me over this bauble of a title—he started looking for a scrap of laurel in the wedding cake in these same mountains of Amanus. The result was that he lost his entire First Cohort, including a Chief-Centurion, Asinius Dento, a distinguished man in his own class, and the other Centurions of the cohort, also a Military Tribune, Sex. Lucilius, whose father T. Gavius Caepio is a man of wealth and standing. It was certainly a nasty reverse, both in itself and as coming when it did.

5   For my part I marched on Pindenissum, a strongly fortified town of the Free Cilicians which had been in arms as long as anyone can remember. The inhabitants were wild, fierce folk, fully equipped to defend themselves. We drew a rampart and moat round the town, erected a huge mound with penthouses and a high tower, plenty of siege artillery and a large number of archers. In the end, with a great deal of labour and apparatus and many of our own men wounded but none killed, we finished the job. The Saturnalia was certainly a merry time, for men as well as officers. I gave them the whole of the plunder excepting the captives, who are being sold off today, 19 December. As I write there is about HS 120,000 on the stand. I am handing over the army to my brother Quintus, who will take it into winter quarters in unsettled country. I myself am returning to Laodicea.

---

[1] Lit. 'the illusions of war': see Commentary.

6   Haec adhuc. sed ad praeterita revertamur. quod me maxime hortaris et quod pluris est quam omnia, in quo laboras ut etiam Ligurino Μώμῳ satis faciamus, moriar si quicquam fieri potest elegantius. nec tamen ego hanc continentiam appello, quae virtus voluptati resistere videtur; ego in vita 5 mea nulla umquam voluptate tanta sum adfectus quanta adficior hac integritate, nec me tam fama, quae summa est, quam res ipsa delectat. quid quaeris? fuit tanti. me ipse non noram nec satis sciebam quid in hoc genere facere possem. recte πεφυσίωμαι: nihil est praeclarius. interim haec λαμπρά: 10 Ariobarzanes opera mea vivit, regnat; ἐν παρόδῳ consilio et auctoritate et quod insidiatoribus eius ἀπρόσιτον me, non modo ἀδωροδόκητον, praebui regem regnumque servavi. interea e Cappadocia ne pilum quidem. Brutum abiectum quantum potui excitavi; quem non minus amo quam tu, 15 paene dixi quam te. atque etiam spero toto anno imperi nostri terruncium sumptus in provincia nullum fore.

7   Habes omnia. nunc publice Romam litteras mittere parabam. uberiores erunt quam si ex Amano misissem. at te Romae non fore! sed est totum ⟨in eo positum⟩, quid Kal. Mart. futurum sit; vereor enim ne, cum de provincia agetur, si Caesar resistet, nos retineamur. his tu si adesses, nihil timerem. 5

8   Redeo ad urbana, quae ego diu ignorans ex tuis iucundissimis litteris a. d. ⟨x⟩v Kal. Ian. denique cognovi. eas diligentissime Philogenes, libertus tuus, curavit perlonga et non satis tuta via perferendas. nam quas Laeni pueris scribis datas

---

6, 4 tamen s: tam Ω: iam Bosius   10 πεφυσίωμαι Victorius: ΠΕΦΕϹΙѠΑΙ vel sim. Ω: πεφύσημαι Lamb. (marg.)   11 regnat NP: -na EORΔ   14 pilum ϛ: pil(l)eum Ω   17 provincia Nb: -am ORΔ   7, 1 habes omnia s: -eo somnia Ω   romam litteras NOR: l- r- Δ (rom(a)e bds)   2 quam si NPs: quasi ORM: quas si bdm at Nm: ac ORΔ   3 in eo positum addidi (in eo Boot)   4 sit m: est Ω   agetur NP: ageretur OR: ger- Δ   8, 1 ex P: et Ω: et e bd: e ms   2 xv cod. Bod.: v Ω

6   So far, so much. But to return to the past. So far as concerns the capital object of your exhortations, the most important point of all, in which you are anxious that I should satisfy even that Ligurian Momus, well, confound me if anything could be more fastidiously correct! But I don't talk of 'restraint' in this connexion, a word which suggests virtuous resistance to pleasurable temptation. Never in all my life have I gained so much pleasure as I do from my integrity here, and it is not so much the *réclame*, which is enormous, as the practice itself that gratifies me. In a word, it has been worth it. I did not know myself, I never quite realized my capabilities in this line. I have a right to a swollen head. It is a fine achievement. Meanwhile here is a scintillation: Ariobarzanes owes his life and throne to me. Just *en passant* I rescued king and kingdom, by good judgement and influence and by showing those who were plotting against him that they could not get near me, much less their money. All the while not a straw was lifted from Cappadocia. I have cheered poor Brutus up as far as I could—I am as fond of him as yourself, I almost said 'as of yourself'. And I hope too that in my entire year of office the province will not be charged a penny.

7   That is all I have to tell. I am now setting about sending an official letter to Rome. There will be more matter in it than if I had written from the Amanus. But to think that you won't be in Rome! Everything depends however on what happens on the Kalends of March. I am afraid that if Caesar is recalcitrant when the question of his command comes up I may be kept on. If you were on the spot I should have no fears.

8   I come back to the affairs of the town, of which I had for a long while been in ignorance until I learned of them on 16 December from your most agreeable letter. Your freedman Philogenes took great trouble to ensure its safe delivery over a very long and not too safe route. The one you say you gave to

non acceperam. iucunda de Caesare et quae senatus decrevit 5
et quae tu speras; quibus ille si cedit, salvi sumus. incendio
Plaetoriano quod †Leius† adustus est minus moleste fero.
Lucceius de Q. Cassio cur tam vehemens fuerit et quid actum
sit aveo scire.

9   Ego cum Laodiceam venero Quinto sororis tuae filio
togam puram iubeor dare; cui moderabor diligentius.
Deiotarus, cuius auxiliis magnis usus sum, ad me, ut scripsit,
cum Ciceronibus Laodiceam venturus erat. tuas etiam
Epiroticas exspecto litteras, ut habeam rationem non modo 5
negoti verum etiam oti tui. Nicanor in officio est et a me
liberaliter tractatur; quem, ut puto, Romam cum litteris
publicis mittam, ut et diligentius perferantur et idem ad me
certa de te et a te referat. Alexis quod mihi totiens salutem
adscribit est gratum; sed cur non suis litteris idem facit quod 10
meus ad te Alexis facit? Phemio quaeritur κέρας. sed haec
hactenus. cura ut valeas et ut sciam quando cogites Romam.
etiam atque etiam vale.

10   Tua tuosque Thermo et praesens Ephesi diligentissime
commendaram et nunc per litteras ipsumque intellexi esse
perstudiosum tui. tu velim, quod antea ad te scripsi, de domo
Pammeni des operam ut quod tuo meoque beneficio puer
habet cures ne qua ratione convellatur; utrique nostrum 5
honestum existimo, tum mihi erit pergratum.

---

5 iucunda *Ernesti*: –de Ω   7 leius *GPMm*: levis *HNOR*: lenis *bds* ambustus
Ernesti 9 aveo δ: habeo Ω   **9**, 3 Deiotarus *Z*: *om.* Ω   5 epiroticas *GP*δ: –cus
ENORM 11 Phemio *Victorius*: phameo Ω*C*   **10,** 5 ne qua *N*δ: neque
GORM cum *ante* utrique *add. Lambinus,* id cum *Buecheler, fort. recte*
6 honestum *Z*ᵇ*c*: *om.* Ω existimo tum *Nbds* (existimo *etiam Z*ᵇ): ex his
motum *HRMm*: motum *G*

Laenius' boys I have not received. The Senate's resolutions on Caesar and your own expectations make pleasant reading. If he yields to them, we are saved. I am the less distressed about Plaetorius' fire because * has been scorched. I'm longing to know why Lucceius took such a strong line about Q. Cassius and what happened.

9 I am under instructions to give your nephew Quintus his white gown when I get to Laodicea. I shall keep him on a tighter rein. Deiotarus, from whom I have had a large military contingent, has written that he will come to me at Laodicea with the boys. I am looking forward to a letter from Epirus, so that I can keep track of your holidays as well as of your business. Nicanor is doing good work and I am treating him handsomely. I think I shall send him to Rome with my official dispatch; that will ensure careful delivery and at the same time he can bring me back reliable news of and from you. I am obliged to Alexis for so often adding his salutations, but why does he not do it in a letter of his own, as *my* Alexis does to you? We are looking for a *cor* for Phemius. But enough. Look after your health and see that I am told when you mean to return to Rome. Again best wishes for your health.

10 I was most careful to recommend your affairs and your people to Thermus when I saw him at Ephesus, and I have now done so again by letter; and I found Thermus himself most anxious to oblige you. I wrote to you some time ago about Pammenes' house; please do your best to see that nothing is done to upset the boy's tenure, which he owes to your favour and mine. I think this will be to our joint credit, moreover it will much oblige me.

114 (V. 21)

Scr. Laodiceae Id. Febr. an. 50 (§9)

CICERO ATTICO SAL.

1 Te in Epirum salvum venisse et, ut scribis, ex sententia navigasse vehementer gaudeo, non esse Romae meo tempore pernecessario submoleste fero. hoc me tamen consolor uno: spero te istic iucunde hiemare et libenter requiescere.

2   Cassius, frater Q. Cassi familiaris tui, pudentiores illas litteras miserat de quibus tu ex me requiris quid sibi voluerit quam eas quas postea misit, quibus per se scribit confectum esse Parthicum bellum. recesserant illi quidem ab Antiochia ante Bibuli adventum, sed nullo nostro εὐημερήματι; hodie vero 5 hiemant in Cyrrhestica, maximumque bellum impendet. nam et Orodi, regis Parthorum, filius in provincia nostra est nec dubitat Deiotarus (cuius filio pacta est Artavasdis filia, ex quo sciri potest) quin cum omnibus copiis ipse prima aestate Euphraten transiturus sit. quo autem die Cassi litterae victrices 10 in senatu recitatae sunt, id est Non. Dec., eodem meae tumultum nuntiantes. Axius noster ait nostras auctoritatis plenas fuisse, illis negat creditum. Bibuli nondum erant adlatae; quas certo scio plenas timoris fore.

3   Ex his rebus hoc vereor, ne, cum Pompeius propter metum rerum novarum nusquam dimittatur, Caesari nullus honos a senatu habeatur, dum hic nodus expediatur, non putet senatus nos ante quam successum sit oportere decedere nec in tanto motu rerum tantis provinciis singulos legatos praeesse. hic ne 5

Ep. 114] **1**, 3 uno *Madvig*: non Ω   **2**, 1 C. Cassius *Boot* pudentiores *Victorius*: pru- Ω   2 voluerint *m*   6 C(h)yrrestica *C*: -cam Ω   7 (h)orodi *P*: -de *EGOR*Δ: -dis *N*   8 Arthavasdis ς: art(h)avadis Ω   10 euphraten *vel* -tem *codd.*   11 id est] datae (*servato* Oct.) *Hofmann* Dec. *Ruete*: oct(obribus) Ω 14 certo *GN*Δ: -te *EOR*   **3**, 3 habeatur *ms*: -etur Ω   expediatur *bs*: experi- Ω

114 (V. 21)

Laodicea, 13 February 51

CICERO TO ATTICUS

1 I am delighted to hear of your safe arrival in Epirus after a 'satisfactory passage', but a little disappointed that you are away from Rome at what is for me a very critical time. However I have this one consolation: I hope you are passing a pleasant winter in Epirus and enjoying the rest.

2 You ask me what Cassius, your friend Q. Cassius' cousin, meant by that dispatch. It was more modest than the one he sent later, in which he claims to have brought the Parthian war to an end. True, they had retreated from Antioch before Bibulus arrived, but not because of any success on our part; and at this moment they are wintering in Cyrrhestica and a major war is in the offing. The son of King Orodes of Parthia is in our province, and Deiotarus, whose son is to marry the daughter of Artavasdes, a good source of information, has no doubt that the king himself will cross the Euphrates with his whole power as soon as summer comes. The same day that Cassius' letter of victory was read out in the Senate, i.e. the Nones of December, my dispatch was read announcing a state of emergency. Our friend Axius says that mine carried a lot of weight and that Cassius' was not believed. No dispatch from Bibulus had then arrived. When one does I know that it will be full of trepidation.

3 What I am therefore afraid of is that, with Pompey not sent out abroad for fear of revolution and the Senate unwilling to make any concessions to Caesar, they may take the view that until this tangle is straightened out we ought not to leave before our successors arrive, and that at so unsettled a time provinces of such importance ought not to be left in charge of a couple

quid mihi prorogetur, quod ne intercessor quidem sustinere
possit, horreo, atque eo magis quod tu abes, qui consilio, gratia,
studio multis rebus occurreres. sed dices me ipsum mihi
sollicitudinem struere. cogor; et velim ita sit, sed omnia
metuo. etsi bellum ἀκροτελεύτιον habet illa tua epistula 10
quam dedisti nauseans Buthroto, 'tibi, ut video et spero,
nulla ad decedendum erit mora'. mallem 'ut video', nihil
opus fuit 'ut spero'.

4　Acceperam autem satis celeriter Iconi per publicanorum
tabellarios a Lentuli triumpho datas. in his γλυκύπικρον
illud: confirmas moram mihi nullam fore, deinde addis, si
quid secus, te ad me esse venturum. angunt me dubitationes
tuae; simul et vides quas acceperim litteras. nam quas Hermoni, 5
centurionis Canulei servo, scribis te dedisse non accepi. Laeni
pueris te dedisse saepe ad me scripseras. eas Laodiceae denique,
cum eo venissem, III Id. Febr. Laenius mihi reddidit datas
a. d. x Kal. Oct. Laenio tuas commendationes et statim verbis
et reliquo tempore ⟨re⟩ probabo.　　　　　　　　　　　10

5　Illae litterae cetera vetera habebant, unum hoc novum de
Cibyratis pantheris. multum te amo quod respondisti M.
Octavio te non putare; sed posthac omnia quae recta non erunt
pro certo negato. Nos enim et nostra sponte bene firmi et
mehercule auctoritate tua inflammati vicimus omnis (hoc tu 5
ita reperies) cum abstinentia tum iustitia, facilitate, clementia.
cave putes quicquam homines magis umquam esse miratos
quam nullum terruncium me obtinente provinciam sumptus

---

11 nauseans *ERm*: -seas *H*: -sias *GNOMbd*　tibi] *nova ep.* Ω: *superiori coniunxit*
Ascensius　12 erit *Z*(b)λc: *om.* Ω　　　4, 2 triumpho *s*: -os Ω　3 addis si ς: addita
Ω　4 esse *NORC*: fore Δ　venturum *M(?)bs*: -ram *NORdm*　angunt *Nm*: ung-
M: pung- *OR*: urgent *bds*　6 Canulei servo *Klotz*: -leiser *R*: -lei sed *N*:
-lcister *P*: -le ipse Δ: caculae ipse *Iunius*　10 re *ms*: *om.* Ω　　　5, 1 ille *OR*:
h(a)e *Nδ*: *om. M*: eae ς　3 recta *GNORCZ¹*: certa Δ　8 nullum terrun-
tium *m*: nullum (nulla(m)) inter(n)u- *vel sim.* Ω　sumptus *sC*: -um Ω

of Legates. In this situation I am terrified of an extension of my term which even a Tribune's veto may not be able to hold up—all the more because you, whose policy, influence, and zeal might forestall many contingencies, are absent. But you will say that I am manufacturing worry for myself. I can't help it. I hope it may be so, but I'm afraid of all manner of things. Still that was a nice tail-piece to the letter you dispatched from Buthrotium with the sea in your stomach: 'As I see and hope, there won't be any difficulty about your leaving'—only I wish you had just said 'as I see'. No need for 'as I hope'.

4   The letter you dispatched to me just after Lentulus' Triumph was delivered to me by the tax-farmers' couriers at Iconium in pretty good time. There is a piece of sweet-and-sour in it: you affirm that there won't be any difficulty; then you add that if anything goes wrong you will join me. Your dubieties put me on the rack. Incidentally you see which letters have come to hand. I have not had the one which you say you gave to Hermo, Centurion Canuleius' slave. You had often mentioned having given a letter to Laenius' boys. This letter, dispatched 21 September, was finally handed to me by Laenius at Laodicea, when I arrived there on 11 February. My words to Laenius at the time and my actions later on will make him appreciate the value of your recommendation.

5   Most of the letter was ancient history, but there was one fresh item about the Cibyra panthers. I am very much obliged to you for telling M. Octavius that you thought not. But in future please give a definite 'no' to any improper requests. For what with my own disposition, which is sufficiently resolute, and, let me add, the stimulus of your encouragement, I have broken all records (yes, you will find it is so) not only for integrity but for justice, affability, and clemency too. Believe me, people have had the surprise of their lives to find that during my governorship not a penny of expense has been incurred by the

factum esse nec in rem publicam nec in quemquam meorum
praeter quam in L. Tullium leg⟨atum⟩. is ceteroqui abstinens, 10
sed Iulia lege †transitam† semel tamen in diem, non ut alii
solebant omnibus vicis (praeter eum semel, nemo), accepit.
hic facit ut mihi excipiendus sit cum terruncium nego sumptus
factum; praeter eum accepit nemo. has a nostro Q. Titinio
sordis accepimus.   15

6   Ego aestivis confectis Quintum fratrem hibernis et Ciliciae
praefeci. Q. Volusium, tui Tiberi generum, certum hominem
et mirifice abstinentem, misi in Cyprum ut ibi pauculos dies
esset, ne cives Romani pauci qui illic negotiantur ius sibi
dictum negarent; nam evocari ex insula Cyprios non licet. 5

7   Ipse in Asiam profectus sum Tarso Non. Ian., non mehercule
dici potest qua admiratione Ciliciae civitatum maximeque
Tarsensium. postea vero quam Taurum transgressus sum,
mirifica exspectatio Asiae nostrarum dioecesium, quae sex
mensibus imperi mei nullas meas acceperat litteras, numquam 5
hospitem viderat. illud autem tempus quotannis ante me fuerat
in hoc quaestu. civitates locupletes ne in hiberna milites
reciperent magnas pecunias dabant, Cyprii talenta Attica CC;
qua ex insula (non ὑπερβολικῶς sed verissime loquor)
nummus nullus me obtinente erogabitur. ob haec beneficia, 10
quibus illi obstupescunt, nullos honores mihi nisi verborum
decerni sino; statuas, fana, τέθριππα prohibeo, nec sum in
ulla re alia molestus civitatibus—sed fortasse tibi qui haec

---

9 meorum *b*: eo- Ω   10 legatum. is ceteroqui *Victorius*: legis ceteros qui Ω
11 sed *del. Baiter*: est sed *Boot*: e *Watt*   transitam *OR*Δ: -tum *N*: translaticia
Watt   12 praeter . . . nemo *delenda censuit Graevius*   13 hic *NOR*: *om.* Δ:
sic *Watt*   6, 1 q(uintum) *vel* que *NORb*: que per Δ   3 et *N*: sed Ω   4 esset
Pius: sed Ω   7, 1 asiam Σ*s*: asia Δ   4 dioecesium *c*: dioce(n)s(i)um Ω
8 Cyprii ⟨: -ri Ω   9 qua *sc*: qu(a)e Ω   10 erogabitur *GNOR*λ: -batur *E*Δ
12 fana, τέθριππα *Scala*: ea nate ΘP- *RM*: ΕΑΝΑΤΕΘP- *m*: ea nate *bds*

province either for public purposes or for any member of my staff, my Legate L. Tullius excepted. He is generally scrupulous, but he did take the ordinary(?) allowance under the lex Julia, only once a day, however, not at every village as used to be the practice of others—and apart from him on the one occasion nobody has done so. So he obliges me to make an exception of him when I say that not a penny of expense has been incurred. Him aside, no one has taken anything. This blot on my copy-book I owe to our friend Q. Titinius.

6   At the end of the campaigning season I put my brother in charge of winter quarters and Cilicia. I sent Q. Volusius, your friend Tiberius' son-in-law, a reliable man and also exceptionally scrupulous, to Cyprus for two or three days so that the few Roman citizens who carry on business there should not say they had no one to try their cases—Cypriots cannot legally be summoned out of the island.

7   I myself left Tarsus for Asia on the Nones of January amid really indescribable enthusiasm among the Cilician communities, especially the people of Tarsus. After crossing the Taurus I found a marvellous eagerness for my arrival in the districts of Asia under me, which in the six months of my administration had not received a single letter of mine or seen a compulsory guest. Before my time that part of the year had regularly been occupied with profiteering of this sort. The richer communities used to give large sums to avoid having troops quartered on them. The Cypriots gave 200 Attic talents. While I am governor the island will not be asked for a penny—that is not hyperbole, it is the naked truth. In return for these benefits, which dumbfound the provincials, I allow none but verbal honours to be decreed to me. I forbid statues, temples, chariots. Nor do I impose myself upon the communities in any other way—but

praedicem de me. perfer, si me amas; tu enim me haec facere
voluisti.   15

8   Iter igitur ita per Asiam feci ut etiam fames, qua nihil
miserius est, quae tum erat in hac mea Asia (messis enim nulla
fuerat), mihi optanda fuerit; quacumque iter feci, nulla vi,
nullo iudicio, nulla contumelia, auctoritate et cohortatione
perfeci ut et Graeci et cives Romani qui frumentum com- 5
presserant magnum numerum populis pollicerentur.

9   Id. Febr., quo die has litteras dedi, forum institueram agere
Laodiceae Cibyraticum et Apamense, ex Id. Mart. ibidem
Synnadense, Pamphylium (tum Phemio dispiciam κέρας),
⟨Lyc⟩aonium, Isauricum; ex Id. Mai. in Ciliciam, ut ibi
Iunius consumatur, velim tranquille a Parthis. Quintilis, si erit 5
ut volumus, in itinere est per provinciam redeuntibus con-
sumendus; venimus enim in provinciam Laodiceam Sulpicio
et Marcello consulibus prid. Kal. Sext., inde nos oportet
decedere a. d. III Kal. Sext. primum contendam a Quinto
fratre ut se praefici patiatur, quod et illo et me invitissimo 10
fiet. sed aliter honeste fieri non potest, praesertim cum virum
optimum Pomptinum ne nunc quidem retinere possim; rapit
enim hominem Postumius Romam, fortasse etiam Postumia.

10 Habes consilia nostra; nunc cognosce de Bruto. familiaris
habet Brutus tuus quosdam creditores Salaminorum ex
Cypro, M. Scaptium et P. Matinium, quos mihi maiorem in
modum commendavit. Matinium non novi. Scaptius ad me in
castra venit. pollicitus ei sum curaturum me Bruti causa ut 5

9, 2 apamense δ: -em Ω   3 synadense s: -em Ω   tum R: cum NOPΔ
Phemio *Victorius*: se- Ω   dispiciam Nd (desp- N): -ceam ORΔ   κέρας C: KEPACA
Ω   4 Lycaonium *Mongault*: aon- C: omnium Ω   5 Iunius ς: in ius Ω   Quintilis ς:
-tius Ω   9 III *Manutius*: IIII Ω   primum δ: -mas Ω   11 sed c: et ORΔ: om. N:
at *Ascensius*   13 enim hominem Nδ: h- e- ORM   **10**, 2 tuus HNPm: tuos
GORΔ   3 matinium HORM: vat- GNPδ (*itidem fere infra*)   5 ei NOR: om.
GΔ   causa G: -am ORΔ: casum N

70

perhaps I do upon you when I blow my own trumpet like this. Put up with it if you love me; after all it was you who wanted me to act so.

8 Well then, I have travelled through Asia in such a fashion as to make even that most dreadful of calamities, famine, which was rampant in my part of Asia after the total failure of the harvest, a thing from my point of view to be desired. Wherever I passed I induced both natives and Roman citizens who had hoarded corn to promise large quantities to the public, not by any violence or legal proceedings or harsh language but by influence and encouragement.

9 On the Ides of February, the date of this letter, I have arranged to hold assize at Laodicea for the districts of Cibyra and Apamea; from the Ides of March, also at Laodicea, for Synnada, Pamphilia (I'll spy out a *cor* for Phemius then), Lycaonia, and Isauria. After the Ides of May I shall go to Cilicia to spend June there, I trust without interruption from the Parthians. July, if all goes well, will be occupied in the return journey through the province. I entered it at Laodicea on 31 July in the Consulship of Sulpicius and Marcellus, so I ought to leave it on 30 July. In the first instance I shall try to get my brother to let himself be left in charge, though that will be very far from the wishes of either one of us. But it is the only seemly course, especially as I cannot keep the excellent Pomptinus even now. Postumius is hurrying him to Rome, perhaps Postumia also.

10 So much for my plans. Now let me tell you about Brutus. Your friend Brutus is on close terms with certain creditors of the people of Salamis in Cyprus, M. Scaptius and P. Matinius. He warmly recommended them to me. Matinius I don't know. Scaptius came to me in camp. I promised to see to it for Brutus' sake that the Salaminians paid him his money. He

ei Salamini pecuniam solverent. egit gratias; praefecturam petivit. negavi me cuiquam negotianti dare, quod idem tibi ostenderam (Cn. Pompeio petenti probaram institutum meum, quid dicam Torquato de M. Laenio tuo, multis aliis?); sin praefectus vellet esse syngraphae causa, me curaturum ut 10 exigeret. gratias egit, discessit. Appius noster turmas aliquot equitum dederat huic Scaptio per quas Salaminos coerceret, et eundem habuerat praefectum; vexabat Salaminos. ego equites ex Cypro decedere iussi. moleste tulit Scaptius.

11 Quid multa? ut ei fidem meam praestarem, cum ad me Salamini Tarsum venissent et una Scaptius, imperavi ut pecuniam solverent. multa de syngrapha, de Scapti iniuriis. negavi me audire; hortatus sum, petivi etiam pro meis in civitatem beneficiis ut negotium conficerent, dixi denique 5 me coacturum. homines non modo non recusare sed etiam hoc dicere, se a me solvere; quod enim praetori dare consuessent quoniam ego non acceperam, se a me quodam modo dare, atque etiam minus esse aliquanto in Scapti nomine quam in vectigali praetorio. collaudavi homines. 'recte' inquit 10 Scaptius, 'sed subducamus summam.' interim cum ego in edicto translaticio centesimas me observaturum haberem cum anatocismo anniversario, ille ex syngrapha postulabat quaternas. 'quid ais?' inquam, 'possumne contra meum edictum?' at ille profert senatus consultum Lentulo Philippoque 15 consulibus, 'ut qui Ciliciam obtineret [et] ius ex illa 12 syngrapha diceret.' cohorrui primo; etenim erat interitus

---

9 quid ς: quod Ω   sin P: sim Ω   11, 2 una GNORbds: in iis M: in his m: om. H   4 petivi OR: det- Mm: decium Nbd   5 dixi denique GNOR: dedi- Δ   7 consuessent s: -sem Ω   10 collaudavi s: -it Ω   13 anatocismo Corradus: antiochi(i)s Ω: anatocis 'codices manuscripti' teste Bosio: ἀνατοκισμῷ Tyrrell–Purser   14 quaternas Victorius: illo Ω   15 edictum cod. Bod.: di- Ω   16 coss. ς: consul(e) Ω   et del. Victorius   ius Ps: eius Ω   12, 1 etenim erat R: et erat enim NOPMm

thanked me and requested an appointment as Prefect. I told him that I never gave these appointments to business men, just as I had told you (I explained my rule to Cn. Pompeius when he made a similar request and he approved it, not to mention Torquatus, in the case of your friend M. Laenius, and many others). But I added that if it was because of his bond that he wanted a Prefecture I would see that he got his money. He thanked me and took his leave. Our friend Appius had given some squadrons of horse to this Scaptius with which to put pressure on the Salaminians, and had also made him a Prefect. He was oppressing the Salaminians, so I ordered the troopers to leave Cyprus. Scaptius was not pleased.

11   To cut a long story short: in order to keep my word to him, when the Salaminians came to me at Tarsus and Scaptius too, I ordered them to pay the money. They had much to say about the bond and Scaptius' ill-usage. I refused to listen. I urged them, even besought them in return for my good offices to their community, to settle the business. Finally I threatened compulsion. Far from making any objection, they told me that they were paying out of my pocket, pointing out that as I had not taken what they customarily gave a governor I was in a sense footing the bill. In fact the amount owing to Scaptius was, they said, somewhat less than the governor's levy. I commended them. 'Very well' says Scaptius, 'but let us reckon up the sum.' Meanwhile, although I had put in my traditionary edict that I should observe a rate of 1% interest compounded annually, Scaptius asked for 4% according to his bond. 'Come now' said I, 'do you expect me to contravene my own edict?' Scaptius however produced a senatorial decree passed in the Consulship of Lentulus and Philippus providing that 'the governor of Cilicia should give judgement in accordance with
12 that bond'. This gave me a bad shock to start with, for it meant

73

civitatis. reperio duo senatus consulta isdem consulibus de eadem syngrapha. Salamini cum Romae versuram facere vellent, non poterant, quod lex Gabinia vetabat. tum iis Bruti familiares freti gratia Bruti dare volebant quaternis, si sibi 5 senatus consulto caveretur. fit gratia Bruti senatus consultum, 'ut neve Salaminis neve qui eis dedisset fraudi esset'. pecuniam numerarunt. at postea venit in mentem faeneratoribus nihil se iuvare illud senatus consultum, quod ex syngrapha ius dici lex Gabinia vetaret. tum fit senatus consul- 10 tum ut ex ea syngrapha ⟨ius diceretur, hoc est, ut nec deteriore nec meliore iure ea syngrapha⟩ esset quam ceterae sed ut eodem. cum haec disseruissem, seducit me Scaptius; ait se nihil contra dicere, sed illos putare talenta CC se debere; ea se velle accipere; debere autem illos paulo minus. rogat ut eos ad ducenta 15 perducam. 'optime' inquam. voco illos ad me remoto Scaptio. 'quid vos? quantum' inquam 'debetis?' respondent 'CVI'. refero ad Scaptium. homo clamare. 'quid opus est' inquam 'potius quam rationes conferatis?' adsidunt, subducunt; ad nummum convenit. illi se numerare velle, urgere ut acciperet. Scaptius 20 me rursus seducit, rogat ut rem sic relinquam. dedi veniam homini impudenter petenti; Graecis querentibus, ut in fano deponerent postulantibus non concessi. clamare omnes qui aderant nihil impudentius Scaptio, qui centesimis cum anatocismo contentus non esset, alii nihil stultius. mihi autem 25

---

4 iis *Victorius*: is *P*Δ: hi(i)s *NOR*   5 volebant ς: so- Ω   quaternis *intellexit Victorius*: quat(t)uor Ω   8 at *Ernesti*: et Ω: sed *Wesenberg*   11 ius diceretur *add. Malaespina, cetera Sternkopf*   16 voco *Ps*: volo Ω 17 quid? vos quantum *Mueller* CVI *Victorius*: cui Ω   18 potius *NOR*: *om.* Δ   19 ad *NOR*: *om.* Δ   20 et ut *Ascensius*   23 clamare *NOPsC*: id am- *Mbd*: id clam- *m*   24 alii *ante* nihil *add. Sternkopf*   25 alii *O*: aliis *R*Δ: *om.* P

nothing less than ruin for the town. I found that there were two senatorial decrees passed in the same year concerning the same bond. When the Salaminians wanted to raise a loan in Rome they were unable to do so because the lex Gabinia forbade it. Then Brutus' friends, relying on his influence, agreed to lend at 4% providing they were safeguarded by a senatorial decree. Through Brutus' influence a decree was passed indemnifying both the Salaminians and any person from whom they borrowed the money. So they handed over the cash. But later on it occurred to the lenders that this decree was no use to them because the lex Gabinia made the bond legally invalid. Then the Senate passed the decree which provided that judgement should be given according to that bond— not thereby giving this bond a status better or worse than other bonds but the same. When I had explained all this, Scaptius took me on one side and said that he had no objection to offer, but the Salaminians were under the impression that they owed 200 talents. He was ready to accept that sum, but in fact they owed him slightly less. So he asked me to bring them up to 200. 'Very good' said I. Then I summoned the Salaminians, Scaptius having left the room. 'Well gentlemen' I said, 'how much do you owe?' '106 talents' was the answer. I put this to Scaptius. Loud protest. So I said 'The best thing you can do is to compare accounts'. So they sat down together and totted everything up. The figures tallied to a penny. The Salaminians expressed their willingness to pay cash down and pressed Scaptius to accept. Then Scaptius took me aside again and asked me to leave the matter there. It was an impudent request, but I gave the man his way; and when the Greeks protested and demanded leave to deposit the money in a temple, I would not allow it. All present were loud in condemnation of Scaptius' egregious impudence or, as others saw it, stupidity in refusing to be

impudens magis quam stultus videbatur; nam aut bono
nomine centesimis contentus ⟨non⟩ erat aut non bono quaternas centesimas sperabat.

13   Habes meam causam. quae si Bruto non probatur, nescio
cur illum amemus; sed avunculo eius certe probabitur, praesertim cum senatus consultum modo factum sit (puto, postquam tu es profectus) in creditorum causa ut centesimae
perpetuo faenore ducerentur. hoc quid intersit, si tuos digitos 5
novi, certe habes subductum. in quo quidem, ὁδοῦ πάρεργον,
⟨L.⟩ Lucceius M. f. queritur apud me per litteras summum
esse periculum ne culpa senatus his decretis res ad tabulas novas
perveniat; commemorat quid olim mali C. Iulius fecerit
cum dieculam duxerit; numquam rei publicae plus. sed ad 10
rem redeo. meditare adversus Brutum causam meam, si haec
causa est contra quam nihil honeste dici possit, praesertim
cum integram rem et causam reliquerim.

14   Reliqua sunt domestica. de ἐνδομύχῳ probo idem quod
tu, Postumiae filio, quoniam Pontidia nugatur; sed vellem
adesses. a Quinto fratre his mensibus nihil exspectaris; nam
Taurus propter nivis ante mensem Iunium transiri non potest.
Thermum, ut rogas, creberrimis litteris fulcio. P. Valerium 5
negat habere quicquam Deiotarus rex eumque ait ⟨a⟩ se
sustentari. cum scies Romae intercalatum sit necne, velim
ad me scribas certum quo die mysteria futura sint. litteras
tuas minus paulo exspecto quam si Romae esses, sed tamen
exspecto.   10

---

27 non *ante* contentus *add. Ernesti, ante* erat *Purser*   13, 4 creditorum ϛ: -tum Ω   ut *P*: aut Ω   7 L. *add. Ellendt*   10 duxerit *Pius*: dix- Ω
rei p. *cod. Ball.*: res p(ublica) Ω   12 possit *Bayet*: -set *Ps*: -se *NRMbd*: potest *m*
14, 1 quod ϛ: cum Ω   2 filio *Manutius*: -i(a)e Ωλ: -ium *Turnebus*   pontidia *s*:
pon(i)dia *vel* pomdia Ω   5 Thermum *anon. ap. Ascensium*: her- Ω   6 a *add.*
Hervagius   7 sustentare *ms*

satisfied with 1% compound interest. For my part I thought him impudent rather than stupid, either as not satisfied with 1% on a good debt or as hoping for 4% on a bad one.

13 Well, there is my case, and if Brutus does not accept it I fail to see why we should care for him. But his uncle will certainly accept it, especially as the Senate recently passed a decree for creditors, after you left Rome, I think, fixing 1% simple interest as the legal rate. If I know your arithmetical powers, you have already reckoned up the difference. *À propos* and *en passant*, L. Lucceius, son of Marcus, complains in a letter to me that there is a serious risk, for which the Senate is to blame, of a general cancellation of debts resulting from these decrees. He recalls the damage C. Julius did when he allowed a tiny delay in payments—the worst blow, says he, ever dealt the state. But to return. Get up my case against Brutus, if one can speak of a case when there is nothing that can decently be said on the other side, particularly as I have left case and issue quite open.

14 The rest concerns domesticities. About the *arcanum*, I favour the same solution as you, Postumia's son, since Pontidia is trifling. But I wish you were on the spot. You must not expect anything from Quintus in the next few months. Snow makes the Taurus impassable before June. I am bolstering up Thermus as you ask with letters at frequent intervals. King Deiotarus says that P. Valerius hasn't a penny and is subvented by himself. When you know whether or not there has been an intercalation in Rome please write to me definitely the date of the Mysteries. I don't expect to hear from you quite so much as if you were in Rome; but still, expect I do.

115 (VI. 1)

Scr. Laodiceae x Kal. Mart. an. 50 (§26)

CICERO ATTICO SAL.

1 Accepi tuas litteras a. d. v Terminalia Laodiceae; quas legi libentissime plenissimas amoris, humanitatis, offici, diligentiae. iis igitur respondebo, * * * (sic enim postulas), nec οἰκονομίαν meam instituam sed ordinem conservabo tuum. Recentissimas a Cybistris te meas litteras habere ais a. d. 5 x Kal. Oct. datas et scire vis tuas ego quas acceperim. omnis fere quas commemoras, praeter eas quas scribis Lentuli pueris et quas Equo Tutico et Brundisio datas. qua re non οἴχεται tua industria, quod vereris, sed praeclare ponitur, si quidem id egisti, ut ego delectarer; nam nulla re sum delectatus magis. 10

2 Quod meam βαθύτητα in Appio tibi, liberalitatem etiam in Bruto probo, vehementer gaudeo; ac putaram paulo secus. Appius enim ad me ex itinere bis terve ὑπομεμψιμοίρους litteras miserat quod quaedam a se constituta rescinderem. ut si medicus, cum aegrotus alii medico traditus sit, irasci 5 velit ei medico qui sibi successerit si quae ipse in curando constituerit immutet ille, sic Appius, cum ἐξ ἀφαιρέσεως provinciam curarit, sanguinem miserit, quicquid potuit detraxerit, mihi tradiderit enectam, προσανατρεφομένην eam a me non libenter videt sed modo suscenset, [et] modo gratias agit. 10 nihil enim a me fit cum ulla illius contumelia; tantum modo dissimilitudo meae rationis offendit hominem. quid enim

---

Ep. 115] 1, 1 Terminalia *CZ*[1(b)]: ter milia Ω   3 *lac. ind. Victorius:* χρύσεα χαλκείων *add. Leopardus:* non χ- χ- *Wesenberg:* sed non χ- χ- *Watt:* κατὰ μίτον *Boot*   5 Cybistris te *C:* cibi(s) triste(s) *vel sim.* Ω   8 et quas *NOR:* et Δ: *om. c*   9 quod *M:* quam *NPδ:* quam quod *OR*   **2,** 1 liberalitatem *OPΔλ:* libert-*NR*   etiam *s:* et iam *m:* et tam Ω   2 paulo *NORc: om.* Δ   3 enim *NORΔ:* em. *EG*   terve *Hms:* terne Ω   6 medico *del. Boot*   9 eam a *C:* et ama Ω   10 videt *Manutius:* vidi Ω   modo *m:* et modo Ω

115 (VI. 1)

Laodicea, 20 February 50

CICERO TO ATTICUS

1 I got a letter from you on 19 February at Laodicea, and read it with the greatest enjoyment—so full of affection, kindliness, and friendly attentiveness. So I shall answer it in detail(?), since that is what you ask; nor shall I make my own arrangement of topics but shall keep to your order.

You say that the most recent letter you have had from me was dispatched on 21 September from Cybistra, and you want to know which of yours have reached me. Almost all you mention, the exceptions being the one you say you gave Lentulus' boys and those dispatched from Equus Tuticus and Brundisium. So your diligence, so far from going for nothing as you are afraid it may, is excellently invested, at any rate if your object was to give me pleasure. Nothing has ever given me more.

2 I am glad indeed that my self-restraint in the case of Appius and also my readiness to oblige in that of Brutus wins your approval. I had thought it might be somewhat otherwise, for Appius sent me two or three rather querulous letters on his way home, blaming me for rescinding some of his ordinances— as though a doctor whose patient has been handed over to another practitioner were to choose to take umbrage against his successor for changing the treatment. After having kept Cilicia under a lowering régime, cupping and reducing all he could, and handed her over to me in the last stages of exhaustion, he doesn't much relish seeing her fed up again by me, so he takes offence one day and thanks me the next. I do nothing, you see, to cast reflexion upon him; it is simply the difference in my system that disgruntles the man. In fact could any two

79

potest esse tam dissimile quam illo imperante exhaustam
esse sumptibus et iacturis provinciam, nobis eam obtinentibus
nummum nullum esse erogatum nec privatim nec publice? 15
quid dicam de illius praefectis, comitibus, legatis etiam? de
rapinis, de libidinibus, de contumeliis? nunc autem domus
mehercule nulla tanto consilio aut tanta disciplina gubernatur
aut tam modesta est quam nostra tota provincia. haec non
nulli amici Appi ridicule interpretantur, qui me idcirco 20
putent bene audire velle ut ille male audiat et recte facere
non meae laudis sed illius contumeliae causa. sin Appius,
ut Bruti litterae quas ad te misit significabant, gratias nobis
agit, non moleste fero, sed tamen eo ipso die quo haec ante
lucem scribebam cogitabam eius multa inique constituta et 25
acta tollere.

3   Nunc venio ad Brutum, quem ego omni studio te auctore
sum complexus, quem etiam amare coeperam; sed ⟨plane⟩
dico, me revocavi ne te offenderem. noli enim putare me
quicquam maluisse quam ut mandatis satis facerem nec ulla
de re plus laborasse. mandatorum autem mihi libellum dedit, 5
isdemque de rebus tu mecum egeras. omnia sum diligentissime
persecutus. primum ab Ariobarzane sic contendi, ut talenta
* * * quae mihi pollicebatur illi daret. quoad mecum rex fuit,
perbono loco res erat; post a Pompei procuratoribus sescentis
premi coeptus est. Pompeius autem cum ob ceteras causas 10
plus potest unus quam ceteri omnes, tum quod putatur ad
bellum Parthicum esse venturus. ei tamen sic nunc solvitur:
tricesimo quoque die talenta Attica XXXIII, et hoc ex tributis;
nec id satis efficitur in usuram menstruam. sed Gnaeus noster

---

15 er(r)ogatum *ERPΔ*: rog- *GNOC*   19 haec *Manutius*: hanc Ω   21 putant *s*
3, 2 plane dico *scripsi*: dico Ω: illico *s*: cito *Orelli*: idcirco *vel* ideo *Kahnt*
3 me revocavi Σ*c*: r- me Δ   4 satis *EHOP*δ: *om. GNRM*   7 c talenta *Purser*
9 post a *EORms*: -tea a *N*: -tea *M*: post *Gbd*   14 id] ita *Orelli*: inde *Otto*
efficit *Ernesti*

systems differ more widely? When he was governor the province was drained dry with charges and disbursements, while since I took over not a sixpence has been paid out either privately or publicly. Need I speak of his Prefects and staff, his Legates too? The robberies, the outrages, the indignities? Whereas now I really don't think you could point to a private household so wisely and strictly run or so well-behaved as my entire province. Certain friends of Appius put an absurd construction on all this, fancying that I am desirous of a good reputation in order to give him a bad one, and that I am an honest governor not to gain credit for myself but to cast reflexion on him. However if Appius says he's grateful to me, as intimated in Brutus' letter to you, so much the better. But this same day that is about to dawn as I write I propose to cancel many of his unjust ordinances and proceedings.

3 Now I come to Brutus, whose friendship at your prompting I eagerly embraced, of whom I had even begun to be fond—but I tell you plainly, I checked myself for fear of offending *you*. I do assure you that I wanted above all things to execute his commissions and that there is nothing over which I have taken greater trouble. He gave me a memorandum of these, and you had already raised the same matters with me. I have followed them all up most faithfully. First I persuaded Ariobarzanes to give Brutus the * talents which he was ready to promise to myself. As long as the king was with me the affair was in excellent train, but afterwards droves of Pompey's agents began to put pressure on him. Now Pompey can do more than the rest of the world put together because, besides all the other reasons, it is thought that he will be coming out to take command against the Parthians. Yet he is now being paid at the rate of 33 Attic talents every 30 days, and that out of taxes, which is not enough to cover the monthly interest. However our Gnaeus

clementer id fert; sorte caret, usura nec ea solida contentus 15
est. alii neque solvit cuiquam nec potest solvere; nullum
enim aerarium, nullum vectigal habet. Appi instituto tributa
imperat; ea vix in faenus Pompei quod satis sit efficiunt. amici
regis duo tresve perdivites sunt, sed ii suum tam diligenter
tenent quam ego aut tu. equidem non desino tamen per 20

4 litteras rogare, suadere, accusare regem. Deiotarus etiam
mihi narravit se ad eum legatos misisse de re Bruti; eos sibi
responsum rettulisse illum non habere. et mehercule ego ita
iudico, nihil illo regno spoliatius, nihil rege egentius. itaque
aut tutela cogito me abdicare aut, ut pro Glabrione Scaevola, 5
faenus et impendium recusare. ego tamen quas per te Bruto
promiseram praefecturas M. Scaptio, L. Gavio, qui in regno
rem Bruti procurabant, detuli; nec enim in provincia mea
negotiabantur. tu autem meministi nos sic agere ut quot
vellet praefecturas sumeret, dum ne negotiatori; itaque duas 10
ei praeterea dederam, sed ii quibus petierat de provincia de-
cesserant.

5   Nunc cognosce de Salaminis, quod video tibi etiam novum
accidisse, tamquam mihi. numquam enim ex illo audivi illam
pecuniam esse suam; quin etiam libellum ipsius habeo in
quo est 'Salamini pecuniam debent M. Scaptio et P. Matinio,
familiaribus meis'. eos mihi commendat; adscribit etiam et 5
quasi calcar admovet intercessisse se pro iis magnam pecuniam.
confeceram ut solverent centesimis †sexenni† ductis cum
renovatione singulorum annorum. at Scaptius quaternas
postulabat. metui, si impetrasset, ne tu ipse me amare desineres;

---

15 sorte *Hervagius*: fo- Ω   19 ii (hi(i) *EGR*) su(u)m (*om. G*) *EGOR*: usum *N*Δ
4, 11 pr(a)eterea *NMC*: pr(a)efecturas *EOR*δ   **5, 2** illam *NOR*: ul- Δ
7 biennii *Sternkopf* (*vide comm.*)

is being quite reasonable about it—he foregoes his principal and is content with interest, and less than the full interest. The king is paying nobody else, nor can he—he has no treasury, no regular revenue. He levies taxes on Appius' model and they hardly produce enough to pay Pompey's interest. Two or three of his friends are very wealthy men, but they take as good care to keep their own as you or I. For my part I am none the less constantly writing to the king with requests and persuasions

4 and reproaches. Deiotarus also told me that he had sent envoys to him about Brutus' affair, and that they had come back with the reply that the king did not have the wherewithal. My own honest opinion is that the kingdom is stripped to the bone and the king an absolute pauper. So I am thinking of renouncing my trusteeship, or else of doing what Scaevola did for Glabrio and refusing to pay interest or let it accumulate (?). However I gave M. Scaptius and L. Gavius, who are looking after Brutus' interests in Cappadocia, the Prefectures which I had promised Brutus through you, seeing that they are not doing business in my province. You remember the line I took, that he could have as many Prefectures as he wanted so long as they were not for business men. I had accordingly granted him two others as well, but the persons for whom he asked them had left the province.

5 Now let me tell you about the Salaminians—I see it has come as a surprise to you just as it did to me. I never once heard him say that the money was his own. In fact I have his own memorandum which says:—'The Salaminians owe money to my friends M. Scaptius and P. Matinius'. He recommends them to me and adds by way of extra stimulus that he had gone surety for them for a large sum. I had arranged for payment by the debtors with interest calculated at 1% per month for * years, interest to be added to the principal annually. Scaptius however demanded 4%. I was afraid that if I let him have it

nam ab edicto meo recessissem et civitatem in Catonis et in 10
ipsius Bruti fide locatam meisque beneficiis ornatam funditus
perdidissem.

6　　Atque hoc tempore ipso impingit mihi epistulam Scaptius
⟨a⟩ Bruto rem illam suo periculo esse, quod nec mihi umquam
Brutus dixerat nec tibi, etiam ut praefecturam Scaptio deferrem.
id vero per te exceperamus, ⟨ne⟩ negotiatori; quod si
cuiquam, huic tamen non. fuerat enim praefectus Appio, et 5
quidem habuerat turmas equitum, quibus inclusum in curia
senatum Salamine obsederat, ut fame senatores quinque
morerentur. itaque ego, quo die tetigi provinciam, cum mihi
Cyprii legati Ephesum obviam venissent, litteras misi ut
equites ex insula statim decederent. his de causis credo 10
Scaptium iniquius de me aliquid ad Brutum scripsisse. sed tamen
hoc sum animo: si Brutus putabit me quaternas centesimas
oportuisse decernere, cum tota provincia singulas observarem
itaque edixissem idque etiam acerbissimis faeneratoribus
probaretur, si praefecturam negotiatori denegatam queretur, 15
quod ego Torquato nostro in tuo Laenio, Pompeio ipsi in
Sex. Statio negavi et iis probavi, si equites deductos moleste
feret, accipiam equidem dolorem mihi illum irasci sed multo
maiorem non esse eum talem qualem putassem.

7　　Illud quidem fatebitur Scaptius, me ius dicente sibi omnem
pecuniam ex edicto meo auferendi potestatem fuisse. addo
etiam illud, quod vereor tibi ipsi ut probem: consistere usura
debuit, quae erat in edicto meo; deponere volebant: impetravi

---

6, 2 a Bruto *Watt*: bruto Ω: -ti ς 4 ne *add. Manutius* 5 Appii *Corradus*
13 cum *GNb*: quin *ORMd*: qui *Ems* 14 itaque *NORΔ*: idque *E* edixissem *Eδ*:
dix- *NORM* 18 feret *Ems*: ferret *GNORΔ* **7,** 4 quae Ω: idque *vel* itaque
Sternkopf: quod *Watt*

you yourself would turn against me. It would have meant departing from my edict and utterly ruining a community which was under Cato's and Brutus' own patronage and on which I had conferred favours.

6   Now just at this present juncture Scaptius thrusts a letter of Brutus' into my hand stating that he himself was the party concerned, a thing Brutus had never told me nor you either, and asking me to give Scaptius a Prefecture. But I had already through you made the reservation that no business man should be appointed; and if I had been prepared to make an exception it would not have been for Scaptius. He had been Prefect under Appius and had some squadrons of horse at his disposal, with which he had shut up the senate at Salamis in their senate-house and besieged them, so that five senators starved to death. The day I set foot in my province (the Cypriot envoys having met me at Ephesus) I sent a letter ordering the troopers to leave the island immediately. For these reasons I suppose Scaptius has written something unpleasant about me to Brutus. However, my feeling is as follows: if Brutus is going to think that I ought to have imposed a rate of 4% when I recognized 1% all over the province and had so stated in my edict to the contentment of even the harshest usurers, if he is going to complain of my refusing a Prefecture to a business man as I refused our friend Torquatus in the case of your friend Laenius and Pompey himself in that of Sex. Statius, both approving my action, if he is going to make a grievance of the recall of the troopers—why, I shall be sorry to have incurred his displeasure, but far sorrier to find that he is not the man I took him for.

7   Scaptius will at least admit that under my ruling he had the chance of taking the whole of the money on the terms laid down in my edict. I will add another thing, of which I doubt whether you yourself will approve. The interest, the rate in my edict,

a Salaminis ut silerent. veniam illi quidem mihi dederunt, 5
sed quid iis fiet si huc Paulus venerit? sed totum hoc Bruto
dedi; qui de me ad te humanissimas litteras scripsit, ad me
autem, etiam cum rogat aliquid, contumaciter, adroganter,
ἀκοινονοήτως solet scribere. tu autem velim ad eum scribas
de his rebus, ut sciam quo modo haec accipiat; facies enim 10
me certiorem.

Atque haec superioribus litteris diligenter ad te perscri-
pseram, sed plane te intellegere volui mihi non excidisse illud
quod tu ad me quibusdam litteris scripsisses, si nihil aliud
de hac provincia nisi illius benevolentiam deportassem, mihi 15
id satis esse. sit sane, quoniam ita tu vis, sed tamen cum eo,
credo, quod sine peccato meo fiat. igitur meo decreto soluta
res Scaptio statim. quam id rectum sit tu iudicabis; ne ad
8 Catonem quidem provocabo. sed noli me putare ἐγκελεύσματα
illa tua abiecisse, quae mihi in visceribus haerent. flens mihi
meam famam commendasti; quae epistula tua est in qua
mentionem ⟨non⟩ facias? itaque irascatur qui volet, patiar;
'τὸ γὰρ εὖ μετ' ἐμοῦ', praesertim cum sex libris tamquam 5
praedibus me ipse obstrinxerim, quos tibi tam valde probari
gaudeo. e quibus unum ἱστορικὸν requiris de Cn. Flavio,
Anni filio. ille vero ante decemviros non fuit, quippe qui aedilis
curulis fuerit, qui magistratus multis annis post decemviros
institutus est. quid ergo profecit, quod protulit fastos? 10
occultatam putant quodam tempore istam tabulam, ut dies
agendi peterentur a paucis; nec vero pauci sunt auctores
Cn. Flavium scribam fastos protulisse actionesque composuisse,

---

5 a Salaminis *num delendum?* 12 diligenter ad te Σ: ad te d- Δ   15 mihi id
NOPΔ: id m- *R*: m- *EG*   18 esset *post* res *add. Purser*   id rectum *Manutius*:
decretum ΩΖ¹   8, 4 non *add.* ς: non (ς) eius (*ante* mentionem) *Koch*   6 ipse
Manutius: ipsum Ω   probari] *hic desinit G*   10 profecit *Pius*: -ficit Ω
13 actionesque *N*: auct- *ORΔ*: autoresque *E*   exposuisse *Schilling*

ought to have stopped. The Salaminians wanted to deposit the money; I got them to keep quiet. They agreed as a favour to me, but what will become of them if Paulus comes out here? But I did this entirely as a concession to Brutus. And Brutus, who writes about me so kindly to you, is apt in his letters to me to take a brusque, arrogant, ungracious tone even when he is asking a favour. I should be glad if you would write to him about these matters so that I know how he reacts—you'll inform me.

In my last letter I gave you a detailed account of all this, but I wanted you fully to realize that I have not forgotten the remark in one of yours that if I bring nothing back from this province but Brutus' good will I may be well satisfied. So be it, since you will have it so, but with the proviso surely that I keep my hands clean. Accordingly by my ruling Scaptius was paid on the nail. Of its propriety you shall be the judge. I shall 8 not even appeal to Cato. But you must not suppose I have put out of mind those tally-hoes of yours—they have sunk deep into my heart. You appealed to me with tears in your eyes to take care of my good name. Is there a single one of your letters which does not mention it? Very well then. Take offence who will; I shall put up with it. 'For right is with me', particularly as I have in a manner of speaking pledged myself with six volumes as my guarantors—I'm glad you like them so much. You raise a historical query in one of them concerning Cn. Flavius, son of Annus. He did *not* live before the Decemvirs, for he became Curule Aedile, an office created long after that time. So what did he achieve by publishing the Calendar? The answer is that at one time the list is supposed to have been kept a secret so that business days could only be known by application to a few persons. There are plenty of authorities for the statement that Cn. Flavius the Secretary published the Calendar

ne me hoc vel potius Africanum (is enim loquitur) commen-
tum putes. οὐκ ἔλαθέ σε illud de gestu histrionis? tu sceleste 15
suspicaris, ego ἀφελῶς scripsi.

9 De me imperatore scribis te ex Philotimi litteris cognosse;
sed credo te, iam in Epiro cum esses, binas meas de omnibus
rebus accepisse, unas a Pindenisso capto, alteras Laodicea,
utrasque tuis pueris datas. quibus de rebus propter casum
navigandi per binos tabellarios misi Romam publice litteras. 5

10 De Tullia mea tibi adsentior scripsique ad eam et ad
Terentiam mihi placere; tu enim ad me iam ante scripseras
'ac vellem te in tuum veterem gregem rettulisses'. correcta
vero epistula Memmiana nihil negoti fuit; multo enim
malo hunc a Pontidia quam illum a Servilia. qua re adiunges 5
Saufeium nostrum, hominem semper amantem mei, nunc
credo eo magis quod debet etiam fratris Appi amorem erga
me cum reliqua hereditate crevisse, qui declaravit quanti me
faceret cum saepe tum in Bursa. ne tu me sollicitudine magna
liberaris.   10

11 Furni exceptio mihi non placet; nec enim ego ullum aliud
tempus timeo nisi quod ille solum excipit. sed scriberem ad
te de hoc plura, si Romae esses. in Pompeio te spem omnem
oti ponere non miror; ita res est, removendumque censeo
illud 'dissimulantem'. sed [enim] οἰκονομία si perturbatior 5
est, tibi adsignato; te enim sequor σχεδιάζοντα.

12 Cicerones pueri amant inter se, discunt, exercentur; sed
alter, ut Isocrates dixit in Ephoro et Theopompo, frenis eget,

---

15 Ἔλαθέ σε Malaespina: -θες ORΔ   interrog. agnovit Shuckburgh   9, 3 laodicea
NOR: a l- Δ   4 casus Wesenberg   5 publice litteras NORc: l- p- Δ
10, 6 Saufeium Buecheler: aufium Ω   mei Pius: me Ω   11, 1 enim ego NΔc:
ego enim HOR   3 pompeium bdsZᵇ   4 otii ponere Nδ: p- o- HOR: p- M
5 illud 'duo codd.' ap. Malaespinam: -um Ω   enim del. Wesenberg   12, 2 ut(i)
isocrates (uti soc-) dixit HNORc: uti dixit (i)soc- Δ

and drew up a list of the formulae of judicial procedure, so you need not think that I, or rather Africanus since he is talking, made this up.—It did not escape you, didn't it, that bit about the actor's miming? Your suspicions are villainous; I wrote quite without *arrière pensée*.

9 You say you have learned from a letter of Philotimus' about my having been saluted general. But I think you will now have got two letters after your arrival in Epirus containing all my news, both given to your boys, one after the capture of Pindenissum, the other from Laodicea. I sent an official dispatch about these matters to Rome by two sets of couriers, having regard to the hazard of the voyage.

10 I agree with what you say about my Tullia, and have written to her and to Terentia to say that I approve—you had already written to me 'but I wish you had gone back to your old gang'. Once the Memmius letter was corrected there was no difficulty, for I much prefer Pontidia's candidate to Servilia's. So please get our friend Saufeius to help you. He was always a good friend of mine, all the better now, I imagine, because he has presumably inherited his brother Appius' affection for me along with the rest of his estate. Appius showed his regard for me on many occasions, notably over Bursa. You will certainly be lifting a big load off my mind.

11 I don't like Furnius' saving clause, for the single contingency which he reserves is the only one I am afraid of. But I should write more on this head if you were in Rome. I don't wonder you put all your hopes of peace on Pompey. That's the way it is, and in my opinion the word 'insincerely' ought to be deleted.—If my arrangement of topics is rather confused, you must blame yourself. I am following your impromptu.

12 The boys are fond of one another, are learning their lessons and taking their exercise. But as Isocrates said about Ephorus

alter calcaribus. Quinto togam puram Liberalibus cogitabam
dare; mandavit enim pater. ea sic observabo quasi intercalatum non sit. Dionysius mihi quidem in amoribus est. 5
pueri autem aiunt eum furenter irasci; sed homo nec doctior
nec sanctior fieri potest nec tui meique amantior.

13 Thermum, Silium vere audis laudari; valde se honeste
gerunt. adde M. Nonium, Bibulum, me si voles. iam Scrofa
vellem haberet ubi posset; est enim lautum negotium. ceteri
firmant πολίτευμα Catonis. Hortensio quod causam meam
commendas valde gratum. de Amiano, spei nihil putat esse 5
Dionysius. Terenti nullum vestigium agnovi. Moeragenes
certe periit; feci iter per eius possessionem, in qua animal
reliquum nullum est. haec non noram tum cum ⟨de ea re cum⟩
Democrito tuo locutus sum. Rhosica vasa mandavi. sed heus
tu, quid cogitas? in felicatis lancibus et splendidissimis 10
canistris holusculis nos soles pascere: quid te in vasis fictilibus
appositurum putem? κέρας Phemio mandatum est. reperietur,
modo aliquid illo dignum canat.

14 Parthicum bellum inpendet. Cassius ineptas litteras misit,
necdum Bibuli erant adlatae; quibus recitatis puto fore ut
aliquando commoveatur senatus. equidem sum in magna
animi perturbatione. si, ut opto, non prorogatur nostrum
negotium, habeo Iunium et Quintilem in metu. esto; duo 5
quidem mensis sustinebit Bibulus. quid illo fiet quem re-
liquero, praesertim si fratrem? quid me autem, si non tam
cito decedo? magna turba est. mihi tamen cum Deiotaro
convenit ut ille in meis castris esset cum suis copiis omnibus;

5 amoribus *Hervagius*: mor- Ω   13, 1 laudari ς: -re Ω se *NOR*: *om.* Δ
2 iam] *fort.* nam   3 ceteri firmant *scripsi*: ceter inf- *N*: ceteri inf- *OR*: ceterum
f- Δ 8 de ea re (*vel* de eo) *add. Lehmann*, cum *Bosius* 9 democrito *Nδ*:
demo erit *ORM*   Rhosiaca (*vel* -ica) vasa *Z*: rhosi(i) (trahosi *N*) causa(m) Ω
10 in filicatis (*sic*) *Iunius*: infelicitatis Ω   14, 3 in ΣC: *om.* Δ   5 duo *HNOR*λ:
duos *E*Δ   7 quid *M corr.*: qui Ω

and Theopompus, one of them needs the rein, the other the spur. I propose to give Quintus his white gown at the Liberalia, as his father asked me to do. I shall keep the day on the assumption that there has been no intercalation. *I* am delighted with Dionysius. The boys say he has a furious temper; but no one could be more learned or high principled or more attached to you and me.

13 What you hear about Thermus and Silius being well spoken of is true enough. They are doing very creditably. Add M. Nonius, Bibulus, myself if you will. As for Scrofa, I wish he had somewhere that gave him an opportunity—he's an excellent creature. The rest are strengthening Cato's policy. I am very grateful to you for commending my cause to Hortensius. As to Amianus, Dionysius thinks there is no hope. I have not found a trace of Terentius. Moeragenes is certainly dead. I marched through his country, and there isn't a living thing left. I did not know this when I talked about the matter to your man Democritus. I have ordered the Rhosian ware—but see here, what are you up to? You give us bits of cabbage for dinner on fern-pattern dishes and in magnificent baskets. What can I expect you to serve up on earthenware? A *cor* has been ordered for Phemius and will be found. His playing had better be worthy of it.

14 A Parthian war is threatening. Cassius sent a silly dispatch, and none had by then arrived from Bibulus. When his is read out I think the Senate will at last sit up and take notice. For my part I am in great anxiety of mind. If, as I pray, my job is not extended, I have June and July to fear. All right—Bibulus will hold out for a couple of months anyway. But what about the man I leave in charge, especially if he is my brother? And what about me if I don't leave so soon? It's a pretty kettle of fish. However I have agreed with Deiotarus that he and his whole

habet autem cohortis quadringenarias nostra armatura xxx, 10
equitum cɔɔ cɔɔ. erit ad sustentandum quoad Pompeius
veniat, qui litteris quas ad me mittit significat suum negotium
illud fore. hiemant in nostra provincia Parthi; exspectatur
ipse Orodes. quid quaeris? aliquantum est negoti.

15 De Bibuli edicto, nihil novi praeter illam exceptionem de
qua tu ad me scripseras 'nimis gravi praeiudicio in ordinem
nostrum'. ego tamen habeo ἰσοδυναμοῦσαν sed tectiorem ex
Q. Muci P. f. edicto Asiatico, 'extra quam si ita negotium
gestum est ut eo stari non oporteat ex fide bona'; mul- 5
taque sum secutus Scaevolae, in iis illud in quo sibi libertatem
censent Graeci datam, ut Graeci inter se disceptent suis
legibus. breve autem edictum est propter hanc meam δι-
αίρεσιν, quod duobus generibus edicendum putavi; quorum
unum est provinciale, in quo inest de rationibus civitatum, de 10
aere alieno, de usura, de syngraphis, in eodem omnia de publicanis; alterum quod sine edicto satis commode transigi
non potest, de hereditatum possessionibus, de bonis possidendis, magistris faciendis, ⟨bonis⟩ vendendis, quae ex
edicto et postulari et fieri solent. tertium de reliquo iure 15
dicundo ἄγραφον reliqui. dixi me de eo genere mea decreta
ad edicta urbana accommodaturum, itaque curo, et satis
facio adhuc omnibus. Graeci vero exsultant quod peregrinis
iudicibus utuntur. 'nugatoribus quidem' inquies. quid refert?
ii se αὐτονομίαν adeptos putant. nostri enim, credo, gravis 20
habent, Turpionem sutorium et Vettium mancipem.

---

12 litteris Eδ: -ras HNORM   15, 3 tectiorem M: cert- Rδ: rect- N
4 Mucii Hervagius: municipi(i) Ω   6 in iis Manutius: misi ORΔ: nisi NP
10 inest] est Mm   14 bonis add. Watt   20 (h)ii se N: ipse R: tu se Δ: tamen se
Brunus (M⁴)   nostri ϛ: ves- ΩC   21 Vettium Malaespina: ve(c)t- OΔ: vec-
N: tuct- R

forces shall serve in my army. He has 30 cohorts of 400 men armed Roman fashion and 2,000 horse. There will be enough to hold the fort until Pompey comes. He indicates in letters to me that this is going to be his concern. The Parthians are wintering in our province and Orodes in person is expected. Yes, it's quite a coil.

15 About Bibulus' edict, the only novelty is the saving clause of which you wrote to me that it constituted 'a very serious precedent against our order'. But I have a clause to the same effect, only more guardedly phrased, which I took from Quintus (son of Publius) Mucius' edict in Asia: 'except the transaction has been such that in good faith its terms ought not to be respected'. Indeed I have followed many of Scaevola's provisions, including that one which the natives regard as their charter of liberty, that cases between natives should be tried under their own laws. The edict is short because of the way I divided it up. I thought best to make it up under two heads. One is specifically provincial, including municipal finances, debt, interest, bonds, also all items connected with tax-farmers. The other comprises such matters as cannot conveniently be handled without an edict, as possession of inheritances, possession of property, appointment of receivers, sale of property, things which are usually both litigated and otherwise transacted in accordance with edict. The third category, containing all else to do with the administration of justice, I left unwritten, stating that my rulings under this head would conform to the edicts published in Rome; and so I manage, and so far everyone is satisfied. The natives indeed are jubilant because they have alien judges. Irresponsibles, you may say. Well, what of it? They feel they have won home rule just the same. And our countrymen have such very impressive ones—Turpio the shoemaker and Vettius the broker!

16 De publicanis quid agam videris quaerere. habeo in deliciis,
obsequor, verbis laudo, orno: efficio ne cui molesti sint. τὸ
παραδοξότατον: usuras eorum quas pactionibus adscripserant
servavit etiam Servilius; ego sic: diem statuo satis laxam,
quam ante si solverint, dico me centesimas ducturum, si non 5
solverint, ex pactione. itaque et Graeci solvunt tolerabili
faenore et publicanis res est gratissima, si illa iam habent
pleno modio, verborum honorem, invitationem crebram.
quid plura? sunt omnes ita mihi familiares ut se quisque
maxime putet; sed tamen μηδὲν αὐτοῖς—scis reliqua.   10
17 De statua Africani (ὦ πραγμάτων ἀσυγκλώστων! sed me id
ipsum delectavit in tuis litteris), ain tu? Scipio hic Metellus
proavum suum nescit censorem non fuisse? atqui nihil
habuit aliud inscriptum nisi 'cos.' ea statua quae ab Opis
parte postica in excelso est. in illa autem quae est ad Πολυ- 5
κλέους Herculem inscriptum est 'cos. ⟨cens.⟩'; quam esse
eiusdem status, amictus, anulus, imago ipsa declarat. at mehercule ego, cum in turma inauratarum equestrium quas hic
Metellus in Capitolio posuit animadvertissem in Sarapionis
subscriptione Africani imaginem, erratum fabrile putavi, 10
18 nunc video Metelli. o ἀνιστορησίαν turpem! nam illud de
Flavio et fastis, si secus est, commune erratum est; et tu belle
ἠπόρησας et nos publicam prope opinionem secuti sumus,
ut multa apud Graecos. quis enim non dixit Εὔπολιν τὸν τῆς
ἀρχαίας ab Alcibiade navigante in Siciliam deiectum esse in 5
mare? redarguit Eratosthenes; adfert enim quas ille post id

16, 3 a(d)scripserant *M corr.*: -at Ω   4 Servilius ς: -vicius (-vit-) Ω   7 illa
ORm: -am *HN*Δ   17, 1 id *NR*: *om. HO*Δ   4 cos. (consul) ea *Malaespina*:
censorea *vel sim.* Ω   5 postica *Urlichs*: posita Ω   Πολυκλέους *Mommsen*: ΠΟΔΛΥ-
*vel sim. R*Δ   6 cos. cens. *Purser*: consul Ω   7 ipsa] *accedit W*   9 sarapionis
MnW: ser- *NOR*δ   18, 1 o *Bosius*: ω (ὠ, ὤ) *R*Δ*W*   6 post *O*Δ: potest
NRW

16 You seem to want to know how I manage about the tax-farmers. I dote upon them, defer to them, butter them up with compliments—and arrange so that they harm nobody. Most surprising of all: the rates of interest specified in their agreements with the provincials were maintained even by Servilius. My system is this: I fix a date, giving plenty of time, and say that if they pay before that date I shall apply a rate of 1%; if not, then the rate in the agreement. So the natives pay a tolerable interest and the tax-farmers are delighted with the arrangement, since they now get verbal compliments and frequent invitations to their hearts' content. In a word they are all my friends and each man thinks himself preeminently so. All the same 'in them let not . . .'—you know how it goes on.

17 About Africanus' statue (what a rag-bag this is! But that was just what I liked about your letter), you don't say so! Doesn't this Scipio Metellus know that his great-grandfather never held the Censorship? While the statue which stands on the high ground behind the Temple of Ops has no caption except 'cos.', the one that stands by the Hercules of Polycles is inscribed 'cos. cens.'; and the stance, the drapery, the ring, the likeness itself declares it to be of the same man. Upon my word, when I saw Africanus' likeness over Sarapio's name in the cavalcade of gilded equestrian statues which this Metellus set up on the Capitol, I thought it was a workman's blunder. Now I see **18** the blunder was Metellus'. What disgraceful ignorance! That statement of mine about Flavius and the Calendar, if it is wrong, is an error in common currency. You were right to be puzzled, while on my side I followed the more or less received opinion. There are many such things in Greek authors, e.g. everybody spoke of Eupolis (him of the Old Comedy) as having been thrown into the sea by Alcibiades on the voyage to Sicily. Eratosthenes disproved the story by instancing plays which he

tempus fabulas docuerit. num idcirco Duris Samius, homo in
historia diligens, quod cum multis erravit, irridetur? quis
Zaleucum leges Locris scripsisse non dixit? num igitur iacet
Theophrastus si id a Timaeo, tuo familiari, reprehensum est? 10
sed nescire proavum suum censorem non fuisse turpe est,
praesertim cum post eum consulem nemo Cornelius illo vivo
censor fuerit.

19 Quod de Philotimo et de solutione HS $\overline{\text{xxdc}}$ scribis, Philotimum circiter Kal. Ian. in Chersonesum audio venisse; at mi
ab eo nihil adhuc. reliqua mea Camillus scribit se accepisse. ea
quae sint nescio et aveo scire. [sed] verum haec posterius et
coram fortasse commodius.   5

20 Illud me, mi Attice, in extrema fere parte epistulae com-
movit; scribis enim sic, 'τί λοιπόν;', deinde me obsecras
amantissime ne obliviscar vigilare et ut animadvertam quae
fiant. num quid de quo inaudisti? etsi nihil eius modi est;
πολλοῦ γε καὶ δεῖ. nec enim me fefellisset nec fallet. sed ista 5
admonitio tua tam accurata nescio quid mihi significare
visa est.

21 De M. Octavio, iterum iam tibi rescribo te illi probe re-
spondisse; paulo vellem fidentius. nam Caelius libertum ad
me misit et litteras accurate scriptas et de pantheris et * * *
a civitatibus. rescripsi ⟨ad⟩ alterum me moleste ferre, si ego in
tenebris laterem nec audiretur Romae nullum in mea pro- 5
vincia nummum nisi in aes alienum erogari, docuique nec mihi
conciliare pecuniam licere nec illi capere, monuique eum, quem

---

7 *anne* ἐν ἱστορίᾳ? **19**, 2 at ς: ac ΩW mi ΔW: me N: mihi OR   3 Camillus
ς:-ilis ΩW   4 aveo *ms*: haveo W: habeo N: ab eo ORΔ   sed *del. Pius*   **20**, 4
inaudisti NRΔ: aud-OW   **21**, 3 pantheris (pand- W) et NW: -ris sed *vel*
sim. HORΔZᵇ   *lac. agnovit Sjögren (vide comm.)*   4 ad *addidi*

says were produced by him after that time. We don't on that account laugh at Duris of Samos, a conscientious historian, because he made the same mistake as many others. Everybody spoke of Zaleucus as the author of the legal code at Locri. Is Theophrastus discredited because your friend Timaeus found fault with that tradition? But it *is* disgraceful not to know that one's great-grandfather was never Censor, especially as no Cornelius became Censor after his Consulship and during his lifetime.

19 With regard to what you say about Philotimus and the payment of the HS 20,600, I hear that Philotimus arrived in the Chersonese about the Kalends of January, but I have had no word from him as yet. Camillus writes that he (Camillus) has received the sums due to me. What these are I don't know, and am very anxious to know. But of this later, and better perhaps when we meet.

20 I was disturbed by a phrase almost at the end of your letter. You write '*quoi encore?*' and then beg me affectionately to remember to keep my eyes open and to watch what goes on. Have you heard something about somebody? Not that there is anything of the kind, *il s'en faut beaucoup*. It would not have escaped my notice, nor will. But I felt that so deliberate an admonition from you pointed *somewhere*.

21 As for M. Octavius, I answer you once again, your reply to him was right and proper—I could wish it had been a little more confidently put. Caelius has sent me a freedman and an elaborate letter both about panthers and about raising money from the townships. I replied to the latter point that I was sorry to find that my light was so much under a bushel and that people in Rome were unaware of the fact that in my province not a sixpence is disbursed except in payment of debt; and I told him that I was not entitled to raise money nor he to take

plane diligo, ut cum alios accusasset cautius viveret; illud autem
alterum alienum esse existimatione mea, Cibyratas imperio
meo publice venari.   10

22 Lepta tua epistula gaudio exsultat; etenim scripta belle est
meque apud eum magna in gratia posuit. filiola tua gratum
mihi fecit quod tibi diligenter mandavit ut mihi salutem
adscriberes, gratum etiam Pilia, sed illa officiosius quod me,
quem iam pridem ⟨amat⟩, numquam vidit; igitur tu quoque 5
salutem utrique adscribito. litterarum datarum dies prid. Kal.
Ian. suavem habuit recordationem clarissimi iuris iurandi quod
ego non eram oblitus; Magnus enim praetextatus illo die fui.
habes ad omnia; non, ut postulasti, 'χρύσεα χαλκείων' sed paria
paribus respondimus.   10

23 Ecce autem alia pusilla epistula, quam non relinquam
ἀναντιφώνητον. bene mehercule ⟨pro⟩posuit Lucceius Tusculanum, nisi forte (solet enim) cum suo tibicine; et velim
scire qui sit eius status. Lentulum quidem nostrum praeter
Tusculanum * * * proscripsisse audio. cupio hos expeditos 5
videre, cupio etiam Sestium, adde sis Caelium; in quibus
omnibus est 'αἴδεσθεν μὲν ἀνήνασθαι, δεῖσαν δ' ὑποδέχθαι'.
de Memmio restituendo ut Curio cogitet te audisse puto. de
Egnati Sidicini nomine nec nulla nec magna spe sumus.
Pinarium, quem mihi commendas, diligentissime Deiotarus 10
curat graviter aegrum. respondi etiam minori.

24 Tu velim dum ero Laodiceae, id est ad Id. Mai., quam
saepissime mecum per litteras colloquare et cum Athenas
veneris (iam enim sciemus de rebus urbanis, de provinciis,

22, 1 lepta *W*: lecta Ω: *anne* Lepta lecta? 4 me *scripsi*: mihi Ω 5 amat *hoc
loco Watt, ante* iam *add. Koch* vidit *Pms*: videt ΩW 6 litterarum datarum ϛ:
-am daturum ΩW dies *om.* Δ 23, 2 proposuit *Bentivoglio*: poruit *W*(?):
potuit Ω 4 qui *ORW*: quis *N*Δ eius status *NORW*: s- e- Δ omnia *ante*
praeter *add. Lambinus,* Pompeianum *vel sim. post* Tusculanum *Watt* 6 adde
sis *W*: -e(s) iis (his) Δ: -es hic *N*: adsis *R* in *ORW*: *om. N*Δ 9 nomine *NOPs*:
-inet *RW*: -ine et Δ 11 curat *P*Δ: cura *NORW*

it and advised him (for I really like him) that as one who had prosecuted others he should be more careful of his conduct. As for the panthers I said it would not help my reputation to have the people of Cibyra hunting publicly on my orders.

22 Lepta is perfectly delighted by your letter. Indeed it is admirably phrased and has put me very high in his good books. I am much beholden to your little daughter for so carefully instructing you to give me her love, and to Pilia also; but the former's attention is more remarkable in that she is so affectionate all this time to someone she has never seen. So on your side please give my love to both. The date of your letter, 29 December, contained an amiable reminder of the famous oath, which I had not forgotten. That day I was Magnus in mufti. Well, there is all answered, not in 'gold for bronze' as you asked, but *quid pro quo*.

23 But here comes another tiny letter! I shall not leave it *sans réponse*. Upon my word Lucceius has done well to put up his place at Tusculum for sale—unless perhaps he was just talking at large (?), as he is apt to do. I should like to know how he stands. I hear that our friend Lentulus has advertised *, besides his Tusculan place. I very much want to see them out of the wood, and Sestius too, and Caelius if you like. With all of them it's a case of 'Durst not for shame refuse, for fear accept'. I expect you have heard how Curio is thinking about restoring Memmius. About Egnatius Sidicinus' debt I have some hope but not much. Deiotarus is taking great care of Pinarius, whom you recommend to me. He is seriously ill. The smaller letter too is answered.

24 I hope you will talk to me by letter as often as you can so long as I am in Laodicea, i.e. until the Ides of May, and that when you come to Athens (we shall know soon about affairs in Rome, including the provinces, all of which are down for

quae omnia in mensem Martium sunt collata) utique ad me
25 tabellarios mittas. et heus tu, †genua† vos a Caesare per
Herodem talenta Attica ʟ extorsistis? in quo, ut audio, magnum
odium Pompei suscepistis; putat enim suos nummos vos
comedisse, Caesarem in Nemore aedificando diligentiorem
fore. haec ego ex P. Vedio, magno nebulone sed Pompei 5
tamen familiari, audivi. hic Vedius mihi obviam venit cum
duobus essedis et raeda equis iuncta et lectica et familia magna,
pro qua, si Curio legem pertulerit, HS centenos pendat necesse
est; erat praeterea cynocephalus in essedo nec deerant onagri.
numquam vidi hominem nequiorem. sed extremum audi. 10
deversatus est Laodiceae apud Pompeium Vindillum; ibi sua
deposuit cum ad me profectus est. moritur interim Vindillus.
quod res ad Magnum Pompeium pertinere putabatur, C.
Vennonius domum Vindilli venit. cum omnia obsignaret, in
Vedianas res incidit. in his inventae sunt quinque imagunculae 15
matronarum, in quibus una sororis amici tui, hominis bruti
qui hoc utatur, et ⟨uxoris⟩ illius lepidi qui haec tam neglegenter
ferat. haec te volui παριστορῆσαι; sumus enim ambo belle
curiosi.

26 Vnum etiam velim cogites. audio Appium πρόπυλον
Eleusine facere; num inepti fuerimus si nos quoque Academiae
fecerimus? 'puto' inquies. ergo id ipsum scribes ad me. equidem
valde ipsas Athenas amo; volo esse aliquod monumentum, odi
falsas inscriptiones statuarum alienarum. sed ut tibi placebit, 5

24, 5 tabellarios . . . Caesare *erasa in W*   25, 1 et Ω: sed *Zᵇ* genuarios
ΩC: iamne vos *Zᵇ* (*sed vide comm.*)   4 Nemore aedificando *Turnebus*: mentor
ed- *EM*: merito reed- *Nδ*: mente reed- *H*: ventorem ed- *R Ant*.   6 mihi
obviam venit *ΣW*: v- m- o- Δ   8 centenos *ORW*: -nas *HNΔ*: -na *m*
11 Vindillum *Sjögren*: vidi illum Ω*W*: Vindullum *Victorius*   12 vindillus *HORW*:
-diliis *N*: -dullus *M*: -dulus δ; *itidem fere infra*   13 quod *W*: qu(a)e Ω
15 imagunculae *Victorius*: iam gun- *W*: langun- Ωλ   17 uxoris *add. Schütz*
18 te] tibi *R*   26, 2 inepti *C*: in epi *W*: in epiro (epyro) Ω   academiae *ms*:
acam- *RMW*: acan(n)e *HNP*   4 monumentum meum *Boot*: mei mon- *Kayser*

settlement in March) you will send me couriers without fail.
25 And look here, has Herodes really squeezed 50 Attic talents out
of Caesar on behalf of your adopted country? I hear that you
Athenians have got into very bad odour with Pompey because
of that. He thinks you have squandered *his* cash and that Caesar
will press on all the harder with his building in the Forest. I
heard all this from P. Vedius, a feather-brained ass but a friend
of Pompey's. This Vedius met me with two gigs and a coach
and horses and a litter and a crowd of servants, for which if
Curio carries his law he will have to pay 100 sesterces per head.
There was a baboon as well in one of the gigs, and some onagers
for good measure. I never saw such a coxcomb. But listen to
the end of the tale. He lodged in Laodicea with Pompeius
Vindillus and left his belongings there when he set out to meet
me. In the meanwhile Vindillus dies. Since the Great Pompey
was supposed to have a claim on his estate, C. Vennonius went
to the house, and as he was putting everything under seal he
came upon Vedius' luggage. In this were discovered five
ladies' portraits in miniature, including one of your friend's
sister, you know whose wife—they live up to their names both
of them, the one by having aught to do with the fellow, the
other by tolerating these goings on so easily. I thought I'd tell
you this *en passant*. We are both fond of a piece of scandal.

26   There is one other thing I should like you to think over. I
hear that Appius is making a gateway at Eleusis. Would it be
out of the way if I did the same for the Academy? 'I think it
would', you'll say. Very well, just write and tell me so. I am
really very fond of Athens, the actual city. I want to have some
memorial there, and I hate false inscriptions on other people's

faciesque me in quem diem Romana incidant mysteria certiorem et quo modo hiemaris. cura ut valeas. post Leuctricam
pugnam die septingentesimo sexagesimo quinto.

116 (VI. 2)

Scr. Laodiceae ex. m. Apr., ut. vid., an. 50

CICERO ATTICO SAL.

1 Cum Philogenes, libertus tuus, Laodiceam ad me salutandi
causa venisset et se statim ad te navigaturum esse diceret, has
ei litteras dedi, quibus ad eas rescripsi quas acceperam a Bruti
tabellario. et respondebo primum postremae tuae paginae, qua
mihi magnae molestiae fuit quod ad te scriptum est a Cincio 5
de Stati sermone; in quo hoc molestissimum est, Statium dicere
a me quoque id consilium probari. ⟨ego⟩ autem de isto hactenus
dixerim, me vel plurima vincla tecum summae coniunctionis
optare, etsi sunt amoris artissima; tantum abest ut ego ex eo
2 quo astricti sumus laxari aliquid velim. illum autem multa de
istis rebus asperius solere loqui saepe sum expertus, saepe etiam
lenivi iratum; id scire te arbitror. in hac autem peregrinatione
militiave nostra saepe incensum ira vidi, saepe placatum. quid
ad Statium scripserit nescio; quicquid acturus de tali re fuit, 5
scribendum tamen ad libertum non fuit. mihi autem erit
maximae curae ne quid fiat secus quam volumus quamque
oportet. nec satis est in eius modi re se quemque praestare, ac
maximae partes istius offici sunt pueri Ciceronis sive iam adulescentis; quod quidem illum soleo hortari. ac mihi videtur valde 10

---

7 leu(c)tricam *ms*: lect- *HOΔW*: lett- *N*
Ep. 116] 1, 2 venisset] *hic desinit W*   4 qua *scripsi*: qu(a)e Ω   7 ego *add. Watt*
de isto autem *cod. Ball.*   9 etsi *Pius*: et Ω   sunt ϛ: sint Ω   amoris *O*: -ri
HNΔ   abest *bs*: adest Ω   **2, 3** *anne* leniri?   5 scripserit *Ns*: ads- *HOΔ*
9 pueri *Brunus* (*M*⁴): veri Ω   10 valde matrem ut *HNO*: m- ut valde Δ

statues. But as you think best. And you'll let me know what day the Roman Mysteries fall and what sort of a winter you have had. Look after yourself. On the seven hundred and sixty-fourth day after the battle of Leuctra.

116 (VI 2)

Laodicea, latter part of April (?) 50

CICERO TO ATTICUS

1 Your freedman Philogenes has come to pay his respects to me in Laodicea and says he is returning to you at once by sea, so I am giving him this letter in reply to yours delivered by Brutus' courier. And first I shall reply to your last page, where the account in Cincius' letter to you of his conversation with Statius vexed me deeply. The most vexatious thing about it was that Statius should say that I approve this idea. On that let me say only one thing: so far from wishing the bond between us to be in any way relaxed, I should welcome as many and as intimate links with you as possible, though those of affection, and of

2 the closest, exist already. As for *him*, I have often found that he is apt to speak rather harshly in these matters, and again I have often mollified his irritation. I think you know this. During this foreign trip or rather service of ours I have repeatedly seen him flare up and calm down again. What he may have written to Statius I cannot say. Whatever step he proposed to take in such a matter he ought not to have written to a freedman. I shall do my utmost to prevent any action contrary to our wishes and to what is right. But in a matter of this sort it is not enough to answer for oneself, and a large share of this responsibility falls upon the boy, or young man as he now is. This I am in the habit of urging upon him. He does seem to me to be

matrem, ut debet, amare teque mirifice; sed est magnum illud quidem verum tamen multiplex pueri ingenium; quod ego regendo habeo negoti satis.

3   Quoniam respondi postremae tuae paginae prima mea, nunc ad primam revertar tuam. Peloponnesias civitates omnis maritimas esse hominis non nequam sed etiam tuo iudicio probati, Dicaearchi, tabulis credidi. is multis nominibus in Trophoniana Chaeronis narratione Graecos in eo reprehendit quod maritima 5 secuti sint, nec ullum in Peloponneso locum excipit. cum mihi auctor placeret (⟨et⟩enim erat ἱστορικώτατος et vixerat in Peloponneso), admirabar tamen et vix adcredens communicavi cum Dionysio. atque is primo est commotus, deinde, quod de deo [cum] isto Dicaearch⟨e⟩o non minus bene existimabat 10 quam tu de C. Vestorio, ego de M. Cluvio, non dubitabat quin ei crederemus. Arcadiae censebat esse Lepreon quoddam maritimum; Tenea autem et Aliphera et Tritia νεόκτιστα ei videbantur, idque τῷ τῶν νεῶν καταλόγῳ confirmabat, ubi mentio non fit istorum. itaque istum ego locum totidem verbis 15 a Dicaearcho transtuli. 'Phliasios' autem dici sciebam et ita fac ut habeas; nos quidem sic habemus. sed primo me ἀναλογία deceperat, Φλιοῦς, Ὀποῦς, Σιποῦς, quod Ὀπούντιοι, Σιπούντιοι; sed hoc continuo correximus.

4   Laetari te nostra moderatione et continentia video. tum id magis faceres, si adesses. atque hoc foro quod egi ex Id. Febr. Laodiceae ad Kal. Mai. omnium dioecesium praeter Ciliciae mirabilia quaedam effecimus; ita multae civitates omni aere

---

11 debet ς: debeat Ω   12 quod Ω: quo ς: in quo *Lamb.* (*marg.*)   **3,** 5 maritima *scripsi*: mare tam *O*Δ: maretani *N*   6 sint *O*: sunt *N*Δ   cum ς: quin *O*Δ: qui *N*: quum *c*   7 etenim erat ς: enim erat Ω: erat enim *s*   8 accredens *Bosius*: adgredens *M*: -diens *NO*δ: *fort.* credens   9 de deo isto *scripsi*: de deo cum isto *M*: cum de isto δ: cum isto *N*: de isto *Orelli*: de *Watt*: de Chaerone isto *Purser*   10 Dicaearcheo *Purser*: -cho Ω   11 M. Cluvio *Manutius*: incluino *vel sim.* Ω   13 tenea *NO*λc: tene Δ   **4,** 4 effecimus *bms*: effic- Ω

very fond of his mother, as he should be, and extraordinarily fond of you. But the boy's nature, though gifted, is complex, and I have plenty to do guiding it.

3   Having answered your last page with my first, I shall now come back to your first. I took the statement that all the Peloponnesian communities adjoin the sea from the accounts of Dicaearchus, no scamp but a man approved by your own judgement. In the course of Chaeron's story about Trophonius he takes the Greeks to task under many heads for clinging to the coast, and makes no exception of any place in the Peloponnese. Though I thought him a good authority (after all he was extremely well-informed and had lived in the Peloponnese), I was surprised and almost incredulous, so I consulted Dionysius. He was taken aback at first, but afterwards, having as high an opinion of this Dicaearchian deity as you have of C. Vestorius or I of M. Cluvius, he was satisfied that we ought to trust him. He thought that Arcadia included a place on the coast called Lepreon, while Tenea, Aliphera, and Tritia were recent foundations in his opinion, which he supported by the Catalogue of Ships, where they are not mentioned. So I took the passage over from Dicaearchus just as it stood. As for 'Phliasians', I know that this is the correct form, and please put it in your copies as I have done in mine. But I was deceived at first by the analogy of Phlius with Opus and Sipus, which make 'Opuntians', 'Sipuntians'. But I corrected this at once.

4   I see that you are pleased with my moderation and disinterestedness. You would be even more so if you were on the spot. At this assize which I have been holding in Laodicea from the Ides of February to the Kalends of May for all my Districts except those of Cilicia I have produced some astonishing results. A great number of communities have been entirely

alieno liberatae, multae valde levatae sunt, omnes suis legibus 5
et iudiciis usae αὐτονομίαν adeptae revixerunt. his ego duobus
generibus facultatem ad se aere alieno liberandas aut levandas
dedi: uno quod omnino nullus in imperio meo sumptus factus
est; nullum cum dico non loquor ὑπερβολικῶς: nullus inquam,
ne terruncius quidem. hac autem re incredibile est quantum 10
5 civitates emerserint. accessit altera: mira erant in civitatibus
ipsorum furta Graecorum quae magistratus sui fecerant. quae-
sivi ipse de iis qui annis decem proximis magistratum gesserant;
aperte fatebantur. itaque sine ulla ignominia suis umeris
pecunias populis rettulerunt. populi autem nullo gemitu 5
publicanis, quibus hoc ipso lustro nihil solverant, etiam
superioris lustri reddiderunt; itaque publicanis in oculis sumus.
'gratis' inquis 'viris.' sensimus. iam cetera iuris dictio nec
imperita et clemens cum admirabili facilitate. aditus autem ad
me minime provinciales. nihil per cubicularium; ante lucem 10
inambulabam domi ut olim candidatus. grata haec et magna
mihique nondum laboriosa ex illa vetere militia.

6 Non. Mai. in Ciliciam cogitabam; ibi cum Iunium mensem
consumpsissem (atque utinam in pace! magnum enim bellum
impendet a Parthis), Quintilem in reditu ponere. annuae enim
mihi operae a. d. III Kal. Sext. emerentur. magna autem in spe

---

6 usae *C*: su(a)e Ω 7 ad *ms*: a(b) Ω 9 inquam ς: unq- (umq-) Ω **5, 2** sui
Manutius: vi HOΔ: vim *N* 7 reliqua *post* lustri *add. Wesenberg*

cleared of debt, many others substantially relieved. All have
come to life again with the acquisition of home rule under
their own laws and courts. I have enabled them to free themselves wholly or partially from debt in two ways. First no
expense whatsoever has been incurred during my term as
governor—and when I say 'no expense' I am not speaking in
hyperbole, I mean literally none, not a penny. You would
hardly believe how much that has helped to drag the communi-
5 ties out of the mire. Then there is another thing. The natives
themselves were responsible for an astonishing number of
peculations in the communities, committed by their own
magistrates. I personally investigated those who had held office
in the last ten years. They admitted it quite frankly. So without
any open disgrace they put back the money with their own
hands into the various public purses. The civic bodies for their
part, which had paid the tax-farmers nothing in this present
quinquennium, have now without any moaning paid the
arrears of the previous quinquennium as well. So I am a prime
favourite with the tax-farmers. 'Grateful gentry' you may say.
I have experienced their gratitude. Then the rest of my admini-
ration of justice has been sufficiently expert on the one hand
and merciful on the other, and my affability makes a great
impression. Access to me is not at all after the usual provincial
fashion. Nothing is done through my valet. I am up and about
in my residence before daybreak, just as in the days when I was
a candidate. These things are appreciated and thought much
of; and being an old campaigner I have not so far found them
irksome.

6   On the Nones of May I propose to leave for Cilicia. After
spending June there (I only hope in peace, for a major war is
threatening from Parthia), I shall devote July to my return
journey, since my year's term will have been served on 30 July.

sum mihi nihil temporis prorogatum iri. habebam acta urbana 5
usque ad Non. Mart.; e quibus intellegebam Curionis nostri
constantia omnia potius actum iri quam de provinciis. ergo, ut
spero, prope diem te videbo.

7   Venio ad Brutum tuum, immo nostrum (sic enim mavis).
equidem omnia feci quae potui aut in mea provincia perficere
⟨aut⟩ in regno experiri. omni igitur modo egi cum rege et ago
cottidie, per litteras scilicet; ipsum enim triduum quadridu-
umve mecum habui turbulentis in rebus quibus eum liberavi. 5
sed et tum praesens et postea creberrimis ⟨litteris⟩ non destiti
rogare et petere mea causa, suadere et hortari sua. multum
profeci, sed quantum, non plane, quia longe absum, scio.

Salaminos autem (hos enim poteram coercere) adduxi ut
totum nomen Scaptio vellent solvere, sed centesimis ductis a 10
proxima quidem syngrapha nec perpetuis sed renovatis quotannis. numerabantur nummi: noluit Scaptius. ⟨quid⟩ tu, qui
ais Brutum cupere aliquid perdere? 'quaternas habebat in
syngrapha'. fieri non poterat nec, si posset, ego pati possem.
audio omnino Scaptium paenitere. nam quod senatus con- 15
sultum esse dicebat ut ius ex syngrapha diceretur, eo consilio
factum est quod pecuniam Salamini contra legem Gabiniam
sumpserant. vetabat autem ea lex ius dici de ita sumpta pecunia;
decrevit igitur senatus ut ius diceretur ⟨ex⟩ ista syngrapha. nunc
8 ista habet iuris idem quod ceterae, nihil praecipui. haec a me

---

6, 7 ergo *Mm*: ego *HNObds*   7, 2 aut *cod. Bod.*: autem Ω   3 aut *cod. Bod.*:
om. Ω experiri omni *Nms*: -re omnia *HΔ*   4 triduum *HNOC*: *om.* Δ   5 -ve *C*:
nec Ω   6 litteris *F*: *om.* Ω   7 mea *HOms*: in ea *NMbd*   8 scio ς: sciam Ω
12 quid tu *Schütz*: quid *N*: qui *OΔ*: *alii aliter*   18 ea lex ius *Hervagius*: alexius Ω
19 ex *add. Hervagius*   8, 1 hec ς: hoc *N*: hac *ORΔ*

I am very hopeful that there will be no prorogation. I have the City Gazette up to the Nones of March, from which I gather that through our friend Curio's firmness any business is more likely to be dealt with than the provinces. So I hope I shall be seeing you soon.

7   I come to your friend Brutus, or rather our friend, since you prefer it so. On my side everything I could manage in my province or attempt in the kingdom I have done. I have taken the matter up with the king in every possible way and am still doing so daily—by correspondence naturally, since I only had him with me for three or four days during a crisis from which I extricated him. But both on that occasion in person and afterwards in letter after letter I have never ceased asking and demanding on my account, advising and urging on his own. I have made considerable progress, but just how much I cannot at this distance say.

As for the Salaminians, with whom I could use compulsion, I brought them to the point that they were willing to pay Scaptius the entire debt, but at 1% interest calculated from the last renewal of the bond, not simple but compounded annually. The money was ready to put down: Scaptius refused. What have you to say, who tell me that Brutus is only too willing to accept some loss? That he had 4% in the bond? That was not possible, and even if it had been, *I* could not have tolerated it. To be sure I hear that Scaptius is sorry now. As for his statement that a senatorial decree ordered judgement to be given in accordance with the bond, it was passed only because the Salaminians had broken the lex Gabinia in borrowing the money, which law prohibited judicial cognizance of money so borrowed. Therefore the Senate decreed that judgement be given according to this bond. It now has the same legal status as any other, no more, no less. I think I shall satisfy Brutus that

8

ordine facta puto me Bruto probaturum, tibi nescio, Catoni
certe probabo.

Sed iam ad te ipsum revertor. ain tandem, Attice, laudator
integritatis et elegantiae nostrae? 'ausus es hoc ex ore tuo' 5
(inquit Ennius), ut equites Scaptio ad pecuniam cogendam
darem me rogare? an tu si mecum esses, qui scribis morderi te
interdum quod non simul sis, paterere me id facere si vellem?
'non amplius' inquis 'quinquaginta.' cum Spartaco minus multi
primo fuerunt. quid tandem isti mali in tam tenera insula non 10
fecissent? ⟨non fecissent⟩ autem? immo quid ante adventum
meum non fecerunt? inclusum in curia senatum habuerunt
Salaminum ita multos dies ut interierint non nulli fame; erat
enim praefectus Appi Scaptius et habebat turmas ab Appio. id
me igitur tu, cuius mehercule os mihi ante oculos solet versari 15
cum de aliquo officio ac laude cogito, tu me, inquam, rogas
praefectus ut Scaptius sit? at hoc statueramus, ut negotiatorem
neminem, idque Bruto probamus. habeat is turmas? cur potius
9 quam cohortis? sumptu iam nepos evadit Scaptius. 'volunt'
inquit 'principes.' scio; nam ad me Ephesum usque venerunt
flentesque equitum scelera et miserias suas detulerunt. itaque
statim dedi litteras ut ex Cypro equites ante certam diem
decederent, ob eamque causam tum ob ceteras Salamini nos 5
in caelum decretis suis sustulerunt. sed iam quid opus equitatu?
solvunt enim Salamini; nisi forte id volumus armis efficere, ut
faenus quaternis centesimis ducant. et ego audebo legere
umquam aut attingere eos libros quos tu dilaudas, si tale quid
fecero? nimis, ⟨nimis⟩ inquam, in isto Brutum amasti, 10

---

2 tibine *Orelli, fort. recte*   6 ut inquit *Wesenberg*   7 rogare an tu si *Rms*: -rent tu(i)
vel sim. HNMbd   11 non fecissent *add. M corr.*   13 interirent *E*   17 at *Hbds*:
ad *NOR: alias Mm: anne* at iam?   18 probaramus *Wesenberg* (-averamus
Victorius)   19 sumptu *NOMmC*: -um *Rbds* : -ui *H*   nepos evadit *C*: ne
(non *Nbds*) posse vadit Ω   9, 5 tum *s*: cum Ω   6 equitatu *P*: -tatus Ω   9 tu
dilaudas *OPMm*: tu lau- *NRbds*: studiose laudas *H*: tu s- l- *E*   10 nimis nimis
Z^b: nimis Ω

I have acted correctly in this matter. As to yourself I don't know, but I shall certainly satisfy Cato.

But now to return to yourself. Do you really mean it, Atticus, you, the encomiast of my fastidious rectitude? 'This hast thou dared from thine own lips', as Ennius says, to ask me to give Scaptius mounted troops to extract the money? You tell me it sometimes chafes you that you are not here beside me. Well, supposing you *were* with me, would you let me do that if I wanted? 'Not more than fifty' you say. There were fewer with Spartacus to begin with. What damage would they not have done in so vulnerable an island? I say 'would they not have done'; I should rather say 'what did they not do, before I came on the scene?'. They kept the Salaminian senate shut up in their senate-house for so many days that some of them starved to death. For Scaptius was Appius' Prefect and had troops of horse from him. Well then, are you, whose face I do assure you is in my mind's eye whenever I contemplate any right and creditable act, are *you* asking me to make Scaptius a Prefect? I had already made a rule not to appoint any business man and Brutus approves of it. Troops of horse for that fellow? Why not companies of foot? Quite a spendthrift
9 Scaptius is turning out! 'The notables' says he 'so desire.' I know! They came to me all the way to Ephesus and told me with tears in their eyes of the atrocities of the troopers and their own sufferings. Accordingly I at once sent a letter ordering the departure of the troopers from Cyprus by a certain date, and that among other things is why the people of Salamis have extolled me to the skies in their public resolutions. But what does he want with cavalry *now*? The Salaminians are paying up—unless of course we wish to make them pay interest at 4% by armed force. Shall I ever dare to read or so much as handle the volumes you praise so warmly if I do anything of the sort?

III

dulcissime Attice, nos vereor ne parum. atque haec scripsi ego
ad Brutum scripsisse te ad me.

10   Cognosce nunc cetera. pro Appio nos hic omnia facimus,
honeste tamen sed plane libenter; nec enim ipsum odimus et
Brutum amamus et Pompeius mirifice a me contendit, quem
mehercule plus plusque in dies diligo. C. Coelium huc quaestorem venire audisti? nescio quid sit hominis. [sed] Pammenia 5
illa mihi non placent. ego me spero Athenis fore mense
Septembri. tuorum itinerum tempora scire sane velim.
εὐήθειαν Semproni Rufi cognovi ex epistula tua Corcyraea;
quid quaeris? invideo potentiae Vestori.

Cupiebam etiam nunc plura garrire, sed lucet; urget turba, 10
festinat Philogenes. valebis igitur et valere Piliam et Caeciliam
nostram iubebis litteris et salvebis a meo Cicerone.

117 (VI. 3)

Scr. Tarsum iter faciens m. Mai. vel in. Iun. an. 50

CICERO ATTICO SAL.

1   Etsi nihil sane habebam novi quod post accidisset quam
dedissem ad te Philogeni liberto tuo litteras, tamen cum
Philotimum Romam remitterem, scribendum aliquid ad te fuit.
ac primum illud quod me maxime angebat (non quo me aliquid
iuvare posses; quippe; res enim est in manibus, tu autem abes 5
longe gentium,

'πολλὰ δ' ἐν μεταιχμίῳ
νότος κυλίνδει κύματ' εὐρείης ἁλός'):

---

10 1, facimus *ERbds*: -iamus *HNOMm*: -iemus *Pm*   4 C. Coelium ... audisti
interrog. feci Coelium ϛ: c(a)el- Ω, *et sic alibi*   huc quaestorem *HNOR*: q- huc Δ
5 hominis *c*: *om.* Ω   sed *seclusi*: sed ... (*cum aposiopesi*) *Wesenberg*   7 tempora
Ps: -re *HNORbdm*: tp̄r *M*   8 εὐήθειαν ϛ: ΕΥΘ- *RMmsC*   tua *HNR codd. Mal.*
Z⁽ᵇ⁾: *om.* OΔ

My dearest Atticus, you have really cared too much for Brutus in this matter, and not enough, I fear, for me. However I have written to Brutus telling him what you have written to me.

10 Now for the rest of my news. I am doing everything possible here on Appius' behalf, having regard to what is seemly however—but not at all half-heartedly. I have no ill will towards Appius himself, I am fond of Brutus, and Pompey, for whom I must say my regard increases from day to day, makes a very great point of it. Have you heard that C. Coelius is coming here as Quaestor? I don't know what sort of a fellow he is. I don't like this about Pammenes. I hope to be in Athens in September. I should much like to know the dates of your journeys. I have learned of Sempronius Rufus' naïveté from your letter from Corcyra and can only say that I envy Vestorius his power.

I should love to go on gossiping a while longer, but it is light. The crowd presses, Philogenes wants to be off. All good wishes then, and please give the like to Pilia and our dear Caecilia when you write. My Marcus sends his love.

117 (VI. 3)

En route *to Tarsus, May or beginning of June 50*

CICERO TO ATTICUS

1 I have no news really, nothing subsequent to the letter I gave to your freedman Philogenes, but as I am sending Philotimus to Rome I must write you a line or two. I'll begin with my biggest worry, not that you can be of any help. How should you? The matter is actual and you are far, far away,

'and many a wave between
the south wind rolls over the wide, salt sea'.

obrepit dies, ut vides (mihi enim a. d. III Kal. Sext. de provincia
decedendum est), nec succeditur. quem relinquam qui provin- 10
ciae praesit? ratio quidem et opinio hominum postulat fratrem,
primum quod videtur esse honos, nemo igitur potior; deinde
quod solum habeo praetorium. Pomptinus enim ex pacto et
convento (nam ea lege exierat) iam a me discesserat. quaestorem
nemo dignum putat; etenim est levis, libidinosus, tagax. 15
2 de fratre autem primum illud est: persuaderi ei non posse
arbitror; odit enim provinciam, et hercule nihil odiosius, nihil
molestius. deinde ut mihi nolit negare, quidnam mei sit offici?
cum bellum esse in Syria magnum putetur, id videatur in hanc
provinciam erupturum, hic praesidi nihil sit, sumptus annuus 5
decretus sit, videaturne aut pietatis esse meae fratrem relinquere
aut diligentiae nugarum aliquid relinquere? magna igitur, ut
vides, sollicitudine adficior, magna inopia consili. quid quaeris?
toto negotio nobis opus non fuit. quanto tua provincia melior!
decedes cum voles, nisi forte iam decessisti; quem videbitur 10
praeficies Thesprotiae et Chaoniae. necdum tamen ego
Quintum conveneram, ut iam si id placeret scirem possetne ab
3 eo impetrari; nec tamen, si posset, quid vellem habebam. Hoc
est igitur eius modi.

   Reliqua plena adhuc et laudis et gratiae, digna iis libris quos
dilaudas: conservatae civitates, cumulate publicanis satis
factum; offensus contumelia nemo, decreto iusto et severo 5
perpauci, nec tamen quisquam ut queri audeat; res gestae
dignae triumpho, de quo ipso nihil cupide agemus, sine tuo

Ep. 117] 1, 9 obrepit *Ernesti*: -psit Ω   10 deced- *OPm*: disced- *HNbds*:
descend- *RM*   14 convento *Manutius*: -tu Ω*Z*⁽ᵇ⁾   15 tagax *M*, *Cuiacius ex Z*
(*teste Bosio*): taga *N*: sagax *HOR*δ   **2,** 6 relinquere Ωλ: *del. Manutius*
12 scirem *HNPs*: -re *ORΔ*   **3,** 4 dilaudas *Victorius*: dii(s) l-*EM*: tu l-*NOR*δ:
tu dil- *Schütz*

The day is creeping up, as you see—I must leave the province on 30 July—, and my successor is not appointed. Whom am I to leave in charge of the province? In principle and in the general expectation my brother is the man, firstly because it has the appearance of an honour, so nobody has a better claim; second, because he is the only man of praetorian rank available. Pomptinus has already left me according to covenant—he came out on that condition. Nobody thinks the Quaestor fit for the position. He is irresponsible, licentious, and light-

2 fingered. As for my brother, there is this to begin with: I don't think he could be persuaded. He hates the province, and certainly nothing could be more boring and disagreeable. Second, granted that he might not care to say no to me, where does my duty lie? There is thought to be a major war in Syria which looks as though it will erupt into this province, there is no means of defence here, only one year's credits have been voted. In such circumstances can I as a good brother leave Quintus in charge? And can I as a good public servant leave some nincompoop? So as you see I am in great worry and perplexity. The truth is I ought never to have touched this job. How I envy you *your* province! You will leave when you like— perhaps you have left already. You will place whomever you think fit in charge of Thresprotia and Chaonia. However I have not yet met Quintus so as to know whether he could be brought to agree, if I *should* decide that way. But if he could,

3 I can't tell what I want. So that's about the size of that.

The rest of my administration brings me so far abundance of praise and gratitude, befitting the volumes you eulogize so handsomely: communities saved from bankruptcy, tax-farmers more than satisfied, nobody insulted, only a very few offended by the strict justice of a ruling (but none daring to complain), military achievements worthy of a Triumph. In *that* matter

quidem consilio certe nihil. clausula est difficilis in tradenda provincia; sed haec deus aliquis gubernabit.

4   De urbanis rebus scilicet plura tu scis, saepius et certiora audis; equidem doleo non me tuis litteris certiorem fieri. huc enim odiosa adferebantur de Curione, de Paulo; non quo ullum periculum videam stante Pompeio vel etiam sedente, valeat modo; sed mehercule Curionis et Pauli, meorum familiarium, 5 vicem doleo. formam igitur mihi totius rei publicae, si iam es Romae aut cum eris, velim mittas quae mihi obviam veniat, ex qua me fingere possim et praemeditari quo animo accedam ad urbem; est enim quiddam advenientem non esse peregrinum atque hospitem.   10

5   Et quod paene praeterii, Bruti tui causa, ut saepe ad te scripsi, feci omnia. Cyprii numerabant; sed Scaptius centesimis renovato in singulos annos faenore contentus non fuit. Ariobarzanes non in Pompeium prolixior per ipsum quam per me in Brutum. quem tamen ego praestare non poteram; erat enim rex per- 5 pauper aberamque ab eo ita longe ut nihil possem nisi litteris, quibus pugnare non destiti. summa haec est: pro ratione pecuniae liber⟨al⟩ius est Brutus tractatus quam Pompeius. Bruto curata hoc anno talenta circiter c, Pompeio in sex mensibus promissa cc. iam in Appi negotio quantum tribuerim Bruto 10 dici vix potest. quid est igitur quod laborem? amicos habet meras nugas, Ma⟨ti⟩nium, Scaptium; qui quia non habuit ⟨a⟩ me turmas equitum quibus Cyprum vexaret, ut ante me fecerat,

---

4, 2 doleo] *accedit W*   8 pr(a)emeditari *HNPδW*: predi- *EORM*   **5,** 6 nisi *Pbds*: ni *MmW*: in *R*   8 pecuni(a)e *Ps*: -ia *ΩW*   liberalius *Victorius*: -erius *Ω*: -eius *W*   9 talenta *s*: tanti *ΩW*   12 Matinium *Corradus*: manium (in a- *R*) *ORMdW*: matrium *N*: M. *bms*   a me *Pδ*: me *Ω*: *om. W*   13 vexaret *NPδ*: ex- *ORMW*   ut *Nδ*: quod *P*: *om. ORMW*

I shall do nothing savouring of undue eagerness, and certainly nothing without your advice. The close of the chapter presents difficulty, in handing over the province. But some providence will guide me there.

4   Of home affairs you of course know more than I, you hear more often and more reliably. I am sorry you don't inform *me* by letter, for some disagreeable reports are coming here about Curio and Paulus. Not that I see any danger so long as Pompey stands—or even sits, provided his health holds. But I am really sorry about Curio and Paulus, both friends of mine. So please send me a sketch of the whole political situation if you are already in Rome or when you get there, so that it meets me on my way and I can adjust myself in the light of it and work out beforehand the attitude of mind in which I ought to approach the capital. It's something not to arrive as a foreigner and a stranger.

5   I nearly forgot to add that, as I have often told you, I have done everything in my power for your friend Brutus. The Cypriots were ready to pay cash down, but Scaptius was not satisfied with 1% per month annually compounded. Ariobarzanes is as anxious to pay Brutus for my sake as he is to pay Pompey for Pompey's. However, I can't answer for him. He is a very impecunious monarch and I am too far away to do anything except by letters, with which I have kept up a steady barrage. The long and the short of it is that proportionally to the sums involved Brutus has been treated more handsomely than Pompey. Brutus has been paid about 100 talents this year, Pompey has been promised 200 over six months. Then there is Appius' affair; what I have done in that for Brutus' sake is almost beyond telling. So why should I worry? He has friends who are utter good-for-nothings—Matinius, Scaptius. The latter may be cross because he did not get from me some

fortasse suscenset, aut quia praefectus non est, quod ego nemini
tribui negotiatori (non C. Vennonio, meo familiari, non tuo, 15
M. Laenio), et quod tibi Romae ostenderam me servaturum;
in quo perseveravi. sed quid poterit queri is qui auferre pecuniam cum posset noluit? †aut Scaptius† qui in Cappadocia fuit
puto esse satis factum. is a me tribunatum cum accepisset, quem
ego ex Bruti litteris ei detulissem, postea scripsit ad me se uti 20
nolle eo tribunatu.

6   Gavius est quidam, cui cum praefecturam detulissem Bruti
rogatu multa et dixit et fecit cum quadam mea contumelia, P.
Clodi canis. is me nec proficiscentem Apamea prosecutus est
nec, cum postea in castra venisset atque inde discederet, num
quid vellem rogavit et fuit aperte mihi nescio qua re non amicus. 5
hunc ego si in praefectis habuissem, quem tu me hominem
putares? qui, ut scis, potentissimorum hominum contumaciam
numquam tulerim, ferrem huius adseculae? etsi hoc plus est
quam ferre, tribuere etiam aliquid benefici et honoris. is igitur
Gavius, cum Apameae me nuper vidisset Romam proficiscens, 10
me ita appellavit ⟨ut⟩ Culleolum vix auderem: 'unde' inquit
'me iubes petere cibaria praefecti?' respondi lenius quam
putabant oportuisse qui aderant, me non instituisse iis dare
7   cibaria quorum opera non essem usus. abiit iratus. huius
nebulonis oratione si Brutus moveri potest, licebit eum solus
ames, me aemulum non habebis. sed illum eum futurum esse

---

16 et Ω*W*: id *Corradus*   18 aut scaptius *NW*: an s- *OR*: s- Δ: Scaptio *Manutius*,
alii aliter   19 esse ei *Purser*   **6,** 1 Gavius *Z*ᵇ: gaius Ω: ca- *H*δ (*similis varietas
infra*)   3 apamea *HN*: -me *M*: -meam *EOR*δ   9 aliquid beneficii *NW*:
b- a- *HOR*Δ: b- *E*   11 ut *add. Schütz*   culleonum *W*λ   12 praefecti *WZ*:
profecto Ω   **7,** 2 nebulonis *om. W*   oratione *Corradus*: opera- Ω*W*   solus
Σ*W*: -um Δ

troops of horse to harry Cyprus, as he had done before my time, or because he is not a Prefect, an appointment which I have not given to any business man, neither to my friend C. Vennonius nor to your friend M. Laenius—the rule I told you in Rome I should follow and to which I have kept. But how can a man grumble who would not take his money when he had the chance? As for the Scaptius who was in Cappadocia, I think he has no complaints. He accepted a Tribunate from me which I offered him as requested in a letter of Brutus', but later wrote to me that he did not want to take the appointment up.

6   There is a certain Gavius who, after I had offered him a Prefecture at Brutus' request, often both spoke and behaved in a manner insulting to me—one of the dogs who ran at P. Clodius' heels. He omitted to accompany me when I left Apamea and, when subsequently he visited my camp, went off again without taking leave of me and showed quite openly that he bore me some sort of grudge. If I had counted a fellow like that among my Prefects, what would you take me for? As you know, I have never put up with rudeness from the most powerful personages; was I to tolerate it from this hanger-on? And this is going beyond mere toleration, actually to confer something in the way of a favour and distinction. Well, this Gavius, seeing me recently at Apamea as he was leaving for Rome, accosted me in a tone I should hardly dare to use to Culleolus: 'Where am I supposed to apply for my maintenance allowance as Prefect?' I answered more gently than those present thought proper to the occasion, that it was not my practice to give maintenance allowances to persons whose services I had not used. He left in a huff. If Brutus can be

7   affected by what this scum has to say, you can love him all by yourself, I shall not be your competitor. But I expect he will

puto qui esse debet; tibi tamen causam notam esse volui et ad
ipsum haec perscripsi diligentissime. omnino (soli enim sumus) 5
nullas umquam ad me litteras misit Brutus, ne proxime quidem
de Appio, in quibus non inesset adrogans et ἀκοινονόητον
aliquid. tibi autem valde solet in ore esse.

'Granius autem
non contemnere se et reges odisse superbos.'   10

in quo tamen ille mihi risum magis quam stomachum movere
solet; sed plane parum cogitat quid scribat aut ad quem.

8   Q. Cicero puer legit, ut opinor, et certe, epistulam inscriptam
patri suo; solet enim aperire, idque de meo consilio, si quid
forte sit quod opus sit sciri. in ea autem epistula erat idem illud
de sorore quod ad me. mirifice conturbatum vidi puerum;
lacrimans mecum est questus. quid quaeris? miram in eo pie- 5
tatem, suavitatem humanitatemque perspexi; quo maiorem
spem habeo nihil fore aliter ac deceat. id te igitur scire volui.

9   Ne illud quidem praetermittam. Hortensius filius fuit
Laodiceae gladiatoribus, flagitiose et turpiter. hunc ego patris
causa vocavi ad cenam quo die venit, et eiusdem patris causa
nihil amplius. is mihi dixit se Athenis me exspectaturum
ut mecum decederet. 'recte' inquam; quid enim dicerem? 5
omnino puto nihil esse quod dixit; nolo quidem, ne offendam
patrem, quem mehercule multum diligo. sin fuerit meus
comes, moderabor ita ne quid eum offendam quem minime
volo.

10   Haec sunt. etiam illud: orationem Q. Celeris mihi velim

---

7 esset *W*   et Σ*W*: *om.* Δ   8 solet valde *W*   9 granius *W*: gravius Ω
8, 2 solet *ms*: -es *R*: -eo *HNOPM(?)bd*   3 idem illud *HNORW*:
il- idem Δ   9, 8 quid *HNRW*: quidem OΔ   10, 1 orationem *PbmsW*: -ne
HNORMd

behave as befits him. However I wanted you to know the facts and I have given Brutus a fully detailed account of them. To be sure (I write in confidence) Brutus has never sent me a letter, not even most recently about Appius, that did not contain something arrogant, ungracious. Now one of your favourite sayings is

'Granius now
Knew his own worth and hated proud grandees.'

But this way of his amuses rather than irritates me. All the same he should really take a little more thought about what he writes and to whom.

8   I think, indeed I am sure, that young Quintus has read a letter addressed to his father. He is in the habit of opening them and does so at my suggestion, in case there might be something we ought to know about. This particular letter contained the same item about your sister which you wrote to me. I could see that the boy was dreadfully upset. He cried as he lamented over it to me. In fact I was greatly impressed by the dutiful, affection- ate, thoughtful way he spoke. It makes me the more hopeful that nothing untoward will happen. So I wanted you to know.

9   Another thing I may as well mention is that Hortensius junior was in Laodicea for the gladiators, behaving in a scandalous, disgraceful fashion. For his father's sake I asked him to dine the day he arrived and equally for his father's sake did nothing more. He told me he would wait for me in Athens in order to go back with me to Rome. 'Very good' I said. What else could I say? To be sure I don't suppose that what he said meant anything. I hope not, for I shouldn't like to offend his father, for whom, believe me, I have a great regard. If how- ever he does accompany me, I shall handle it so as not to give offence where I least wish.

10   That's all—except this: would you please send me Q. Celer's

mittas contra M. Servilium. litteras mitte quam primum; si
nihil ⟨erit, id ipsum scribes, nihil⟩ fieri, vel per tuum tabellarium.
Piliae et filiae salutem. cura ut valeas.

118 (VI. 4)

Scr. in itinere med., ut vid., m. Iun. an. 50

CICERO ATTICO SAL.

1 Tarsum veni Non. Iun. ibi me multa moverunt: magnum in
Syria bellum, magna in Cilicia latrocinia, mihi difficilis ratio
administrandi, quod paucos dies habebam reliquos annui
muneris, illud autem difficillimum, relinquendus erat ex senatus
consulto qui praeesset. nihil minus probari poterat quam 5
quaestor Mescinius. nam de Coelio nihil audiebamus. rectissi-
mum videbatur Quintum fratrem cum imperio relinquere; in
quo multa molesta, discessus noster, belli periculum, militum
improbitas, sescenta praeterea. o rem totam odiosam! sed haec
fortuna viderit, quoniam consilio non multum uti licet.   10
2 Tu quando Romam salvus (ut spero) venisti, videbis, ut
soles, omnia quae intelleges nostra interesse, in primis de Tullia
mea, cuius de condicione quid mihi placeret scripsi ad Terentiam cum tu in Graecia esses; deinde de honore nostro. quod
enim tu afuisti, vereor ut satis diligenter actum in senatu sit de 5
litteris meis.
3 Illud praeterea μυστικώτερον ad te scribam, tu sagacius
odorabere. τῆς δάμαρτός μου ὁ ἀπελεύθερος (οἶσθα ὃν λέγω) ἔδοξέ
μοι πρώην, ἐξ ὧν ἀλογευόμενος παρεφθέγγετο, πεφυρακέναι τὰς
ψήφους ἐκ τῆς ὠνῆς τῶν ὑπαρχόντων ⟨τῶν⟩ τοῦ Κροτωνιάτου

---

3 erit . . . nihil *addidi*: nihil *add. Bosius*, fit nihil *Watt*
Ep. 118] 1, 1 veni *HNORW*: -imus Δ   3 reliquos *P*: al- Ω   4 ex] *hic desinit W*
2, 3 de ς: cum Ω   **3**, 3 πεφυρακέναι *Victorius*: πεφωρ- *M corr.*: ΠΕΦΡΑΚΑΙΝΕ
vel sim. RPM: διεφθαρκέναι δ   4 τῶν *add. Wesenberg*

speech against M. Servilius? Send me a letter as soon as you can. If no news, just say that, that there is nothing doing, even if it means sending a courier of your own. My love to Pilia and your daughter. Take care of your health.

118 (VI. 4)

En route, *mid-(?) June 50*

CICERO TO ATTICUS

1 I arrived at Tarsus on the Nones of June. There I found much to disquiet me: a great war in Syria, a great deal of brigandage in Cilicia, a difficult administrative task because I have only a few days left of my year's charge; most difficult of all, somebody must be left in charge under the Senate's decree. No choice could have less to recommend it than Quaestor Mescinius—of Coelius I hear nothing. The most correct course seems to be to leave my brother Quintus with full authority. It involves many disagreeables, our separation, the danger of war, the rascality of the soldiers—there's no end to them. The whole thing is an unmitigated bore. But I must leave all this to luck since there is little room for calculation.

2 Now that you are safely back, I hope, in Rome, would you please attend in your usual way to all you may find to concern me, above all with regard to my dear Tullia—I gave my views about a match for her to Terentia in a letter written when you were in Greece; and secondly with regard to my prospective honour, for I'm afraid that because of your absence my letter did not get sufficiently careful treatment in the Senate.

3 There's something else about which I must write to you *en langue voilée*, and you must lay your nose to the scent. *From the confused and incoherent way he talked the other day, I formed the impression that my wife's freedman (you know to whom I refer) has cooked the accounts relating to the purchase of the Crotonian*

τυραννοκτόνου. δέδοικα δὴ μή τι—νοήσεις δήπου. τοῦτο δὴ 5
περισκεψάμενος τὰ λοιπὰ ἐξασφάλισαι. non queo tantum quantum
vereor scribere; tu autem fac ut mihi tuae litterae volent
obviae.

Haec festinans scripsi in itinere atque agmine. Piliae et
puellae Caeciliae bellissimae salutem dices.   10

119 (VI. 5)

Scr. in castris ad Pyramum v Kal. Quint. an. 50 (§3)

CICERO ATTICO SAL.

1 Nunc quidem profecto Romae es, quo te, si ita est, salvum
venisse gaudeo; unde quidem quam diu afuisti, magis a me
abesse videbare quam si domi esses. minus enim mihi meae
notae res erant, minus etiam publicae. qua re velim, etsi (ut
spero) te haec legente aliquantum iam viae processero, tamen 5
obvias mihi litteras quam argutissimas de omnibus rebus
crebro mittas, in primis de quo scripsi ad te antea. τῆς
ξυναόρου τῆς ἐμῆς οὐξελεύθερος ἔδοξέ μοι θαμὰ βατταρίζων
⟨καὶ⟩ ἀλύων ἐν τοῖς ξυλλόγοις καὶ ταῖς λέσχαις ὑπό τι πεφυρακέναι τὰς ψήφους ἐν τοῖς ὑπάρχουσιν τοῖς τοῦ Κροτωνιάτου. 10
2 hoc tu indaga, ut soles, at hoc magis. ἐξ ἄστεως ἑπταλόφου
στείχων παρέδωκεν μνῶν †καμν† ὀφείλημα τῷ Καμίλλῳ, ἑαυτόν
τε ὀφείλοντα μνᾶς κδ' ἐκ τῶν Κροτωνιατικῶν καὶ ἐκ τῶν Χερ-

---

5 νοήσεις *Watt*: NONCHC EIC *vel sim. RPM*: νοήσης (-ης) ἐν (ἐν) δ (νοήσῃ λ; εἶς *C*, ut vid.*) 6 περισκεψάμενος δ: -ΨΗΜΕΝΟC *vel sim. RPM* queo *s*: quo Ω
Ep. 119] 1, 2 a(b)fuisti *Manutius*: abisti Ω 5 aliquantum *Ps*: alio q- Ω iam *Ernesti*: tam *R*: tamen *HOP*δ: tum *NE: om. s* 6 obviam *H* 9 καὶ *add.* ς ἐν *OR: om. P*Δ 11 at *m*: ast Ω: et *Reid*: sed *Wesenberg* **2**, 1 ἑπταλόφου *c*: ΥΠΓΑ- *vel sim. PMm*: ΥΝΤΑ- *R* 2 μνῶν *Bosius*: ΗΩΜΝ *RMm*: ομὴ *O*: ἡμῶν *c* ΚΑΜΝ *RMmc*: κάμη *O*: κδ', μη' *Bosius* ὀφείλημα τῷ *Lambinus*: -ΜΑΤΩΝ *vel sim. Ωc* 3 κδ' *Victorius*: ΗΔ (Ηδ) *Mc*: ΗΑ *OR*: ΥΑ *P*

tyrannicide's property. I am afraid that something—you'll take my meaning. Please look into it and see that the other matters are put on a safe footing. I can't put all I fear into words. You must see that a letter comes flying to meet me.

I write this in haste, on the road, in fact on the march. Give my love to Pilia and pretty little Caecilia.

119 (VI. 5)

In camp on the Pyramus, 26 June 50

CICERO TO ATTICUS

1 You must surely be in Rome by now. If so, I'm glad of your safe arrival. All the while you have been away from Rome it seemed as though you were farther from me than if you had been at home. I knew less about my own affairs and less about public affairs too. So although by the time you read this I hope to have put some of the road behind me, please send a rapid succession of letters to meet me, as gossipy as you can make them, about this, that and the other, but more especially about what I wrote to you some time ago. *At my meetings and talks with my spouse's freedman, he kept stammering and losing his way, so that I got the impression that he had done some cooking of accounts*
2 *in the matter of the man of Croton's property.* Ferret this out in your usual style, but still more the following:— *On leaving the city of the seven hills he transferred a claim of * minae to Camillus, and himself as owing 24 minae on the Crotonian property and 48 on*

ρονησιτικῶν μη′ καὶ μνᾶς κληρονομῆσαι χμ′ [κμ]. τούτων δὲ
μηδὲ ὀβολὸν διευλυτῆσθαι, πάντων ὀφειληθέντων τοῦ δευτέρου 5
μηνὸς τῇ νουμηνίᾳ. τὸν δὲ ἀπελεύθερον αὐτοῦ, ὄντα ὁμώνυμον
τῷ Κόνωνος πατρί, μηδὲν ὁλοσχερῶς πεφροντικέναι. ταῦτα οὖν
πρῶτον μὲν ἵνα πάντα σώζηται, δεύτερον δὲ ἵνα μηδὲ τῶν τόκων
ὀλιγωρήσῃς τῶν ἀπὸ τῆς προεκκειμένης ἡμέρας. ὅσας ✳ ✳ ✳
αὐτοῦ ἠνέγκαμεν σφόδρα δέδοικα· καὶ γὰρ παρῆν πρὸς ἡμᾶς 10
κατασκεψόμενος καί τι σχεδὸν ἐλπίσας· ἀπογνοὺς δ᾽ ἀλόγως
ἀπ⟨ῆλθ⟩εν ἐπειπών 'εἴκω· "αἰσχρόν τοι δηρόν τε μένειν..."',
meque obiurgavit vetere proverbio 'τὰ μὲν διδόμενα...'.

3 reliqua vide et quantum fieri potest perspice.

Nos etsi annuum tempus [est] prope iam emeritum habebamus (dies enim xxxiii erant reliqui), sollicitudine provinciae
tamen vel maxime urgebamur. cum enim arderet Syria bello
et Bibulus in tanto maerore suo maximam curam belli sustineret 5
ad meque legati eius et quaestor et amici eius litteras mitterent
ut subsidio venirem, etsi exercitum infirmum habebam, auxilia
sane bona sed ea Galatarum, Pisidarum, Lyciorum (haec enim
sunt nostra robora), tamen esse officium meum putavi exercitum
habere quam proxime hostem quoad mihi praeesse provinciae 10
per senatus consultum liceret. sed quo ego maxime delectabar,
Bibulus molestus mihi non erat, de omnibus rebus scribebat
ad me potius. et mihi decessionis dies λεληθότως obrepebat.
qui cum advenerit, ἄλλο πρόβλημα, quem praeficiam, nisi
Caldus quaestor venerit; de quo adhuc nihil certi habebamus. 15

---

4 μη′ O: MN (μν) Mc: MI P: M R μνᾶς Bosius: TINAC RΔ κληρονομῆσαι
Lambinus: -CAC Ω   χμ′ scripsi: XMKM RM: χμ′, χμ′ nescioquis: χμ′, ψμ′ Haywood
9 lac. ind. Watt δὲ κλοπὰς vel sim. excidisse ratus   10 αὐτοῦ Sjögren: AYTO
RM: αὐτὸν Oδ   12 ἀπῆλθεν scripsi: ΑΠΕΝ P: ΑΠΕΗ RM: ἀπέστη δ: ἀπῇει Watt
εἴκω O: IKΩ RM   3, 1 perspice nos C: -ciamus Ω   2 est del. Victorius iam
Manutius: tamen ΩC   emeritum Victorius: me- ΩC   6 eius (alt.) om. E
14 praeficiam nisi ς: presi nisi Δ: pre feci si N: pretermisi R: prefinxi P
15 caldus ΔZ⁽ᵇ⁾: cal(l)idus NOR

*the Chersonesian, also stated amount by legacy as 640 minae. Not
an obol of this alleged to have been cleared, though it was all owing
on the 1st of the second month. His freedman, namesake of Conon's
father, alleged to have paid absolutely no attention. So please see first
that all these sums are taken care of and second don't overlook the
interest accruing from the date agreed. I am much alarmed about how
much I have lost by his pilferings (?). He came to spy out the ground,
and with some sort of expectation of profit. When that was disappointed he left without reason given, remarking 'I give up. "Shame to
stay long ..."', and took me to task with the old saw about*
3 beggars and choosers. As for the other matters, see to them and
explore as far as possible.

I have now got my year's service pretty well over (33 days
remain), but the cares of my office have never weighed on me
so heavily. Fighting has blazed up in Syria, where Bibulus in
his own terrible bereavement has the responsibility of a major
war on his hands. His Legates and Quaestor and friends have
written asking me to come to his assistance. My army is weak—
the auxiliaries are pretty good but are made up of Galatians,
Pisidians, and Lycians; such is the backbone of my force. None
the less I felt it my duty to keep the army as close to the enemy
as possible so long as under the Senate's decree I can legally
remain in charge of the province. But much to my gratification
Bibulus is not troubling me—he writes to me about everything
under the sun rather than this. And the day of my departure
draws imperceptibly nearer. When it comes there is another
problem, whom I am to put in charge, unless Quaestor Caldus
arrives. I have no definite news of him yet.

4   Cupiebam mehercule longiorem epistulam facere, sed nec
erat res de qua scriberem nec iocari prae cura poteram. valebis
igitur et puellae salutem Atticulae tuae dices nostraeque Piliae.

120 (VI. 7)

Scr. Tarsi, ut vid., m. Quint. an. 50

CICERO ⟨ATTICO SAL.⟩

1   Quintus filius pie sane (me quidem certe multum hortante, sed
currentem) animum patris sui sorori tuae reconciliavit. eum
valde etiam tuae litterae excitarunt. quid quaeris? confido rem
ut volumus esse.

Bis ad te antea scripsi de re mea familiari, si modo tibi 5
redditae litterae sunt, Graece ἐν αἰνιγμοῖς. scilicet nihil est
movendum; sed tamen ἀφελῶς percontando ⟨de⟩ nominibus
Milonis et ut expediat ut mihi receperit hortando aliquid aut
proficies ⟨aut certe perspicies⟩.

2   Ego Laodiceae quaestorem Mescinium exspectare iussi, ut
confectas rationes lege Iulia apud duas civitates possim relinquere. Rhodum volo puerorum causa, inde quam primum
Athenas, etsi etesiae valde reflant; sed ✳ ✳ ✳ plane volo his
magistratibus, quorum voluntatem in supplicatione sum ex- 5
pertus. tu tamen mitte, quaeso, mihi obviam litteras num quid
putes rei publicae nomine tardandum esse nobis.

Tiro ad te dedisset litteras, nisi eum graviter aegrum Issi

4, 3 Atticulae (*Malaespina*) tuae *Dahlman*: -colate *Z*¹: articulate Ω: ᾿Αττικωτάτῃ
Madvig
Ep. 120] attico s(alutem) *bd*: *om.* Ω*C* I, 3 etiam *R codd. Mal. Z*⁽ᵇ⁾: me *Hbds*:
om. NOM litterae me *R* 7 de ϛ: *om.* Ω 8 ita ut mihi *Mueller* receperit
NOPΔ: -pit *R* aliquid aut] aliquantum *Manutius*: aliquid tu *Sturmius*: al-
certe *Castiglioni*: al- utique *Watt* 9 aut . . . perspicies *addidi* **2**, 1 exspectare
iussi ϛ: -are (*ut vid.*) missi *Z*¹: -arem is si *NO*: -arem ipse *R*: -are misi Δ ut Δ:
venerit ut *NOR* 2 possim *OΔ*: -sem *N*: -sum *R* 4 reflant *N*: -avi *ORΔ*
post sed *vel* plane *excidisse videtur* Romam (*Purser*) *vel sim.* (*fort.* istuc) plane
NOR: *om.* Δ 6 quaeso mihi *HNOR*: m- q- Δ 8 Issi *Manutius*: esse Ω

4   I should really like to make a longer letter of it, but I have
nothing to write about and am too anxious for jesting. So
keep well and give my love to your little Attica and our dear
Pilia.

120 (VI. 7)

Tarsus (?), July 50

CICERO TO ATTICUS

1   Young Quintus has certainly acted like a good son in reconciling his father's mind towards your sister, not it is true without
a good deal of encouragement from me, but I was spurring a
willing horse. Your letter too has greatly stimulated him.
Altogether I am satisfied that the matter stands as we wish.

I have written to you twice about my finances, if only you
got the letters, in Greek, riddle-fashion. No doubt it's best to
let things stay as they are. But by making innocent enquiries
about the claims due to Milo and urging him to clear the thing
up as he gave me his word he would you will get something
done or at any rate find something out.

2   I have instructed Quaestor Mescinius to wait at Laodicea so
that I can leave my accounts made up in two towns as required
by the lex Julia. I want to go to Rhodes for the boys' sake,
from there as quickly as possible to Athens, though the Etesians
are blowing hard the other way. But I definitely want to get
back while the present magistrates are in office, having had a
sample of their good will in the matter of the Supplication.
However do pray send a letter to meet me and tell me whether
for political reasons you think I ought to dawdle.

Tiro would have sent you a letter but for the fact that I left

reliquissem; sed nuntiant melius esse. ego tamen angor; nihil
enim illo adulescente castius, nihil diligentius.   10

121 (VI. 6)

Scr. Sidae c. iii Non. Sext. an. 50

CICERO ATTICO SAL.

1 Ego dum in provincia omnibus rebus Appium orno, subito
sum factus accusatoris eius socer. 'id quidem' inquis 'di
adprobent!'. ita velim, teque ita cupere certo scio. sed crede
mihi, nihil minus putaram ego, qui de Ti. Nerone, qui
mecum egerat, certos homines ad mulieres miseram; qui 5
Romam venerunt factis sponsalibus. sed hoc spero melius.
mulieres quidem valde intellego delectari obsequio et comitate
adulescentis. cetera noli ἐξακανθίζειν.

2 Sed heus tu, πυροὺς εἰς δῆμον Athenis? placet hoc tibi? etsi
non impediebant mei certe libri; non enim ista largitio fuit in
civis sed in hospites liberalitas. me tamen de Academiae προπύλῳ
iubes cogitare, cum iam Appius de Eleusine non cogitet?

De Hortensio te certo scio dolere. equidem excrucior; 5
decreram enim valde cum eo familiariter vivere.

3 Nos provinciae praefecimus Coelium. 'puerum' inquies 'et
fortasse fatuum et non gravem et non continentem.' adsentior;
fieri non potuit aliter. nam quas multo ante tuas acceperam
litteras in quibus ἐπέχειν te scripseras quid esset mihi faciendum de relinquendo, eae me pungebant. videbam enim quae 5

Ep. 121] 1, 4 quin de *Madvig*   2, 3 non de *c*   4 cum iam *Manutius*:
quoniam Ω   6 valde cum eo *HOR*: cum eo v- *NΔ*   3, 3 sed *ante* fieri *add.*
Watt   4 ἐπέχειν te scripseras *Manutius*: ΕΠΕΧΕ inters- *ORMdm*: inters- *HNbs*
5 e(a)e me Δ: eam *N*: esse me *HR*: me *P*   pungebant *C*: pugnab- Ω

him seriously ill at Issus. But they tell me he is better. Even so I am acutely worried. He is such a well-behaved, conscientious young fellow.

121 (VI. 6)

Side, c. 3 August 50

CICERO TO ATTICUS

1 Here am I in my province paying Appius all manner of compliments, when out of the blue I find his prosecutor becoming my son-in-law! 'Good luck to that', say you. So I hope and I am very sure you so desire. But believe me it was the last thing I expected. I had actually sent reliable persons to the ladies in connexion with Ti. Nero, who had treated with me. They got to Rome after the *fiançailles*. However I hope this is better. The ladies are evidently quite charmed with the young man's attentiveness and engaging manners. For the rest, no black paint please!

2 But what's all this? *Panem populo* at Athens? Do you think that is in order? Not that *my* volumes have anything against it, since it was not a largesse to fellow-countrymen but a piece of generosity to foreign hosts. But do you tell *me* to 'think about' the Academy porch, when Appius has already given up *thinking* about Eleusis?

I am sure you will be grieving about Hortensius. For my own part I am deeply distressed. I had made up my mind to live on really close terms with him.

3 I have put Coelius in charge of the province. You'll say he is a boy, and perhaps a silly boy, without sense of responsibility or self-control. I agree. There was nothing else to be done. The letter I had from you quite a long time ago in which you wrote that you were suspending judgement as to what I ought to do about a deputy struck home. I saw the reasons for your

tibi essent ἐποχῆς causae, et erant eaedem mihi. puero traderem? ⟨id rei publicae non utile⟩. fratri autem? illud non utile nobis. nam praeter fratrem nemo erat quem sine contumelia quaestori, nobili praesertim, anteferrem. tamen, dum impendere Parthi videbantur, statueram fratrem relinquere, aut etiam rei publicae 10 causa contra senatus consultum ipse remanere; qui postea quam incredibili felicitate discesserunt, sublata dubitatio est. videbam sermones: 'hui, fratrem reliquit! num est hoc non plus annum obtinere provinciam? quid quod senatus eos voluit praeesse provinciis qui non praefuissent? at hic triennium.'   15

4   Ergo haec ad populum: quid quae tecum? numquam essem sine cura, si quid iracundius aut contumeliosius aut neglegentius, quae fert vita hominum. quid si quid filius puer et puer bene sibi fidens? qui esset dolor? quem pater non dimittebat teque id censere moleste ferebat. at nunc Coelius non dico 5 equidem 'quod egerit', sed tamen multo minus laboro. adde illud. Pompeius, eo robore vir, iis radicibus, Q. Cassium sine sorte delegit, Caesar Antonium: ego sorte datum offenderem, ut etiam inquireret in eum quem reliquissem? hoc melius, et huius rei plura exempla, senectuti quidem nostrae profecto 10 aptius. at te apud eum, di boni, quanta in gratia posui! eique legi litteras non tuas sed librari tui.

Amicorum litterae me ad triumphum vocant, rem a nobis, ut ego arbitror, propter hanc παλιγγενεσίαν nostram non neglegendam. qua re tu quoque, mi Attice, incipe id cupere, 15 quo nos minus inepti videamur.

---

6 e(a)edem P: eadem Ω   traderem Z^b: -re Ω   7 id . . . utile addidi   illud non rei publicae, hoc non utile nobis Madvig   13 num ds: non Ωλ   4, 1 qu(a)e ORbd: quod Mms: me N   3 fert vita (fertu-) NMmλ: fortu- ORbds   7 illud Δ: illa NOR   8 mandatum C   9 in eum Nλ: meum ORΔ   11 at te Victorius: apte Ω

'suspense of judgement', and they were my reasons too. Should I hand over to a boy? Contrary to public interest. To my brother then? That was contrary to my own (*except* my brother there was no one whom I could put ahead of the Quaestor, a nobleman too, without insulting him). None the less, so long as the Parthians looked like coming down on us, I had decided to leave my brother, or even for the country's sake to stay on myself in contravention of the Senate's decree. But when by an incredible stroke of luck they disappeared, my doubts were removed. I could hear the talk: 'Aha, left his brother, has he? Hardly what one would call governing for one year only, that! Thought the Senate wanted governors without previous service. This chap's had three years of it.'

4   So much for the public ear. For your own, I should never have had a minute's peace of mind for fear of some piece of irritability or rudeness or carelessness—these things happen. Then there's his son, a boy, and a boy with a fine conceit of himself—any incident involving him would be *most* distressing. His father was unwilling to send him away and was annoyed at your advising it. But as things are, Coelius—I won't say 'can please himself', but still I am much less concerned. Another point: Pompey, with all his power and backing, chose Q. Cassius without lots cast, similarly Caesar Antony. Was I to offend an officer assigned to me by lot, and have him spying too on the man I appointed? No, this is the better way; there are more precedents for it and for an old man like me it's clearly more appropriate! As for yourself, I have put you in his best books, tremendously so I assure you, and read him your letter or rather your secretary's.

My friends' letters beckon me to a Triumph, something I feel I ought not to neglect in view of this second birth of mine. So you too, my dear fellow, must start wanting it, so that I shan't look so foolish.

122 (VI. 8)

Scr. Ephesi Kal. Oct. an. 50 (§ 4)

CICERO ATTICO SAL.

1 Cum instituissem ad te scribere calamumque sumpsissem, Batonius e navi recta ad me venit domum Ephesi et epistulam tuam reddidit II Kal. Oct. laetatus sum felicitate navigationis tuae, opportunitate Piliae, etiam hercule sermone eiusdem de 2 coniugio Tulliae meae. Batonius autem meros terrores ad me attulit Caesarianos, cum Lepta etiam plura locutus est, spero falsa sed certe horribilia: exercitum nullo modo dimissurum, cum illo praetores designatos ⟨tris⟩, Cassium tribunum pl., Lentulum consulem facere, Pompeio in animo esse urbem 5 3 relinquere. sed heus tu, num quid moleste fers de illo qui se solet anteferre patruo sororis tuae fili? at a quibus victus!

4   Sed ad rem. nos etesiae vehementissimi tardarunt; detraxit XX ipsos dies etiam aphractus Rhodi. Kal. Oct. Epheso conscendentes hanc epistulam dedimus L. Tarquitio simul e portu egredienti sed expeditius naviganti. nos Rhodiorum aphractis ceterisque longis navibus tranquillitates aucupaturi eramus; ita 5 tamen properabamus ut non posset magis.

5   De raudusculo Puteolano gratum. nunc velim dispicias res Romanas, videas quid nobis de triumpho cogitandum putes, ad quem amici me vocant. ego, nisi Bibulus, qui dum unus hostis in Syria fuit pedem porta non plus extulit quam ⟨consul⟩ domo sua, adniteretur de triumpho, aequo essem animo; nunc 5

Ep. 122] 1 2, Battonius λ (*et sic infra*)   3 II Z: prid(ie) Ω   **2,** 1 meros *Muretus*: miros Ω   3 Caesarem exercitum *c*   4 tris *addidi*   cassium P: -us Ω   tr(i). ORb: pr. (p. r.) EHNΔ   **3,** 1 numquid *HNMs*: inquis id E: inquis OR: num inquit *bd*   2 filii *Pius*: -io Ω   **4,** 1 vehementissimi *Gronovius*: -ime Ω   2 Rhodi *ms*: prodi OΔ: prodii(t) NR: Rhodiorum ς   3 Tarquitio *Ant.* Z⁽ᵇ⁾: -in(i)o Ω   **5,** 1 dispicias *ENc*: desp- HORΔ   4 hostis *Victorius*: hospis Zᵗλ: -pes Ω   consul (*vel olim*) *add. Schütz*   5 adniteretur *Pius*: admir- Ω   essem animo Σ: a- e- Δ

122 (VI. 8)

Ephesus, 1 October 50

CICERO TO ATTICUS

1 I had no sooner set about writing to you and picked up my pen than Batonius arrived at my house in Ephesus straight from shipboard and gave me your letter, on 29 September. I was happy to hear what a good voyage you had, of Pilia's opportune arrival, also let me add of her remarks about my Tullia's
2 marriage. But Batonius brought me quite blood-curdling reports of Caesar, and told Lepta more still—untrue I hope, but certainly enough to make one shiver: that he will on no account give up his army, that three Praetors Designate, Cassius the Tribune, and the Consul Lentulus are on his side, and that
3 Pompey is minded to abandon Rome. And now, my good sir, are you sorry about the personage who is apt to set himself above your sister's son's uncle? To be beaten by such competitors too!

4 But to business. Etesians of unusual strength have held us up. An open boat too cost us twenty clear days at Rhodes. I am giving this letter to L. Tarquitius on the Kalends of October as I take ship from Ephesus. He is leaving port along with ourselves, but has less to cumber his voyage. We shall be waiting for calm spells to suit the Rhodian craft and the other long ships. Not but what we are making all possible haste.

5 Thanks for dealing with the petty cash at Puteoli. Now would you please take a look at affairs in Rome, see what in your opinion I ought to think about the Triumph to which my friends are beckoning me on? If it were not that Bibulus is exerting himself to get one, who so long as there was a single Parthian in Syria did not stir a step from the city gates any more than from his house when he was Consul, *I* should be easy. As

vero 'αἰσχρὸν σιωπᾶν'. sed explora rem totam, ut quo die congressi erimus consilium capere possimus.

Sat multa, qui et properarem et ei litteras darem qui aut mecum aut paulo ante venturus esset. Cicero tibi plurimam salutem dicit, tu dices utriusque nostrum verbis et Piliae tuae 10 et filiae.

123 (VI. 9)

Scr. Athenis Id. Oct. an. 50 (§ 5)

CICERO ATTICO SAL.

1 In Piraeea cum exissem prid. Id. Oct., accepi ab Acasto servo meo statim tuas litteras. quas quidem cum exspectassem iam diu, admiratus sum, ut vidi obsignatam epistulam, brevitatem eius, ut aperui, rursus σύγχυσιν litterularum, quae solent tuae compositissimae et clarissimae esse, ac, ne multa, cognovi ex 5 eo quod ita scripseras te Romam venisse a. d. xii Kal. Oct. cum febri. percussus vehementer, nec magis quam debui, statim quaero ex Acasto. ille et tibi et sibi visum et ita se domi ex tuis audisse ut nihil esset incommodi; id videbatur adprobare quod erat in extremo, febriculam tum te habentem scripsisse. sed 10 te amavi tamen admiratusque sum quod nihilo minus ad me tua manu scripsisses. qua re de hoc satis; spero enim, quae tua prudentia et temperantia est, ⟨et⟩ hercule, ut me iubet Acastus, confido te iam ut volumus valere.

2 A Turranio te accepisse meas litteras gaudeo. παραφύλαξον, si me amas, τὴν τοῦ φυρατοῦ φιλοτιμίαν· αὐτίκα γὰρ hanc, quae mehercule mihi magno dolori est (dilexi enim hominem),

---

8 sat *Schütz*: at Ω

Ep. 123] 1, 8 ita *cod. Bod.*: ista Ω　9 incommodi *Vollgraff*: -de Ω　11 amavi *HOR*λ: cla- *N*Δ: te a- *Wesenberg*　13 et c: om. Ω　iubet s: lu- *N*Δ: libet *OR* **2,** 1 Turranio *Manutius*: turannio *vel sim.* Ω, *et sic alibi*　2 αὐτίκα γὰρ *Watt*: ΑΙΤΟΤΑ *R*: αὐτότατα Δ: -ατος *anon. ap. Iunium*

it is, 'shame to be mute'. But do explore the whole matter so that we can make the decision the day we meet.

That's enough, as I'm in a hurry and the bearer will arrive the same time as myself or only a little before. Marcus sends you his best love. Give the same from us both to Pilia and your daughter.

123 (VI. 9)

Athens, 15 October 50

CICERO TO ATTICUS

1 Immediately on landing at Piraeus on 14 October I received your letter from my slave Acastus. Having waited for one a long time I was surprised when I saw the sealed letter that it was so short, and when I opened it I was again surprised at the irregularity of the writing—yours is usually beautifully precise and legible. And then, to be brief, I learned from your own statement that you had a fever when you arrived in Rome on 19 September. I was greatly alarmed, as was only right and proper, and at once enquired of Acastus. He said that, as you and he both thought and as he had heard from your people at home, there was nothing wrong. That seemed to be confirmed by the remark at the end of your letter that you had 'a slight touch of fever' when you wrote. But I wonder you wrote to me in your own hand just the same, and I appreciate it. So enough about that. Knowing how prudent and self-disciplined you are I hope and indeed am confident, as Acastus tells me to be, that you are by now as well as we wish you.

2 I am glad you have received my letter from Turranius. I beg you earnestly to keep a vigilant eye on the *philotimy* of the Chef. For example, look after Precius' legacy, such as it is (I

procura, quantulacumque est, Precianam hereditatem; prorsus
ille ne attingat. dices nummos mihi opus esse ad apparatum 5
triumphi; in quo, ut praecipis, nec me κενὸν in expetendo
cognosces nec ἄτυφον in abiciendo.

3   Intellexi ex tuis litteris te ex Turranio audisse a me provinciam fratri traditam. adeon ego non perspexeram prudentiam
litterarum tuarum? ἐπέχειν te scribebas: quid erat dubitatione
dignum, si esset quicquam cur placeret fratrem et talem fratrem
relinqui? ἀθέτησις ista mihi tua, non ἐποχή videbatur. monebas 5
de Q. Cicerone puero ut eum quidem neutiquam relinquerem:
'τοὐμὸν ὄνειρον ἐμοί.' eadem omnia quasi collocuti essemus
vidimus. non fuit faciendum aliter, meque ἐπιχρονία ἐποχή
tua dubitatione liberavit. sed puto te accepisse de hac re epistulam scriptam accuratius.   10

4   Ego tabellarios postero die ad vos eram missurus; quos puto
ante venturos quam nostrum Saufeium, sed eum sine meis
5 litteris ad te venire vix rectum erat. tu mihi, ut polliceris, de
Tulliola mea, id est de Dolabella, perscribes, de re publica,
quam provideo in summis periculis, de censoribus, maximeque
de signis, tabulis quid fiat, referaturne. Id. Oct. has dedi litteras,
quo die, ut scribis, Caesar Placentiam legiones IIII. quaeso, 5
quid nobis futurum est? in arce Athenis statio mea nunc placet.

---

5 ille *R*: illa *HΔ*: -am *N*   attingat *P*: -gas *Ω*   **3,** 3 ἐπέχειν *Victorius*: ΕΠΕΙΝ *Ω*
5 ἐποχή ϛ: ΑΠ- *Ω*   6 ut ϛ: et *Ωλ*   8 ἐπιχρονία ϛ: ΕΠΕΧ- *RM*   **5,** 3 provideo
OR: pr(a)er- *HNΔ*   4 referaturne *Pius*: -antur ne *Ω*   6 in arce *HNPsZ¹*:
ma- *RΔ*

am really very sorry to get it; I was fond of him)—don't let *him* get his fingers on it. You can say that I need the money for Triumph expenses. In that matter you shall find me, according to your precept, neither *glorieux* in demanding nor *modeste* in declining.

3   I gather from your letter that Turranius told you I had handed the province over to my brother. Can you suppose I was so blind to the wisdom of your letters? You wrote that you were 'suspending judgement'. What ground would there have been for hesitation if there had been anything to be said *for* leaving my brother in charge, and such a brother? Your suspension of judgement looked to me more like outright rejection. You warned me about young Quintus, not to leave him behind on any account. Great minds! We saw exactly eye to eye, as though we had talked it over together. Any other course would have been wrong, and your long-standing suspension of judgement freed me from any hesitation. But I expect you have received a letter I wrote on the subject in greater detail.

4   I am going to send couriers to you all tomorrow. I expect they will arrive before friend Saufeius, but it would scarcely have been right for him to join you without a letter from me.

5   On your side please write to me as you promise, all about my little Tullia, i.e. about Dolabella, and the political situation, which I foresee to be extremely dangerous, and the Censors, more particularly what is toward about statues and pictures—is there to be a motion in the Senate? I am dispatching this letter on the Ides of October, the day on which you say Caesar is taking four legions to Placentia. Pray what is to become of us? My present station in the citadel at Athens is to my liking.

124 (VII. I)

Scr. Athenis xvii Kal. Nov. an. 50

CICERO ATTICO SAL.

1 Dederam equidem L. Saufeio litteras et dederam ad te unum, quod, cum non esset temporis mihi ad scribendum satis, tamen hominem tibi tam familiarem sine meis litteris ad te venire nolebam; sed, ut philosophi ambulant, has tibi redditum iri putabam prius. sin iam illas accepisti, scis me Athenas venisse 5 prid. Id. Oct., e navi egressum in Piraeum tuas ab Acasto nostro litteras accepisse, conturbatum quod cum febre Romam venisses bono tamen animo esse coepisse quod Acastus ea quae vellem de adlevato corpore tuo nuntiaret, cohorruisse autem in e⟨o⟩ quod tuae litterae de legionibus Caesaris adferrent; et 10 egi[sse] tecum ut videres ne quid φιλοτιμία eius quem nosti nobis noceret; et, de quo iam pridem ad te scripseram, Turranius autem secus tibi Brundisi dixerat (quod ex iis litteris cognovi quas a Xenone, optimo viro, accepi), cur fratrem provinciae non praefecissem exposui breviter. haec fere sunt in illa 15 epistula.

2 Nunc audi reliqua. per fortunas, omnem tuum amorem quo me es amplexus omnemque tuam prudentiam, quam mehercule ego in omni genere iudico singularem, confer iam ad eam curam, ut de omni statu meo cogites. videre enim mihi videor tantam dimicationem, nisi idem deus qui nos melius quam 5 optare auderemus Parthico bello liberavit respexerit rem publicam—sed tantam quanta numquam fuit. age, hoc malum mihi commune est cum omnibus; nihil tibi mando ut de eo cogites, illud meum proprium πρόβλημα, quaeso, suscipe.

Ep. 124] 1, 7 febri *Boot* 9 cohorruisse *Pm codd. Mal.* λ: cor- *Rs*: cum horruisset *HNOMbd* 10 in eo *Mueller*: me Ωλ: eo *Schütz*: me eo *Tyrrell–Purser* 11 egi *scripsi*: egisse Ω 12 Turranius λ: turan(i)us Ω 2, 3 ego Σ: *om.* Δ confer iam *Lambinus*: -r eam *ER*: -ram *HZ*⁽ᵇ⁾: confeceram *N*: confer *P*Δ (te *add. ms*)

124 (VII. I)

Athens, 16 October 50

CICERO TO ATTICUS

1 I gave L. Saufeius a letter for you, and for nobody else, because even though I did not have time enough for writing I was unwilling that so close a friend of yours should join you without a letter from me. But at the rate philosophers move I imagine this will reach you first. If however you have already received the other, you are aware that I arrived at Athens on 14 October; that on disembarking at Piraeus I received a letter from you by our friend Acastus; that my consternation at the news of your arrival in Rome with a fever turned to something more optimistic at Acastus' satisfactory report of your recovery; but that I fell a'shivering at the news in your letter about Caesar's legions; and I asked you to see I came to no harm from the *philotimy* of you know who, and I briefly explained why I had not put my brother in charge of the province, a matter on which I had written to you previously but which Turranius (as I learned from the letter given me by the excellent Xeno) misreported to you at Brundisium. Such more or less are the contents of that letter.

2 Now let me tell you the rest. For mercy's sake, put all your affection, lavished on me as it is, and all your wisdom, remarkable in every field as I do assure you I regard it, into one single concern, the consideration of my position *in toto*. I fancy I see the greatest struggle—unless the same Providence that delivered me from the Parthian war better than I could have dared to hope takes pity on our country—, the greatest that history has ever known. Well, that is a calamity which I shall have to bear along with the rest of the world. I don't ask you to think about that. But do pray take up this personal problem of my own.

videsne ut te auctore sim utrumque complexus [Pompeium et 10
Caesarem]? ac vellem a principio te audisse amicissime
monentem,

'ἀλλ᾽ ἐμὸν οὔποτε θυμὸν ἐνὶ στήθεσσιν ἔπειθες'·
[πατρίδος]

sed aliquando tamen persuasisti ut alterum complecterer quia 15
de me erat optime meritus, alterum quia tantum valebat. feci
igitur, itaque effeci omni obsequio ut neutri illorum quisquam
3 esset me carior. haec enim cogitabamus, nec mihi coniuncto
cum Pompeio fore necesse peccare in re publica aliquando nec
cum Pompeio sentienti pugnandum esse cum Caesare; tanta
erat illorum coniunctio. nunc impendet, ut et tu ostendis et ego
video, summa inter eos contentio. me autem uterque numerat 5
suum, nisi forte simulat alter. nam Pompeius non dubitat; vere
enim iudicat ea quae de re publica nunc sentiat mihi valde
probari. utriusque autem accepi eius modi litteras eodem tempore quo tuas ut neuter quemquam omnium pluris facere quam
me videretur.   10
4   Verum quid agam? non quaero illa ultima (si enim castris res
geretur, video cum altero vinci satius esse quam cum altero
vincere), sed illa quae tum agentur cum venero, ne ratio absentis
habeatur, ut exercitum dimittat. 'dic, M. Tulli.' quid dicam?
'exspecta, amabo te, dum Atticum conveniam'? non est locus 5
ad tergiversandum. contra Caesarem? 'ubi illae sunt densae
dexterae?'; nam ut illi hoc liceret adiuvi, rogatus ab ipso
Ravennae de Caelio tribuno pl. ab ipso autem? etiam a Gnaeo
nostro in illo divino tertio consulatu. aliter sensero? 'αἰδέομαι'
non Pompeium modo sed 'Τρῶας καὶ Τρωάδας'. 'Πουλυδάμας 10

10 Pompeium et Caesarem *del. Victorius* 11 audissem *Lambinus* 14 πατρίδος
del. Schütz 17 effeci Σ: feci et Δ   **4,** 1 illa ultima *C:* illa ultum *ER: om.*
*HNO*Δ 6 tense *E* 7 ut illiϛ: utile Ω adiuvi *Pius:* adivi (adini *N*) Σ *Mbd:* adiu *ms*

You see, don't you, that at your instigation I have made
friends with both the contestants. And I only wish I had
listened to your affectionate admonitions from the first.
'The heart within my breast thou ne'er couldst sway.'
However in the end you persuaded me to make friends with
one of them because of all he had done for me and with the
other because of his power. So I did, and by conciliating them
in every possible way I managed to win as high a place in their
3 several good graces as any other man's. We calculated that on
the one hand joined with Pompey I should never be obliged to
go politically astray, while on the other hand as Pompey's ally
I ought not to be at loggerheads with Caesar—they were so
closely linked. Now, as you represent and as I see myself, there
looms ahead a tremendous contest between them. Each counts
me as his man, unless it be that one of them is only pretending—
for Pompey has no doubts, judging correctly that I strongly
approve of his present politics. Moreover I received letters from
both at the same time as yours, conveying the impression that
neither has a friend in the world he values more than myself.
4 But what am I to do? I don't mean in the last resort—if war
is to arbitrate, I am clear that defeat with one is better than
victory with the other—, I mean in the proceedings that will
be set on foot when I get back to prevent his candidature *in
absentia* and to make him give up his army. 'Speak, M. Tullius!'
What shall I say? 'Be so kind as to wait until I see Atticus'?
There's no room for fence-sitting. Against Caesar then?
'Where are those close-clasped hands?' For I helped to get him
this privilege, as requested by himself at Ravenna in connexion
with Caelius who was Tribune—and not only by him but by
our Gnaeus too in that immortal third Consulship of his. Or
shall I take a different line? 'I fear' not Pompey only but 'the

143

μοι πρῶτος ἐλεγχείην καταθήσει'; quis? tu ipse scilicet, laudator et factorum et scriptorum meorum.

5   Hanc ergo plagam effugi per duos superiores Marcellorum consulatus cum est actum de provincia Caesaris, nunc incido in discrimen ipsum. itaque ut stultus primus suam sententiam dicat, mihi valde placet de triumpho nos moliri aliquid, extra urbem esse cum iustissima causa. tamen dabunt operam ut 5 eliciant sententiam meam. ridebis hoc loco fortasse: quam vellem etiam nunc in provincia morari! plane opus fuit, si hoc impendebat. etsi nil miserius; nam ὁδοῦ πάρεργον volo te hoc scire: omnia illa prima quae etiam ⟨tu⟩ tuis litteris in caelum

6 ferebas ἐπίτηκτα fuerunt. quam non est facilis virtus! quam vero difficilis eius diuturna simulatio! cum enim hoc rectum et gloriosum putarem, ex annuo sumptu qui mihi decretus esset me C. Coelio quaestori relinquere annuum, referre in aerarium ad HS M̄, ingemuit nostra cohors, omne illud putans 5 distribui sibi oportere, ut ego amicior invenirer Phrygum et Cilicum aerariis quam nostro. sed me non moverunt; nam et mea laus apud me plurimum valuit nec tamen quicquam honorifice in quemquam fieri potuit quod praetermiserim. sed haec fuerit, ut ait Thucydides, ἐκβολὴ λόγου non inutilis. 10

7   Tu autem de nostro statu cogitabis: primum quo artificio tueamur benevolentiam Caesaris, deinde de ipso triumpho; quem video, nisi rei publicae tempora impedient, εὐπόριστον. iudico autem cum ex litteris amicorum tum ex supplicatione;

5, 1 ergo ORMm: ego EHNbds   9 tu tuis Bentivolius: tuis Ω: tu Manutius
6, 5 M. HNOΔ: or. R: C̄I̅C̅ Tyrrell–Purser: x (i.e. ⌈x⌉) Graevius

Trojan men and dames'. 'Polydamas will foremost cry me shame.' Being who? You yourself of course, the encomiast of my doings and writings.

5 I escaped this dilemma during the two earlier Marcelline Consulships when the Senate discussed Caesar's command; now I am coming in just at the crisis. Accordingly, 'to let the dunce state his opinion first', I am strongly in favour of my doing something about a Triumph, and so staying outside Rome with the best possible excuse. Even so they will try to draw a statement of my views. You may laugh when I say it, but I wish to heaven I was still back there in my province. It would really have been better, if this was hanging over us. Not that anything could have been more wretched. *En passant*, I want you to know that all those fine things at the start, which you too used to praise sky-high in your letters, were only

6 veneer. How far from easy a thing is virtue, how difficult its simulation for any length of time! I felt it would be a fine and proper thing to leave Quaestor C. Coelius a year's maintenance and to return a million sesterces to the Treasury out of the year's expense allowance decreed to me. My staff set up a wail, thinking the whole amount ought to be disbursed among themselves, so that I, if you please, should show myself up as a better friend to the treasuries of Phrygians and Cilicians than to our own! But they left me unmoved. My own good name came first with me, while on the other hand I have left nothing undone that I could do for anyone in the way of marks of consideration. However let this be, in the words of Thucydides, a not unprofitable digression.

7 Now you must think about my position: first, what device I can use to act up to Caesar's friendliness, second, about the Triumph itself, which, as I see it, will be easy enough to come by, unless political developments intervene. I am judging both

quam qui non decrevit, ⟨plus decrevit⟩ quam si omnis decresset 5
triumphos. ei porro adsensus est unus familiaris meus, Favonius,
alter iratus, Hirrus. Cato autem et scribendo adfuit et ad me de
sententia sua iucundissimas litteras misit. sed tamen gratulans
mihi Caesar de supplicatione triumphat de sententia Catonis,
nec scribit quid ille sententiae dixerit sed tantum supplicatio- 10
nem eum mihi non decrevisse.

8   Redeo ad Hirrum. coeperas eum mihi placare: perfice.
habes Scrofam, habes Silium. ad eos ego etiam antea scripsi et
iam ad ipsum Hirrum. locutus enim erat cum iis commode, se
potuisse impedire sed noluisse; adsensum tantum esse Catoni,
amicissimo meo, cum is honorificentissimam in me sententiam 5
dixisset; nec me ad se ullas litteras misisse, cum ad omnis mit-
terem. verum dicebat; ad eum enim solum et ad Crassipedem
non scripseram.

9   Atque haec de rebus forensibus: redeamus domum. diiun-
gere me ab illo volo; merus est φυρατής, germanus Lartidius.
'ἀλλὰ τὰ μὲν προτετύχθαι ἐάσομεν ἀχνύμενοί περ.' reliqua
expediamus, hoc primum, quae accessit cura dolori meo—sed
tamen hoc, quicquid est, Precianum cum iis rationibus quas 5
ille meas tractat admisceri nolo. scripsi ad Terentiam, scripsi
etiam ad ipsum, me quicquid posset nummorum ad apparatum
sperati triumphi ad te redacturum. ita puto ἄμεμπτα fore;
verum ut libebit. hanc quoque suscipe curam, quem ad modum
expediamur; id tu et ostendisti quibusdam litteris ex Epiro 10
⟨an⟩ Athenis datis et in eo ego te adiuvabo.

7, 5 plus decrevit *add. Brunus* (*M*⁴)   10 ille *OR*: illi *NPΔ*   8, 2 et iam *NO*:
etiam *R*: *om.* Δ   4 tantum *scripsi*: tamen Ω   7 Crassipedem *Brunus* (*M*⁴):
cassi(i) fidem Ω   9, 2 merus *Manutius*: mirus Ω   4 quae *scripsi*: quod Ω: quo
Pius: in quo *Lambinus* curae *anon. ap. Graevium*   5 tamen hoc *HNORs*:
hoc t- Δ   9 lubebit ς: iube- *NΔC*: vide- *HOR*   10 expediamur *Tyrrell-*
Purser: experi- Ω   tu et *NORδ*: et tu *H*: et *M*   11 an *add. Lambinus*: aut
Wesenberg

from my friends' letters and from the Supplication. The man who spoke against the motion gave me more in his own proposal than if he had voted me all the Triumphs in creation. Two members agreed with him, one, Favonius, a friend of mine, the other, Hirrus, with a grudge against me. Moreover Cato witnessed the decree and wrote to me about his motion in the pleasantest way. All the same in congratulating me on the Supplication Caesar is triumphant about Cato's motion, not mentioning *what* he proposed, only that he was against the grant.

8   To come back to Hirrus: you had made a start in mollifying him towards me. Finish the job! You have Scrofa and Silius to help. I wrote to them even before, and I have now written to Hirrus himself. He had spoken them fair, said that he could have obstructed but chose not to do so; he had merely registered support for Cato, a very good friend of mine, in a proposal most flattering to me; and yet I had not written to him, though I had sent letters to everyone else. He was right there. He and Crassipes were the only ones I did not write to.

9   So much for public matters, now let's go back home. I want to dissociate myself from that man. He's nothing but a cooker of accounts, a real Lartidius. 'But let what's past be past, though sore our hearts.' Let us get things straight in future, and this to start with—it's brought me worry on top of grief—, but this Precius inheritance, whatever it amounts to, I don't want it mixed up with the business which *he* is handling on my account. I have written to Terentia and to himself as well that I proposed to hand over to you any money I could to meet the expenses of my prospective Triumph. In this way I hope there won't be any cavilling—but that's as he likes. Please also make it your concern to see how I am to get clear. You said you would in a letter from Epirus (or was it Athens?), and I shall co-operate.

125 (VII. 2)

Scr. Brundisi fort. vi Kal. Dec. an. 50 (§1)

CICERO ATTICO SAL.

1 Brundisium venimus VII Kal. Dec. usi tua felicitate navigandi; ita belle nobis 'flavit ab Epiro lenissimus Onchesmites' (hunc σπονδειάζοντα si cui voles τῶν νεωτέρων pro tuo vendito).

2 Valetudo tua me valde conturbat; significant enim tuae litterae te prorsus laborare. ego autem, cum sciam quam sis fortis, vehementius esse quiddam suspicor quod te cogat cedere et prope modum infringat. etsi alteram quartanam Pamphilus tuus mihi dixit decessisse et alteram leviorem accedere. 5 Terentia vero, quae quidem eodem tempore ad portam Brundisinam venit quo ego in portum mihique obvia in foro fuit, L. Pontium sibi in Trebulano dixisse narrabat etiam eam decessisse; quod si ita est, quod maxime mehercule opto, ⟨gaudeo⟩, idque spero tua prudentia et temperantia te con- 10 secutum.

3 Venio ad epistulas tuas; quas ego sescentas uno tempore accepi, aliam alia iucundiorem, quae quidem erant tua manu; nam Alexidis manum amabam quod tam prope accedebat ad similitudinem tuae, [litterae manum] non amabam quod indicabat te non valere. cuius quoniam mentio facta est, 5 Tironem Patris aegrum reliqui, adulescentem ⟨doctum et diligentem⟩, ut nosti, et adde, si quid vis, probum; nihil vidi melius. itaque careo aegre et, quamquam videbatur se non graviter habere, tamen sum sollicitus maximamque spem habeo in M'. Curi diligentia, de qua ad me scripsit Tiro et multi 10

Ep. 125] 1, 1 usi *Nδ*: ut si *HORM*   2 Onchesmites *Latinus*: anchesmitis *ΩZ¹* 3 vendita *Gronovius*   2, 1 valetudo *RCλ*: inv- *HNOPΔ*   7 obvia in *Nbds*: -am *H*: -am in *ORMm*   8 eam *Pius*: iam *Ωλ*: eam iam *Lambinus*   9 est, est *Bosius* 10 gaudeo *add. nescioquis*   3, 3 manum *b*: animum *ΩZ¹λ*   4 litterae manum *ΩZ¹λ*: *del. Watt*: manum *del. Manutius*   6 doctum et diligentem *addidi* (doctum *Wesenberg*, diligentem *ς*)   8 et *NOR*: *om. Δ*   10 M'. *Manutius*: M. *Ω*

125 (VII. 2)

Brundisium, 25 November (?) 50

CICERO TO ATTICUS

1 We arrived at Brundisium on 24 November, as favoured in the crossing as yourself, with a fair wind behind us. 'Softly, softly, from Epirus blew the Onchesmitic breeze.' There! You can commend that as your own to one or other of the *avant-garde*.

2   I am greatly perturbed about your health, for your letter indicates that you are really unwell. And knowing how brave you are I suspect it must be something truly severe that makes you give way and almost breaks you down. Your man Pamphilus however told me that one of your quartans had left you and the other was coming in a milder form; while Terentia, who arrived at the gates of Brundisium at the same time as I got to the harbour and met me in the market square, says that L. Pontius told her in the Trebula country that this latter had gone too. If that is so, as I most earnestly pray it may be, I am very glad, and I expect it is the reward of your prudence and temperance.

3   I come to your letters, a spate of which reached me simultaneously, each more agreeable than the last—those, that is, which were in your own hand. I liked Alexis' hand because it so nearly resembles your own, but again I didn't like it because it showed you were unwell. *À propos* of him, I have left Tiro at Patrae sick, an accomplished, conscientious young fellow as you know and, you are at liberty to add, an honest one. I never saw a better. So I miss him sorely, and though he did not seem to be very bad I am anxious. My chief hope is in M'. Curius' care, of which Tiro has written to me and many others have

nuntiarunt. Curius autem ipse sensit quam tu velles se a me diligi, et eo sum admodum delectatus. et mehercule est quem facile diligas; αὐτόχθων in homine urbanitas est. eius testamentum deporto trium Ciceronum signis obsignatum cohortisque praetoriae; fecit palam te ex libella, me ex terruncio. in Actio 15 Corcyrae Alexio me opipare muneratus est. Q. Ciceroni obsisti non potuit quo minus Thyamim videret.

4   Filiola tua te delectari laetor et probari tibi φυσικὴν esse τὴν ⟨στοργὴν τὴν⟩ πρὸς τὰ τέκνα. etenim si hoc non est, nulla potest homini esse ad hominem naturae adiunctio; qua sublata vitae societas tollitur. 'bene eveniat!' inquit Carneades, spurce, sed tamen prudentius quam Lucius noster et Patron, qui, cum 5 omnia ad se referant ⟨nec⟩ quicquam alterius causa fieri putent et cum ea re bonum virum esse oportere dicant ne malum habeat, non quo⟨d⟩ id natura rectum sit, non intellegunt se de callido homine loqui, non de bono viro. sed haec, opinor, sunt in iis libris quos tu laudando animos mihi addidisti.   10

5   Redeo ad rem. quo modo exspectabam epistulam quam Philoxeno dedisses! scripseras enim in ea esse de sermone Pompei Neapolitano. eam mihi Patron Brundisi reddidit; Corcyrae, ut opinor, acceperat. nihil potuit esse iucundius; erat enim de re publica, de opinione quam is vir haberet integritatis 5 meae, de benevolentia quam ostendit eo sermone quem habuit de triumpho. sed tamen hoc iucundissimum, quod intellexi te

---

11 se *ORc*: si *N*: *om.* Δ   12 quem *NPbs*: quam *ORMdm*   13 est *om. cod. Bod.*   14 deporto (*Manutius*) trium *Iunius*: detortorium *CZ*: -io Ω 15 libella (*i.e.* lib.?) ϛ: libertum *NORZ*: -tu Δ   me Δ*Z*¹: *om. NORZ*ᵇ   terruncio *c* (-cia *iam* ϛ): taruacus Ω*Z*   16 alexio me *OR*: -iom (-ion) me Δ: -ium *N* 17 thyamim *M*: *varie corrumpunt cett.*   4, 2 στοργὴν τὴν *add. Wesenberg* h(a)ec *Rm*   4 eveniat *EORΔZ*⁽ᵇ⁾: ve- *NPC*   5 patron Δ: -ono *ENR*: -o *PF* 6 nec ϛ: *om.* Ω: numquam *maluit Orelli*   7 esse oportere Σ: o- e- Δ   8 quod *scripsi*: quo Ω   intellegunt *ER*: -gant *NOΔZ*⁽ᵇ⁾ *codd. Mal.*   se *EP*: sed *NORΔ* **5, 3** patro *P*

brought me word. As for Curius himself, he realized how much you wanted me to like him, and I was much taken with him. He is indeed an easy fellow to like—he has a genuine Roman *esprit*. I am bringing his will home, witnessed by three Ciceros and my official staff. He left you one tenth of his estate and me one fortieth, openly. Alexio made royal provision for my entertainment on the Foreland of Corcyra. Nothing would do for our nephew but he must see the Thyamis.

4   I am glad your little daughter gives you pleasure and that you agree that affection for children is part of nature. Indeed if this is not the case there can be no natural tie between one human being and another, and once you abolish that, you abolish all society. 'And good luck!', says Carneades—an abominable thing to say, but not so naïve as the position of our friend Lucius and Patro, when they make self-interest their only yardstick while refusing to believe in any altruistic act and maintain that we should be good only to avoid getting into trouble and not because goodness is naturally right, they fail to see that they are talking about an artful dodger, not a good man. But I think all this is in the volumes which you have encouraged me by praising.

5   To get to business: impatiently indeed did I await the letter you said you had given to Philoxenus, for you wrote that it contained an account of your conversation with Pompey at Naples. Patro gave it to me at Brundisium—he had received it at Corcyra, I believe. It made the pleasantest of reading, covering as it did the political situation, the great man's opinion of my uprightness, and the good will he showed in what he said about my Triumph. But what pleased me most of all was

ad eum venisse ut eius animum erga me perspiceres; hoc mihi,
inquam, accidit iucundissimum.

6   De triumpho autem nulla me cupiditas umquam tenuit ante
Bibuli impudentissimas litteras quas amplissima supplicatio
consecuta est. a quo si ea gesta essent quae scripsit, gauderem
et honori faverem; nunc illum, qui pedem porta quoad hostis
cis Euphratem fuit non extulerit, honore augeri, me, in cuius 5
exercitu spem illius exercitus habuit, idem non adsequi dedecus
est nostrum—nostrum, inquam, te coniungens. itaque omnia
experiar et, ut spero, adsequar. quod si tu valeres, iam mihi
quaedam explorata essent; sed, ut spero, valebis.

7   De rausdusculo Numeriano multum te amo. Hortensius quid
egerit aveo scire, Cato quid agat; qui quidem in me turpiter
fuit malevolus. dedit integritatis, iustitiae, clementiae, fidei
mihi testimonium, quod non quaerebam; quod postulabam
negavit. [id] itaque Caesar iis litteris quibus mihi gratulatur et 5
omnia pollicetur quo modo exsultat Catonis in me ingratissimi
iniuria! at hic idem Bibulo dierum xx. ignosce mihi: non
possum haec ferre nec feram.

8   Cupio ad omnis tuas epistulas, sed nihil necesse est; iam enim
te videbo. illud tamen de Chrysippo (nam de altero illo minus
sum admiratus, operario homine; sed tamen ne illo quidem
quicquam improbius)—Chrysippum vero, quem ego propter
litterularum nescio quid libenter vidi, in honore habui, disce- 5
dere a puero insciente me! mitto alia quae audio multa, mitto
furta; fugam non fero, qua mihi nihil visum est sceleratius.

---

9 accidit *HR*Δ: accedit *ENOP*   **6,** 2 amplissima *Pius*: -me Ω   3 essent
Corradus: sunt Ω   5 extulit *Ant.*   7 coniungens *P*: -es Ω   **7,** 2 aveo
ms: habeo Ω   qui quidem *P*: quid eq- *Mbd*: quidum (qui dum) q- *EHNms*
5 itaque *E*: id itaque *NOR*Δ id *ante* negavit *transponere noluit Graevius*
c(a)esar iis (his *E*) *E*δ: -ris *NORM*   7 dierum ϛ: D (d.) Ωλ: dies *Klotz*   xx] x
T. Frank   **8,** 1 est iam *Hervagius*: sestiam Ω   5 lit(t)erularum *ORMm*:
-rarum *HN*Δ

to perceive that you had visited him in order to ascertain his sentiments towards me. I repeat, that pleased me most of all.

5   With regard to the Triumph, I was never in the least eager until Bibulus sent that quite shameless letter which resulted in a Supplication in the most handsome terms. If he had done what he claimed I should be delighted and wish him the honour. As it is, if Bibulus is honoured, who did not stir a foot outside the town gate so long as there was a Parthian this side Euphrates, while I, whose army was *his* army's hope and stay, am not similarly honoured, why, we are humiliated—and I mean 'we', you as well as I. So I shall try all I know and I trust I shall succeed. If you were well, I should already have been safe on certain points. But you *will* be well, I trust.

7   With regard to Numerius' bit of money I am very much obliged to you. I am longing to know what Hortensius has done and what Cato is doing. To me he has been disgracefully spiteful. He gave me an unsolicited testimonial for uprightness, justice, clemency, and honourable dealing, while what I asked for he refused. Accordingly Caesar, in a letter of congratulation in which he promises me full support, is fairly cock-a-hoop at Cato's 'most ungrateful' ill-usage. And the same Cato votes twenty days to Bibulus! You must forgive me, I cannot and will not swallow such things.

8   I should like to answer all your letters, but there is no need as I shall be seeing you in no time. One thing though about Chrysippus—I am less surprised about the other, a mere mechanic, though he too is a thorough-paced scamp. But Chrysippus, whom for the sake of a smattering of letters he had I liked to have about me and made much of, to leave the boy without my knowledge! His other misdeeds, plenty of which are coming to my ears, his pilferings, I leave; but his absconding I won't stand, it's the most blackguardly thing I ever met with.

itaque usurpavi vetus illud Drusi, ut ferunt, praetoris in eo qui
eadem liber non iuraret, me istos liberos non addixisse, praesertim cum adesset nemo a quo recte vindicarentur. id tu, ut 10
videbitur, ita accipies; ego tibi adsentiar.
   Vni tuae disertissimae epistulae non rescripsi, in qua est de
periculis rei publicae. quid rescriberem? valde eram perturbatus.
sed ut nihil magno opere metuam Parthi faciunt, qui repente
Bibulum semivivum reliquerunt.   15

126 (VII. 3)

Scr. in Trebulano Ponti v Id. Dec. an. 50 (§ 12)

CICERO ATTICO SAL.

1 A. d. VIII Id. Dec. Aeculanum veni et ibi tuas litteras legi quas
Philotimus mihi reddidit; e quibus hanc primo aspectu volup-
tatem cepi, quod erant a te ipso scriptae, deinde earum accuratis-
sima diligentia sum mirum in modum delectatus. ac primum
illud in quo te Dicaearcho adsentiri negas: etsi cupidissime 5
expetitum a me est et te adprobante ne diutius anno in provincia
essem, tamen non est nostra contentione perfectum. sic enim
scito, verbum in senatu factum esse numquam de ullo nostrum
qui provincias obtinuimus quo in iis diutius quam ex senatus
consulto maneremus, ut iam ne istius quidem rei culpam 10
sustineam, quod minus diu fuerim in provincia quam fortasse
2 fuerit utile. sed 'quid si hoc melius?' saepe opportune dici
videtur, ut in hoc ipso. sive enim ad concordiam res adduci

---

9 liberos ς: libros Ω
Ep. 126] 1, 5 te *cod. Bod.*: de Ω 6 est *Wesenberg*: sit Ω et *om. H* te appro-
bante *HC*: ap- *NORM*: ap- te δ 11 fuerim *H*Δ: -ram *NOR* **2,** 1 saepe
*Z*ᵇ: *om.* Ω

So I have followed the precedent of Drusus the Praetor, so they say, in the case of the slave who would not retake the oath after manumission, and have denied giving them their freedom—all the more easily as no competent Claimant was present on the occasion. You will react to this as you think proper and I shall assent to your judgement.

I have not replied to one very eloquent letter of yours in which the dangers to the commonwealth are discussed. What could I reply? I am greatly disturbed. However when I think of how the Parthians all of a sudden left Bibulus half-dead I am not very much afraid of anything.

126 (VII. 3)

Near Trebula, 9 December 50

CICERO TO ATTICUS

1 On 6 December I arrived at Acculanum, where I read your letter delivered to me by Philotimus. The first glance at it gave me pleasure, for the writing was your own; and then I was wonderfully gratified by the trouble you had taken to write in such detail. To begin with the point on which you say you disagree with Dicaearchus, it is true I did my very utmost, and with your approval, to avoid being kept more than a year in my province, but the result was not due to any effort of mine. You may take my word for it that not a word was said in the Senate at any time about any of us governors of provinces to countenance us remaining in them beyond the time specified by its decree. So I cannot even be held to blame for not staying in my province as long as might perhaps have been expedient.

2 But the common saying 'It may be all for the best' seems to apply here, as so often. For if matters can be brought either to

potest sive ad bonorum victoriam, utriusvis rei me aut adiu-
torem velim esse aut certe non expertem; sin vincuntur boni,
ubicumque essem, una cum iis victus essem. qua re celeritas 5
nostri reditus ἀμεταμέλητος debet esse. quod si ista nobis
cogitatio de triumpho iniecta non esset, quam tu quoque
adprobas, ne tu haud multum requireres illum virum qui in
sexto libro informatus est. quid enim tibi faciam, qui illos
libros devorasti? quin nunc ipsum non dubitabo rem tantam 10
abicere, si id erit rectius. utrumque vero simul agi non potest,
et de triumpho ambitiose et de re publica libere. sed ne dubi-
taris quin, quod honestius, id mihi futurum sit antiquius.

3   Nam quod putas utilius esse, vel mihi quod tutius sit vel
etiam ut rei publicae prodesse possim, me esse cum imperio, id
coram considerabimus quale sit; habet enim res deliberationem,
etsi ex parte magna tibi adsentio⟨r⟩. de animo autem meo erga
rem publicam bene facis quod non dubitas, et illud probe 5
iudicas, nequaquam satis pro meis officiis, pro ipsius in alios
effusione illum in me liberalem fuisse, eiusque rei causam vere
explicas; †et eis† quae de Fabio Caninioque acta scribis valde
consentiunt. quae si secus essent totumque se ille in me pro-
fudisset, tamen illa quam scribis custos urbis me praeclarae 10
inscriptionis memorem esse cogeret nec mihi concederet ut
imitarer Vulcatium aut Servium, quibus tu es contentus, sed
aliquid nos vellet nobis dignum et sentire et defendere; quod
quidem agerem, si liceret, alio modo ac nunc agendum est.

4   De sua potentia dimicant homines hoc tempore periculo

---

3 utriusvis *P*: utrumvis Ω   11 agi *E*ς: ac *NORM*   13 quod *Ebd*: quo
NORMms   **3, 4** adsentior *M corr.*: -io Ω*C*   7 causas *Bayet*   8 haec eis
Watt: *fort.* et ea   12 volcatium *ORΔ*: -acium *EN*

a peaceful settlement or to victory for the honest men, I should in both of these two cases wish to help or at any rate not to be on the outside. On the other hand if the honest men lose the day, I should have lost it with them wherever I was. Therefore my returning so quickly should be no matter for regret. In fact if this notion of a Triumph, which you too approve, had not been put into my head, you really would not have much cause to desiderate the ideal sketched in my sixth volume. What, after all, as an eager reader of that work, would you want me to do? Why even at this stage I shall not hesitate to throw away the great prize, if that turns out to be the right thing. Certainly the two roles of candidate for a Triumph and independent statesman are not to be played simultaneously. But rest assured that honour will come first with me.

3   As for your view that it is more expedient (either as safer for me personally or perhaps as enabling me to render service to the state) that I retain my military authority, we shall go into that together. It's quite a question, though I agree with you to a large extent. You do well to have no doubts of my patriotism. You are quite right too in your judgement that Caesar has not behaved by any means as handsomely to me as he ought in view of my services and his own lavishness towards others, and you explain the reason for this correctly. What you write of his dealings with Fabius and Caninius chimes very well. But even if this were otherwise and he had showered upon me everything he had to offer, the Protectress of Rome to whom you refer would not let me forget her noble inscription or allow me to make Vulcatius or Servius my model, whom you think good enough. She would wish me to take and maintain some line worthy of myself. That is what I should do, if I were able, in a way different from what circumstances now prescribe.

4   What we now see is a struggle for personal power at the

civitatis. nam si res publica defenditur, cur ea consule isto ipso
defensa non est? cur ego, in cuius causa rei publicae salus
consistebat, defensus postero anno non sum? cur imperium illi
aut cur illo modo prorogatum est? cur tanto opere pugnatum 5
ut de eius absentis ratione habenda decem tribuni pl. ferrent?
his ille rebus ita convaluit ut nunc in uno civi spes ad resistendum sit; qui mallem tantas ei viris non dedisset quam nunc tam
5 valenti resisteret. sed quoniam res eo deducta est, non quaeram,
ut scribis, 'ποῦ σκάφος τὸ τῶν 'Ατρειδῶν;': mihi σκάφος unum
erit quod a Pompeio gubernabitur. illud ipsum quod ais, 'quid
fiet cum erit dictum "dic, M. Tulli?"': σύντομα, 'Cn.
Pompeio adsentior'. ipsum tamen Pompeium separatim ad 5
concordiam hortabor; sic enim sentio, maximo in periculo
rem esse. vos scilicet plura, qui in urbe estis; verum tamen haec
video, cum homine audacissimo paratissimoque negotium esse,
omnis damnatos, omnis ignominia adfectos, omnis damnatione
ignominiaque dignos illac facere, omnem fere iuventutem, 10
omnem illam urbanam ac perditam plebem, tribunos valentis
addito Q. Cassio, omnis qui aere alieno premantur, quos pluris
esse intellego quam putaram (causam solum illa causa non habet,
ceteris rebus abundat); hic omnia facere omnis ne armis
decernatur, quorum exitus semper incerti, nunc vero etiam in 15
alteram partem magis timendi.

Bibulus de provincia decessit, Veientonem praefecit; in
decedendo erit, ut audio, tardior. quem cum ornavit Cato

4, 2 isto] illo O   6 ut Σ: est ut Δ   7 civi ORΔZ¹⁽ᵇ⁾: cive ENP   spes Lambinus:
res ΩZ¹: vires E, Klotz   8 sit ΩZ¹: sint Klotz   5, 2 ut tu c   4 cum Eδ: dum
NORM   7 rem p(ublicam) Moricca   h(a)ec ΩC: hoc δ   12 Q. Corradus: C.
Ω: del. Manutius   quos Eδ: quod NOM: quo(m) RP   15 vero etiam
ORbd: e- v- ENMm: v- s   17 Veientonem Victorius: vele- Ω

community's risk and peril. If it is in defence of the constitution, why was the constitution not defended when Caesar himself was Consul? Why was I, with whose cause the survival of the constitution was bound up, not defended in the following year? Why was his command extended, and in such a fashion? Why was there such pressure to get the ten Tribunes to bring in the law about his candidature *in absentia*? By these steps he has become so strong that hope of resistance now depends on one man; and I would rather that *he* had not given Caesar such formidable strength in the first place than that he should resist 5 him now that he is so powerful. However, since that is the pass we have come to, I shall not in your phrase ask 'Where the bark of Atreus' sons?' The only bark for me will be the one that has Pompey at the helm. As for your question 'What will happen when the word comes "Speak, M. Tullius"?', *tout court* 'I agree with Cn. Pompeius'. Pompey himself however I shall privately urge to peace. For my feeling is that things are in a very parlous state indeed. No doubt you people in Rome are better informed. All the same I see this much: we are dealing with a man who fears nothing and is ready for anything. All persons under legal sentence or censorial stigma, and all who deserve the one or the other, are on his side, so are pretty well all the younger people, all the desperate city rabble, some sturdy Tribunes, Q. Cassius now included, all the debt-ridden, who I find are worth more than I supposed!—Caesar's side lacks nothing but a cause, all else they have in abundance. Here I find everyone moving heaven and earth against decision by war, the results of which are always unpredictable and now may even be apprehended as more likely than not to turn out wrong.

Bibulus has quitted his province, leaving Veiento in charge. I hear that he will not hurry himself on the return journey. In doing him honour Cato made it plain that he confines his

declaravit iis se solis [non] invidere quibus nihil aut non multum
ad dignitatem posset accedere.   20

6   Nunc venio ad privata; fere enim respondi tuis litteris de re
publica et iis quas in suburbano et iis quas postea scripsi⟨sti⟩.
ad privata venio. unum etiam, de Caelio: tantum abest ut
meam ille sententiam moveat ut valde ego ipsi quod de sua
sententia decesserit paenitendum putem. sed quid est quod ei 5
vici Luccei sint addicti? hoc te praetermisisse miror.

7   De Philotimo, faciam equidem ut mones. sed ego †mihi† ab
illo hoc tempore non rationes exspectabam quas tibi edidit,
verum id reliquum quod ipse in Tusculano me referre in
commentarium mea manu voluit quodque idem in Asia mihi
sua manu scriptum dedit. id si praestaret, quantum mihi aeris 5
alieni esse tibi edidit, tantum et plus etiam mihi ipse deberet.
sed in hoc genere, si modo per rem publicam licebit, non
accusabimur posthac; neque hercule antea neglegentes fuimus
sed et amicorum ⟨et publicorum negotiorum⟩ multitudine
occupati. ergo utemur, ut polliceris, et opera et consilio tuo, 10
nec tibi erimus, ut spero, in eo molesti.

8   De serpirastris cohortis meae, nihil ⟨est⟩ quod doleas; ipsi
enim se collegerunt admiratione [in te] integritatis meae. sed
me moverat nemo magis quam is quem tu minime putas.
idem et initio fuerat et nunc est egregius; sed in ipsa decessione
significavit sperasse se aliquid et id quod animum induxerat 5

---

19 non *del. Manutius: anne* nunc?   **6,** 1 venio ad privata *del. Madvig*
2 scripsisti *P:* -si Ω   3 ad privata venio *ante* de (7,1) *transp. Purser; delere mallet
Watt:* igitur *post* privata *add. Lehmann*   5 ei vici *ORZ¹λ:* ei nici *N:* evuci
(enuci) Δ   6 Lucceii *Z¹λ:* lucci *N:* lu(c)ceis *ORΔ*   **7,** 1 mihi *fort. delendum
vel* egomet *scribendum*   2 hoc tempore *Zᵇc* (*sed ante* ab illo *c*): *om.* Ω   tibi
OR: ibi *NΔ*   6 mihi ipse *NOR:* i- m- Δ   8 posthac *Rbms:* post hanc
HNOMd   9 et . . . negotiorum *addidi* (*olim* in re p. *et post* sed et)
8, 1 est *add.* ς   2 in te *OΔ:* vit(a)e *Rb: om. N*   3 minime *Watt* (*sed vide comm.*):
nemo Ω: non *Faërnus:* nullus *ego olim*

jealousy to those whose prestige admits of little or no enlarge-
ment.

6   Now I come to private matters—I have answered your political letters more or less, both the one you wrote at your place
near Rome and the later one. I come to private matters. One
thing more, about Caelius: so far from letting him influence
my views, I think it a great pity for himself that he has changed
his. But what is this about Lucceius' properties being knocked
down to him? I am surprised you didn't mention it.

7   About Philotimus, I shall certainly do as you advise. But it's
not the accounts he produced to you that I am expecting from
him now but the balance which he himself asked me at Tusculum to enter in my memorandum in my own hand and
which he also gave me in writing under his own hand in Asia.
If he were paying that, *he* would owe me as much as and even
more than my total debts as he represented them to you. Well,
in future I shall not be found wanting in this department, that
is if the state of the country allows, nor indeed have I been
negligent in the past, but preoccupied by the multitude of
affairs, both of state and of my friends. So I shall avail myself
of your services and advice, which you kindly promise, though
I hope I shan't put you to too much trouble in that way.

8   As for the knee-splints for my staff, you need not distress
yourself. They pulled themselves together of their own accord,
in admiration of my uprightness. But none of them disturbed
me more than the one whom you think 'the last man'. And
yet he had behaved admirably to begin with and does now.
But just as we were leaving he intimated that he had hoped for

paulisper non tenuit, sed cito ad se rediit meisque honorificentissimis erga se officiis victus pluris ea duxit quam omnem pecu-
uniam.

9　Ego a Curio tabulas accepi, quas mecum porto. Hortensi
legata cognovi; nunc aveo scire quid †hominis† sit et quarum
rerum auctionem instituat; nescio enim cur, cum portam
Flumentanam Caelius occuparit, ego Puteolos non meos
faciam.　　　　　　　　　　　　　　　　　　　　　　　　5

10　Venio ad 'Piraeea', in quo magis reprehendendus sum quod
homo Romanus 'Piraeea' scripserim, non 'Piraeum' (sic enim
omnes nostri locuti sunt), quam quod addiderim ⟨'in'⟩; non
enim hoc ut oppido praeposui sed ut loco; et tamen Dionysius
noster et qui est nobiscum Nicias Cous non rebatur oppidum 5
esse Piraeea. sed de re videro. nostrum quidem si est peccatum,
in eo est quod non ut de oppido locutus sum sed ut de loco,
secutusque sum non dico Caecilium, 'mane ut ex portu in
Piraeum' (malus enim auctor Latinitatis est), sed Terentium
(cuius fabellae propter elegantiam sermonis putabantur a C. 10
Laelio scribi), 'heri aliquot adulescentuli coiimus in Piraeum';
et idem, 'mercator hoc addebat, captam e Sunio'; quod si
δήμους oppida volumus esse, tam est oppidum Sunium quam
Piraeus.

Sed quoniam grammaticus es, si hoc mihi ζήτημα persolveris, 15
11 magna me molestia liberaris. ille mihi litteras blandas mittit;
facit idem pro eo Balbus. mihi certum est ab honestissima
sententia digitum nusquam; sed scis illi reliquum quantum sit.

---

6 meisque *Brunus* (*M*⁴): in iis qu(a)e Ω　9, 2 aveo *s*: habeo Ω　hominis] *fort.*
heredis: in animo hominis (*melius* homini) *Watt*　3 autionem *Brunus* (*M*⁴): act-
ΩC　10, 1 Piraeea ς: pirea *vel sim.* Ω (*itidem fere vv.* 2 *et* 6)　3 quam *Pms*: cum Ω
in *N*: *om.* ORΔ　5 et NOR: *om.* Δ　non *b*: noen Δ: noenu OR: non enim *N*
6 re δ: reo Ω　11 coiimus *Wesenberg*: coimus Pδ: cum imus *vel sim.* ΩC
12 sunio δ: *varie corruptum in* Ω　13 sunium δ: sum(i)um Ω　15 ζήτημα ς: zetema
Ω

something, and fell for a little while below the standard he had set himself. But he was soon his own man again. My compliments and attentions won him over, and he valued them more than any amount of money.

9   I have received the will from Curius and am bringing it with me. I note Hortensius' legacies. Now I am longing to know what the heir (?) gets and what items he's putting up to auction. Since Caelius has occupied the Flumentane Gate, I don't see why *I* shouldn't acquire Puteoli.

10   Now I come to Piraeus, in which matter as a Roman I am more open to criticism for writing *Piraeea* instead of *Piraeum*, the form universally used by our countrymen, than for adding the preposition. I prefixed it not as to a town but as to a locality—and after all our friend Dionysius and Nicias of Cos, who is with us, think Piraeus is *not* a town. But the matter of fact I leave for further enquiry. If I *have* made a mistake it is in speaking as of a locality instead of a town, and I had for precedent I won't say Caecilius ('when I went early from the harbour to Piraeus[1]'), for his Latinity is not much to go by, but Terence, whose plays were supposed from the elegance of their diction to be the work of C. Laelius: 'Yesterday a party of us young fellows went to Piraeus[1]' and 'The trader added that she was taken from Sunium[2]'—if we are going to say that Demes are towns, then Sunium is as much a town as Piraeus.

   But since you have turned schoolmaster, perhaps you will once for all solve my problem for me and take a big load off my
11 mind. Caesar sends me smooth letters and Balbus does the same on his behalf. I am determined not to stray an inch from the path of strict honour. But you know how much I still owe

---

[1] *in Piraeum*   [2] *e Sunio*

putasne igitur verendum esse ne aut obiciat id nobis aliquis, si
languidius, aut repetat, si fortius? quid ad haec reperis? 'solva- 5
mus' inquis. age, a Caelio mutuabimur. hoc tu tamen consideres
velim. puto enim, in senatu si quando praeclare pro re publica
dixero, Tartessium istum tuum mihi exeunti, 'iube sodes
nummos curare'.

12 Quid superest? etiam: gener est suavis mihi, Tulliae, Terentiae; quantumvis vel ingeni vel humanitatis †satis†; reliqua,
quae nosti, ferenda. scis enim quos †aperierimus†; qui omnes,
praeter eum de quo per te egimus, reum me facerent. ipsis enim
expensum nemo ferret. sed haec coram; nam multi sermonis 5
sunt.

Tironis reficiendi spes est in M'. Curio, cui ego scripsi tibi
eum gratissimum facturum. data v Id. Dec. a Pontio ex
Trebulano.

127 (VII. 4)

Scr. in Cumano, ut vid., c. Id. Dec. an. 50

CICERO ATTICO SAL.

1 Dionysium flagrantem desiderio tui misi ad te, nec mehercule
aequo animo, sed fuit concedendum. quem quidem cognovi
cum doctum, quod mihi iam ante erat notum, tum sanctum,
plenum offici, studiosum etiam meae laudis, frugi hominem,
ac, ne libertinum laudare videar, plane virum bonum. 5
2 Pompeium vidi IIII Id. Dec.; fuimus una horas duas fortasse.
magna laetitia mihi visus est adfici meo adventu; de triumpho

---

11, 9 curari *Corradus*   12, 1 quid *Manutius*: qui Ω   gener *R*: -re *NO*Δ
2 satis *del. Pius*: -is est *Mommsen*: -is sit *Tyrrell–Purser*   3 aperierimus *OR*Δλ:
apperuie- *N*: aperue- *cod. Ball.*: abiecerimus *Boot*: *anne* praeterierimus?
4 facerent *NOR*: -re rentur Δ   5 ferret *OPFAnt.*: feret *RN*: offer(r)et Δ
7 M'. *Manutius*: M. Ω   Curio ς: curione(m) Ω
Ep. 127] 1, 5 ne ut *Bouhier*

him. Don't you think there is a danger of having it thrown in my teeth by someone or other if I take a weak line or payment demanded if I take a strong one? What do you suggest? 'Pay up' perhaps. All right, I'll borrow from Caelius! But I would like you to give it your consideration. I suppose that if I ever make a fine patriotic speech in the Senate your friend from Tartessus will politely ask me for a banker's draft on my way out!

12 Now, let me see. Oh yes, my son-in-law. We all find him charming, Tullia, Terentia, myself. He is as clever and agreeable as you please. Other characteristics, of which you are aware, we must put up with. After all you know what the rejected suitors were like (?). Every man of them, except the one in whose case you were intermediary, would have put me into debt—nobody would advance *them* a penny. But of all this when we meet; it will take a good deal of talking over.

My hope of getting Tiro back to health lies in M'. Curius, to whom I have written that he will oblige you greatly. Dispatched on 9 December from Pontius' house near Trebula.

127 (VII. 4)
Cumae (?), c. 13 December 50
CICERO TO ATTICUS

I am sending you Dionysius, who is on fire with impatience to see you; reluctantly I must say, but I had to agree. I have found him not only a good scholar, which I already knew, but upright, serviceable, zealous moreover for my good name, an honest fellow, and in case that sounds too much like commending a freedman, a really fine man.

I saw Pompey on 10 December. We were together for something like two hours. He seemed very happy to see me back;

hortari, suscipere partis suas, monere ne ante in senatum
accederem quam rem confecissem, ne dicendis sententiis aliquem tribunum alienarem. quid quaeris? in hoc officio sermone 5
eius nihil potuit esse prolixius. de re publica autem ita mecum
locutus est quasi non dubium bellum haberemus: nihil ad spem
concordiae; plane illum a se alienatum cum ante intellegeret,
tum vero proxime iudicasse; venisse Hirtium a Caesare, qui
esset illi familiarissimus, ad se non accessisse et, cum ille a. d. 10
VIII Id. Dec. vesperi venisset, Balbus de tota re constituisset
a. d. VII ad Scipionem ante lucem venire, multa de nocte eum
profectum esse ad Caesarem. hoc illi τεκμηριῶδες videbatur esse
3 alienationis. quid multa? nihil me aliud consolatur nisi quod
illum, cui etiam inimici alterum consulatum, fortuna summam
potentiam dederit, non arbitror fore tam amentem ut haec in
discrimen adducat. quod si ruere coeperit, ne ego multa timeo
quae non audeo scribere. sed ut nunc est, a. d. III Non. Ian. ad 5
urbem cogito.

128 (VII. 5)

Scr. in Formiano med. m. Dec. an. 50

CICERO ATTICO SAL.

1 Multas uno tempore accepi tuas, quae mihi, quamquam
recentiora audiebam ex iis qui ad me veniebant, tamen erant
iucundae; studium enim et benevolentiam declarabant.
valetudine tua moveor et Piliam in idem genus morbi delapsam

---

5 hoc iudicio (inditio) et officio *R Ant.*   sermone eius *Jørgensen*: -onis Ω
11 venisset et *Madvig*   **3**, 3 dederit *Pius*: -rat Ω
Ep. 128] 1, 1 accepi *HN*: litteras a- *OR*: a- epistolas Δ   4 valetudine (valit-)
NRC: inval- *HO*Δ

encouraged me about the Triumph, promised to do his part, and advised me not to attend the Senate before I had got the matter settled for fear I might make an enemy of some Tribune or other in the course of debate. In fact on this personal matter his language could not have been more forthcoming. On the political situation he talked as though we were certainly in for war, nothing to suggest a hope of agreement. He told me that although he had previously been aware of Caesar's complete estrangement from himself, a very recent incident had confirmed his opinion. Hirtius, a very close friend of Caesar's, had come from him to Rome, but had not approached himself; he had arrived on the evening of 6 December, and Balbus had arranged to call at Scipio's before dawn on the 7th for a talk on the whole situation. But Hirtius had left to join Caesar in the middle of the night. This seemed

3 to Pompey proof positive of estrangement. In short, my only comfort is that I don't believe that Caesar, given a second Consulship even by his enemies and immense power by the grace of fortune, will be mad enough to put all this in jeopardy. But if he does start plunging, then indeed I fear much that I dare not write down. Anyway as matters stand I propose to come to Rome on 3 January.

128 (VII. 5)

Formiae, mid-December 50

CICERO TO ATTICUS

1 I have received a number of letters from you all at once. Though I am getting more recent news from my visitors here, I was glad to have them, for they showed your warm interest in my welfare. I am much concerned to hear of your illness, and I know how much more anxious you must be now that

curam tibi adferre maiorem sentio. date igitur operam ut 5
valeatis.

2   De Tirone video tibi curae esse; quem quidem ego, etsi
mirabilis utilitates mihi praebet, cum valet, in omni genere vel
negotiorum vel studiorum meorum, tamen propter humanitatem et modestiam malo salvum quam propter usum meum.

3   Philogenes mecum nihil umquam de †lusgenio† locutus
est; de ceteris rebus habes Dionysium. sororem tuam non
venisse in Arcanum miror. de Chrysippo, meum consilium
probari tibi non moleste fero. ego in Tusculanum nihil sane
hoc tempore (devium est τοῖς ἀπαντῶσιν et habet alia δύσ- 5
χρηστα), sed de Formiano Tarracinam prid. Kal. Ian., inde
Pomptinum †summam†, inde Albanum Pompei; ita ad urbem
III Non., natali meo.

4   De re publica cottidie magis timeo. non enim boni, ut
putant⟨ur⟩, consentiunt. quos ego equites Romanos, quos
senatores vidi, qui acerrime cum cetera tum hoc iter Pompei
vituperarent! pace opus est. ex victoria cum multa mala tum
certe tyrannus exsistet. sed haec prope diem coram.   5

    Iam plane mihi deest quid ad te scribam; nec enim de re
publica, quod uterque nostrum scit eadem, et domestica nota
5   sunt ambobus. reliquum est iocari, si hic sinat; nam ego is sum
qui illi concedi putem utilius esse quod postulat quam signa
conferri; sero enim resistimus ei quem per annos decem aluimus
contra nos. 'quid senti⟨e⟩s igitur?' inquis. nihil scilicet nisi de

---

3, 1 Luscenio *c, Pius*: Tuscenio *Manutius*: *fort.* HS c̄ (centū) *vel* HS ↀ
ↁↁ   7 summam *NRMZ¹*: -ma *H*: sumam *EOms*: invisam *Corradus* Pomptini
in Setinum *Purser*   **4,** 2 putantur *Mueller*: putant Ω   5 tyrannis ς   6 mihi
deest quid *HNORΔ*: nihil est quod *Em*   **5,** 4 senties *Wesenberg*: -is Ω

Pilia has contracted the same sort of complaint. Try both of you to get well.

2 I see you are not forgetting Tiro. He is extraordinarily useful to me when well in all sorts of ways, both in business and in my literary work, but I hope for his recovery more because he is such a nice, modest fellow than for my own convenience.

3 Philogenes never said a word to me about the HS 15,000 (?). On other matters you can consult Dionysius. I am surprised your sister has not gone to Arcanum. I am glad you approve of the course I took about Chrysippus. No, I don't intend to go to Tusculum at all at the present time (it's out of the way for people coming to meet me and has other inconveniences), but shall leave Formiae for Tarracina on 29 December, from there go to ✳ in the Pontine marshes, and from there to Pompey's place at Alba, thus reaching Rome on my birthday, 3 January.

4 The political situation alarms me more every day. It is not as though the honest men, as they are reckoned, were agreed. You would hardly credit me if I told you of the Roman Knights and Senators too I have heard using the bitterest language about the conduct of affairs in general and this trip of Pompey's in particular. Peace is what is wanted. Victory will bring many evils in its train, including the certainty of a despot. But we shall talk of this together soon.

Just now I have really nothing to write to you about—not politics because we both have the same information, and dom-
5 estic matters too are known to both of us. Jokes are all that's left, with *his* kind permission—for I am one of those who hold it more expedient to concede his demands than to join battle. It is late in time for us to resist a force which we have been building up against ourselves for ten years. 'What line will you take then?', you may ask. None of course which you do not

sententia tua, nec prius quidem quam nostrum negotium aut 5
confecerimus aut deposuerimus. cura igitur ut valeas; aliquando
ἀπότριψαι quartanam istam diligentia quae in te summa est.

129 (VII. 6)

Scr. in Formiano c. xiii Kal. Ian. an. 50

CICERO ATTICO SAL.

1 Plane deest quid ad te scribam. nota omnia tibi sunt, nec ipse
habeo a te quod exspectem. tantum igitur nostrum illud sol-
lemne servemus, ut ne quem istuc euntem sine litteris dimit-
tamus.

2   De re publica valde timeo, nec adhuc fere inveni qui non
concedendum putaret Caesari quod postularet potius quam
depugnandum. est illa quidem impudens postulatio, opinione
†valentior†. cur autem nunc primum ei resistamus? ʻοὐ γὰρ δὴ
τόδε μεῖζον ἔπι κακὸνʼ quam cum quinquennium prorogaba- 5
mus, aut cum ut absentis ratio haberetur ferebamus, nisi forte
haec illi tum arma dedimus ut nunc cum bene parato pugnare-
mus. dices ʻquid tu igitur sensurus es?ʼ non idem quod dicturus.
sentiam enim omnia facienda ne armis decertetur, dicam idem
quod Pompeius, neque id faciam humili animo. sed rursus hoc 10
permagnum rei publicae malum, esse quodam modo mihi
praeter ceteros non rectum me in tantis rebus a Pompeio
dissidere.

Ep. 129] 1, 1 nihil est quod *E*   **2,** 2 quod *Lambinus*: quid Ω   3 sed is qui
postulat *post* postulatio *add. Lehmann*   4 valentior] *fort.* tamen lenior   resistamus *P*: -am Ω   δὴ *Schütz*: ΛΗ *M*: ΑΗ *R*: ἂν δ   5 ἔπι *O*: ΕΠΕΙ (ἔπει) *RM*δ: ἔπει
Victorius   11 esse *scripsi*: est et *HNOR*Δ: est *E*   12 me *secl. Boot*

advise and none before I have either settled my own affair or given it up. Look after your health therefore, and take pains (no man better) to shake off this quartan of yours at long last.

129 (VII. 6)

Formiae, c. 18 December 50

CICERO TO ATTICUS

1 I have really nothing to write to you about. You know all there is to know, and I on my side have nothing to expect from you. So let me just keep up my old-established habit of not letting anyone go your way without a letter.

2   The political situation alarms me deeply, and so far I have found scarcely anybody who is not for giving Caesar what he demands rather than fighting it out. The demand is impudent no doubt, but more moderate than was expected (?). And why should we start standing up to him now? 'Sure, 'tis no worse a thing' than when we gave him his five years extension or when we brought in the law authorizing his candidature *in absentia*. Or did we put these weapons into his hands only to fight him now that he is equipped and ready? You will ask me what line I shall take in the House. Not the same as in my own mind. *There* I shall vote for peace at any price, but in the House I shall echo Pompey, and I shall not do it in a spirit of sub-servience either. But it is yet another major misfortune for the country that for me especially there is in a way something wrong in dissenting from Pompey on such high matters.

130 (VII. 7)

Scr. in Formiano xii, ut vid., Kal. Ian. an. 50

CICERO ATTICO SAL.

1 'Dionysius, vir optimus, ut mihi quoque est perspectus, et doctissimus tuique amantissimus, Romam venit xv Kal. Ian. et litteras a te mihi reddidit.' tot enim verba sunt de Dionysio in epistula tua; illud putato non adscribis, 'et tibi gratias egit'. atqui certe ille agere debuit et, si esset factum, quae tua est 5 humanitas, adscripsisses. mihi autem nulla de eo παλινῳδία datur propter superioris epistulae testimonium. sit igitur sane bonus vir; hoc enim ipsum bene fecit, quod mihi sui cognoscendi penitus etiam istam facultatem dedit.

2 Philogenes recte ad te scripsit; curavit enim quod debuit. eum ego uti ea pecunia volui quoad liceret; itaque usus est menses XIIII.

3 Pomptinum cupio valere et, quod scribis in urbem introisse, vereor quid sit; nam id nisi gravi de causa non fecisset. ego, quoniam IIII Non. Ian. compitalicius dies est, nolo eo die in Albanum venire, ne molestus sim familiae; veniam III Non. Ian. igitur, inde ad urbem prid. Non. tua λῆψις quem in diem 5 incurrat nescio, sed prorsus te commoveri incommodo valetudinis tuae nolo.

4 De honore nostro, nisi quid occulte Caesar per suos tribunos molitus erit, cetera videntur esse tranquilla; tranquillissimus autem animus meus, qui totum istuc aequi boni facit, et eo magis quod iam a multis audio constitutum esse Pompeio et eius consilio in Siciliam me mittere quod imperium habeam. 5

Ep. 130] 1, 3 te mihi ς: me tibi Ω   4 putato ΩZ^b: puta tu *Bosius*   5 tua est ς: tu si Ω   7 sit δ: sed Ω   3, 4 ne Z^b: *om.* Ω   sim Z^b: *om.* Ω   veniam *delendum coniecit Orelli*   4, 1 quid Eδ: quod *HNORM*

130 (VII. 7)

Formiae, 19 (?) December 50

CICERO TO ATTICUS

1 'The excellent Dionysius, as I also know him to be, a fine scholar too with a warm affection for you, arrived in Rome on 16 December and gave me a letter from you.' That, no more and no less, is what you write about Dionysius in your letter. You don't add, let us say, 'and he expressed his gratitude to you'. And yet he certainly ought to have done so, and if he had it would have been unlike your kindly self not to have added it. However I can't recant about him after the testimonial in my earlier letter. Agreed then that he is a very fine fellow. Indeed I actually feel beholden to him for giving me this insight among others into his character.

2 Philogenes was correct in what he wrote to you. He paid what he owed. I wanted him to put the money to use for the time allowed. Accordingly he did so for fourteen months.

3 I hope Pomptinus is getting well. You say he has entered Rome, which makes me uneasy. He would not have done so without a strong reason. 2 January being Crossways Day I don't want to go to Alba that day in case my arrival might be troublesome for the staff. That shall be for the 3rd therefore, and from there to Rome on the 4th. I don't know what day your fever is due, but I wouldn't have you think of making a move to the detriment of your health.

4 With regard to my Triumph, unless Caesar gets up something underhand through his Tribunes, all seems to be calm water. Calmest of all is my own mind, which takes the whole business philosophically, all the more so as I hear from many quarters that Pompey and his council have settled to send me to Sicily because I have military authority. That is senseless. I have no

id est 'Αβδηριτικόν; nec enim senatus decrevit nec populus
iussit me imperium in Sicilia habere; sin hoc res publica ad
Pompeium refert, qui me magis quam privatum aliquem
mittit? itaque si hoc imperium mihi molestum erit, utar ea
porta quam primam videro.   10

5   Nam quod scribis mirificam exspectationem esse mei neque
tamen quemquam bonorum aut satis bonorum dubitare quid
facturus sim, ego quos tu bonos esse dicas non intellego. ipse
nullos novi, sed ita, si ordines bonorum quaerimus. nam
singulares sunt boni viri; verum in dissensionibus ordines 5
bonorum et genera quaerenda sunt. senatum bonum putas,
per quem sine imperio provinciae sunt (numquam enim Curio
sustinuisset, si cum eo agi coeptum esset; quam sententiam
senatus sequi noluit, ex quo factum est ut Caesari non succede-
retur), an publicanos, qui numquam firmi sed nunc Caesari 10
sunt amicissimi, an faeneratores, an agricolas, quibus optatissi-
mum est otium? nisi eos timere putas ne sub regno sint qui id
numquam, dum modo otiosi essent, recusarunt.

6   Quid ergo? exercitum retinentis cum legis dies transierit
rationem haberi placet? mihi vero ne absentis quidem; sed cum
id datum est, illud una datum est. annorum autem decem
imperium et ita latum ⟨placet⟩? placet igitur etiam me expulsum et agrum Campanum perisse et adoptatum patricium a 5
plebeio, Gaditanum a Mytilenaeo, et Labieni divitiae et
Mamurrae placent et Balbi horti et Tusculanum. sed horum
omnium fons unus est. imbecillo resistendum fuit, et id erat

---

9 mittit *Zc*: -tat Ω   utar ea *Victorius*: utar e *vel sim*. *RN*Δ: utar *E*
10 primam *Popma*: -mum Ω   5, 3 facturus *CZ*: sensu- Ω 8 esset *EPb*: est
*HNOR*Δ 12 qui id *HNORC*: quid id *M*: quod *E*δ   6, 1 dies Σλ: diem Δ
3 autem *scripsi*: enim Ω 4 placet *add.* ς

mandate either from Senate or Assembly to hold command in Sicily. If on the other hand the state leaves this to
Pompey, why send me rather than a private individual? So if
this military authority is going to be a nuisance, I shall walk
in by the first gate I see.

5   You say my advent is awaited with extraordinary interest,
but that none of the honest, or fairly honest, men have any
doubt about what I shall do. I don't understand whom you
mean by 'the honest men'. *I* don't know of any, that is if we
are thinking in terms of classes. There are honest *individuals*,
but in political conflicts one has to look for honest men by
classes and categories. Do you reckon the Senate as 'honest'?
It is thanks to them that the provinces now have no governors.
Curio would never have stood out if representations had been
started with him. But the Senate would not support the
proposal, with the result that no successors to Caesar were
appointed. Well then, the tax-farmers—never reliable, now
warmly attached to Caesar—, or the capitalists, or the farmers,
whose first prayer is for peace? Or do you suppose they are
frightened of living under an autocracy? They never have
objected to that, so long as they were left in peace.

6   You may ask whether I approve of allowing a commander
who retains his army after the expiry of the term legally assigned to stand for office. I disapproved even of allowing his
candidature *in absentia*; but the one concession implied the
other. Do we approve of the ten years' command and the way
it was conferred? Then we also approve of my expulsion and
the loss of the Campanian land and the adoption of a patrician
by a plebeian and of a man from Gades by a man from Mytilene; and we approve of the fortunes of Labienus and Mamurra
and of Balbus' estates in the suburbs and at Tusculum. But the
root of all these things is one and the same. We should have

facile; nunc legiones XI, equitatus tantus quantum volet,
Transpadani, plebes urbana, tot tribuni pl., tam perdita iuven- 10
tus, tanta auctoritate dux, tanta audacia. cum hoc aut depug-
7 nandum est aut habenda e lege ratio. 'depugna' inquis 'potius
quam servias.' ut quid? si victus eris, proscribare, si viceris,
tamen servias? 'quid ergo' inquis 'acturus es?' idem quod pe-
cudes, quae dispulsae sui generis sequuntur greges; ut bos
armenta, sic ego bonos viros aut eos quicumque dicentur boni 5
sequar, etiam si ruent. quid sit optimum male contractis rebus
plane video; nemini est enim exploratum cum ad arma ventum
sit quid futurum sit, at illud omnibus, si boni victi sint, nec in
caede principum clementiorem hunc fore quam Cinna fuerit
nec moderatiorem quam Sulla in pecuniis locupletum. ἐμπο- 10
λιτεύομαί σοι iam dudum, et facerem diutius nisi me lucerna
desereret. ad summam, 'dic M. Tulli'. 'adsentior Cn. Pompeio',
id est T. Pomponio.

Alexim, humanissimum puerum (nisi forte, dum ego absum,
adulescens factus est; id enim agere videbatur), salvere iubeas 15
velim.

131 (VII. 8)

Scr. in Formiano vi aut v Kal. Ian. an. 50

CICERO ATTICO SAL.

1 Quid opus est de Dionysio tam valde adfirmare? an mihi nutus
tuus non faceret fidem? suspicionem autem eo mihi maiorem
tua taciturnitas attulerat, quod et tu soles conglutinare amicitias

---

7, 6 sit *Mueller*: est Ω   8 sint ϛ: sunt Ω   10 sulla *ENORbms*: -am *HMdλ*
locupletum *HNRΔ*: -tium *EO*   13 tito *P*: p. Ω
Ep. 131] 1, 1 nutus *Mm*: notus *Z¹*: nuntius *HNORbms*

stood up to him when he was weak, and that would have been easy. Now we have to deal with eleven legions, all the cavalry he may want, the Gauls beyond Po, the city populace, all these Tribunes, our demoralized youth, and a leader strong in prestige and hardihood. We must either fight him or allow

7 his candidature as by law authorized. 'Better fight than be a slave', you say. For what? Proscription if you're beaten and if you win slavery just the same? What am I going to do then? What stray cattle do when they follow droves of their own species. As an ox follows the herd, so I shall follow the honest men or whoever may be called such, even if they plunge. The *best* course in the straits to which we are reduced I see clearly enough. For nobody can be sure what will happen once the fight is on, but everybody can assume that if the honest men are beaten Caesar will be no more merciful than Cinna in the slaughter of leading men and no more temperate than Sulla in plundering the rich. Well, I have been inflicting my political views on you all this while, and I should go on doing so if the lamp were not going out. To sum up: 'Speak, M. Tullius!'. 'I agree with Cn. Pompeius', i.e. with T. Pomponius.

Please greet Alexis for me, a most courteous lad, unless he has become a young man while I have been away—he seemed to be heading that way.

131 (VII. 8)

Formiae, 25 or 26 December 50

CICERO TO ATTICUS

1 There is really no need to be so emphatic about Dionysius, as though a nod from you would not satisfy me. Your silence made me the more suspicious because it is a practice of yours to cement friendships by your testimonials and because I am

testimoniis tuis et illum aliter cum aliis de nobis locutum audiebam. sed prorsus ita esse ut scribis mihi persuades; itaque ego 5
is in illum sum quem tu me esse vis.

2   Diem tuum ego quoque ex epistula tua quadam quam incipi-
ente febricula scripseras mihi notaveram et animadverteram
posse pro re nata te non incommode ad me in Albanum venire
III Non. Ian. sed, amabo te, nihil incommodo valetudinis feceris.
quid enim est tantum in uno aut altero die?   5

3   Dolabellam video Liviae testamento cum duobus coheredibus
esse in triente sed iuberi mutare nomen. est πολιτικὸν σκέμμα
rectumne sit nobili adulescenti nomen mutare mulieris testamento. sed id φιλοσοφώτερον διευκρινήσομεν cum sciemus
quantum quasi sit in trientis triente.   5

4   Quod putasti fore ut ante quam istuc venirem Pompeium
viderem, factum est ita; nam VI Kal. ad Lavernium ⟨me⟩
consecutus est. una Formias venimus et ab hora octava ad
vesperum secreto collocuti sumus. quod quaeris ecquae spes
pacificationis sit, quantum ex Pompei multo et accurato ser- 5
mone perspexi, ne voluntas quidem est. sic enim existimat, si
ille vel dimisso exercitu consul factus sit, σύγχυσιν τῆς πολιτείας
fore, atque etiam putat eum, cum audierit contra se diligenter
parari, consulatum hoc anno neglecturum ac potius exercitum
provinciamque retenturum; sin autem ille fureret, vehementer 10
hominem contemnebat et suis et rei publicae copiis confidebat.
quid quaeris? etsi mihi crebro 'ξυνὸς Ἐνυάλιος' occurrebat,
tamen levabar cura virum fortem et peritum et plurimum

2, 1 tua quadam *HNOR*: q- t- Δ   3, 3 nomen mutare *HNOR*: m- n- Δ
4, 2 me *add.* ς   4 quod Δ: quid Σ   ecquae ς: et q- Ω

told he has talked about me different ways to different people. But you quite convince me that it is as you say, and so I feel towards him as you wish.

2   I too had made a note of your day from one of your letters which you wrote me as a touch of fever was coming on and had observed that it would not be inconvenient, relatively speaking, for you to visit me at Alba on 3 January. But don't, I beg you, do anything to the detriment of your health. After all one or two days are not so important.

3   I see that Dolabella is down for a third share in Livia's will along with two co-heirs, but is required to change his name. It is a question in political ethics whether it is right for a young man of noble family to change his name under a lady's will. But we shall solve the problem more scientifically when we know approximately how much a third share of a third share amounts to.

4   Your forecast that I should be seeing Pompey before I came your way has proved correct. On the 25th he overtook me near Lavernium. We went back to Formiae together and talked privately from two o'clock till evening. The answer to your question whether there is any hope of a pacification, so far as I could see from Pompey's talk, which lacked neither length nor detail, is that there isn't even the desire for one. His view is that if Caesar is made Consul, even after giving up his army, it will mean the subversion of the constitution; and he further thinks that when Caesar hears that preparations against him are energetically proceeding he will forego the Consulate this year and prefer to retain his army and province. But should Caesar take leave of his senses, Pompey is quite contemptuous of anything he can do and confident in his own and the Republic's forces. All in all, though I often thought of 'Mars on both sides', I felt relieved as I heard such a man, courageous,

auctoritate valentem audiens πολιτικῶς de pacis simulatae
5 periculis disserentem. habebamus autem in manibus Antoni
contionem habitam x Kal. Ian., in qua erat accusatio Pompei
usque a toga pura, querela de damnatis, terror armorum. in
quibus ille 'quid censes' aiebat 'facturum esse ipsum, si in
possessionem rei publicae venerit, cum haec quaestor eius 5
infirmus et inops audeat dicere?' quid multa? non modo non
expetere pacem istam sed etiam timere visus est. ex illa autem
sententia relinquendae urbis †movet† hominem, ut puto. mihi
autem illud molestissimum est, quod solvendi sunt nummi
Caesari et instrumentum triumphi eo conferendum; est enim 1
ἄμορφον ἀντιπολιτευομένου χρεωφειλέτην esse. sed haec et
multa alia coram.

132 (VII. 9)

Scr. in Formiano iv Kal. Ian. an. 50

CICERO ATTICO SAL.

1 'Cottidiene' inquis 'a te accipiendae litterae sunt?' si habebo
cui dem, cottidie. 'at iam ipse ades.' tum igitur cum venero
desinam. unas video mihi a te non esse redditas, quas L.
Quinctius, familiaris meus, cum ferret ad bustum Basili vul-
2 neratus et despoliatus est. videbis igitur num quid fuerit in iis
quod me scire opus sit. et simul hoc διευκρινήσεις πρόβλημα
sane πολιτικόν:—

Cum sit necesse aut haberi Caesaris rationem illo exercitum
vel per senatum vel per tribunos pl. obtinente, aut persuaderi
Caesari ut tradat provinciam atque exercitum et ita consul fiat,

---

5, 8 relinquend(a)e *NOR*: īrel- *M*: infra (*vel* ita) rel- δ　9 molestissimum est
Δ: est m- *OR*: m- *NP*
Ep. 132] *novam ep. Corradus: superiori coniungunt codd.*　　1, 2 ades *O*: -st
*HN*Δ　　**2, 2** simul *C*: si multo Ω: simul tu *Victorius*

experienced, and powerful in prestige, discoursing statesman-
5 wise on the dangers of a false peace. We had in front of us
a speech made by Antony on 21 December containing a
denunciation of Pompey from the day he came of age, a protest
on behalf of the persons condemned, and threats of armed
force. Talking of which Pompey remarked: 'How do you
expect Caesar to behave if he gets control of the state, when his
feckless nobody of a Quaestor dares to say this sort of thing?'
In short, far from seeking the peaceful settlement you talk of,
he seemed to dread it. I think * move him from the idea of
abandoning Rome. What irks me the most is that Caesar must
be paid his money and the wherewithal for my Triumph
diverted to that purpose. It does not look well to be in debt to
a political opponent. But of this and much else when we are
together.

132 (VII. 9)

Formiae, 27 December 50

CICERO TO ATTICUS

1 You may wonder whether you have to expect a letter from
me every day. The answer is 'yes', provided I have people to
take them. And if you point out that I shall be with you in
person very soon, I answer that when I am I shall stop writing.
I notice that one letter of yours has miscarried. Its bearer, my
friend L. Quinctius, was robbed with violence at Basilus' tomb.
2 So please see whether it contained anything I ought to know
and at the same time please solve the following problem which
is nothing if not political:—
The possibilities are as follows:— (1) Caesar's candidature
may be admitted while he still retains his army either by favour
of the Senate or of the Tribunes. (2) Caesar may be persuaded
to hand over his province and army and so become Consul.

aut, si id ei non persuadeatur, haberi comitia sine illius ratione
illo patiente atque obtinente provinciam, aut, si per tribunos
pl. non patiatur ⟨et⟩ tamen quiescat, rem adduci ad interregnum, aut, si ob eam causam quod ratio eius non habeatur 10
exercitum adducat, armis cum eo contendere, illum autem
initium facere armorum aut statim nobis minus paratis aut tum
cum comitiis amicis eius postulantibus ut e lege ratio habeatur
impetratum non sit, ire autem ad arma aut hanc unam ob
causam quod ratio non habeatur aut addita causa si forte 15
tribunus pl. senatum impediens aut populum incitans notatus
aut senatus consulto circumscriptus aut sublatus aut expulsus
[sit] dicensve se expulsum ad illum confugerit, suscepto autem
bello aut tenenda sit urbs aut ea relicta ille commeatu et reliquis
copiis intercludendus—quod horum malorum, quorum aliquod 20
certe subeundum est, minimum putes.

3   Dices profecto persuaderi illi ut tradat exercitum et ita consul
fiat. est omnino id eius modi ut, si ille eo descendat, contra dici
nihil possit, idque eum, si non obtinet ut ratio habeatur retinentis exercitum, non facere miror; nobis autem, ut quidam
putant, nihil est timendum magis quam ille consul. 'at sic malo' 5
inquies 'quam cum exercitu.' certe; sed istuc ipsum 'sic' [o]
magnum malum putat aliquis, neque ei remedium est ullum;
cedendum est, si id volet. 'vide consulem illum iterum quem

---

9 et *add. Lambinus*   14 impetratum *EPδ:* imper- *NORM*   18 sit *seclusi*
3, 5 putat *Tunstall*   6 sic *Manutius:* sic, dico *Tunstall:* dico *Ernesti:* sic malo
Koch: sic, scio *Sternkopf*

(3) If he be not so persuaded, elections may be held without admission of his candidature, he not obstructing and meanwhile retaining his province. (4) Should he obstruct this by means of Tribunes but not resort to violence, there will be an interregnum. (5) If he brings up his army because his candidature is not accepted we must fight him. Now he may begin military operations (a) at once, before we are properly ready, or (b) at the elections, when his friends demand that his candidature be admitted according to the law and the demand is rejected. Further he may resort to arms either (a) on the single pretext of the rejection of his candidature or (b) on some additional pretext, if it should happen that a Tribune obstructing the Senate or stirring up the people and being censured or curtailed in his functions by senatorial decree or removed from office or expelled or claiming to have been expelled should take refuge with him. War once begun, either (a) Rome would have to be held or (b) Rome would have to be abandoned and Caesar cut off from his supplies and his remaining forces. Of these evils, one of which is inevitable, which do you consider the least?

3   No doubt you will say that he be persuaded to hand over his army and so become Consul. True, this would be a course against which, if he were to bring himself to it, nothing could be said, and I am surprised that he does not do so if his claim to stand while retaining his army is not allowed. From our standpoint however, as certain persons think, no prospect is more formidable than Caesar as Consul. 'Better thus' you will say, 'than with an army at his back.' Assuredly, but this very 'thus' is, I know, considered a disaster by somebody; and yet there is no help for it. If that is what he wants we must let him have it. 'You have put up with him as Consul before, put up

vidisti consulatu priore.' 'at tum imbecillus plus' inquit 'valuit
quam tota res publica. quid nunc putas?' et eo consule Pompeio 10
certum est esse in Hispania. o rem miseram! si quidem id ipsum
deterrimum est quod recusari non potest, et quod ille si faciat,
iam a bonis omnibus summam ineat gratiam.

4   Tollamus igitur hoc quo illum posse adduci negant; de
reliquis quid est deterrimum? concedere illi quod, ut idem dicit,
impudentissime postulat. nam quid impudentius? tenuisti
provinciam per annos decem non tibi a senatu sed a te ipso per
vim et per factionem datos; praeteriit tempus non legis sed 5
libidinis tuae, fac tamen legis; ut succedatur decernitur; impedis
et ais 'habe meam rationem'. habe tu nostram. exercitum tu
habeas diutius quam populus iussit, invito senatu? 'depugnes
oportet, nisi concedis.' cum bona quidem spe, ut ait idem, vel
vincendi vel in libertate moriendi. iam si pugnandum est, quo 10
tempore, in casu, quo consilio, in temporibus situm est. itaque
te in ea quaestione non exerceo. ad ea quae dixi adfer si quid
habes. equidem dies noctesque torqueor.

---

9 at *Ebs*: ac *NORMdm* inquis δ 13 iam a *Sturmius*: iam iam Ω: iamiam a
Manutius   **4,** 2 quod *post* dicit *libenter transposuerim* 4 annos decem (x)
Σ: d- (x) a- Δ 5 legis *C*: -it *EORM*: legas *N*: legitimum δ sed . . . legis
C: *om.* Ω 7 habe tu *c*: -et tu *N*: -et *ORM*: -e *E*δ nostram *Graevii operae*
(*in Var. Lect.*): -rum Ω

with him again.' 'Ah, but he was weak then' comes the answer, 'and yet stronger than the entire state. What do you think he will be like now?' And if he is Consul, Pompey is resolved to stay in Spain. A wretched situation indeed if the worst of all contingencies is something which cannot be refused and which, should he accept it, would make all the honest men immediately and heartily grateful to him!

4   Well then, let us eliminate this possibility which they say he cannot be brought to accept. Which is the worst of those that remain? Surely to concede what the same person calls his most impudent demands. For could impudence go further? You have kept a province for ten years, years given you not by the Senate but by yourself through factious violence. The time is up, the time set not by law but by your own whim—but grant it was by law. The appointment of your successor is resolved. You obstruct and say 'admit my right to stand'. What about *our* rights? Who are you to keep an army longer than the people have ordained, against the will of the Senate? 'You will have to fight if you don't give me what I want.' Very well, fight we will, in good hope (as the same person says) of victory or of death as free men. War once decided, the time depends on chance, the plan of campaign on circumstances. So I won't take up your time on that question. If you have any views on what I have said, let me know them. For my part I have no peace day or night.

COMMENTARY

94 (V. 1)

May 51 found Cicero in the earliest stages of a reluctant journey to a belated province. That was in consequence of a law passed by Pompey in his third Consulship under which Consuls and Praetors, instead of proceeding to provincial commands immediately after their terms of office, had for the future to wait five years. Caesar maintained (*B.C.* 1. 85. 9) that the law was directed against himself. More probably it was part of Cato's πολίτευμα (115 (VI. 1). 13) to improve provincial administration—Dio says (XL. 56. 1) that a decree of the Senate to the same effect had been passed not long beforehand. To fill the gap thus created, Consulars and *praetorii* who for one reason or another had never governed a province were called in (cf. Mommsen, *St.* II, pp. 248 f). C.'s portion was Cilicia, where Ap. Pulcher was coming to the end of two years' misgovernment. At this period (from 56 to 50) the province included, besides Cilicia proper, Lycia, Pamphylia, Pisidia, Isauria, Lycaonia, and Cyprus, together with the three Phrygian 'dioceses' (*conventus*; cf. 108 (v. 15). 3 n.) of Laodicea, Apamea, and Synnada, which were normally part of the province of Asia.

To C. the appointment was all the less attractive because he might be called upon to cope with a serious military situation. Since Carrhae (June 53) the threat of a Parthian invasion had hung over the eastern frontier. It materialized this summer; but Syria, not Cilicia, was the target, and though the province was overrun, the invaders eventually withdrew with loss. This however lay in the uncertain future. Against what might befall C. took three experienced soldiers on his staff, his brother, C. Pomptinus (cf. 92 (IV. 18). 4 n.), and M. Anneius (cf. 97 (v. 4). 2 n.). It also included his Quaestor, L. Mescinius Rufus, and one other Legate, L. Tullius.

Writing for dispatch on 7 May Atticus had not received this letter (96 (v. 3). 2). He dispatched his reply to it on 8 May (*ibid.* 1 *tertio abs te die*). As letters from Minturnae took at least two days to arrive in Rome, this must have been dispatched not later than the 6th.

1, 1 discessu At Tusculum (§3).

meo For the dative cf. *Quinct.* 37 *quis huic rei testis est?* and Sjögren, *Comm. Tull.* pp. 86 f.

2 ne...decernatur C. remained in continual dread of a prorogation of his term of office by the Senate.

3 ne plus sit annuum Cf. K.–S. II, p. 471.

2, 1 Annio Saturnino Milo having gone into exile after his condemnation in 52 his goods were sold, and C., through Philotimus, became a purchaser, possibly using Terentia's dowry: cf. 101 (v. 8). 2. From his cognomen the person here named will have been a connexion or client of Milo's rather than a freedman.

satis dando Cf. 4 (I. 8). 1 n. Atticus is asked to make the guarantees, as C.'s *procurator*, in what transactions we cannot say.

3 **satisdationes secundum mancipium** Guarantees 'connected with *mancipatio*, probably a formal promise (*stipulatio*) by the seller to deliver the immovable alienated with all proceeds and profits he had derived therefrom in the time between the *mancipatio* and the effective delivery' (A. Berger, *Encycl. Dict. of Roman Law*, p. 690).

Mennianorum...Atilianorum Mennius (Menius) is an attested name, though rare: see Münzer, *RE.* xv. 896 and 404 (xv. 26). 5 n. Nothing is known of these properties, which were presumably sold by C. to Mennius and Atilius. The latter was probably the Roman Knight to whose difficulties C. refers in a letter some six months later (*Fam.* XIII. 62). From 112 (v. 19). 1 it seems that he owed C. money, perhaps as a result of this sale.

4 **Oppio** Cf. 89 (IV. 16). 8 n.

de $\overline{\text{DCCC}}$ A loan from Caesar to C., which the latter was now anxious to repay: cf. 97 (v. 4). 3 *de Oppio, bene curasti quod ei de* $\overline{\text{DCCC}}$ *exposuisti.* The preposition seems desirable: cf. *ad Her.* II. 50 *si de clementia, humanitate, misericordia nostra, qua in alios usi sumus, aperiemus*; Pacuv. 364 (Ribbeck[3]) *Graiugena: de isto aperit ipsa oratio.* A direct accusative would rather suggest that Oppius did not know about the loan; but it was surely C.'s intentions, not the loan itself, which Atticus explained.

3, 1 transversum Along the margin, crosswise to the main column.

8 **sumpta** *sumptus* has better authority; but *ex ratione sumptus* is a strange phrase, and we hear nothing elsewhere of Pomponia's extravagance. *sumpta offensio*, to which Orelli took exception, seems perfectly natural (cf. *sumere obsequium (animo), constantiam, arrogantiam*, etc.).

ille sic dies Sc. *abiit* (cf. D. Brutus, *Fam.* XI. 13. 1 *hic dies hoc modo abiit. postero die* sqq.); for the ellipse cf. *ad Brut.* 5. 3 *itaque ille dies silentio*; *Verr.* II. 4. 66 *dies unus, alter, plures; non referri.*

9 **Arcano** From Arx, between Aquinum and Arpinum. The preposition, with respect to the villa, is normal: cf. 128 (VII. 5). 3 *in Arcanum*; 192 (X. 2). 1 *in Arcano fratris.* But the locative *Arcani* in Q. *Fr.* III. 3. 1 and perhaps II. 6. 4 shows that Arcanum could be regarded as a place name.

10 **dies** Sc. *festus*, probably that of 1 May to the Lares. This called for Quintus' presence at Arpinum, but not for C.'s at Aquinum; therefore a stop or semi-colon should follow *fecit*, not the comma of modern editions.

ego Aquini Sc. *mansi.*

12 **mulieres...pueros** The servants and farm-workers. *viros* (Malaespina) is quite needless; besides, Quintus might probably not care to call slaves *viri.*

14 **vultu** Cf. §4 *verbis vultuque*; Ov. *Fast.* v. 503 *addidit et vultum verbis.*

16 **Statius** Cf. 38 (II. 18). 4 n.

4, 1 **quaeso** *quasi* might be defended by 131 (VII. 8). 3 *cum sciemus quantum quasi sit in trientis triente*, where however the quantitative pronoun makes it easier.

2 **me ipsum** As well as the victim, Quintus. *idque* (Watt) for *itaque* is not an improvement.

4 **dolens** Inwardly smouldering, as it were.

10 **cum discessura esset** Pomponia evidently left, probably for Rome, early the following morning.

5, 2 **Pomptinum** See introd. note. He caught up with C. in Athens (103 (V. 10). 1).

5 **A. Torquatum** A. Manlius Torquatus belonged to the younger branch of his house, being only distantly related to Lucius (cf. 92 (IV. 18). 3 n.). He was also much older, Quaestor in 81 and Praetor in 70. Like Lucius a Pompeian in 49, he seems to have been among those who gave up the struggle after Pharsalia. At any rate he was in Athens in 46-45, where he received several consolatory letters from C. (*Fam.* VI. 1-4). Efforts were made through Dolabella to obtain permission for him to return to Italy (cf. 317 (XIII. 9). 1 n.), whether successfully or not is uncertain. After Caesar's death at any rate he was back, and active in the republican cause. His friend Atticus helped him after Philippi (Nep. *Att.* 11. 2; cf. 15. 3). In *Fin.* II. 72 C. warmly acknowledges his loyalty and zeal in the dark days of his own exile.

Minturnis Perhaps we should write *Menturnis*, the older spelling: cf. Mommsen, *C.I.L.* X, p. 595.

6 **cui...velim** Cf. 45 (II. 25). 1. The sense is sufficiently clear without *de se.*

95 (V. 2)

1, 2 **Trebulano** The *ager Trebulanus* (cf. *Fam.* XI. 27. 3; Liv. XXIII. 14. 13) bordered the Via Appia between Saticula and Suessula in the country of the Hirpini, some 25 miles from Pompeii: see Constans, III, p. 188, n. 2; Philipp, *RE.* VIA. 2284. Several other Trebulae are recorded in central Italy and Campania. *Trebulanum* is probably a neuter substantive (cf. Solonium (23 (II. 3). 3 n.), Vescinum, Picenum). If C. had meant 'in Pontius' Trebulan villa' he would have written *in Ponti Trebulano.*

Pontium L. Pontius appears elsewhere as entertaining C. and Terentia on the way to or from Brundisium. He is not otherwise identifiable.

3 **iusta itinera** C. arrived at Brundisium on 22 May (*Fam.* III. 3. 1), travelling about 25 Roman miles a day apart from a halt at Tarentum (cf.

Constans III, p. 192, n. 3)—decidedly slow progress (cf. Friedländer, *Sittengeschichte Roms*[10], I, p. 335).

7 **provinciam** Manutius has two explanations of the plural *provincias*: that it refers to other commands as well as C.'s, and that part of Asia as well as Cilicia was under C.'s jurisdiction (see introd. note). Constans preferred to suppose that *nobis* includes the Quaestor and Legates. In view of C.'s normal usage the failure of all these defences is apparent, and no less so the source of corruption, the preceding plural *nobis*.

10 **Furnium** Cf. 111 (v. 18). 3 *amicos consules habemus, nostrum tribunum pl. Furnium.* C. Furnius, Tr. pl. 50, Pr. 42(?), governor of Asia 36–35, was a steady friend of C.'s, though a Caesarian in the Civil War and later a supporter of M. and L. Antonius. Pardoned and dignified by Augustus, he lived to see his son Consul in 17. Two letters to him as Plancus' Legate in 43 survive (*Fam.* X. 25, 26).

2, 2 **Rufio** Contemptuous diminutive of *Rufus* (cf. Kühner–Holz-weissig, *Ausf. lat. Gramm.* p. 989), hence a common slave name. The person referred to is C. Sempronius Rufus (perhaps Asellio Rufus: see Münzer, *RE.* IIA. 1436 f.), known only from C.'s correspondence and Horace's scholiasts. From the latter it appears that he attained the Praetorship and was credited with introducing stork-chicks as a culinary fashion (see Münzer, *l.c.*). He appears to have been condemned later this year on an unknown charge (cf. Caelius, *Fam.* VIII. 8. 1) and gone into exile, but may have been restored by Antony after Caesar's death (cf. 368 (XIV. 14). 2). The circumstances of his quarrel with Vestorius cannot be made out from Caelius' corrupt reference (*l.c.*) or from C.'s in 116 (VI. 2). 10; probably he owed Vestorius money. Nor is anything known about C.'s claims upon his gratitude (see below).

se...observari From what follows we gather that there was in fact no great difficulty in finding Rufus abroad, and the explanation offered by C. for the man's discourtesy in failing to visit him is plainly facetious. The following comparison with Hortensius implies that it was really simply negligence on Rufus' part. *me* for *se* may be right, but if so *observari* means 'cultivated', not 'watched'.

5 **tam longe** Presumably from his villa at Bauli (cf. J. H. D'Arms, *Am. Journ. Phil.* 88 (1967), pp. 195 f.)

et Hortensius Cf. Q. *Fr.* I. 2. 15 *adulescens nullius consili, sed tamen civis Romanus et Cato*; *Nat. Deor.* II. 2 *et philosophi et pontificis et Cottae*; Val. Max. II. 9. 2 *et censor ⟨et⟩ Cato*, III. 3 *Ext.* 2 *et tyranno et Phalari.* Hortensius had property in Puteoli: cf. 126 (VII. 3). 9 n.

9 **iussi valere** 'Said good-bye to him': cf. 88 (IV. 14). 2 *Dionysium iube salvere.* So *bene vale* answers *numquid vis?* in Plaut. *Curc.* 516. In the next sentence C. pretends ironically to take the common formula (cf. Q. *Fr.* III. 1. 22 *ne*

num quid vellem quidem rogavit) literally; what more could a man do for his benefactor than ask how he could serve him?

3, 3 ex consuetudine aliorum Cf. the jest in *Leg.* III. 18 CIC. *sed iam, si placet, de provinciis decedatur in urbemque redeatur. ATT. nobis vero placet, sed iis qui in provinciis sunt minime placet.* Quintus however had felt the same way in Asia (cf. 36 (II. 16). 4 n.).

6 opus sit scire Cf. with Watt 117 (VI. 3). 8 *si quid forte sit quod opus sit sciri*; 132 (VII. 9). 2 *videbis igitur num quid fuerit in iis quod me scire opus sit*; 193 (X. 3) *si quid erit aliud quod scire opus sit*; *Q. Fr.* II. 10. 2 *si quid erit quod te scire opus sit.*

8 de auctoritate perscripta A senatorial decree vetoed by a Tribune might be recorded as an *auctoritas* (cf. 71 (III. 26) n. and Caelius, *Fam.* VIII. 8. 4 *senatus consultum quod tibi misi factum est auctoritatesque perscriptae,* 6 *si quis huic s.c. intercesserit, senatui placere auctoritatem perscribi*). Caesar, who had for a long time been advocating full citizenship for the Transpadanes (Suet. *Iul.* 8), had just founded Novum Comum as a Roman colony, but the Consul M. Marcellus refused to recognize it as such (cf. 104 (V. 11). 2 n.). The vetoed decree probably took the same line.

9 IIII viros The normal board of magistrates in a *municipium*: cf. 26 (II. 6). 1 n.

10 Pompeio C. was to meet him at Tarentum (98 (V. 5). 2).

96 (v. 3)

1, 2 tertio abs te die C. is thinking of the second letter. The first, dispatched on the 7th (§2), arrived on the fourth day.

3 litteras 95 (V. 2).

6 de his If this refers to the rumours or = *de his rebus*, then *quando* is incomprehensible. One cannot ask 'when' about unspecified reports or situations. Constans suggests that *quando* refers to the date proposed for Caesar's recall from Gaul, a matter raised in the Senate by M. Marcellus in April; but this seems impossibly obscure. Nor is *cogitare (de aliquo)* in the sense of *existimare* normal Ciceronian usage. The questions must surely be understood as relating to Atticus' forthcoming journey: cf. 196 (X. 5). 3 *tu de tuo itinere quid et quando cogites velim me certiorem facias*; 138 (VII. 14). 3 *tu ipse cum Sexto scire velim quid cogites de exeundo*; 167 (IX. 1). 4 *tu quid cogites de transeundo in Epirum scire sane velim.* None of the proposed corrections of *his* (*viis, villis, dis⟨cessu⟩, itinere*) convinces. Probably something has fallen out, as suggested in the apparatus.

2, 3 †publi mihi P. *Licini* remains the most plausible reconstruction. C. might well wish to consult the edict of so eminent a jurisconsult as P.

Licinius Crassus Mucianus, Pontifex Maximus and governor of Asia (131–130); and Atticus as an antiquary might well supply a copy. C. did consult that of Q. Mucius Scaevola, governor of Asia in 94 (? cf. 110 (v. 17). 5 n.), but Q. *Muci P. f.* (Purser) would hardly have produced the paradosis. *P. Lentuli* (Schiche) might, but one would think a copy of Lentulus Spinther's edict as governor of Cilicia in 56–54 would have been obtained from him direct.

3, 1 Lentulum Presumably Lentulus Spinther, apparently a common friend (cf. 115 (VI. 1). 23 *Lentulum. . .nostrum*). But I suspect that a less familiar name may be concealed, perhaps *lenium*, i.e. Atticus' friend M. Laenius (cf. 113 (v. 20). 8 n.), who was going to Cilicia (or already there) on business (114 (v. 21). 10). Atticus would naturally recommend him and wish C. to say that he had done so: cf. 104 (v. 11). 6 *apud Patronem. . .te in maxima gratia posui*.

Dionysius Cf. 82 (IV. 8*a*). 1 n. He accompanied his pupils, the young Ciceros, to Asia.

2 Nicanor Probably a slave lent by Atticus, perhaps for book-keeping or secretarial work (cf. 113 (v. 20). 9).

3 esse So W. S. Watt, *Mnem.* Ser. 4, 16 (1963), p. 364, comparing 87 (IV. 13). 1 *Romae a. d. XIII Kal. volumus esse*; *Fam.* XVI. 10. 1 *ego in Formiano a. d. III Kal. esse volo*. A dative, such as *cunctis* (Graevius: cf. 106 (v. 13). 1 *omnibusque satis faciemus*; 115 (VI. 1). 15 *satis facio adhuc omnibus*), is not required in the next sentence. Watt points to 34 (II. 14). 2 *satis fiet a nobis* and *Q. Fr.* II. 4. 1 *cumulatissime satis fecimus* (sc. *exspectationi hominum*).

97 (v 4)

1, 2 superioribus Cf. 96 (v. 3). 2. Atticus' letter just received at Beneventum was *written* before the two received at Trebula; to obviate misunderstanding C. adds *ad quas. . .Pontio*.

4 Funisulanus Two years later he is found again carrying a letter from Atticus to C., and owing money to the latter. A L. Funisulanus was eminent under the Flavian emperors.

5 scriba Tullius So 329 (XIII. 22). 4 *Tullium scribam* and *Fam.* V. 20. 1 *M. Tullius, scriba meus*. The usual assumption (cf. Mommsen, *St.* I, p. 346, n. 1) that he was a freedman of C.'s is wrong, the only evidence for it being *Fam.* V. 20 2 *a meo servo scriba*; but *servo = liberto* is incredible and should be expelled with Wesenberg. Freedmen were not usually referred to by their gentile names with cognomen, nor described by their patrons as *necessarii*; C. so describes this Tullius to Pompey in 161B (VIII. 11B). 4 (cf. *Div. in Caec.* 29 *Potamonem, scribam et familiarem tuum*). And it is not at all likely that a freedman would have been entrusted with the important task of arranging

C.'s accounts with his Quaestor and his Quaestor's cousin, as was Tullius in 50 (*Fam. l. c.*). Finally the appellation *scriba* proves that he was no ordinary *librarius*. C. calls the Senators who took down the Catilinarian depositions *scribae mei* (*Sull.* 44), and *scribae* are distinguished from *librarii* in *Leg. Agr.* II. 32. Note that the designation *scriba meus* occurs only in C.'s letter to his Quaestor (*Fam.* v. 20). The conclusion is obvious that Tullius was a *scriba quaestorius* seconded from the Treasury in the customary way to serve with C. during his Proconsulate. Such officials could be called the *scribae* of the governor himself or of his Quaestor (Mommsen, *St.* I, p. 348, n. 2: see also on 44 (II. 24). 2 (*C. Septimium*)). The proposed identification with M. Tullius Laurea (cf. Drumann–Groebe VI, p. 355) must therefore be abandoned.

6 mandato To resist any prorogation (95 (v. 2). 3).

7 ac †me...labat C. would hardly have written *ac de illo* (i.e. the choice of a third husband for Tullia), but something to this effect is needed —perhaps *ac de ⟨pus⟩illa* (cf. 90 (IV. 15). 4 fin.) or *ac de illo ⟨ἐνδομύχῳ⟩* (cf. 107 (V. 14). 3 *illud* ἐνδόμυχον; 114 (v. 21). 14 *de* ἐνδομύχῳ), with Kayser's *illuc quidem labor* (cf. 80 (IV 5). 2 *ne qua mihi liceret⟨re⟩labi ad illos*) to follow. Watt's ἀσμένιστὸν *illud quod laudas* would imply a degree of approval both on C.'s side and on Atticus' which the context does not support.

8 non quo— Something like *illud nimium placeat* is implied.

eo Probably that protégé (son ?) of Pontidia who appears as the younger Ser. Sulpicius' rival in 114 (v. 21). 14 and 115 (VI. 1). 10; not Dolabella, who is never mentioned in subsequent letters to Atticus until the announcement of his engagement to Tullia over a year later (121 (VI. 6). 1) and then in terms which do not suggest that Atticus had known of him for long as a probable choice. The credit for dispersing most of the fog in this and related passages belongs to J. H. Collins (*Cl. Journ.* 47 (1951), pp. 164 ff., 186).

illo altero He remains anonymous. He can hardly be the younger Servius (see below), for (*a*) *nam* suggests a fresh departure; (*b*) the objection to Servius was not that Tullia did not like him (at least the later references give no hint of this) but the difficulty of conducting negotiations in C.'s and Atticus' absence ; (*c*) if *eo* is Pontidia's man, a mere *eques* (115 (VI. 1). 10), there was on the face of it more than a little to choose between him and Servius.

11 †habebis mirationem The only classical occurrence of *miratio* is in *Div.* II. 49 *causarum enim ignoratio in re nova mirationem facit*, where *admirationem*, the normal term (cf. *Mur.* 69 *quid habet ista multitudo admirationis?* et sim.), could easily be substituted. Here however the sense is unsatisfactory. One would expect C. to object the difficulty of coming to an arrangement in his and Atticus' absence rather than the surprise it would cause. Watt suggests *res⟨haerebit⟩* (so Palmer). *habes meam rationem*, comparing 14 (v. 21). 13 *habes meam causam* and *Fam.* IX. 2. 4 *habes rationem mei consili*, where however lengthy expositions precede.

12 **Servilia** Born about 100. Her father was Q. Servilius Caepio, Livius Drusus' adversary in 91, her mother Drusus' sister Livia, who by a second marriage became the mother of Cato Uticensis. She had children by three husbands, M. Brutus by the first. On her relations with Caesar cf. 44 (II. 24). 3 *nocturnam deprecationem*. One of the great ladies of the period, she doubtless counted for something in politics, if not for so much as Münzer would have us believe (cf. *Cl. Quart.* N.S. 10 (1960), p. 267). She was on friendly terms with Atticus before and after her son's death (Nep. *Att.* 11. 4: cf. Introd. p. 7), presumably also with Servius' mother, Postumia (see below, and cf. 115 (VI. 1). 10).

13 **Servio** Ablative, as in *quid hoc homine facio?* cf. K.–S. 1, p. 321. Ser. Sulpicius Rufus the Younger, of patrician family on both sides (cf. 114 (v. 21). 9 n.), seems to have been old enough in 63 to join his father (now Consul) in prosecuting Murena (cf. Münzer, *RE.* IVA. 860 f.). Though nothing came of the matrimonial project C. remained on friendly terms with him (cf. *Fam.* XIII. 27. 4 (to his father) *ego cum tuo Servio iucundissime et coniunctissime vivo*). In March 49 he was serving in Caesar's army at Brundisium with his father's permission (cf. 187 (IX. 18). 2 n.), but whether he remained a Caesarian or accompanied his father to Greece is unrecorded. A republican after Caesar's death, he probably perished in the proscriptions.

si iam = *ut iam*, 'even supposing': cf. *Thes.* VII. 128. 1.

2, 1 **de Marcello** M. Claudius M. f. Marcellus, Consul this year with Sulpicius Rufus. C. Marcellus (cf. 75 (IV. 3). 5 n.), Cos. 50, was his cousin, another Gaius, Cos. 49, his brother. His political record was consistent: support for C. in 63 (*Catil.* I. 21; Plut. *Cic.* 15), steady though not fanatical opposition to Caesar before and during the Civil War down to Pharsalia (cf. *Cl. Quart.* N.S. 10 (1960), p. 253, n. 7; 162A (VIII. 12A). 4 n.), and dignified reluctance to solicit Caesar's pardon thereafter (*Fam.* IV. 7. 3). C. was on good terms with the whole family (*ibid.* XV. 11. 1), and Atticus wrote its history (cf. Introd. p. 9, n. 11). Four of C.'s letters to M. Marcellus remain and one from Marcellus himself, also the *pro Marcello* of 45. On his murder, which took place that year, cf. 318 (XIII. 10). 1 n.

2 **senatus consultum** Atticus had evidently made interest with the Consul to obtain a decree authorizing a grant to C. as Proconsul. This is now generally thought to have been a grant of troops, on the strength of *Fam.* III. 3. 1 of c. 24 May, where C. informs Ap. Pulcher of a proposal to authorize levies in Italy for himself and Bibulus and its frustration by

senatorial obstruction. But his words here are not to be so understood, for he assumes that even should the decree not pass Atticus will none the less 'put the matter through'. If it were a question of troops, Atticus could hardly be expected to manage this. With *attribui oportebit* (note the future) understand with Corradus *pecuniam publicam*: cf. *Thes.* II. 1163. 82. Even without a senatorial decree, C. implies, the Treasury could and should issue the money, which was no doubt to pay the existing forces (cf. 107 (v. 14). 1 fin.) or for other public purposes: cf. e.g. *Pis.* 86 *nonne sestertium centiens et octogiens. . .ex aerario tibi attributum Romae in quaestu reliquisti?* When C. wrote that the proposed grant would save public money he must have had in mind something practical and specific (we cannot say what), not a wiseacre generality ('si vis pacem, para bellum'). Watt, who prints his conjecture *populis* ('the provincial communities (of Cilicia and Syria)'), doubts whether C. would have used *populus* to connote the Roman state-treasury (*Mnem. l. c.* p. 365). But *vectigalia (pecunia) populi Romani* is a stock phrase in his speeches. On the other hand it may be doubted whether he would have used *populi* for *socii* without such help from the context as is forthcoming in 114 (v. 21). 8 and 116 (vi. 2). 5. Watt's point that the provincial communities would be better able to meet their financial obligations to the Romans if relieved of excessive expenditure for military purposes would apply only to the *populi liberi* of *Fam.* xv. 4. 3; as a reason for the Senate's authorizing additional troops who would have to be paid for directly from the Roman treasury it looks unimpressive.

3 tamen Even without a decree.

6 de Torquato Atticus will have duly passed on the compliment in 94 (v. 1). 5.

de Masone The Masones come into view early in the third century as a branch of the patrician gens Papiria. Later they appear to have sunk into the plebs (Münzer, *RE.* XVIII (3). 1064. 18). In 58 one M. Papirius, a distinguished *eques, publicanus,* and friend of Pompey, lost his life in a Clodian riot. His brother or cousin Aelius Ligus, though a follower of Clodius and though left out of Papirius' will, showed some disposition to avenge his death (*Dom.* 49). Putting the data together, Münzer (*ibid.* 1065. 13) plausibly suggests that the Maso mentioned here was the son of the murdered Knight, whose name was therefore M. Papirius Maso. His (and Ligus') business with C. is unknown.

Ligure Aelius Ligus, Tr. pl. 58, gets opprobrious notice in the speeches of 57–56 as an obscure partisan of Clodius; that he was an Aelius, claiming descent from P. Aelius Ligus, Cos. 172, is certain from *Sest.* 69 *qui cognomen sibi ex Aeliorum imaginibus adripuit* and 94 *Numerium, Serranum, Aelium, quisquilias seditionis Clodianae.* C. was sceptical of such claims by political opponents, as in the case of Servilius Rullus (*Leg. Agr.* II. 19) and perhaps P. Decius (*Phil.* XI. 13, though this may be merely facetious): cf. what he says of Atilius Serranus in *Sest.* 72. The association with Maso suggests that this is the same man. He may also be the *Ligurinus* Μῶμος of 113 (v. 20). 6; whereas the wealthy L. Ligus of 142 (VII. 18). 4 could be the *Ligus noster* with whom C. stayed at Fundi in 44 (360 (XIV. 6). 1). But it is all a long way from certain. There were Octavii Ligures as well as Aelii.

7 **cum venerint**   Sc. (probably) *Romam, rem conficies.*

Chaerippus   Cf. 77 (IV. 7). I n.

8 πρόσνευσιν **sustulisti**   To render 'since you have suppressed your own *penchant*' is unsatisfactory in the context and linguistically difficult. *sustulisti* should mean 'removed', i.e. 'taken out of the case, ruled out' (cf. Sen. *Ben.* II. 18. 7 *si necessitas tollet arbitrium*), not merely 'made no mention of'. I see two possibilities: (*a*) Atticus may have written 'no matter what your inclination (πρόσνευσις), you had better do what these fellows want'. If Ligus was indeed the Tribune of 57, C. might well have no πρόσνευσις in his direction. Such a metaphorical use of the word seems to be unique; elsewhere it occurs as an astronomical term. (*b*) πρόσνευσις may = κατάνευσις, 'consent': cf. ἀπάνευσις = ἀνάνευσις. L.-S.-J. quote from Plotinus, v. 1. 6 οὐ προσνεύσαντος οὐδὲ βουληθέντος where προσνεύσαντος should surely be rendered 'consent' ('annuente', Creuzer), not 'have an inclination or tendency'. Atticus might be said to have taken C.'s consent out of the question by committing him in advance. The linguistic evidence seems to favour (*b*).

10 **'consule!' aut 'numera!'**   By *'consule!'* members of the Senate demanded a discussion as opposed to a vote *per discessionem*, by *'numera (senatum)!'* a count to show the presence or absence of a quorum; the usual object being to block the passage of a decree (Fest. (Lindsay), p. 174; Mommsen, *St.* III, p. 984). C.'s meaning may be that Chaerippus must be conciliated so far as necessary to prevent his friends in the Senate obstructing the aforementioned decree. But it seems odd that he should be credited with so much influence. Alternatively the danger may have been that if Chaerippus' business was not taken care of it might come up in the Senate in association with C.'s and cause controversy which might lead to the obstruction of the latter. But the construction is doubtful. The traditional assumption that *ad senatum = in senatu* has, as Watt (*l.c.* p. 366) points out, no basis in usage (my suggestion on *Fam.* v. 8. 1 (*Philol.* 105 (1960), p. 75) must be withdrawn). *ad senatum* properly applies to non-members appearing before the house or otherwise present or just outside: cf. *Acad.* II. 137 *cum Carneades et Stoicus Diogenes ad senatum in Capitolio starent; Pis.* 28 *deprehensus denique cum ferro ad senatum is quem ad Cn. Pompeium interi-*

mendum collocatum fuisse constabat. But bystanders would hardly take such liberties. If the text is kept, *veniat* may be understood with *ne quid* and '*consule!*' *aut* '*numera!*' taken separately (cf. 130 (VII. 7). 7 *ad summam*, '*dic, M. Tulli*') as describing what was likely to ensue. Or we could read *ne*, ⟨*si*⟩ *quid ad senatum* (sc. *de me referetur*), '*consule!*' *aut* '*numera!*' (sc. *dicat aliquis*). Gronovius' *ne quis* does not help. Watt prints *ne quid ad* '*senatum consule!*' *aut* '*numera!*' (sc. *veniat*): ' "that no decree (touching my interests) should encounter obstruction" ' (*l.c.* p. 367), pointing out that 'the ellipse of a verb of motion is almost too common in the Letters to call for comment'. But *veniat* thus would be no ordinary verb of motion, and I do not think many readers will find this text easy to understand, particularly as *venire ad* = 'encounter, come up against' is unusual Latin.

de ceteris Sc. presumably *minus curo*. *ceteris* may be 'other persons (less influential than Chaerippus)' or, as I think more likely, 'the other items', i.e. such of Chaerippus' requests as did not involve the risk of trouble in the Senate.

11 **cum Scrofa** Sc. *egisti*. Cn. Tremellius Scrofa, of an old praetorian family (Varro, *R.R.* II. 4. 2), was Crassus' Quaestor in 71, Tribune in 69, a member of Caesar's agrarian board in 59, and therefore presumably Praetor some year in between. Like C. he was belatedly charged with a province, Crete and Cyrene, as appears from 115 (VI. 1). 13. A leading character in Varro's dialogue on agriculture, he knew more about the subject than any man living, if the author did not flatter (cf. *R.R.* I. 2. 10, II. 1. 2, 11). The business which Atticus had discussed with him is of course unknown.

13 **fuerint** *sint* or *futuri sint* would be regular, unless we translate 'need not have been' instead of 'need not be'; in that case the oratio recta would run *si...futurus est, minus urgendi fuerunt*. *sit* is a case of *attractio modi* (K.-S. II. p. 203).

M. Anneius et Tullius Legates. The first, like C.'s other two Legates Pomptinus and Q. Cicero, was an experienced soldier (*Fam.* XIII. 57. 1). L. Tullius appears from 104 (V. 11). 4 and 107 (V. 14). 2 to have been a friend of Atticus, but from 114 (V. 21). 5 to have owed his appointment to the recommendation of Q. Titinius. He could be the Caesarian *quaestorius* Tullius Rufus who was killed by his own men after Thapsus (*Bell. Afr.* 85. 7).

3, 1 de Sicinio A Pompeian *monetalis*, Q. Sicinius, struck coins in 49 (Münzer, *RE.* IIA. 2198), but there is nothing to connect him with C. T.-P. may be right in suggesting *Mescinio*.

2 **exceptio** In C.'s provincial edict: cf. the definition in *Thes.* V (ii). 1223. 55 '*clausula* formulae, legi sim. inserta, *per quam* aliquid vel aliquis

excipitur'. For illustration cf. *Leg. Agr.* I. 10; *Balb.* 32. The legal technicalities surrounding the term are not relevant here.

4 **quinque praefectis**   To be appointed by Pompey in each of his two Spanish provinces: cf. 100 (v. 7) *ait se Pompeius quinos praefectos delaturum novos vacationis iudiciariae causa. quinque* may be used carelessly for *quinis*, or perhaps C. did not realize that there were to be ten appointments in all. Magistrates appear to have been at liberty to nominate Prefects either with functions, usually military, assigned or simply in order to confer official status. A *praefectura* for a Knight (Senators were never appointed) thus corresponded to a *legatio* for a Senator, except that the latter was in theory a senatorial appointment (cf. Mommsen, *St.* III, p. 557). Presumably Atticus had candidates to recommend (cf. 104 (v. 11). 6 n.).

6 **exposuisti**   Cf. 94 (v. 1). 2 n.

8 **ut ne tecum agam amplius**   Cf. (with Watt) 20 (I. 20). 1 *ut...te hortari amplius non debeam*; 111 (v. 18). 2 *sed turpe est me pluribus verbis agere tecum. ut agam amplius* could mean 'to do more' (cf. Val. Max. I. 8. 8 *quid enim amplius agam si occidisse parum est?*), but not, as Watt apparently takes it, 'to go further'. The less said of other interpretations the better.

4, 2 **captio**   I.e. *fraus, damnum*; ordinarily a trick or quibble, especially in an agreement, or the loss resulting.

3 **aufer**   Cf. Hor. *Sat.* II. 3. 236 *aufer! | sume tibi decies, tibi tantundem.*

CC   Sc. *chartas*. Others understand *scapos* or *sestertios* with *ducentos*. But Constans observes that being short of space C. would naturally use figures.

parsimoniam   Cf. *Fam.* VII. 18. 2 *nam quod in palimpsesto, laudo equidem parsimoniam.*

4 **paginae**   Here inexactly but naturally for the writing on the page.

dum ades   Sternkopf compared 99 (v. 6). 2 *dum adesse putabo* and 104 (v. 11). 1 *dum ades*. But he should not have extruded *acta*: cf. 53 (III. 8). 3 n. *dumtaxat* (for *dum acta et*), *diu*, and *dudum* (cf. 80 (IV. 5). 1 n. (*iam dudum*)) are poor efforts.

5 **litteras...dabis**   Sc. *ut ad me ferant* (not 'you will write'). C. hoped that Pomptinus would join him at Brundisium (98 (v. 5). 1).

98 (v. 5)

1, 3 **iocandi**   Jokes being a recognized ingredient of letters: cf. 119 (VI. 5). 4; 128 (VII. 5). 5; *Fam.* II. 4. 1.

8 **diem**   The Kalends of June (97 (v. 4). 2).

2, 1 **διαλόγους de re publica**   Almost a *iocus*, with Plato, etc., in mind. Unfortunately this promise was not fulfilled (cf. 100 (v. 7)), no doubt because of uncertainty as to Atticus' whereabouts (cf. 99 (v. 6). 2).

2 **id ipsum** *ipsum* implies that the point arises out of what has just been said (cf. 76 (IV. 4) n.).

6 **illud** Perhaps add *de*, though the neuter with reference to a sum of money is common (K.–S. I, p. 62).

$\overline{XX}$ **et** $\overline{DCCC}$ Could = *milia viginti et octingenta*. But from 102 (V. 9). 2 *de* $\overline{XX}$ *et de* $\overline{DCCC}$ it seems likely that the 20,000 is a separate sum (perhaps interest, as Boot suggests).

7 **auctore te** Cf. 106 (V. 13). 3.

99 (V. 6)

From §1 it is clear that C. had already seen Pompey, probably on the day after his arrival at Tarentum, i.e. 19 May.

1, 3 **Pompeio** The respectful tone, quite free from irony, reflects the change that had come about in Pompey's political position: cf. 100 (V. 7) n. and contrast 85 (IV. 9). 1.

4 **ut. . .cottidie** This suggests daily visits. But from the next letter C. would seem to have stayed at Pompey's house.

100 (V. 7)

1 **vel potius in dies singulos** This amendment is hardly translatable. I do not think C. meant that *cottidie = in dies singulos* was *incorrect*, for he immediately uses it in just the same way. Expressions like *cottidie pluris facio, cottidie maiora praemia* are standard: cf. *Thes.* IV. 1092. 18. But it struck him as he wrote that *in dies singulos* would put his meaning more clearly, because *cottidie breviores litteras mitto* could be understood 'every day I write rather short letters' (or 'shorter than formerly').

4 **quinos praefectos** Cf. 97 (V. 4). 3 n.

6 **triduum** The natural implication is that C. had three clear days (19–21 May) at Tarentum: cf. *Fam.* III. 5. 5 *triduum illud quod ego Ephesi commoratus sum* (he was at Ephesus from 22–26 July: cf. 106 (V. 13). 1; 107 (V. 14). 1 introd. note) and L. W. Hunter, *Journ. Rom. Stud.* 3 (1913), p. 97. He arrived at Brundisium on 22 May (*Fam.* III. 3. 1). The distance between the two towns, 45 Roman miles, makes an exceptionally long day's travel. But as T.–P. point out, C. performed a like feat in 58 (51 (III. 6); 52 (III. 7). 1; see however Vol. II, Appendix I, p. 232). The going was flat, and there may have been no convenient stopping-place.

8 **egregium** So six weeks later to Caelius (*Fam.* II. 8. 2) *tantum habeto, civem egregium esse Pompeium et ad omnia quae providenda sunt in re publica et*

animo et consilio paratum...iam idem illi et boni et mali cives videntur qui nobis videri solent.

9 cum ut...tum ut Sjögren (*Comm. Tull.* p. 138) includes *cum ut...tum ubi sis* in the category of 51 (III. 6) *et ut...et* and the like. But this seems a particularly awkward case.

101 (v. 8)

1, 3 duodecimum Probably including the day of arrival: cf. 106 (v. 13). 1 n. (*sexagesimo*).

2, 1 vehementer With *velim*. The context decides in such cases: cf. on the one hand *Verr.* II. 1. 103 *his omnibus...me vehementer excusatum volo* and on the other 426 (XVI. 15). 2 *agi prorsus vehementer et severe volo*.

4 socius...in bonis Cf. *Fam.* XIII. 30. 1 *est hodie in bonis.* After Milo's condemnation and exile in 52 his property was sold for a fraction of its value as it was heavily encumbered by debts (Ascon. 54. 20). Philotimus was a purchaser; not, as Manutius and others, joint purchaser with C., for in that case Milo would have named C. himself (cf. also §3 *ne sit invito Milone in bonis*; if Milo's objection had been to Philotimus apart from C., the reasons offered by the latter would be irrelevant). He must have been acting as C.'s agent (cf. 118 (VI. 4). 3; 119 (VI. 5). 2; Caelius, *Fam.* VIII. 3. 2), perhaps in association with Duronius.

C. Duroni Otherwise unknown. The family was senatorial.

8 malus 'Sharp', cf. *malitia* (40 (XV. 26). 4 *nisi tua malitia adfuisset*), *homo minime malus* et sim. (*Thes.* VIII. 223. 39). Not 'evilly-disposed'; that would make *alienus* superfluous, unless we read *vel alienus*. The conjunction of *malus* and *alienus* is however rather odd; *alius* (sc. *praeter nos*) would be an easy change.

9 Faustae Twin sister of Faustus Sulla, married to Milo early in 52 after divorce by her previous husband, C. Memmius; her son by the latter, who appeared in court to supplicate the jury on behalf of Scaurus (Ascon. 28. 20), may have been still a boy. Her infidelities were notorious (see Münzer, *RE.* 1599. 52).

quod If *cui* (*quoi*) is read, *ratum esset* is impersonal (cf. *Dom.* 79 *de agris ratum est*); but *quod* is clearer.

3, 2 maiora Sc. *quam re vera sunt*: cf. *ad Brut.* 4. 6 *si quod amas eum eo maiora facis; Tusc.* III. 54 *usus docet minora esse ea quae sint visa maiora*; Symm. *Ep.* IV. 38 *longa obsequiorum eius faciet inspectio ut me iudices minora dixisse.*

5 nihil...tanti Cf. 20 (I. 20). 2 *nullam rem tanti aestimassem*; 354 (XIII. 42). 1 *nunc nihil mihi tanti est.* The vulgate *fuerat* (= *fuisset*: cf. K.–S. I, p. 173) is a needless change, the future (cf. *ibid.* p. 148) being as relevant as the past.

6 **leviora**   Sc. *quam scribuntur*: cf. 195 (x. 4). 6 *velim ea quae ad nos delata sint aut falsa esse aut minora*; Tac. *Ann.* III. 44. 4 *an compererat modica esse et vulgatis leviora.*

Camillum   C. Camillus is often mentioned in financial contexts from this point on; he was now probably acting as C.'s procurator in Rome. An expert on business law (*Fam.* v. 20. 3; cf. 310 (XIII. 6). 1) and a notable quidnunc (330 (XIII. 33*a*). 1), he was regarded by C. as a personal friend (*Fam. ibid.*, IX. 20. 2). His gentile name is unknown, but it seems highly improbable that he belonged to the patrician Furii. No Furius Camillus is on record after the fourth century until the cognomen reappeared under the principate, no doubt as an antiquarian revival like Cossus, Gracchus, etc.

7 **Caelium**   M. Caelius Rufus, C.'s friend and correspondent, also, as Tribune in 52, *studiosissimus Milonis* (Ascon. 36. 13). We happen to know that C. wrote to him about Milo's property (*Fam.* VIII. 3. 2), so this is one *asyndeton bimembre* which even Sjögren was willing to sacrifice.

Lamiam   L. Aelius Lamia, the first conspicuous member of a family whose nobility had become proverbial by Juvenal's time (Juv. IV. 154; cf. Hor. *Od.* III. 17. 1), was a hereditary friend of C.'s, *equestris ordinis princeps* (*Fam.* XI. 16. 2). Exiled by Gabinius in 58 for his activity in C.'s cause he subsequently entered the Senate, was Aedile in 45 (cf. 337 (XIV. 45). 1 n.), and a candidate, probably successful, for the Praetorship in 43. Caesar's letters of support to D. Brutus survive (*Fam.* XI. 16, 17).

9 **reque**   A noteworthy addition, especially in view of Asconius' information about the proceeds of Milo's sale (see above).

102 (v. 9)

1, 2 **Sybotis**   Probably the town of Sybota on the Thesprotian coast, opposite the little archipelago of the same name between Corcyra and the mainland.

muneribus   Cf. 125 (VII. 2). 3 *in Actio Corcyrae Alexio me opipare muneratus est*, also Val. Max. v. 1. 1 fin.

Araus...Eutychides   Of the former no more is known. Eutychides is Atticus' enfranchised slave mentioned in 89 (IV. 16). 9 and 90 (IV. 15). 1.

5 **commodissime...sed**   So Constans (and Moricca). *incommodissime ...et* is generally printed; but *et...decorum* then follows awkwardly upon *qui...navigassemus.* For the concessive force of the latter cf. K.–S. II, pp. 294 f.

6 **actuariis**   Rapid transport vessels, using sail and oar simultaneously (so Isid. *Etym.* XIX. 1. 24); but the term seems to have covered a variety of

203

types (cf. Luebeck, *RE*. i, 331). Elsewhere C. has the diminutive *actuariola* (202 (x. 11). 4; 413 (xvi. 3). 6; 414 (xvi. 6). 1).

9 **currentem**   *currentem hortari (incitare)* is a common saying: cf. Otto, *Sprichwörter*, pp. 102 f.

11 **extraordinarium**   Cf. 94 (v. 1), introd. note.

Parthus   After their victory at Carrhae the Parthians continued to menace Rome's eastern provinces. An incursion into Syria in 52 had been easily repulsed by the Proquaestor C. Cassius Longinus, but it was repeated this year on a larger scale: cf. 114 (v. 20). 3.

12 **praestabimus**   The future is used as in English, 'I'll guarantee'. So often in the Letters, as 271 (xii. 32). 2 *praestabo nec Bibulum nec Acidinum...* *maiores sumptus facturos*; Q. Fr. iii. 1. 3 *praestabo sumptum nusquam melius posse poni*; *Fam*. vi. 8. 1, vii. 17. 2, viii. 10. 5 (Caelius).

2, 2 **de** $\overline{\text{DCCC}}$ *de* is sometimes omitted, but cf. 98 (v. 5). 2 n.

4 **quoniam...rescripsisti**   *abes* and *aderis...rescripsisti* add up to a single idea (Greek would use μέν and δέ), 'you are now away, but will be back'. *recepisti* is needless. Atticus will have offered this reassurance in reply to 187 (v. 4). 1 *sed tua profectio spem meam debilitat*.

9 **intercaletur**   Intercalary months were inserted into the calendar at the discretion of the Pontifices (Marquardt, *Röm. Staatsverwaltung*, iii, pp. 285 f.).

103 (v. 10)

1, 1 **VII**   C. says he spent ten clear days (*decem ipsos dies*) in Athens and left on 6 July (cf. 104 (v. 11). 4 n.; *Fam*. ii. 8. 3). That gives 24 June as the day of his arrival and 27 June as the probable date of this letter.

3 **totus...tecum**   So Ter. *Eun*. 195 *me speres, me te oblectes, mecum tota sis*; Prop. iv. 8. 48 *Lanuvii ad portas (ei mihi!) totus (solus* codd.) *eram*.

crede mihi   Abnormal in C. for *mihi crede*. The six examples are all in letters, and all but one in letters to Atticus (cf. K.–S. ii, p. 616).

4 **vestigiis**   'Quia diu Atticus vixerat Athenis, multamque et iucundam sui memoriam reliquerat' (Manutius): cf. *Leg*. ii. 4 *movemur enim nescio quo pacto locis ipsis in quibus eorum quos diligimus aut admiramur adsunt vestigia*.

2, 2 **adhuc**   Usually taken with what follows.

3 **lege Iulia**   Passed by Caesar as Consul to restrain extortion in the provinces. Among other provisions it limited requisitioning by travelling officials to certain essentials (cf. 109 (v. 16). 3).

8 **perorata**   'Cicéron parle plaisamment de son activité de proconsul en des termes empruntés à son métier d'avocat' (Constans).

3, 3 **ἔρδοι τις**   ἣν ἕκαστος εἰδείη τέχνην (Aristoph. *Vesp*. 1431; cf.

Leutsch-Schneidewin, *Corp. Paroem. Gr.* II, p. 219). Cf. *Tusc.* I. 41 *bene enim illo Graecorum proverbio praecipitur 'quam quisque norit artem, in hac se exerceat'* (sim. Hor. *Ep.* I. 14. 44).

5 **plane scio** Cf. 116 (VI. 2). 7 *non plane. . .scio*; 180 (IX. 13). 3 *nec quam ob causam plane scio*; Plaut. *Truc.* 490 *qui vident, plane sciunt. sane scio* is not a common combination; I can only quote Symm. *Ep.* II. 11 *et sane scio litteras meas tibi haud longas ab urbe reddendas.* Tyrrell's *ne ego scio* is quite possible, though the supposed abbreviation *neĕscio* could hardly have been in the archetype.

6 **etiam** With *bellissime*; but perhaps read *et* or *et id.* Had it not been for *equidem* preceding C. might well have written *et quidem.* Watt explains as = *adhuc*, which would be awkward after *dices. . .restare* and hard to understand.

ut puto et volo Sjögren compares Caelius, *Fam.* VIII. 4. 2 *ut spero et volo.* The old reading *vultu* is an unnecessary conjecture, though it may easily be right: cf. 367B (XIV. 13B). 1 *ex vultu et oculis et fronte, ut aiunt*; *Fam.* I. 9. 17 *fronte atque vultu*; *Comm. Pet.* 44 *vultu ac fronte, quae est animi ianua* (cf. 90 (IV. 15). 7 n.).

bellissime Sjögren compares 92 (IV. 18). 2 *dices 'tu ergo haec quo modo fers?' belle mehercule et in eo me valde amo.* But the paradosis rather supports the superlative (see App. Crit.).

8 **et dicuntur et aguntur** 'A comitibus meis, ineptis hominibus' (Manutius). The credit for reviving *aguntur* belongs to Watt.

10 **δυσεκλάλητα** This remains by far the most satisfactory correction. Dionysius of Halicarnassus (*Lys.* 11) uses the compound in exactly the same way, πολλῶν καὶ καλῶν πραγμάτων δυσεκλαλήτων ἀπαιτῶν λόγον.

βαθύτητα Cf. 83 (IV. 6). 3 n.

4, 1 **ergo haec quoque** *ergo*, as Constans says, because Atticus would be able to judge for himself when C. returned. *quoque* alludes to the end of §2.

4 Milonis Since *Caesaris* certainly refers to what C. owed Caesar, this presumably refers to money he owed Milo, as purchaser of his property through Philotimus. There is no evidence that Milo's goods were forfeited to the state.

5 ne Roma quidem *sed* need not be added: cf. K.–S. II, p. 66. *ut sciremus. . .ageretur* refers to *ne Roma quidem*; any traveller from Rome would have brought news of *public* affairs. Further interference in this sentence is quite uncalled for.

5, 3 in nos *et* of previous editions is rightly discarded by Watt; the contrast between *amore* and *benevolentia* is more effective without it.

sed mutata multa *multa in* for *mult(a)e et*, printed by Watt (cf.

Mnem. l.c. pp. 367 ff.), is certainly an improvement on previous guesses, which do not bear repetition. But it seems to me likely that C. was thinking of the state of philosophy in general rather than of particular aspects, especially in view of his next remark.

4 si quid est, est This is really the paradosis (*quidem = quid ē*): cf. *de Orat.* II. 122 *si quid est in me. . .ex eo est quod* sqq.; 126 (VII. 3). 10 *nostrum quidem si est peccatum, in eo est quod* sqq. Watt's text *si quidem aestimes Aristo* is a verbal improvement on *si quidem est in Aristo* (Manutius), but I do not believe that C. so wrote of his *hospes et familiaris* (*Brut.* 332), particularly as slighting criticism of a friend of Brutus (see below) might have jarred upon his correspondent. ἀγροικία was not among his failings.

Aristo Aristus of Ascalon, brother of Antiochus (cf. 320 (XIII. 12). 3 n.) and his successor as head of the so-called Fifth Academy, was the friend and teacher of M. Brutus (Plut. *Brut.* 2). *Tusc.* v. 22 *nuper cum Athenis imperator apud eum deversarer* is generally supposed to refer to a second visit by C. paid on his way home from Cilicia, after the title of *imperator* had been conferred upon him by his army (cf. 113 (v. 20). 3 n.). But from 123 (VI. 9). 5 it would appear that C. did not lodge with Aristus on his return journey, so *imperator* in *Tusc.* v. 22 probably = *cum imperio ὤν*.

5 Xenonem Subsequent references suggest that he looked after Atticus' affairs in Athens. 104 (v. 11). 6 does not prove him an Epicurean.

8 ubi quoque tempore Cf. 102 (v. 9). 2 *ubi quoque tempore futurus sis . . .cura ut sciamus.*

104 (v. 11)

1, 1 totiensne. . .darem? An echo of Atticus' complaint. Such sentences are often printed as exclamations, but *ne* has its proper interrogative force, 'can it be that. . .?': cf. K.–S. I, p. 720.

2 frustra. . .dem Cf. 98 (v. 5). 2 *ne dem frustra*. P. T. Eden (*Mnem.* 4th Ser. 15 (1962), pp. 398 ff.) points out that the expression here is not entirely logical. But C. means 'I will rather send a letter and take the chance of it going astray than, etc.' *recte* does not imply 'a reliable messenger who will reach you', but simply 'a suitable messenger', who might however fail to deliver because he might be going the wrong way.

4 per fortunas 'In re misera modus obtestandi' (Manutius). The plural no doubt referred in origin to the double aspect (*virilis* and *muliebris*) under which Fortuna was worshipped: cf. O. J. Brendel, *Am. Journ. Arch.* 64 (1960), pp. 41 ff. Hence Bayet and Watt print with a capital. But C. did not know he was invoking the goddess, as appears from *Fam.* XIV. 1. 5 *per fortunas miseras nostras*; cf. 200A (x. 19A). 1 (Caelius) *per fortunas tuas, Cicero, per liberos te oro et obsecro.*

6 **quam vix. . .feram** Cf. *Sest.* 109 *leges. . .quae feruntur ita vix ut* sqq.

2, 1 **foede de Comensi** Almost the paradosis. Caesar had founded Novum Comum, probably as a Roman colony under the lex Vatinia (see How's note *ad loc.*). The Consul M. Marcellus, denying the validity of the law, had ordered a citizen of the place to be flogged, to show what he thought of its claim to the Roman franchise (Plut. *Caes.* 29; App. *B.C.* II. 26). The Transpadanes in general possessed the *ius Latii*, which admitted the four chief magistrates of a township to the full franchise. There seems to have been some doubt as to whether Marcellus' victim was an ex-magistrate (so Appian) or merely a decurion (ἕνα τῶν ἐκεῖ βουλευτῶν, Plutarch). The subjunctive *gesserit*, unwisely changed to *gesserat* (Pantagathus) in some editions, leaves that question open: cf. K.–S. II, p. 440. In the former case the Consul's action was illegal on any showing; in the latter, if not illegal (granting his objection to the lex Vatinia), it was still 'ugly', and likely to offend Pompey as well as Caesar. It would also have been illegal on a different ground if, as maintained by M. O. B. Caspari (*Cl. Quart.* 5 (1911), pp. 115 ff.), the bill of Livius Drusus in 122 which provided that Latin citizens should in all circumstances be exempt from flogging (Plut. *C. Gracch.* 9) had become law. But *foede* does not establish this; and if Roman and Latin rights *had* been the same in that respect, Marcellus would not have made his point.

3, 1 **Varronem** Still apparently in Rome; in 49 he is found governing part of Spain as one of Pompey's Legates.

4 **illud nusquam discedere** Usually printed with a comma after *illud*, perhaps rightly so: cf. 174 (IX. 7). 3 *video tibi placere illud, me* πολίτευμα *de pace suscipere*; Mart. VI. 59. 7 *quanto est humanius illud, | mense vel Augusto sumere gausapinas!* But cf. *Fin.* II. 9 *non delere. . .istud* et sim. (K.–S. I, p. 666). Atticus or Varro may have used the phrase. Of course *illum* may have been what C. wrote.

5 **auctoritas** Cf. 177 (IX. 10). 5 *quem. . .hominis prudentis et amici tali admonitu non moveret auctoritas?* et sim. But a note of irony is perceptible here.

4, 2 **Cn. Volusius** Possibly, as Corradus suggested, *Cn.* should be *Q.*: cf. 114 (V. 21). 6 n. But there is nothing to prove this, and the particularity with which Q. Volusius is introduced points the other way. At least one other contemporary Volusius (M.) is recorded (*Fam.* XVI. 12. 6; cf. Val. Max. VII. 3. 8).

3 **quaestor** L. Mescinius Rufus. C. did not think much of him in this capacity (117 (VI. 3). 1), and some difficulties arose between them in connexion with the provincial accounts; cf. *Fam.* V. 20. But as the other two

letters addressed to him (*ibid.* 19, 21) show, they remained on friendly terms.

unus Tullius Cf. 97 (v. 4). 2 n.

aphracta Undecked or partially undecked vessels without any protective screen for the upper rowers (θρανῖται).

5, 3 **causam** 'Case, situation'; cf. 224 (XI. 13). 4 n.

5 οἷαπερ ἡ δέσποινα τοία χἠ κύων; cf. Leutsch–Schneidewin, *Corp. Paroem. Gr.* II. p. 44. 'The manuscript evidence suggests that Cicero wrote, in violation of the metre, οἷα τᾶν [= τοι ἂν] δέσποινα'; so Watt, *l.c.* p. 369, and so in his text. But was C. likely to violate metre in a well-known saying?

8 **dulces** Cf. Hor. *Sat.* I. 4. 135 *sic dulcis amicis / occurram.*

10 †ανεζιαν ἀνεξίαν of O used to be understood as 'patience' (cf. ἀνέχω), but the context makes this impossible. C. says in effect that he can only keep it (whatever ανεζια stands for) up for a year; if he is forced to stay in office any longer than that he may 'prove a rascal', i.e. take to making money out of the provincials. Clearly it is not patience that keeps him (or indeed his staff) from doing so. The sense required is 'abstinence, incorruptibility', but the word remains doubtful, all the more so as it was evidently not in general use (*ut Siculi dicunt*). My suggestion ἀνιξίαν (cf. ἱξός = *avarus*, Aristoph. fr. 718) has been followed by Watt's ἀθιξίαν, neither being attested words. Not impossibly ἀν-εξία (cf. μειονεξία) meant 'abstinence' in Sicily. The late E. A. Barber communicated ἀφεξίαν. Add ἀ⟨πλεο⟩νεξίαν.

6, 1 **redeo** C. returns to the contents of Atticus' letter, from which the last two paragraphs digressed.

excusatio ne sit *excusatio* is usually taken as referring to exemptions from jury-service: cf. 100 (v. 7) *ait se Pompeius quinos praefectos delaturum novos vacationis iudiciariae causa.* Hence Watt by a combination of previous conjectures reads *nunc. . .mandasti. praefectos excusationis causa quos voles deferto.* But *causa* for *his* or *(h)iis* is not the slightest of changes. The reading in my text follows the MSS, with the addition of two letters which could very easily have fallen out. The sense is 'don't put off those who want you to get them the title'. In the case of Appuleius Atticus' recommendation had evidently been overlooked by C. He may therefore have written that in future he would excuse himself when such requests came his way. There need be no direct connexion with Pompey's Prefects referred to in 97 (v. 4). 3 and 100 (v. 7).

2 **iis quos voles deferto** Sc. *praefecturas.* This might seem to give Atticus *carte blanche.* But he had already been told (114 (v. 21). 10 *quod idem tibi ostenderam*) of C.'s resolution not to give the title to business men

operating in his own province. Brutus, through Atticus, was offered as many Prefectures as he liked under the same proviso (115 (VI. 1). 4).

μετέωρος Not 'high and mighty' but, as elsewhere in C., 'absent-minded, *distrait*': cf. 402 (XV. 14). 4; 410 (XVI. 5). 3.

3 **Appuleio** Possibly the *praediator* of 251 (XII. 14). 2.

Xenonem *Not*, apparently, one of the *barones*.

4 **Patronem** Successor of Phaedrus (cf. 342 (XIII. 39). 2 n.) as head of the Epicurean school at Athens, and an old friend and protégé of C.'s (cf. *Fam.* XIII. 1. 2). The matter at issue is explained in an extant letter to C. Memmius (*ibid.* 3), now an exile resident in Athens. He owned a site in the deme Melita (cf. 112 (v. 19). 3) which contained the ruins of the house where Epicurus had lived and which he had left to his friends (Diog. Laert. x. 17). Memmius had at one time proposed to build there himself and appears to have obtained authority from the Areopagus to do away with the remains. But Patro, with typical Epicurean *pietas*, wished to rescue them by getting the decree rescinded.

barones C. could never forgive the Epicureans for their professed ἀπαιδευσία: cf. *Pis.* 70; *Fin.* I. 26; *Nat. Deor.* I. 72 f. He is fond of sneering at their founder's alleged ignorance or stupidity (*Pis.* 69; *Acad.* II. 97; *Nat. Deor.* I. 85; *Div.* II. 103; *Tusc.* III. 50). If Atticus had taken his own Epicurea-nism seriously, 'blockheads' would have been a discourteous term to use of the principal members of the sect; but cf. Introd. p. 8, n. 5. In his *de Finibus* (II. 76) C. makes the Epicurean spokesman say ironically *nos barones*, and when he wrote *barones* in a letter to another Epicurean, Pansa (*Fr. Epp.* v. 4), it was probably in the same context. Cf. also *Fam.* IX. 26. 3.

5 **et hercule. . .feci** The irony here has been missed. C. cannot mean that Atticus' courtesy in informing Patro of C.'s interest in the case was really much of a service to himself. Rather he hints that Atticus had over-stated the case when he told Patro that he, C., 'had looked into the matter' (cf. 106 (v. 13). 2 *tua negotiola Ephesi curae mihi fuerunt*) 'in accordance with his, Patro's, letter' (sc. to Atticus; *ex illius litteris* goes with *curae fuisse*, not with *scripsisse*). In fact, as the next sentence shows, C. had done nothing about it until he arrived in Athens, and had then refused Patro's request that he should ask the Areopagus to revise its decree, merely agreeing to write to Memmius. Failing the latter's concurrence, which was doubtful, he evidently did not mean to go any further. *post ipsi Patroni* implies that Patro was less than satisfied at the time.

6 **is** *h* of *hister* may be due to *mihi* preceding, *ter* perhaps to an antici-patory *te* (cf. Müller, pp. x ff.). Editors prior to Watt intrude an Epicurean Hister, an odd name for a Greek. Obviously Atticus would be in touch with the head of the school on such a matter (cf. *Fam.* XIII. 1. 5). Watt reads *iste*

but the netural *is*, pointing to the person just named, seems preferable.

8 **vestro**   Cf. 16 (I. 16). 4 n. (*tui cives*).

ὑπομνηματισμόν   C. uses the same word to Memmius (*Fam.* xⅢ. 1. 5).

9 **Polycharmo praetore**   *praetor* = στρατηγός. Polycharmus became Archon later on (Dinsmore, *Archons of Athens*, pp. 280, 292).

10 **me**   Perhaps to be placed after *Patroni* (Pius; so Watt); but cf. Sjögren, *Eranos* 19 (1920), pp. 152 f.

15 **Patroni iratus**   Cf. *Fam.* xⅢ. 1. 4 *si qua offensiuncula facta est animi tui perversitate aliquorum.*

7, 3 ad Quintum   Since the letter was addressed to Quintus, C. would naturally say so; and *attuli* is at least as likely to have arisen from *ad Q. abstuli* as from simple *abstuli* (cf. 142 (vⅡ. 18). 1 *ad me pertulerunt | attulerunt*). Boot suggested *ad Tulliam* (for *attuli*), but we then have to assume that the letter got into the parcel by mistake. With respect to C.'s conduct in opening it editors compare his tampering with his brother's correspondence in 47 (220 (xⅠ. 9). 2), but on that occasion he was careful to explain how it occurred. However his admission in 118 (vⅠ. 3). 8 that he had advised Quintus junior to read letters addressed to his father is no less nonchalant. One is left wondering how the broken seals were explained or concealed.

Pilia's letter is generally supposed to have referred to Quintus' difficulties with Pomponia. If so, it seems odd that Atticus should be told without further explanation to give her a message of consolation from C.; and it would surely have been difficult for him to do this without mentioning the intercepted letter. The wording would be much more intelligible if Pilia required consolation on her own account, which is after all quite possible; for example she might have wished that her daughter, born about this time (cf. 112 (v. 19). 2), had been a son. But in that case συμπαθῶς should be ἐμπαθῶς, as Boot proposed on other and nugatory grounds.

5 **datas**   Cf. 312 (xⅢ. 5). 1 *videlicet* (sc. *Sp. Mummium) fratri fuisse* (sc. *legatum*). The accusative and infinitive construction after *videlicet* and *scilicet* is found in Varro, Sallust, and Lucretius as well as in Comedy: cf. K.–S. 1, p. 699.

6 †νομαηαρια me   An expression having to do with pressure of business would be in order (cf. Sen. *Ep.* 106. 1 *tardius rescribo ad epistulas tuas, non quia districtus occupationibus sum. hanc excusationem cave audias*), but nothing at all plausible has been suggested. Atticus may have quoted something à propos in his letter, in which case an author's name (*Menandri a me?*) may be concealed. Watt reads *aliam* (Schiche) *a me*, excluding NOMAHAPI as a 'dittography' of *nam aliam*.

105 (v. 12)

1, 3 Zostera Cape Zoster, half-way between Piraeus and Sunium. Smith (*Dict. of Gr. and Rom. Geogr.*, 1, p. 330 b) quotes from Leake: 'The hill of Zoster terminates in three capes; that in the middle is a low peninsula, which shelters in the west a deep inlet called *Vuliasméni.*'

5 citius quam vellemus Watt (*l.c.* p. 370) explains that C. had enjoyed his voyage and would have wished it prolonged. On the contrary C. means that a slower voyage (from Ceos onward), with no *saevus ventus* to speed it, would have been safer (cf. Ov. *A.A.* III. 584 *saepe perit ventis obruta cumba suis:* see also 122 (VI. 3). 4 n.) and less uncomfortable (cf. 414 (XVI. 6). 1 *magis commode quam strenue navigavi; remis enim magnam partem, prodromi nulli*).

6 iam nosti '*iam* 'means "moreover", not (as Tyrrell–Purser and others) "by this time" ' (Watt, *l.c.*). Cf. however 14 (I. 14). 4 *nosti iam in hac materia sonitus nostros;* 18 (I. 18). 6 *ceteros iam nosti; Cluent.* 109 *iam insolentiam noratis hominis; Rab. Post.* 36 *iam nostis insulsitatem Graecorum;* Ov. *Met.* 1. 605 *ut quae* / *deprensi totiens iam nosset furta mariti.* Not but that *nam* would be fully appropriate, since the remark explains why running before the gale was so disagreeable.

8 ἄκρα Γυρέων From Archilochus, fr. 56. 2 (Diehl) ἀμφὶ δ᾽ἄκρα Γυρέων ὀρθὸν ἵσταται νέφος, | σῆμα χειμῶνος. Γυραί or Γυρά was the highest peak in the mountains of Tenos, which closed the view from Delos to the north: see F. H. Sandbach, *Cl. Rev.* 56 (1942), pp. 63 ff.

2, 1 Messalla Messalla Rufus (Cos. 53) had been defended *de ambitu* by his uncle Hortensius and acquitted. The verdict was unpopular, and Hortensius was hissed in the theatre for the first time in his life (Caelius, *Fam.* VIII. 2. 1). Soon afterwards (*ibid.* VIII. 4. 1) Messalla was accused and convicted under the lex Licinia *de sodaliciis.*

autem...Hortensium On the readings see *Towards a Text,* p. 22 and Watt, *Cl. Rev.* N.S. 13 (1963), pp. 129 ff. *a te...audivi,* of news received from his correspondent's letter, would be contrary to C.'s usage, as Watt demonstrates. His supplement *et erat* is apt to the next sentence, and I therefore prefer it to my proposal *et ad ipsum ⟨et (id⟩ consilium nostrum) etiam ad Hortensium,* though I do not agree that the parenthesis would necessarily be without point. If in fact Atticus had suggested a letter to Messalla, C. might stress that the further letter to Hortensius was an idea of his own.

5 meos...libros *de Republica.*

6 †Thallumeto This strange name can scarcely be right; it may be identical with 'Halimetus' of 81 (IV. 12).

7 Helonius Unknown. *gravissimus* is used in two senses, 'responsible' (cf. *Rosc. Com.* 49 *quem hominem? levem? immo gravissimum*) and 'tedious'; possibly three, if Helonius was physically heavy. Cf. Ov. *Am.* III. 1. 35 '*quid gravibus verbis, animos a Tragoedia,' dixit/ 'me premis? an numquam non gravis esse potes?'*

9 **consules** I.e. *designatos*: cf. 11 (I. 2). 1 n.

3, 3 **plane rogo** As the text stands *sis* should be taken with *rogo*, since the independent second personal subjunctive for imperative is probably inadmissible (cf. Watt, *Hermes*, 92 (1964), pp. 406 f.). The bricks and the aqueduct must in that case be connected. But the sentence would read better with *et* to follow *plane rogo*.

de aqua Probably at Tusculum. Some years later C. wrote to Tiro about the possibility of bringing the Aqua Crabra there (*Fam.* XVI. 18. 3), but by that time the water supply was more than he needed (*etsi nunc quidem etiam nimium est aquae*).

4 **de aqua** Editors delete. But Atticus may have been fond of holding forth about the importance of a good water supply (n.b. *tuis sermonibus*). Possibly there is an implication that he was ὑδροπότης, which would suit his economical habits.

5 **tu id** There seems nothing to choose between this correction and Watt's deletion of *quid*, which he explains as an erroneous anticipation (*l.c.* p. 370).

6 **Philippus** Somehow concerned in the matter of the aqueduct (cf. 106 (V. 13). 3), possibly as C.'s *vilicus* or, as Watt thinks almost certain, as a contractor carrying out the work.

8 **in medio mari** Not that, as some have supposed, §§2 and 3 are a postscript written after the resumption of the voyage, but in contrast to *cum constitero* (for which cf. 165A (VIII. 15A). 1 *cum constiterit et timere desierit*; 177 (IX. 10). 7 *si salvus sit Pompeius et constiterit alicubi*; 107 (V. 14). 1 *ante quam aliquo loco consedero*). At Delos C. was in mid-Aegean: cf. *Man.* 55 *insula Delos, tam procul a nobis in Aegaeo mari posita*.

106 (V. 13)

C. spent three days at Ephesus (*Fam.* III. 5. 5), arriving on the 22nd and leaving on the 26th. This letter was written before dawn (see below, *de nocte*) on the day of his departure.

1, 1 **sexagesimo sqq.** Clodius was killed near Bovillae on 18 January 52 (Ascon. 31. 12); cf. 115 (VI. 1). 26 n. The addition of an intercalary month of 23 days (cf. Marquardt, *Röm. Staatsverwaltung*, III, p. 285) in 52 gives a total of 378 days. 199 days of the year 51 had elapsed up to and including 22 July. 199 + 378 − 17 = 560. C. includes both *termini* in his calculation.

7 **quid ad te attinet?** Reading *me* with the MSS scholars have regarded this as an imaginary quotation from Atticus (sc. *inquies*); cf. 13
(I. 13). 6 '*quid id ad me?*' *inquis* and 89 (IV. 16). 8 *dices '*quid mihi hoc monumentum
proderit?*' Shuckburgh and Constans are exceptions, but their interpretations
are rightly rejected by Watt (*l.c.* pp. 370 ff.), who explains: 'Cicero means:
"either you have heard (from other people) or if you haven't it is of no
importance to me that you should hear [Cicero affects to set little store by
such demonstrations] and you will therefore not hear from me." ' That
would be rather ungracious. C. might modestly suggest that Atticus could
not be expected to interest himself in such a trifle as his own reception in
Ephesus (which in fact delighted him, as he confesses in a subsequent letter
(113 (V. 20). 1)); but to say that he, C., did not care a jot whether Atticus
heard of it or not would savour more of arrogance than of modesty. But Watt
seems to be justified in objecting to the ordinary view that there is nothing
here to indicate a quotation. *inquies* is lacking in 188 (VIII. 9). 2 '*num igitur
peccamus?*' *minime vos quidem*, but there the context makes it unnecessary.

quasi ad se venissem Editors are content to add *quasi* only. But
C. *had* arrived *cum imperio*, though the governor of Asia (Q. Minucius
Thermus), who was in Ephesus at the time (cf. 113 (V. 20). 10; *Fam.* XIII. 55.
1, 57. 2), had *maius imperium*; cf. Rosenberg, *RE.* IX. 1209. 40. A further supplement therefore seems to be needed, and *ad se* makes the point that it was
not the Romans in Ephesus whom C. had come to govern. But ⟨*quasi aequo*⟩
or⟨*quasi maiore*⟩ *venissem cum imperio* might do as well. M. Antonius in 74 and
Pompey in 67 were given *imperium* equal to that of the local governors in all
coastal regions of the empire, Brutus and Cassius had *imperium infinitum
maius* (Rosenberg, *l.c.* 56; H. Last, *Journ. Rom. Stud.* 37 (1947), pp. 157 ff.).

8 **Ephesio** I.e. *Asiae*, somewhat as Ptolemy is called *rex Alexandrinus*.
I think C. used this unusual expression because he had in mind that the
'Greeks', unlike the *decumani*, were natives of the city. For *praetori* cf. 90
(IV. 15). 2.

10 **ostentationes** Of good will to *publicani* on the one hand and provincials on the other.

13 **pactiones** Between the tax-farmers and the provincial communities,
cf. *Fam.* XIII. 65. 1 *ut pactiones cum reliquis civitatibus conficiat.* As we learn in
that letter, C. did attempt to settle some outstanding agreements of this kind
for his friend Terentius Hispo, but the Ephesians, who were or represented
the other parties involved, would have none of his intervention.

sed hactenus So in 174 (IX. 7). 3 and 371 (XIV. 17). 2 (cf. 317 (XIII. 9).
1), if the MSS are to be trusted; but *haec* may easily have fallen out. On the
other hand there is no such doubt in Ov. *Her.* XVII (*Ep. Helenae*) 265
hactenus. arcanum furtivae conscia mentis | littera iam lasso pollice sistat opus.

213

14 **nuntiarit** Sjögren would explain *nuntiaret* as implying that the message was delivered as C. wrote ('cum cenabam, mihi nuntiabat'). It is true that C. wrote letters not only at his own but at other people's dinner-tables (cf. *Fam.* IX. 26. 1). But since Cestius was not leaving till dawn (see below) he would have had plenty of time to spare.

Cestius Perhaps the Knight C. Cestius, who seems to have been a tax-farmer in Asia in 62 (*Flacc.* 31).

de nocte Before daybreak: cf. 75 (IV. 3). 4 n. 'Cestius' ship would naturally leave at dawn to catch the morning breeze' (L. W. Hunter, *Journ. Rom. Stud.* 3 (1913), p. 77).

2, 1 Thermoque Q. Minucius Q. f. Thermus, Tribune and supporter of Cato in 62, now governor of Asia. The date of his Praetorship is uncertain. C. thought well of him as a governor (115 (VI. 1). 13), and wrote him a number of recommendatory letters in that capacity (*Fam.* XIII. 53–57). A Pompeian in the Civil War, he escaped proscription to join Sex. Pompeius and, subsequently, Antony.

3 **Philogenem** Freedman and agent of Atticus (113 (V. 20). 8).

Seium M. Seius, Knight, possibly son of a Curule Aedile. Primarily a man of business, scattered references show him to have been a supporter of Caesar; in 46 he is reckoned as one of the dominant clique (*Fam.* IX. 7. 1). Ap. Pulcher, Varro, and D. Brutus (cf. 249 (XII. 11) n.) were among his acquaintance. A noted producer of poultry, etc. (Varro, *R.R.* III *passim*; Plin. *N.H.* x. 52), he may possibly be the poet 'Sueius' (cf. Morel, *Fr. Poet. Rom.* p. 53). Of Xeno of Apollonia (in Lydia) nothing else is known.

tradidi. . .commendavi *tradidi* seems to imply personal introduction as opposed to recommendation in absence. The two terms are however often combined, as in *Fam.* VII. 17. 2.

5 **rationem. . .edidi** Cf. 108 (V. 15). 2. Philogenes will have been concerned in cashing the draft and arranging for its repayment: cf. 130 (VII. 7). 2 n.

3, 1 redeo So in 113 (V. 20). 8 *redeo ad urbana*, Rome and its doings being the centre of C.'s world from which his present activities as it were digressed.

3 **intercaletur** Cf. 102 (V. 9). 2 n.

4 **scrupulo** 'Worry', not 'hitch'. C. refers to the question of a husband for Tullia (cf. 97 (V. 4). 1 n.).

5 **quam** I.e. *qua de re*, a common type of attraction. *cuius* is generally read and understood as by T.-P., 'and on your suggestion I am eagerly desirous of this'—'this' being the repayment of Caesar's loan (cf. 94 (V. 1). 2; 97 (V. 4). 3). But the neuter comes awkwardly after *Caesare*, which looks like the antecedent and has actually been so taken. *quam* is better Latin and

palaeographically more likely to be the original of *cum*: cf. 31 (II. 10); 32 (II. 11). 1; 38 (II. 18). 3; 69 (III. 24). 1; 126 (VII. 3). 10; 223 (XI. 12). 1.

8 sed diligentissime Possibly to be taken with what follows. More probably *sed* = *et quidem*, a Plautine usage (see Sonnenschein on *Rud.* 799), no doubt colloquial, which reappears in Silver Latin. Cf. *Fam.* XIII. 43. 3 *velim. . .des litterarum aliquid quae tibi in provincia reddantur, sed ita conscribas ut tum cum eas leges facile recordari possis huius meae commendationis diligentiam.*

9 num quid. . .laboret Cf. 105 (V. 12). 2 *de ipsis iudiciis.* The wording is zeugmatic, since the state of *past* trials (or courts) could hardly be called unsatisfactory ('in trouble'). C. seems to mean 'tell me about the trials, both past and future, and whether the administration of justice is in a bad way'.

10 de aqua sqq. Cf. 105 (V. 12). 3 n. The former vulgate, *de aqua, si curae est, si quid Philippus aget, animadvertes* is implausible in form and content. Boot rewrote: *de aqua tibi curae esto* (*sit* in his first edition). *quid Philippus agat, animadvertes*; but the same result can be gained with less disturbance. Watt prints *eget* from Cratander's text, supposing that Atticus is asked to provide Philippus with necessary funds. This may be right, though I have the feeling that C. would have written *si quid opus erit* as in 154 (VIII. 6). 5 *ego autem Curium nostrum si quid opus esset rogaram* (which Watt cites).

107 (V. 14)

C. probably spent the night of the 26th at Magnesia, and wrote this letter after his arrival at Tralles next day. He could however have written *en route* (cf. §1 *iter conficiebamus*), *dedi* being the epistolary equivalent of *dabo*.

1, 6 ex ea die See Neue-Wagener, *Formenlehre*[3], I, pp. 1015 f. Cf. however 108 (V. 15). 1 *ex hoc die.*

παράπηγμα ἐνιαύσιον commoveto I.e. 'count my year of office from then and see that it is not extended': so 108 (V. 15). 1 *ex hoc die clavum anni movebis.* Constans notes that a fragment of a calendar of the type indicated, with movable pegs to mark the date, was discovered at Pozzuoli (*Notizie degli Scavi*, Ser. 6, 4 (1928), pp. 202 ff.).

2, 3 magno timore No need for *in*. Such ablatives are a feature of C.'s writing: cf. 115 (VI. 1). 23 *nec nulla nec magna spe sumus*; *Fam.* VI. 4. 4 *quanto fuerim dolore*, XII. 16. 3 *etiam si odio pari fuerit in eos*; *Planc.* 22 *nec minore nunc sunt sollicitudine quam tum erant studio*; *Sull.* 36 *essentne eadem voluntate.* See also on 29 (II. 9). 1 (*ulla esse invidia*).

3, 7 subtiliores Cf. 13 (I. 13). 4 *sed haec ad te scribam alias subtilius*; *ad Brut.* 23. 1 *subtilius ut explicem quae gerantur.*

108 (v. 15)

1, 1 clavum anni Cf. 107 (v. 14). 1 n.

4 campum. . .cursus Cf. *Mur.* 18 *nullum enim vobis sors campum dedit in quo excurrere virtus cognoscique posset*; *Phil.* XIV. 17 *magnus est in re publica campus. . .multis apertus cursus ad laudem*; *Thes.* III. 221. 17. Cf. also *Brut.* 332 *etsi cursum ingeni tui, Brute, premit haec importuna clades civitatis. cursus* fits the metaphor of *campum*; in Asia C.'s talents and energy are like stalled horses.

5 praeclara Not in self-praise. *opera* = *opera forensis*, a noble employment: cf. Plin. *Ep.* v. 9. 6 *rem pulcherrimam.*

6 A. Plotius A. Plotius or Plautius (cf. Münzer, *RE.* XXI. 7. 29) was Praetor, evidently Urbanus or Peregrinus, in 51. He can be identified with a Legate of Pompey's in 67–63, was Tribune in 56, Curule Aedile in 54 (as generally supposed; in 55 according to L. R. Taylor, *Athenaeum*, 42 (1964), pp. 12 ff.), and perhaps governor of Bithynia in 49–48 (cf. *Fam.* XIII. 29. 4). C. calls him *ornatissimo homini, familiari meo* in *Planc.* 17.

7 noster amicus Cf. 33 (II. 13). 2 *noster amicus Magnus*; 104 (v. 11). 2 *nostro*. Pompey commanding a large army from the neighbourhood of Rome is contrasted with C. commanding a small one in Cilicia.

8 lucem Cf. 52 (III. 7). 1 n.; *Fam.* II. 12. 2 *urbem, urbem, mi Rufe, cole et in ista luce vive.*

2, 3 permutavi Cf. 106 (v. 13). 2.

4 Appi I.e. *ab Appio imposita*: cf. 110 (v. 17). 6.

3, 3 Moeragene A local chieftain, who was duly extinguished (115 (VI. 1). 13). Apparently a runaway slave belonging to Atticus had taken refuge with him.

4 clitellae. . .onus Ribbeck, *Com. Rom. Fr.*[2], p. 122. Quintilian and Ammianus quote the proverb (cf. Otto, *Sprichwörter*, p. 57).

5 sit annus *sim. . .annuus* is supported by 106 (v. 13). 3 *ut simus annui* and 110 (v. 17). 5 *ut annui essemus*; *sit annuum* by §1, *sit modo annuum*. But this may be a third variant.

9 alias Cf. 13 (I. 13). 4 *sed haec ad te scribam alias subtilius*; 17 (I. 17). 10 *scribam alias. . .plura*; 20 (I. 20). 3 *aut scribam ad te alias*; *Fam.* II. 7. 3 *scribam ad te plura alias*, VII. 6. 2 *sed plura scribemus alias*, VII. 30. 2 *sed haec alias pluribus*, XII. 24. 2 *sed hac de re alias ad te pluribus.*

10 C. Andronico By his name a freedman or descendant of one.

12 magistros. . .portus Cf. 221 (XI. 10). 1 *operas in portu et scriptura Asiae pro magistro dedit.* The *magistri* of the companies would be in Rome.

dioecesium Cf. 94 (v. 1) introd. note. διοίκησις = *conventus*, an administrative and assize district called after its capital town; cf. D. Magie, *Roman Rule in Asia Minor*, pp. 1059 ff.

109 (v. 16)

The date assigned to this letter, written on the first day of C.'s journey from Synnada to Philomelium, depends on the time allowed for his stops in Apamea and Synnada. On this see below, also Appendix I.

1, 1 discedebant It would seem that the postmen on their way to Rome and C. bound for the east travelled together some distance from Synnada. On Constans' sketch map (Vol. IV) this looks natural enough: the road runs south from Synnada for about 15 miles till it joins the main route from Apamea to Philomelium. But according to W. M. Ramsay (*Historical Geography of Asia Minor*, pp. 23 and 330 (maps)) there were two roads from Synnada joining this route at different points about 50 miles apart (cf. Murray's Classical Atlas, Map 12 and Hunter, *l.c.* p. 83, n. 1). Why then did not the postmen take the western and C. the eastern? The difficulty disappears if we suppose that C. met the postmen coming from the opposite direction, but *discedebant* suggests that they had been in his company.

2 surripiendum C. had to sacrifice some progress by calling a halt on the road in order to write before the couriers left his party. Hunter (*l.c.* p. 84, n. 3) remarks that writing in a moving vehicle without springs would be quite impossible.

3 mandati tui Not to neglect an opportunity of sending a letter.

2, 1 et plane. . .provinciam An accidental senarius.

3 triduum Writing to Cato between four and five months later C. says that he spent two days (*biduum*) at Laodicea, four (*quadriduum*) at Apamea, and three (*triduum*) at Synnada (*Fam.* xv. 4. 2). About the same time he makes the same statement to Atticus (113 (v. 20). 1), except that *quinque dies* replaces *quadriduum*—not really a discrepancy since expressions like *quinque dies* (unless qualified by *ipsos*) can include the days of arrival and/or departure; similarly C. gives his stay at Philomelium as *triduum* in writing to Cato (*triduum Synnadis, totidem dies Philomeli*) but as *quinque dies* in his letter to Atticus. But *triduum* and *quadriduum* would normally mean three and four clear days, and C.'s two later statements that he spent four days in Apamea seem as likely to be an inaccuracy on his part as another way of expressing the period, which was in fact three clear days (see Hunter, *l.c.* p. 82). There remains the problem of *triduum Laodiceae*. We know from the preceding letter that C. arrived at Laodicea on 31 July and left on 3 August, so that *biduum* in the two later letters is correct. Hunter observes that 'he might well call a stay from 31 July to 3 August a three days' stay, if he arrived at Laodicea early enough on the 31st to open his *conventus* the same day': cf. 161B (VIII. 11B). 2 n. (*triduum*). Better perhaps to cut the knot with *biduum* for *triduum*. If the latter were sound would not C. have written *triduum Laodiceae, totidem dies Apameae, totidem Synnade*?

Laodiceae...Apameae...Synnade The chief towns of the three Phrygian dioceses attached to C.'s province. On the form *Synnas* cf. Ruge, *RE.* IVA. 1411. 2.

4 ἐπικεφάλια Poll-taxes. The form in -αιον seems to be either alternative or non-existent.

5 ὠνὰς omnium venditas The most recent explanation is Broughton's (*Am. Journ. Phil.* 57 (1936), p. 174): 'The phrase means that the local tax-contracts of all the cities have been let, and the gist of the complaint to Cicero was as follows: The cities told Cicero through their representatives that they could not pay the poll-taxes which the demands of Appius (*Fam.* III. 7. 2) had made necessary, and since the contracts for the revenues had been let no new revenues beyond the sums named in the contracts could be expected.' In support of ὠνὰς venditas thus interpreted he cites *inter alia* an Olbian inscription of c. 230 B.C. (Dittenberger, *Syll. Inscr. Gr.* 495, l. 50) τρὶς ἀναπραθείσης τῆς ὠνῆς. This seems nearer the mark linguistically than Mommsen's view that ὠναί were debts due from individuals in respect of taxes imposed by local magistrates in order to meet tributary obligations, such tax-debts being sold to a contractor in the event of non-payment (*Röm. Geschichte* II⁷ (Book IV. Ch. XI), p. 383 n.)—to say nothing of the hallucinations of T.-P. and others. But it quite fails to take account of the parallel passage in *Fam.* III. 8. 5 *ne in venditionem tributorum et illam acerbissimam exactionem, quam tu non ignoras, capitum atque ostiorum inducerentur sumptus minime necessarii.* There *venditio tributorum* is plainly not the ordinary process of tax-collection but something imposed on the communities either by the governor's orders or by the necessity to raise money to pay his exactions. I should therefore suppose that instead of raising their taxes in the usual way (whatever precisely that was) the communities were forced to let them to *publicani* for ready cash, perhaps for a year or more ahead.

3, 3 **lege Iulia** Cf. 103 (V. 10). 2 n.

4 **quattuor lectos** Three for the dining-room (*triclinium*) and one for the bedroom?

8 **ex oppidis omnibus** Cf. Liv. XXXVII. 54. 15 *illi agrum, hi vicos, hi oppida, hi portus...ut possideant*, also *Man.* 38; *Flacc.* 74; *Pis.* 51; *post Red.* 24. Editors used to prefer *ex domibus omnibus*, an absurd exaggeration which spoils the series (in ascending order of population) 'country, villages, towns', but better than *ex domibus ex omnibus* or Gurlitt's *ex domibus [omnibus]* (as though villages did not contain houses). '*nominibus* was originally *omnibus*, and was preceded by *oppidis*, which dropped out of the text because of homoeoarchon' (Watt, *l.c.* p. 372).

et omnes C. probably never began a sentence with *mehercule* (cf.

27 (II. 7). 3 n.). Hence Sjögren transferred *itaque* from below, but *itaque* is more easily disposed of by Watt's *cognita quae*.

4, 2 forum agit Appius had no business to do this with a successor known to be already in the province or on the point of arrival: cf. C.'s remonstrance in *Fam.* III. 6. 4.

silentium est Cf. 105 (v. 11). 4 *de Parthis erat silentium.* C. seems to mean that there was no talk of a Parthian invasion of Cilicia.

6 in castra At Philomelium. This was not the main camp of C.'s army, which was near Iconium in Lycaonia, but 'the temporary rendezvous of five cohorts without officers, who had mutinied and marched westwards, possibly to meet the governor and have the first word with him' (Hunter, *l.c.* p. 85; cf. *Fam.* XV. 4. 2).

7 bidui Writing the following day (110 (v. 17). 1) C. again says the camp was two days' journey away (*bidui*). But it is not necessary to change to *tridui* here or to suppose that C. was mistaken about the distance or that he later decided to add a stage to his journey. If he had already travelled half a day or more he could naturally speak of the remaining two and a half (or less) as two days rather than three.

110 (V. 17)

1, 3 sedens in raeda Probably just before setting off on the next day's journey (cf. Hunter, *l.c.* pp. 83 f.).

5 habebam Hardly = *habiturus eram*: this is to be distinguished from cases like 113 (v. 20). 5 *ipse me Laodiceam recipiebam,* where the epistolary imperfect stands for a present expressive of intention ('I am returning'). If the paradosis is retained it must imply that the couriers were, so to speak, in hand, i.e. the arrangements were already made: cf. 111 (v. 18). 3 *amicos consules habemus.* If so, they do not seem to have materialized, since the next extant letter was written nearly two months later.

2, 1 tamen The implication is 'though I am not going to write at length still I will say this much. . .'.

5 Lepta Q. Paconius Lepta of Cales (the *nomen gentile* and place of origin rest on Münzer's plausible deductions in *RE.* XII. 2071) was C.'s *praefectus fabrum* (*Fam.* III. 7. 4) in Cilicia and remained friendly and serviceable thereafter (*Fam.* IX. 13. 1 *nostri familiarissimi*).

3, 1 Deiotarus filius The elder Deiotarus, originally Tetrarch of the Tolistobogii, eventually absorbed almost all Galatia under his rule. He had been the friend and ally of a succession of Roman generals, notably Pompey, on whose side he fought at Pharsalus (cf. *Phil.* XI. 33 f.). Caesar, before whom C. defended him in 45, and later Antony continued to favour him, and a timely defection to the Triumvirs after the first battle of Philippi kept him on his throne until his death in 40, in extreme old age. His son of the same name, whose royal title had presumably been granted by the Senate as a favour to his father (cf. *Deiot.* 36), probably predeceased him.

4, 2 cura Tullia's betrothal.

5, 2 in Cumano Cf. 95 (v. 2). 1.

4 hunc locum muni Cf. 106 (v. 13). 3 *illud praefulci atque praemuni*; *Verr.* I. 43 *cui loco...consulite ac providete.*

6 Scaevolae The Pontifex. The date of his celebrated Asian Proconsulate (97 or 94?) is disputed: see Broughton, *Suppl.* p. 42.

6, 2 forum agit Cf. 109 (v. 16). 4.

5 quod...contumelia Cf. 115 (vi. 1). 2 *nihil enim a me fit cum ulla illius contumelia.*

6 Bruto Now Appius' son-in-law.

III (v. 18)

The date is established by the next letter (§1). Over a month had elapsed since C.'s arrival at Philomelium on 16 August. Somehow he managed to pacify the mutinous cohorts there (see 109 (v. 16). 4 n.), and sent them ahead with his Legate M. Anneius to rejoin their comrades in Iconium (*Fam.* xv. 4. 2). He himself set out on the 20th after holding his usual three-day *conventus* in Philomelium, and reached Iconium on the 23rd (cf. 113 (v. 20). 1 n.), there to hold another *conventus* and to review his army (on the 28th: *ibid.*). At the beginning of September, with reports of a Parthian invasion of Syria coming in (cf. 113 (v. 20). 2 n.), C. set off with his army eastwards, and on the 18th encamped at Cybistra in the south-western corner of Cappadocia, from where he could at once protect Cilicia proper, hold Cappadocia, and watch for any untoward movement among the neighbouring client princes (*Fam.* xv. 1. 6, 2. 2, 4. 4). There he probably remained till the 22nd (113 (v. 20). 2 n.; Hunter, *l.c.* pp. 90 ff.). While at Cybistra he received a visit from the young ruler of Cappadocia (from 52–42), Ariobarzanes III, to whom he brought the Senate's recognition (*Fam.* II. 17. 7) and gave support against a conspiracy which came to light during his stay (113 (v. 20). 6; *Fam.* xv. 2. 4 ff., 4. 6).

1, 5 Pacoro, Orodis...filio Arsaces XIII Orodes reigned from 57 to 37 B.C. According to Dio (XL. 28. 3) his son Pacorus was only nominally in command of the invading forces, Osaces (cf. 113 (v. 20). 3) being the real general. Justin (XLII. 4. 5) says that Pacorus was recalled on suspicion of disloyalty, but if so he was back in command by February 51 (114 (v. 21). 2; cf. Dio, XL. 29. 3). He became co-ruler with his father and died in battle with Ventidius in 38.

cunctis fere copiis *cum* (Baiter) is not needed: cf. K.–S. I, pp. 407 f.

6 **Cassius** C. Cassius Longinus (the tyrannicide) had served as Crassus' Quaestor in 53, and after retreating from Carrhae with the remnant of the Roman army had organized the defence of Syria. As Proquaestor in 52 he drove back an invading force without difficulty, and scored a brilliant success (unfairly depreciated by C. in 114 (V. 21). 2 and 115 (VI. 1). 14) against the renewed attempt this year, pursuing and defeating the enemy as they withdrew from Antioch (113 (V. 20). 3). His later fortunes are familiar. C. had long been on good terms with him (cf. *Fam.* XV. 14. 2 of October 51 *te, quem iam diu plurimi facio*), and wrote him fifteen extant letters; four of his to C. also survive (*Fam.* XII. 1–13, XV. 14–19).

7 **Antiochia est** = -*ia ē*. The appositional genitive could hardly stand in C.; cf. K.–S. I, p. 419. *portum Caietae* in *Man.* 33 may be a standard name (cf. *Thes.* Suppl. I. 60. 62) or may correspond to *Verr.* II. 5. 95 *Syracusarum moenia ac portus*. Sulpicius Rufus however has *in nobilissimo orbi terrarum gymnasio Academiae* (*Fam.* IV. 12. 3).

10 **putesne reddendas** The letter *was* read to the Senate, probably on 5 December (114 (V. 21). 2 n.), and is extant (*Fam.* XV. 1). It was natural that governors of remote provinces should leave it to friends on the spot to decide whether official letters written long previously ought to be read without change on their arrival, and Roman practice appears to have sanctioned this procedure. Thus in 43 Plancus, D. Brutus, and Cassius submitted such letters to C. (*Fam.* X. 12. 2, XI. 19. 1, XII. 12. 1; cf. *ibid.* III. 3. 2 and *ad Brut.* 5. 3). In *Pis.* 39 C. suggests that Piso's friends suppressed a laurelled dispatch from him when governor of Macedonia.

12 **inter caesa et porrecta** Sc. *exta*: cf. Varro, *L.L.* VI. 16 *inter cuius exta caesa et proiecta*, 31 *medio tempore inter hostiam caesam et exta proiecta*. From Varro and Macrobius (*Sat.* I. 16. 3) it appears that on certain days, called *intercisi*, business could be transacted between the slaughter of a victim in the morning and the offering of the entrails in the evening. The proverbial application here can only be made out from the context. Various explanations have been proposed: 'at the wrong time', 'at the last moment', 'verebatur ne, quo tempore discessurus esset, eo tempore eiusmodi quid accideret ne posset discedere'. None of these quite fits, because the dreaded prorogation had always been on the cards, even apart from any awkward development, and would be objectionable at any time (C. had served less than three of his twelve months). The idea seems rather to be simply of a 'danger period', in which what is feared may occur.

2, 2 **stamus** I.e. *firmi sumus* (*stas animo?* in Hor. *Sat.* II. 3. 213 means 'are you of sound mind?'). T.–P. remark on 'the different views Cicero expresses as to his military situation in this section and in §1'. But there is no real conflict. He does not want to be responsible for what may happen next year.

For the present his best resource is the approaching winter, but he feels fairly confident of his ability to defend himself until it comes. After that he hopes that Pompey, or at any rate somebody, may be sent out to cope with the Parthians as generalissimo.

3 speramus   Sc. *nos stare*.

4 a frumento   Lit. 'from the side of' (i.e 'on the score of') 'corn'.

5 expedito ad mutandum loco   The position could easily be changed if that seemed desirable, i.e. the routes leading from the camp were easy to travel in a hurry. Watt prefers *ad dimicandum* (Koch).

6 Deiotari   Cf. 110 (V. 17). 3 n.

7 sociis. . .usus est   The apparent contradiction to the words of the previous paragraph, *inopia sociorum, praesertim fidelium*, seems not to have been noticed, much less explained. It is apparent only. In §1 *sociorum* refers to non-subject allies like Deiotarus. Here, as the following words show, *sociis* refers to the provincials.

9 nostra et   Sjögren (*Comm. Tull.* p. 138) defends the paradosis *et nostra*. There is no security on such points.

3, 5 consules   In the coming year (L. Aemilius Paulus and C. Claudius Marcellus).

6 Furnium   Cf. 95 (V. 2). 1 n.

4, 4 et ut. . .et   Cf. 51 (III. 6) n.

5 rem   Money lent by Brutus to King Ariobarzanes: cf. 115 (VI. 1). 3 n. The Senate had placed the latter under C.'s protection (*Fam.* XV. 2. 4); hence, facetiously, *pupillum*: cf. 115 (VI. 1). 4 *tutela cogito me abdicare*.

6 exhibeo   I.e. *in iudicio sisto* (*Thes.* V (ii). 1418. 51).

7 negotia   Cf. 12 (I. 12). 1 n.

8 tibi quidem   Cf. 167 (IX. 1). 3 *in conviviis, tempestivis quidem*; *Acad.* II. 76 *quid inventum sit, paulo post videro, te ipso quidem iudice. et* or *ac tibi quidem* would be more usual (cf. 175 (IX. 8). 1 *cenantibus III Id. nobis, ac noctu quidem*; *Tusc.* IV. 3 *philosophi sumus exorti, et auctore quidem nostro Platone* et sim.).

112 (V. 19)

Written shortly after the last, perhaps the following morning. Both letters were probably dispatched on 21 September, along with *Fam.* XV. 1 and 2, official letters to the Magistrates and Senate (cf. 115 (VI. 1). 1 n.).

1, 3 Apellae   Freedman (*Fam.* VII. 25. 2) of C.'s friend M. Fabius Gallus (cf. 162 (VIII. 12). 1 n.), who was in the East at this time—perhaps he had just arrived from Syria to join C. (cf. *Fam.* XV. 14. 1). Presumably Apella had been left in charge of his affairs in Rome.

septimo quadragesimo die   Apella then dispatched his courier on 3 August. As Hunter (*l.c.* p. 91) says, this was good time, better than others recorded: 'In *Att*. VI, 2 [116], 6, written at the beginning of May, 50 from Laodicea, Cicero mentions that he has the Urban Gazette up till the nones of March: this means a journey of not over 60 days, even supposing it was sent off at once. A letter of Atticus from Epirus written on 29 Dec. reached Cicero at Laodicea on 19 Feb., 48 days' journey in winter; but a double journey to Epirus from Cybistra and back to Laodicea took from 21 Sept. to 19 Feb. (*Att*. VI, 1 [115], 1, 22).'

4 **tam longe** Sc. *veniens*: cf. 95 (v. 2). 2 *cum Hortensius veniret et infirmus et tam longe*; Sen. *Ep*. 106. 2 *tam longe venientem*.

5 **et** Preferable, I think, to *tu*, even though R's authority is of small account. *et* brings out the relationship between the clauses—on the one hand Atticus will not have left Rome until Pompey's return, on the other he *will* have left by now.

6 **Arimino** Caelius writes on 1 August (*Fam*. VIII. 4. 4) *nam Ariminum ad exercitum Pompeius erat iturus et statim iit*.

magisque vereor As generally understood C. means that Atticus' letter made him take an even gloomier view than before of the political outlook. If that were the sense he would surely have written *magisque etiam* for clarity, and even then it would not have been very happily expressed—it would be odd for C. to imply that even before reading the letter he had been uneasy about Atticus' peace of mind in Epirus. I think his drift is that he does not now have to worry about whether Atticus is still in Rome or not (cf. the opening of the previous letter), but rather whether, now that he is on holiday, he is not as burdened with anxiety over the political future (if that, and not some local distraction is what *sollicitus* implies) as C. himself with the cares of his Proconsulate.

9 **Atiliano nomine** Atilius owed C. money, apparently for some property he had purchased (cf. 94 (v. 1). 2 n.). The day for settlement having arrived, he was unable to meet his obligations. C.'s next step as creditor would normally be to call on Atilius' sureties; but in the present case he did not propose to do so, at least so far as Messalla was concerned, no doubt because of the latter's recent condemnation (cf. 105 (v. 12). 2 n.).

2, 3 **iam Romae** Atticus' daughter was probably born after or shortly before C. set out for the East, since he had never seen her. The birth may have taken place somewhere outside Rome, but Atticus had written that the child was now at his town house and giving him pleasure. True, by the time C. replied Atticus had, as he supposed, already left for Epirus; but he had Atticus' letter in mind, and may be repeating Atticus' actual words. If the text were clearly corrupt, the preference among many conjectures ought probably to go to the one adopted by Watt, *tam ⟨ca⟩ram ac iucundam* (Koch).

4 etiam atque etiam vale   See on 113 (v. 20). 9.

3, 1 de Patrone sqq.   A postscript. On the matter of Epicurus' house see 104 (v. 11). 6 n.

    Melita   A deme, west of Athens.

    3 eum qui...certaret   M. Calidius. See Appendix II.

    6 τὸ νεμεσᾶν interest τοῦ φθονεῖν   On the construction cf. 14 (I. 14). 4 n. (*auditori*). Aristotle (*Rhet.* II. 9) draws this distinction, defining τὸ νεμεσᾶν as τὸ λυπεῖσθαι ἐπὶ ταῖς ἀναξίαις εὐπραγίαις, which he considers to be characteristic of a good nature (ἤθους χρηστοῦ). C. did not wish Calidius ill out of malice, but because he thought the man 'ought' to be taken down.

113 (v. 20)

C.'s stay at Cybistra was abbreviated by news that the Parthians were outside Antioch (*Fam.* xv. 4. 7). He therefore moved south to protect Cilicia, reaching Tarsus on 5 October. What followed he describes in this letter (§§3 ff.), written on 19 December (§5) from the captured mountain stronghold of Pindenissum (not Pindenissus: the gender is determined by 115 (VI. 1). 9 and *Fam.* xv. 4. 10). It was dispatched by Atticus' *tabellarii*, who had arrived three days previously (§8).

    1, 1 Saturnalibus   I.e. on the first day of the festival, 17 December.

    septimo...die   *quinquagesimo* is confirmed by *Fam.* xv. 4. 10. The siege of Pindenissum therefore began on 12 October.

    3 quid, malum? isti...sunt?   Editors read *qui malum! isti...sunt?* But cf. Plaut. *Amph.* 403 *quid, malum? non sum ego servos Amphitruonis Sosia?*; *Pseud.* 1165 *quid, malum? id totum tuom est.*

    6 nunc   The vulgate *nec hoc exercitu ⟨nec⟩ hic* entails the awkward necessity of understanding 'my exploits' from the context as antecedent to *quae*, which the reader would naturally take with *negotia*. Furthermore the emphatic *hoc iam sic habeto* ought to introduce something less feeble. The point which C. would wish to put as forcibly as possible is that his achievements, both political and military, fully matched his opportunities, limited as these were. *tanta* (sc. *quanta gessi*) = 'so big (and no bigger)'.

    7 proximis litteris   Received three days previously; see on §8. It was probably written in mid-October, certainly after 21 September; again see on §8 *Laeni*.

    8 Ephesum...nosti   Cf. 106 (v. 13). 1.

    10 oppidis   The ablative is to be distinguished from such examples as Caes. *B.G.* II. 3. 3 *oppidis recipere* (cf. K.–S. I, p. 353); 'towns' here stands for their inhabitants: cf. *Sest.* 131 *cunctae itinere toto urbes Italiae festos dies agere adventus mei videbantur.*

quae erant Variously changed or supplemented, the text may be defended with Lehmann as implying that there were few towns on C.'s route between Ephesus and Laodicea: cf. with Sjögren *Fam.* II. 11. 2 *eas* (sc. *pantheras*) *quae sunt*. There were in fact only three of any importance, Magnesia ad Maeandrum, Tralles, and Nysa. As for the imperfect, in Latin as in other languages a past tense can be used of something which exists in the present if it is connected with the past in the writer's mind: cf. 415 (XVI. 7). 1 *erat enim villa Valeri*; K.-S. I, p. 123.

11 **biduum** Cf. 109 (v. 16). 2 n.

12 **revellimus** 'Plucked out', like thorns from flesh.

13 **quod idem** *dein* in Δ seems to be dittography; Watt (*l.c.* p. 376) points out that this form is not used before a word beginning with a vowel. After *idem* M has a gap of seven letters in which Schiche proposed to insert *Colossis*; but 'apart from the difficulties of date this would create, it is unlikely that C. would hold another *conventus* at Colossae, as Laodicea was the chief town in the Lycus valley' (Hunter, *l.c.* p. 82, n. 1). There is also an argument *ex silentio* from 109 (v. 16), 2 and *Fam.* XV. 4. 2.

14 **Philomeli...Iconi** Philomelium was the centre of the Isaurian *conventus*, Iconium of the Lycaonian.

quinque dies Cf. 109 (v. 16). 2 n.

Iconi decem Apparent discrepancies in C.'s statements about his halt at Iconium, which had led editors to introduce two false dates at *Fam.* III. 6. 6 and XV. 4. 3, were reconciled by Hunter (*l.c.* pp. 80 f.). According to his reconstruction C. arrived there on 23 August, and joined the camp outside the town on the 24th. On the 28th he reviewed his army and struck camp on the 29th (*Fam.* III. 6. 6 *castra movi ab Iconio prid. Kal. Sept.*). After spending the night in the town he started for Cilicia the following day (*Fam.* XV. 4. 3); but shortly after midnight there arrived a slave from Ap. Pulcher, now on his return journey to Rome, giving notice that his master would be at Iconium before dawn (*Fam.* III. 7. 4). C. therefore turned back on 2 September to meet Appius (whether the meeting took place or not is doubtful: see Hunter, *l.c.* pp. 88 f.). On 3 September he left Iconium for good.

16 **gravius** Not 'dignified', but balancing *lenius*; mercy was tempered with justice: see on 116 (VI. 2). 5 *cetera iuris dictio nec imperita et clemens*.

2, 1 **VII Kal. Sept.** Cf. *Fam.* XV. 4. 3.

2 **cum...venirent** Cf. *Fam.* XV. 1. 2, 2. 1, 4. 4.

3 †**et ceris** Either of Watt's conjectures (*l.c.* pp. 376 f. See App. Crit.) may be right. For the first he compares *Fam.* XV. 2. 1. *cum...nuntiique et litterae de bello a Parthis in provinciam Syriam illato cottidie fere adferrentur.*

4 **et ut...et** Cf. 51 (III. 6). n.

5 **Artavasdes**   Son and co-regent of Tigranes (cf. 24 (II. 4). 2 n.), now sole king of Armenia. After Carrhae he forsook the Roman alliance and married his daughter to Pacorus. Later he returned to it, but was dethroned and led in triumph by Antony in 34. After Actium Cleopatra had him executed.

6 **dies quinque**   So in *Fam.* xv. 4. 6, but cf. *Fam.* xv. 2. 3 *tempus eius tridui quod in iis castris morabar*. According to Hunter's reckoning C. was at Cybistra from 18–22 August, so that as in §1 *quinque* includes the days of arrival and departure.

Cybistra Cappadociae   C. is anxious to make the geography as clear as he can. For the genitive Sjögren points to 125 (VII. 2). 3 *in Actio Corcyrae*, where however one Actium is distinguished from another. Livy uses such genitives freely simply to indicate locality, e.g. XXXVI. 13. 3 *Malloeam Perrhaebiae*, 20. 5 *Cenaeum Euboeae*, 21. 5 *Patras Achaiae*. Pliny has *Claudiopolim Cappadociae* (*N.H.* v. 85).

3, 3 **sempiternorum**   Cilicia had been a Roman province for less than half a century. Perhaps C. had vaguely in mind the mountaineers' resistance to previous governments; cf. *Fam.* xv. 4. 10 *qui ne regibus quidem umquam paruissent.*

hic. . .appellati sumus   In his letter to Cato (*Fam.* xv. 4. 8 f.) C. gives further details of this operation. From his camp at Epiphanea, a day's march from the Amanus, his army had marched rapidly through the night of 12–13 October and as day was beginning to break ascended the mountains in three detachments, commanded severally by himself and his brother, by Pomptinus, and by the other two Legates, Anneius and Tullius. There was little opposition except in Pomptinus' area, where the principal place, 'more of a city than a village', along with two others named, put up a short resistance from dawn till afternoon. We gather that C. joined Pomptinus in time to complete the capture. A number of other forts were stormed and burned.

6 **imperatores**   By a custom dating back at least a century and a half Roman commanders called themselves by this title after a victory. In C.'s time the initiative was generally left to the troops on the battlefield or to the Senate (Mommsen, *St.* I, p. 124).

castra   *in radicibus Amani apud Aras Alexandri* (*Fam.* xv. 4. 9).

paucos dies. . .dies quinque   To Cato (*ibid.*) C. says *quadriduum*. Probably he spent five nights in the camp and five days in laying waste the surrounding district.

8 **haud paulo melior**   Cf. Hor. *Sat.* II. I. 29 *Lucili ritu, nostrum melioris utroque.*

11 τὰ κενὰ τοῦ πολέμου   A proverbial expression: cf. *Corp. Paroem. Gr.*

1, p. 300. Aristotle (*Nic. Eth.* III. 8. 6) explains that courage may be only a matter of experience; veteran soldiers are not taken in by appearances which alarm the tiro: δοκεῖ γὰρ εἶναι πολλὰ κενὰ (v.l. καινά) τοῦ πολέμου, ἃ μάλιστα συνεωράκασιν οὗτοι· φαίνονται δὴ ἀνδρεῖοι ὅτι οὐκ ἴσασιν οἱ ἄλλοι οἷά ἐστιν. Quintus Curtius (VII. 11. 25) provides an excellent illustration in his account of how the Sogdians defending Petra were shocked into surrender by the sudden apparition of a few Macedonian soldiers on the pinnacle of their rock-fortress, together with the sound of trumpets and shouting from the Macedonian camp: *ea res, sicut pleraque belli vana et inania, barbaros ad deditionem traxit; quippe occupati metu paucitatem eorum qui a tergo erant aestimare non poterant.* Similarly Tacitus speaks of the Gallic auxiliaries in Vitellius' army as *ingens numerus et prima statim defectione inter inania belli adsumptus (Hist.* II. 69)—these masses were of no value except *in terrorem.* In C.'s letter the report which (as he alleges) turned the tables in Syria was true in so far as his army had indeed approached the Syrian border; but it was κενός in that both Romans and Parthians reacted far more violently than the facts justified, supposing mistakenly that he intended to march further south. In a much disputed passage of Thucydides, III. 30. 4, I think the phrase τὸ κενὸν (v.l. καινὸν) τοῦ πολέμου refers to the factor of illusion in military events and operations, which affects morale either irrationally or at least out of due proportion (cf. 'psychological' (or 'nerve') 'warfare'). In the context this is closely related to the factor of surprise, but to read καινὸν (cf. C. P. Bill, *Cl. Phil.* 32 (1937), pp. 160 f.) or κοινὸν defies the later evidence.

12 **Antiochia tenebatur** Cf. K.-S. I, p. 352.

14 **Osaces** Cf. III (v. 18). 1 n. (*Pacoro*).

4, 1 appellatione Sc. *imperatoris.*

2 **loreolam...quaerere** I.e. to look for glory on easy terms. The saying, not found elsewhere, alludes of course to the victor's (or Triumphator's) laurel crown: cf. *Fam.* II. 10. 2 *tantum modo ut haberem negoti quod esset ad loreolam satis.* Cato the Elder's recipe for a wedding cake contains laurel bark (bark rather than leaves: *de virga lauri deradito, eodem addito),* and the cake was cooked on laurel leaves (*R.R.* 121).

3 **centurionemque primi pili** The senior Centurion of the legion (*primipilus*). He was the senior of the two Centurions of the *triarii* of the first cohort (*pili = manipuli*).

4 **nobilem sui generis** *nobilis* is sometimes used of gladiators (e.g. *Rosc. Am.* 17). For *generis* cf. *Verr.* II. 2. 174 *ab homine non nostri generis, non ex equestri loco profecto.* Presumably Asinius was distinguished not only by his rank but by personal qualities and reputation.

5 **Sex. Lucilium** His father may have been a *tribunicius* of the same

name who was thrown from the Tarpeian Rock by the Marians in 86 (Vell. II. 24. 2). If so, *filius* may mean stepson (so Münzer, *RE.* XIII. 1639. 48); but Gavius could have been his natural father and Lucilius adoptive. C.'s description of the former suggests a Knight, *splendidus* being an epithet he generally applies to Knights or provincials.

5, 2 omnium   C. may have written *omni*, as in *Har. Resp.* 37. He surely would have done so if he had meant 'as long as history records' (cf. *hostium sempiternorum* in §3). He would not have written *hominum* (Orelli: *omni hominum* might be possible). But if he wanted to say 'in living memory', *omnium*, i.e. all local people, would be natural here instead of the customary *nostra* or *hac*, which could not well be used in connexion with a place of which few Romans had ever heard.

3 cinximus sqq.   Cf. the parallel passages in letters to Caelius (*Fam.* II. 10. 2) and Cato (*Fam.* XV. 4. 10).

8 captivis   For variety's sake somewhat preferable to *mancipiis*. Horses (*equis*) appear in most texts down to 1870 and in some since. Wesenberg's two arguments to the contrary (*Emend. Cic. Epist.* p. 37) are of unequal weight. It is certainly unlikely that horses should have been found in any quantity at a mountain stronghold like Pindenissum. It might be possible, on the other hand, for C. to say that all the booty except the horses went to the soldiers and then to add that the captives were sold for the state, if he regarded the latter as apart from the booty: cf. Liv. VII. 27. 8 *praeda omnis militi data. extra praedam quattuor milia deditorum habita; eos vinctos consul ante currum triumphans egit; venditis deinde, magnam pecuniam in aerarium redegit.* But *equis* becomes even less plausible in the light of normal Roman practice. What this was appears from a series of passages in Livy of which XXIII. 37. 12 will serve as a specimen: *ex Hirpinis oppida tria, quae a populo Romano defecerant, vi recepta. . .supra quinque milia captivorum sub hasta venierunt; praeda alia militi concessa.* That is the usual pattern whenever a town or camp is taken by storm; the people are slaughtered, or kept in custody for a Triumph, or sold then and there. It is repeated with a few minor variations in Liv. IV. 34. 4, V. 21. 17, VI. 13. 6, VII. 27. 8, X. 31. 4, XXIV. 16. 5, XLIII. 19. 12, also Tac. *Ann.* XIII. 39. 7. One exception: after the battle of Sutrium in 310 the enemy's gold and silver were brought to the Consul (Liv. IX. 37. 10). Hannibal, after Cannae, it is true, reserved the Roman captives, horses, and silver (*id.* XXII. 52. 5).

9 cum haec scribebam   Sometimes taken with the previous sentence.

10 HS $\overline{\text{CXX}}$ '$\overline{|\text{CXX}|}$ veri similius quam $\overline{\text{CXX}}$' Watt. I disagree. Horace (*Ep.* II. 2. 5) quotes *HS* 8,000 as the price of a handsome, well-educated young slave born at Tibur or Gabii; these barbarians, sold off to dealers in the wilds, would fetch nothing like so much. And the auction may not have been in progress long. If 120,000 is thought too little, it would be better to emend to $\overline{XXI}$.

11 **dabam**   Epistolary for *do*, 'I am giving (intend to give)'.

6, 3 Ligurino Μώμῳ   Cf. 97 (V. 4). 2 n. Atticus' letter apparently referred to Ligus, perhaps in the same words. Editors print μώμῳ, though some at least have understood that C. is thinking of the god, not 'âpreté critique'.

4 **nec tamen**   Better than the vulgate *nec iam*. Atticus will have used the word *continentia* in his letter. Notwithstanding his demurrer, C. uses it himself in 116 (VI. 2). 4.

11 **Ariobarzanes sqq.**   Cf. 111 (V. 18), introd. note.

14 **abiectum**   In despair of getting his money back: cf. 111 (V. 18). 4 n. For the phrase cf. *Cluent*. 68 *promissis suis eum excitavit abiectum*; *Brut*. 13 *quasi iacentem excitavit*, et sim. No doubt C. had written to Brutus in encouraging terms.

7, 1 publice   To the Magistrates and Senate: cf. *Fam*. III. 9. 4. The letter does not survive.

3 **in eo positum**   This (or *in eo situm*) accounts for the lacuna better than simple *in eo*: cf. 266 (XII. 27). 1 *est enim totum positum in te*; 305 (XIII. 32). 1 *in eo enim totum est positum id quod cogitamus*; 152 (VII. 9). 4 *quo consilio, in temporibus situm est*. Similarly in 218 (XI. 7). 5 better *totum ⟨in eo est positum⟩* than *totum ⟨in eo est⟩* or *⟨in eo est⟩ totum*.

Kal. Mart.   The question of the consular provinces, involving Caesar's position in Gaul, was to be taken up on 1 March 50 in accordance with a decision taken by the Senate on 29 September (Caelius, *Fam*. VIII. 8. 5).

8, 1 redeo ad urbana   Cf. 106 (V. 13). 3 n.

diu ignorans   Caelius' letter *Fam*. VIII. 8, written at the beginning of October, could not have reached C. at Pindenissum much before the end of November. Probably he had not yet received it. His reference below to the Senate's decrees suggests that he got first news of them from Atticus. In *Fam*. VIII. 8. 10 Caelius implies that Curio had already been elected Tribune; but C.'s congratulatory letter to Curio (*Fam*. II. 6) was written about the same time as this to Atticus (cf. Constans, IV. p. 24).

2 **a.d. xv Kal. Ian.**   Recent editors keep the date *a.d. v* supposing that the last three paragraphs of the letter were added a week later, an untenable theory. It is improbable that C. would have written at all on the 19th if he had not been able to dispatch his letter, and even more improbable that he would have added a postscript to a letter already a week old without a word to explain what he was doing and why (contrast *Q. Fr*. III. 1. 17, 19, 23). *redeo ad urbana* implies continuity, and §§1–7, if written as a complete letter,

would not have lacked a reference to the absence of news from Rome (cf. *diu ignorans* above). That absence of news would also make it necessary to suppose that Atticus' letter to which C. replies in §6 and which he mentions in §1 (*proximis litteris*) had been received a long time previously. Could he have omitted to say when it arrived and why he had not answered sooner? In 115 (VI. 1). 9 C. refers to 113 (V. 20) as dispatched *a Pindenisso capto*.

3 Philogenes Cf. 106 (V. 13). 2 n.

4 Laeni Not C.'s friend M. Laenius Flaccus (cf. *Fam.* XIV. 4.2), but a friend of Atticus (115 (VI. 1). 6 *tuo Laenio*) on business in Cilicia. C. finally received the letter, which had been dispatched on 21 September, when he got back to Laodicea in February (114 (V. 21). 4).

6 quae tu speras Caelius too had been in hopes that Caesar was ready to submit (*Fam.* VIII. 8. 9).

incendio Plaetoriano The Plaetorius concerned could be C.'s friend M. Plaetorius Cestianus (cf. *Fam.* I. 8. 1; *Font.* 36), but this is by no means certain. Nor is anything known of his 'fire', though the word has suggested a judicial conviction: cf. *Brut.* 90 *isque* (sc. *Galba, a Catone accusatus*) *se tum eripuit flamma*; Liv. XXXIX. 6. 4 *ne. . .incendio alieni iudicii, quo L. Scipio damnatus erat, conflagraret* (also *id.* XXII. 35. 3, 40. 3; *Har. Resp.* 45, where the metaphor is much elaborated; Plin. *Ep.* III. 11. 3). But that he was condemned for extortion and that 'Seius, who shared the plunder, was tried on the charge *quo ea pecunia pervenerit*, and was compelled to pay part of the fine' is a commentator's fable. Quite possibly after all the fire was not metaphorical; it may have happened to the Plaetorius who is mentioned as a neighbour of Atticus' in 44 (394 (XV. 17). 1).

7 †Leius The former vulgate *Seius* has been left by Watt in the limbo to which I relegated it in *Philol.* 108 (1964), p. 106. Whatever the man's real name, he seems to have been no friend of C.'s, if *minus moleste fero* has its natural sense of 'I am less upset (than I should otherwise have been)', not 'I am not much upset'.

adustus Cf. Quint. *Decl.* XII. 5 *cum finitimas quoque civitates incendium nostrum* (sc. *fames*) *adussisset*. Even if C. had used *amburo* metaphorically in *Verr.* II. 1. 70 and *Har. Resp.* 4 (so, wrongly, *Thes.* I. 1878. 1), he could still have written *adustus* here.

8 Q. Cassio Q. Cassius Longinus was (probably) C. Cassius' cousin, and a friend of Atticus' (114 (V. 21). 2). He had been Pompey's Quaestor by special choice (120 (VI. 7). 4), but as Tribune in 49 fled with Antony to Caesar's camp. A discreditable and disastrous career as Caesarian Propraetor of Further Spain ended in 47 at the mouth of the Ebro, where he was drowned along with the plunder he was transporting to Rome. Nothing is known about the incident mentioned here, unless it may be deduced from

C.'s letter to C. Cassius (*Fam.* XV. 14. 4 *si quae sunt onera tuorum*) that Q. Cassius had been on trial.

9, 2 togam puram The *toga virilis*, without the purple border. Young Quintus' sixteenth birthday fell about this time (cf. 6 (I. 10). 5). The following remark shows that reports of his conduct in Galatia had not been satisfactory: cf. 115 (VI. 1). 12.

3 auxiliis 'Auxiliary troops', as in 119 (VI. 5). 3. Deiotarus had marched in person with his entire force, but while on the way had received word from C. telling him to return to Galatia (*Fam.* XV. 4. 7).

5 Epiroticas Atticus apparently did not go to Epirus in August, as planned (111 (V. 18). 1; 112 (V. 19). 1); he probably arrived there late in December (cf. 114 (V. 21). 1 n.).

6 oti Cf. 1 (I. 5). 4 n.

Nicanor Cf. 96 (V. 3). 3 n.

9 Alexis Atticus' secretary, called *imago Tironis* four years later (247 (XII. 10)).

11 meus...Alexis I.e. Alexis' counterpart Tiro, since his manumission (in April 53: cf. *Fam.* XVI. 14. 2) M. Tullius Tiro. I do not find it possible to believe with Groebe (*RE.* VIIA. 1319) on the authority of the Eusebian Chronicle that Tiro, called *adulescens* in 120 (VI. 7). 2 and 125 (VII. 2). 3, was now in his fifties. Alexis was hardly more than a boy (130 (VII. 7). 7).

ad te *ad* rather than *in* or *erga* because the idea of writing a letter is in mind.

Phemio A musical slave of Atticus' (cf. 89 (IV. 16). 7), named after the minstrel of Odysseus. His 'horn' was doubtless a kind of flute (Kroll, *RE.* XI. 262. 62). From 114 (V. 21). 9 it seems that the particular type needed came from Pamphylia (which however included Pisidia and Lycia).

13 etiam atque etiam vale Not 'good-bye, and yet again good-bye'. Nor does *etiam atque etiam* look back to the supposed division of the letter at §8. It looks back no further than the previous sentence, to *cura ut valeas*, as in *Fam.* XVI. 5. 2 *cura igitur nihil aliud nisi ut valeas; cetera ego curabo. etiam atque etiam vale* (cf. *ibid.* IX. 24. 3, XIV. 7. 3, XVI. 7. 9, 14. 2). In 112 (V. 19). 2 the same formula is used because that letter was written as a pendant to another just sealed (the latter does not actually contain a reference to health, but C. may have thought it did); and, as here, a postscript follows. On 412 (XVI. 2). 6 see *ad loc.*

10, 1 Thermo Cf. 106 (V. 13). 2 n.

4 Pammeni...puer A rhetor of this name, *vir longe eloquentissimus Graeciae*, is mentioned as Brutus' teacher in *Brut.* 332. He lived in Athens and the boy may have been his son or grandson. If C.'s memory is correct, the previous letter to which he refers is lost.

6 tum Cf. Ter. *Phorm.* 328 *quot me censes homines iam deverberasse usque ad necem,* | *hospites, tum civis?*; *Phil.* III. 7 *veteranorumque, fortissimorum virorum, tum legionis Martiae quartaeque mirabilis consensus.* Of course a preceding *cum* may easily have fallen out.

114 (v. 21)

After the capture of Pindenissum C. appears to have settled in Tarsus until 5 January (§7), when he left for Laodicea. He arrived there on 11 February (§4) and stayed till 7 May (116 (VI. 2). 6).

1, 1 ut scribis Not in the letter brought by Laenius' couriers (§4), which was written before Atticus went to Epirus (cf. 113 (v. 20). 8), nor in that received at Iconium (§4), but probably in the one referred to in §3 as *illa tua epistula quam dedisti nauseans Buthroto.* C. presumably got it at Laodicea, so it may have been written towards the end of December (cf. 112 (v. 19). 1 n.).

ex sententia Cf. *Acad.* II. 100 *se ex sententia navigaturum;* 88 (IV. 14). 2 *totoque itinere ⟨ feliciter ex⟩ sententiaque confecto.*

2 pernecessario Cf. 111 (v. 18). 3 *tempus est necessarium.*

2, 1 Cassius Perhaps the praenomen should be inserted; but with it there would be less reason for C. to have added *frater. . . tui.* Cf. 122 (VI. 8). 2.

Q. Cassi Cf. 113 (v. 20). 8 n.

pudentiores *prudentes litterae* is questionable Latin. C.'s depreciation of Cassius' achievement here can be contrasted with *Phil.* XI. 35 *magnas ille res gessit ante Bibuli, summi viri, adventum, cum Parthorum nobilissimos duces, maximas copias fudit Syriamque immani Parthorum impetu liberavit.*

4 recesserant Cf. 113 (v. 20). 3.

7 Orodi So in *Fam.* XV. 1. 2, but *Orodis* in v. 18 .1: cf. Neue–Wagener, *Formenlehre*[3], I, p. 511.

8 Artavasdis Cf. 113 (v. 20). 2 n.

10 victrices I.e. *laureatae*: cf. Ov. *Am.* I. 11. 25 *victrices lauro redimire tabellas.*

11 id est Non. Dec. C.'s dispatch (*Fam.* XV. 1) probably left Cybistra on 22 September (cf. 112 (v. 19), introd. note). Some editors read *datae Non. Oct.,* but the dispatch date of Cassius' letter would be of no particular interest. T.–P.'s statement that C. uses *hoc est* far more commonly than *id est* is not true.

3, 2 nullus honos. . .habeatur 'No consideration be paid to him' (i.e. to his demands): cf. *Font.* 15 *quibus neque propter iracundiam fidem neque propter infidelitatem honorem habere debetis.*

4 nos   I.e. *Bibulum et me*, as *tantis provinciis* shows.

6 quod. . .possit   The pressure might be so strong that even the veto of a friendly Tribune (Furnius is no doubt in view: cf. 95 (v. 2). 1 n.) would not stop the dreaded prorogation. The Senate had ways of dealing with recalcitrant Tribunes (cf. 130 (VII. 7). 5). How's statement that exercise of the veto was illegal in matters relating to consular provinces is erroneous; had that been so, Curio's activities this year would have been impossible and Furnius' good will of small account. *Prov. Cons.* 17, upon which this doctrine relies, only shows that the veto did not apply to the Senate's assignment of such provinces under the lex Sempronia in advance of the elections.

9 cogor; et velim ita sit   'Displicet illud *cogor*; nam quis hominem cogit sollicitudinem sibi ipsum struere? deinde illud *cogor* non bene coit cum sequentibus *et velim ita sit*' (Schütz). Watt (*l.c.* p. 377) finds this unanswerable and pronounces it no answer 'to misinterpret *cogor* as "non possum non facere" (J. F. Gronovius *ap.* Boot) or "kann ich anders?" (Wieland)'. The misinterpretation is not on Gronovius' side, for this is just what *cogor* does imply here, much as in 172 (IX. 6). 4 *sollicitus eram et angebar, sicut res scilicet ipsa cogebat* or 233 (XI. 19). 1 *cogis me sperare quod optandum vix est* (C. means that he cannot help hoping, though he knows well enough that he is hoping for the impossible). Quite often *cogere* denotes something considerably short of rigorous compulsion. I see nothing unnatural in the text, bearing in view that C. is writing a letter, not a logical exercise. He admits that he *is* 'manufacturing his own worry', i.e. that the dangers he has just been conjuring up may be unreal (cf. 167 (IX. 1). 1 *sed haec fortasse* κενόσπουδα *sunt*), but says that he is *driven* to do this (by the lack of up-to-date information which might prove his fears groundless). He adds, 'and I hope it *is* so', i.e. 'I hope I *am* worrying myself over nothing'. Lehmann's *ut* robs *cogor* of all point. Watt prints his own conjecture *struere cog⟨itati⟩one*, 'a more colourful equivalent of *fingere cogitatione* (cf. *T.L.L.* III, 1452, 52 ff.)'— but the added substantive is neither elegant nor helpful.

11 nauseans   Atticus had just landed. Since his crossing had been *ex sententia*, perhaps *nauseans* in his letter was not meant seriously; or it may have had nothing to do with the voyage (cf. 362 (XIV. 8). 2; 364 (XIV. 10). 2).

4, 1 acceperam. . .datas   The tense shows that this letter was received before the one from Buthrotrum, though it was probably dispatched before Atticus left Rome. If it reached C. at Iconium about the end of January, it will have started on its 'fairly rapid' progress about the beginning of December.

2 a Lentuli triumpho   Lentulus Spinther, governor of Cilicia from

56–53, must have had between two and three years to wait before he was allowed to celebrate his Triumph. The cause of the delay is unknown.

3 **illud** Anticipatory: cf. 118 (VI. 4). 1 n. The 'sweet' is *confirmas. . . fore*, the 'bitter' *si quid secus*. It is also possible (though not, I think, preferable) to punctuate with Watt ('monente E. Fraenkel') *in his* γλυκύπικρον *illud confirmas* sqq. Anyhow, the credit for seeing that punctuation is required belongs to Schütz.

6 **Laeni pueris** Cf. 113 (V. 20). 8.

7 **saepe** Perhaps three times.

10 **probabo** 'I'll prove the validity of. . .': cf. Ov. *Met.* III. 350 *exitus illam* (sc. *vocem*) / *resque probat*. Similarly *comprobare* in Caes. *B.G.* V. 58. 6 *comprobat hominis consilium fortuna*.

5, 2 **M. Octavio** Son of Gnaeus (Cos. 76), and now Curule Aedile along with Caelius Rufus. Caelius too pestered C. for panthers from Cibyra (see below, §9 n.) for his games (115 (VI. 1). 21; *Fam.* VIII. 4. 5, etc.), and perhaps got them (*ibid.* II. 11. 2). In the Civil War Octavius was active as a Pompeian admiral in the Adriatic and later in Africa. He probably perished after Thapsus.

9 **nec in rem publicam** I.e. not for any public purpose, over and above ordinary taxation. Appius is said in 115 (VI. 1). 2 to have drained the province dry *sumptibus et iacturis*. *sumptus* means expense incurred by provincials: cf. 103 (V. 10). 2.

11 **†transitam** The most popular conjecture, *transitans*, is worse than dubious; the verb does not occur in literary Latin and assorts oddly with *praeter eum semel* below. *transita* may well conceal an object to *accepit* such as *translaticia* (Watt).

14 **praeter. . .accepit** These words are often omitted on account of the emphatic reiteration below; but C. may be allowed to labour his point. If they stand, the parenthesis ends with *nemo* (so Watt), not with *accepit*; *hic* clearly begins a new sentence. *semel* = 'on one occasion', i.e. on one journey; for the combination with *eum* cf. 145 (VII. 21). 2 *sciebat nemo praeter me ex litteris Dolabellae*.

Q. **Titinio** A Senator of long standing (juror in the Verres trial), wealth (cf. 142 (VII. 18). 4), and optimate repute (cf. 172 (IX. 6). 6).

6, 1 **aestivis** In fact the campaign ended with the fall of Pindenissum on 17 December (= 11 November by the sun).

2 **Q. Volusium** Cf. 104 (V. 11). 4. n. The financial transactions none too perspicuously described in *Fam.* V. 20. 3 f. (see *Philol.* 105 (1961), pp. 76 f.) suggest that his *abstinentia* was not carried to the point of indifference— if the Volusius there is the same. He reappears in a letter of Vatinius' in 44 as defending an Illyrian pirate (*Fam.* V. 10. 2): *defenditur a Q. Volusio, tuo*

discipulo, si forte ea res potuit adversarios fugare. Of his father-in-law Tiberius nothing is known. C. would hardly have used the simple praenomen unless his name too had been Volusius.

3 **misi in Cyprum**   Probably as *praefectus*, but not *praefectus fabrum*, the post held by Lepta. Normally a commander seems to have had only one of the latter; that Pompey in 49 had at least two (cf. 174 (IX. 7c). 2) does not disprove the rule.

5 **evocari...non licet**   The Sicilians had the same privilege (*Verr.* II. 2. 32, 3. 38). The Cyprian towns enjoyed some degree of autonomy under Roman rule: cf. Oberkummer, *RE.* XII. 105. 67.

7, 4 **dioecesium**   The three 'dioceses' detached from the province of Asia; cf. 94 (v. 1), introd. note. The genitive is not easy to range. It seems to be loosely possessive, the whole expression amounting to 'that part of Asia which belongs to my districts' (cf. *in hac mea Asia* below).

5 **litteras**   Requisitioning letters of one sort or other: cf. *Q. Fr.* I. 2. 7 f.

6 **illud...tempus**   The summer. *in hoc quaestu* refers back, to the sending of requisitionary letters by the Proconsul, himself on campaign; not forward to what follows, as Constans, Watt and others take it.

fuerat   I.e. *posita erat* (cf. 116 (VI. 2). 6 *Quintilem in reditu ponere*). Pliny (*N.H.* VII. 132) has *cum interim illa hora in gaudio fuit.* Generally there is a personal subject, as in *Verr.* II. 4. 137 *in negotio curaque fueram*; Caes. *B.G.* IV. 1. 8 *multumque sunt in venationibus*; Hor. *Ep.* I. 1. 1. 11 *omnis in hoc sum* et sim.

8 **talenta Attica cc**   About 4,800,000 sesterces.

9 ὑπερβολικῶς   Cf. 106 (VI. 3). 4; Q. *Fr.* II. 15. 4 *non dico* ὑπερβολάς.

12 **fana**   Such amenities were quite usual. Already in 60 C. had declined a temple voted by the communities of Asia (*Q. Fr.* I. 1. 26).

τέθριππα   Statues in chariots, of bronze or marble (Juv. VIII. 3, etc.).

8, 3 **optanda**   Candid philanthropy!

9, 2 **Cibyraticum**   The district of Cibyra in the extreme south of Phrygia was formed into a *conventus* after its conquest by L. Murena in 84, and Laodicea, a much less important town but one conveniently situated, detached from the *conventus* of Apamea to become its capital: cf. A. H. M. Jones, *Cities of the Roman Eastern Provinces*, p. 74. C. will have preferred not to write *Laodiceae Laodicense.*

3 **Synnadense**   If *ex Id. Apr.* fell out, it was probably before *Pamphylium* rather than after, for (*a*) Pamphylia, Lycaonia, and Isauria form a natural unit; (*b*) the conventus of Synnada was very large (Jones, *op. cit.* p. 65); (*c*) a whole month would not be needed for the sparsely populated districts of Lycaonia and Isauria. But C. may have left out the date, either because it had not yet been fixed or because he felt that to repeat *ibidem*

would be clumsy, while not to repeat it (after a new date) might be misleading. The assizes for all these areas were held at Laodicea between the Ides of February and the Kalends of May (116 (vi. 2). 4).

Phemio Cf. 113 (v. 20). 9.

10 **invitissimo** Because of the separation involved and other disagreeables: cf. 118 (vi. 4). 1. No criticism of Quintus is implied.

13 **Postumius** Probably not the man mentioned in 139 (vii. 15). 2 (see *ad loc.*) and certainly not the *adulescens gravis* of *Sest.* 111, who was dead by 56. Clearly a relative of Postumia (see below), he must have belonged to the patrician house of the Postumii Albini. Its only male member otherwise known at this period is D. Brutus Albinus, who appears to have been Postumia's nephew by adoption (cf. 261 (xii. 22). 2; he was *consobrinus* of her son Ser. Sulpicius (*Fam.* xi. 7. 1)). Elsewhere he is called by his pre-adoptive name; but not to have called him Postumius here (if, as I should suppose, he is the person in question) would have spoiled C.'s jest. Though still *adulescens* (Caes. *B.G.* iii. 11. 5, vii. 9. 1, 87. 1), probably therefore not yet of quaestorian rank, he had served with distinction in Gaul, and was now back in Rome. Caelius informs C. in April/May of his forthcoming marriage to the recently divorced Paula Valeria, sister of Triarius (*Fam.* viii. 7. 2). Possibly Pomptinus' return was connected with the wedding plans, of which a friend of the family might have had notice even though Paula's divorce can hardly have already taken place.

Postumia Wife of Ser. Sulpicius Rufus, mentioned again in §14. The innuendo is obvious and fits in with the story of her intrigue with Caesar (Suet. *Iul.* 50. 1) and her appearance in Catullus as *magistra* of a dinner-party, *ebriosa acina ebriosior* (27. 3; the identity cannot of course be proved). She must by now have been well past youth; hence perhaps the respectability of later allusions in the Letters and her title *fidelissima coniunx* in *Phil.* ix. 5.

10, 1 **cognosce de Bruto** Atticus had probably mentioned this topic in his last letter, having heard of the refusal of a Prefecture to Scaptius.

2 **Salaminorum** On this form cf. Mommsen, *Hermes*, 34 (1899), p. 150. Sjögren refers also to *C.I.L.* iii. 12104. *ex Cypro* distinguishes the Cypriot Salaminians from their namesakes in Greece.

3 **M. Scaptium** A trusted agent, as C. was later to discover, and *familiaris* (115 (vi. 1). 5; Brutus to Caesar *ap.* Charis. *G.L.K.* i. 130. 15) of Brutus, whose affairs in Cappadocia were handled by a namesake (115 (vi. 1). 4). One of the two reappears in 44–43, still in connexion with Brutus (416 (xv. 13). 4; *ad Brut.* 4. 1, 26. 1).

P. Matinium Otherwise unknown, apart from the references in 115 (vi. 1). 6.

7 **negavi sqq.** Cf. 115 (VI. 1). 4, 6.

8 **petenti** On behalf of one Sex. Statius (115 (VI. 1). 6).

9 **Torquato** Aulus (cf. 94 (V. 1). 5 n.) rather than Lucius (cf. 92 (IV. 18). 3 n.), in view of the former's contact with C. just before he left Italy (94 (V. 1). 5).

11 **turmas** Cf. 116 (VI. 2). 8.

14 **iussi** The sequence of events might have been made plainer. The letter ordering the troopers out of Cyprus was dispatched on 31 July, the day C. entered his province (115 (VI. 1). 6). Scaptius' visit *ad castra* and the refusal of his request for a Prefecture may have taken place at Cybistra in September (cf. 111 (V. 18). 4). The incidents described in §11 happened during C.'s residence at Tarsus between *c.* 25 December and 5 January.

11, 2 **una** Intrinsically better than *in iis*, which associates Scaptius too closely with his victims.

7 **praetori** Cf. 90 (IV. 15). 2 n.

12 **centesimas** Sc. *partis*, i.e. 1% per month.

15 **Lentulo Philippoque consulibus** I.e. in 56.

12, 4 **lex Gabinia** Presumably brought in by A. Gabinius either as Tribune in 67 or as Consul in 58. Its provisions, known only from C.'s references here and in 116 (VI. 2). 7, forbade under penalty of fine and rendered invalid loans raised from Roman citizens by representatives of provincial communities in Rome (Mommsen, *Str.* pp. 885 f.). That, as sometimes stated, they went further, barring all loans from Romans to provincials, is unproven.

11 **ex ea syngrapha** The gist of what has fallen out of the text at this point is plain from 116 (VI. 2). 7 *ut ius diceretur ⟨ex⟩ ista syngrapha. nunc ista habet iuris idem quod ceterae, nihil praecipui.*

14 **illos. . .debere** Why should Scaptius tell C. a lie which the Salaminians were certain to contradict? It looks as though there was some misunderstanding in this conversation.

15 **ad ducenta perducam** Cf. *Verr.* II. 2. 69 *hominem ad HS LXXX perducit*; Liv. XXXVIII. 14. 14 *ad centum talenta est perductus*; 268 (XII. 29). 2 *quoad possunt adducito.* Since the amount of interest already paid is unknown it is impossible to reckon back to the original sum, though attempts have not been lacking.

17 **CVI** Scaptius will have calculated at 4% monthly compound interest, the Salaminians at 12% annually.

25 **alii** A correlative *alii* may have fallen out after *aderant* above; but cf. 75 (IV. 3). 3 *ut. . .homines eductis gladiis, alios cum accensis facibus eduxerit.* Furneaux on Tac. *Ann.* I. 63. 7 points out that in such cases a smaller body

is distinguished from a larger. Cf. also *ibid.* XIII. 39. 7 *cetera* (sc. *castella*) *terrore et alia sponte incolarum in deditionem veniebant.*

27 **non**   Most editors recognize that a negative has to be inserted, since in fact Scaptius was *not* content with 12%. But the resulting text makes sense only when it is realised that the two *aut* clauses do not present alternative *explanations* of Scaptius' conduct, but only different aspects of it. He *both* refused 12% *and* hoped for 48%. You could either look at what he rejected or at what he wanted. He rejected 12% on a good claim, i.e. on one that was sure to be paid (cf. *Fam.* V. 6. 2 *ut bonum nomen existimer*; Sen. *Ben.* VII. 29. 2 *quaedem nomina bona lentus ac sapiens creditor fecit*; Colum. *R.R.* I. 72 *optima nomina non appellando fieri mala*: cf. *Font.* 18; Ov. *A.A.* III. 45. 3 (?)). That was impudent, because 12% was a proper rate, but not stupid—he might in the end get more. On the other hand, he hoped for 48% on a claim which would not be 'good', the prospect of payment being doubtful: impudent again, because the rate was excessive, but again not necessarily stupid. Under another governor he might get it (cf. 115 (VI. 1). 7 *quid iis fiet si huc Paulus venerit?*). Note that C. was apparently still unaware that Brutus was the real creditor (*ibid.* 5 n.).

13, 2 avunculo   Cato, half-brother of Brutus' mother Servilia.

7 **L. Lucceius M. f.**   So distinguished from the historian and Senator (cf. 1 (I. 5). 5 n.), who was Q. f. His praenomen therefore must have been Lucius. He may be the Lucceius referred to in *Fam.* V. 20. 5, in which case he was probably in Cilicia as Pompey's agent (cf. *Philol.* 105 (1961), pp. 77 f.).

9 **C. Iulius**   The reference seems to be to an unrecorded incident in the Curule Aedileship of C. Caesar Strabo (90 B.C.).

10 **dieculam**   So in Comedy (Plaut. *Pseud.* 503; Ter. *Andr.* 710).

11 **si haec causa est sqq.**   Cf. 14 (I. 14). 5 n. (*commulcium. . .si id est commulcium* sqq.). Not 's'il est vrai que ma cause est de celles contre lesquelles on ne peut honnêtement rien dire'.

14, 1 ἐνδομύχῳ   Cf. 107 (V. 14). 3. The two *partis* mentioned are Ser. Sulpicius Rufus the Younger and the person alluded to in 115 (VI. 1). 10 as *hunc a Pontidia*, on whom and on Pontidia see *ad loc.*

5 **P. Valerium**   Probably the man mentioned in *Fam.* V. 20. 3; clearly not the friend (or friends) of *Fam.* XIV. 2. 2, 295 (XII. 53), and 415 (XVI. 7). 1. He seems to have owed money to Atticus or someone in whom Atticus was interested.

8 **mysteria**   These remain mysterious, and the further reference in 115 (VI. 1). 26 *Romana. . .mysteria* does nothing to unveil them. They cannot well be the festival of the foundation of Bona Dea's temple nor yet the Cerialia, since these had fixed dates (Marquardt, *Röm. Staatsverwaltung*, III, pp. 345, 500), which would not be affected by intercalation.

115 (VI. 1)

1, 1 a.d. v Terminalia   19 February, the Terminalia being on the 23rd·
C. does not write *a.d. XI Kal. Mart.* because an intercalary month, if there
was to be one, would start on 24 February. Atticus' letter was dated 29
December (§22).

3 respondebo   In order to fill the obvious gap after this word it is
tempting to look with most editors to §22, *non, ut postulasti,* 'χρύσεα,
χαλκείων' *sed paria paribus respondimus.* But to add 'χρύσεα χαλκείων'
here makes the promise immodest, while *sed non* 'χρύσεα χαλκείων'
somewhat debilitates (by anticipating) the comment in §22. κατὰ μίτον
(Boot, comparing 370 (XIV. 16). 3) seems to me more likely. It better suits
nec οἰκονομίαν. . .*tuum*, and Atticus may easily have written something
like *responde igitur* κατὰ μίτον *et* 'χρύσεα χαλκείων'.

οἰκονομίαν   Here simply 'order of topics': cf. Quint. *Inst.* III. 3. 9
*Hermagoras iudicium, partitionem, ordinem, quaeque sunt elocutionis subicit
oeconomiae, quae Graece appellata ex cura rerum domesticarum et hic per abusionem
posita nomine Latino caret.*

5 a.d. x Kal. Oct. datas   112 (V. 19) being a sort of appendix to 111
(V. 18) and dispatched in the same package the two are treated as one. There
is no need to alter the date to XI Kal. (Schiche): see introd. note to the
former.

7 eas. . .datas   Three letters rather than two; it is unlikely that Atticus
should have found couriers of Lentulus (Spinther) at both places.

8 οἴχεται   *periit*: cf. 37 (II. 17). 1 fin.

2, 1 βαθύτητα   Cf. 83 (IV. 6). 3 n. Atticus will have congratulated C. on
not letting his real opinion of Ap. Pulcher's record as governor appear on
the surface and so making an enemy of him.

liberalitatem   Not exactly 'generosity'; rather 'handsome behaviour', 'obligingness'. A man in C.'s position would not be congratulated
upon 'independence' towards a person far junior to himself in age and official
rank.

2 ac. . .secus   This applies both to Appius and to Brutus. From the
former's letters and other indications (cf. *Fam.* III. 8 and 7) C. had supposed
that in fact he was disgruntled, so that Atticus' congratulations came as
something of a surprise. Similarly Brutus' letters (cf. §7) had shown little
sense of C.'s *liberalitas* in the affairs of Ariobarzanes and Scaptius.

7 ἐξ ἀφαιρέσεως   L.-S.-J. quote Archigenes (2nd century A.D.) for
ἀφαίρεσις = 'amputation', so Constans renders 'chirurgicalement'. Here
however the word is plainly antonymous to πρόσθεσις, which is used of
administration of food in Hippocrates and Galen. Cf. Hippocr. *Vict.* 89

τοῦ τε σίτου τῇ ἀφαιρέσει καὶ προσαγωγῇ; *Salubr.* 1 τὰ ὄψα. . . ἀφαιρεῖν et sim.

16 **legatis etiam** *etiam,* sometimes erroneously taken with what follows, distinguishes the subordinates of high rank (*legati* were always Senators) from the humbler sort.

3, 2 sed. . .offenderem C. must mean that he stopped himself getting too fond of Brutus, i.e. going too far in meeting his wishes, for fear of offending Atticus' high moral standards: cf. §5 *metui si impetrasset, ne tu ipse me amare desineres.* But to make the sentiment effective and easily intelligible something more than a bald enunciation is needed. Hence I prefer ⟨*plane*⟩ *dico* (or ⟨*plane tibi*⟩ *dico*) to corrections like *ideo* or *ilico*: cf. *Catil.* 1. 3 *nos, nos, dico aperte, consules desumus.*

3 enim But for his respect for Atticus, C. implies, his anxiety to oblige Brutus would have known no bounds.

7 Ariobarzane Cf. 111 (v. 18). 4 n.

talenta A figure seems to have dropped out, perhaps, though not necessarily, C (Purser)—the sum actually paid to Brutus in 50 (117 (vi. 3). 5). 100 Attic talents = 2,400,000 sesterces. The tense of *pollicebatur* should be noticed. Out of gratitude (cf. 113 (v. 20). 6) the king offered C. money, in promises, but was told to pay his creditor instead.

13 tricesimo quoque die Probably equivalent to 'every (calendar) month'. C. L. Howard (*Cl. Quart.* N.S. 8 (1958), p. 3) cites *C.I.L.* II. 5181. 25 f. *aena quibus utetur lavare. . .tricensima quaque die recte debeto* and the suggested restoration ⟨*quo*⟩*que mense* in section 49. The literal meaning is 'every 30 days' (rather than 29): 'the larger the number the greater the tendency to adopt the non-inclusive mode of reckoning, particularly where a round figure is involved' (Howard).

talenta Attica XXXIII 792,000 sesterces.

14 id. . .efficitur *ita* or *inde efficitur* or *id efficit* would make an easier phrase. But the text may perhaps be regarded as equivalent to *nec, cum id efficitur, satis efficitur* sqq. For the verb cf. Plaut. *Bacch.* 233 *unde aurum ecficiam*; Liv. XXII. 16. 8 *ad duo milia ferme boum effecta* et sim.

17 vectigal Regular income (cf. 357 (XII. 19). 1 *nihil egeo vectigalibus*). *tributa* were special impositions such as Appius levied in his province.

4, 3 habere Sc. *pecuniam quam Bruto deberet.* There is no need to understand absolutely, 'was without means'.

5 tutela Cf. III (v. 18). 4 n.

pro Glabrione Scaevola This incident is otherwise unrecorded. Glabrio was doubtless M'. Acilius Glabrio, Cos. 67, who was brought up by his grandfather Q. Mucius Scaevola the Augur (see Münzer, *RE.* XVI. 428. 61).

6 faenus et impendium Hardly 'capital and interest'. *faenus* is sometimes used of money lent at interest (cf. *Thes.* VI. 483. 8), but never for *sors* as distinct from *usura*. Moreover repudiation of the entire debt seems too drastic. T.–P.'s view (Vol. III, Appendix IX) that *impendium* means additional expenses charged to the debtor is quite unwarranted; the passages cited in *Thes.* VII. 544. 25 show that *impendium* is interest. Constans takes *faenus* as interest payments, *impendium* as interest accumulating to the principal, which makes tolerable sense though the distinction is not attested elsewhere.

7 M. Scaptio Not the supposed creditor of the Salaminians, from whom he is distinguished in 117 (VI. 3). 5, but presumably a relative—if a son, as Münzer suggests, the fact would surely have been mentioned.

L. Gavio Cf. 117 (VI. 3). 6.

5, 1 novum C. had just learned from a letter handed to him by Scaptius (see below, §6 init.) that Brutus himself was the real creditor. At the same time as he sent this letter (probably addressed to C.) Brutus may be supposed to have written to Atticus in Epirus acquainting him with the true state of affairs.

6 magnam pecuniam For the accusative cf. *Phil.* II. 45 *tantum enim se pro te intercessisse dicebat.*

7 †sexenni The original debt was apparently contracted in 56 (114 (V. 21). 11), but it had been renewed more than once, the unpaid interest being added to the principal. The arrangement proposed by C. was to have dated from the last renewal (116 (VI. 2). 7 *centesimis ductis a proxima quidem syngrapha, nec perpetuis sed renovatis quotannis*). If his statements are to tally, *sexenni*, which takes us back to 56, cannot stand (to refute Gurlitt (*Berl. Phil. Woch.* 20 (1900), 1421, to which Watt appeals) would, as usual, be a waste of time). *bienni* (Sternkopf, *bi-* representing *sex* (*vi*) of the MSS) involves another difficulty, since *singulorum annorum* here and *quotannis* in 116 (VI. 2). 7 imply more than one *renovatio*. Possibly, as Sternkopf suggested, C. was using these terms formulistically (equivalent to *cum anatocismo anniversario* of 114 (V. 21). 11), without regard to the actual number of years. But it is also possible that the corrupt *sexenni* represents a larger number of years than two, as *trienni* (*IIIenni*). We need not take it for granted that the bond had been renewed at regular intervals.

11 fide Cato and Brutus as his assistant having supervised the annexation of Cyprus in 58–56 would naturally become its *patroni.*

meisque beneficiis Cf. 402 (XV. 14). 3 *beneficia autem nostra tueri solemus.*

6, 1 hoc tempore ipso I.e. *nunc ipsum*, as normally: cf. *Verr.* I. 25 *atque hoc ipso tempore Siculis denuntiatum esse audio* sqq., II. 5. 175 *omnium nunc* *oculi coniecti sunt hoc ipso tempore in unum quemque nostrum;* Cluent. 186 *huic tandem ipsi tempori cur non reservata est?* et sim.

3 ut...deferrem Scaptius had already made this request on his own behalf and had it rejected (114 (v. 21). 10).

8 quo die 31 July. The interview with the envoys at Ephesus took place between 22 and 26 July.

16 Torquato Cf. 114 (v. 21). 10 n.

17 Sex. Statio Otherwise unknown. Statius, an Italian praenomen, also appears as a *nomen gentile,* like Vibius, Salvius, Numerius.

7, 4 quae erat *idque* or *itaque,* or *quod* (Watt, *l.c.* pp. 391 f.; correct his apparatus), needlessly changes the sense. C. wants to point out that when he says 'interest' he is not thinking of Scaptius' 4% but of the legitimate 1%. Even that the Salaminians *ought* not to pay in future, but in fact they will. ⟨*ea etiam*⟩ *quae erat* would be clearer, but the text is intelligible as it stands.

5 a Salaminis A gloss? We should expect *deponere volebant Salamini; impetravi ut silerent.*

6 venerit Clearly as C.'s successor. L. Aemilius Paulus (cf. 44 (II. 24). 2 n.), now Consul, was related to Brutus almost as C. to Atticus, his brother M. Lepidus having married Brutus' half-sister Junia. He could not have taken a province in 49 without infringing Pompey's law providing for an interval between urban and provincial office (see 94 (v. 1), introd. note). But C. can hardly be thinking of any but an immediate successor, so Paulus must be supposed to have aimed at exemption on some grounds or other (prompted perhaps by Caesar: cf. Mommsen, *Rechtsfr.* p. 47). Caelius writes in November 51 (*Fam.* VIII. 10. 3) *Paulus porro non humane de provincia loquitur. huius cupiditati occursurus est Furnius noster,* which is generally supposed to concern Caesar's command in Gaul. Probably it concerns Cilicia. Paulus could not arrive there until 49, so that his appointment might have made it harder for C. to leave—hence the loyal Furnius' promise to obstruct the plan, whatever precisely it was.

9 ἀκοινονοήτως The adjective means either 'ignorant of common knowledge' (cf. Cic. *ap.* Gell. XII. 12. 4) or 'tactless, egoistic': cf. Friedländer on Juv. VII. 218, where the scholiast has *communi carens sensu.*

16 cum eo...quod Cf. K.-S. II, pp. 271 f.

17 soluta Perhaps *esset* should be added. But I think C. means that so far as his own ruling went Scaptius had been paid then and there; his refusal to take the money was irrelevant to the decision: cf. 116 (VI. 2). 7 *numerabantur nummi: noluit Scaptius* (sim. 117 (VI. 3). 5); *ibid.* 9 *solvunt enim Salamini.* I doubt whether *soluta res stat* (Madvig), on the meaning of which editors disagree, would be Ciceronian.

18 id *decretum.*

19 **Catonem** Cf. 114 (v. 21). 13; 116 (vi. 2). 8.

8, 1 ἐγκελεύσματα Xenophon (?), the only other authority for this noun in L.–S.–J., uses it of the hunter's cries to his dogs (*Cyn.* vi. 24). So the verb ἐγκελεύειν (*ibid.* IX. 7) = *monere* (Prop. II. 19. 20).

2 **in visceribus** Cf. *Fam.* xv. 16. 2 *qui mihi haeres in medullis; Phil.* I. 36 *o beatos illos qui, cum adesse ipsis. . .non licebat, aderant tamen et in medullis populi Romani ac visceribus haerebant!* Differently Liv. xxxiv. 48. 6 *tyrannum . . .haerentem visceribus nobilissimae civitatis* (cf. *Vat.* 13).

4 **mentionem non facias** *eius* is unnecessary: cf. Quinct. 37 *doce te petisse ab eo istam nescio quam innumerabilem pecuniam, doce aliquando mentionem fecisse; Sest.* 85 *gladiatores. . .emissi a Serrano: mentio nulla.*

5 τὸ γὰρ εὖ μετ' ἐμοῦ Eur. fr. 918 (Nauck); cf. 158 (VIII. 8). 2.

sex libris *de Republica.*

6 **praedibus** Not *sponsoribus* because the 'debt' is to the public: cf. 176 (IX. 9). 4 n.

ipse *ipsum* can be defended (cf. K.–S. I, pp. 631 f.), but cf. *Cael.* 77 *durissimis se ipse legibus iam obligavit.*

7 **requiris** 'Enquire about': cf. 260 (XII. 21). 1 *ea quae requisieras; Tusc.* IV. 10 *sed post requires si quid fuerit obscurius,* v. 21 *habeo paulum quod requiram;* Nep. *Att.* 20. 2 *cum modo aliquid de antiquitate ab eo requireret;* Ov. *Fast.* v. 276 *'ius tibi discendi si qua requiris' ait* et sim. The relevant passage in the *de Republica* is lost.

8 **Anni filio** On the praenomen Annus or Annius see Mommsen, *Röm. Forsch.* I, p. 97, n. 66.

9 **multis annis post decemviros** In 366.

10 **quid. . .fastos?** A new query, not related to the chronological one.

fastos A calendar distinguishing the different categories of days, *fasti, nefasti,* etc.

12 **a paucis** The College of Pontifices.

auctores C. himself is now the earliest authority; see Münzer's list, *RE.* vi. 2527. 58.

15 οὐκ ἔλαθέ σε Atticus probably wrote οὐκ ἔλαθέ με.... The sentence cannot be a statement because C. goes on to deny that there was any ulterior meaning to be discovered.

de gestu histrionis Corradus plausibly suggested that Atticus had thought he detected somewhere in the *de Republica* a hit at Hortensius, of whom it is said in *Brut.* 303 *motus et gestus etiam plus artis habebat quam erat oratori satis.* Whether *histrionis* referred to a particular actor or to actors in general remains doubtful.

9, 1 **imperatore** Cf. 113 (v. 20). 3 n.

Philotimi   Now on his way to Cilicia (§19). He will have written to Atticus (in Epirus) before he left Rome.

2 **binas**   113 (v. 20) and 114 (v. 21).

4 **casum**   Perhaps *casus* (Wesenberg): cf. Ov. *ex Pont*. II. 10. 39 *casus. . . timuisse marinos*; Tac. *Ann*. XII. 43. 4 *navibusque et casibus vita populi Romani permissa est*. If the singular is right *navigandi = navigationis*: cf. *Div*. II. 114 *casum autem proeli nemo nostrum erat quin timeret*.

5 **per binos tabellarios**   Not 'by two different couriers' but 'by two different sets of couriers'. *tabellarii* did not usually travel singly.

litteras   This has not survived.

10, 1 **ad Terentiam**   Cf. 118 (VI. 4). 2 n.

2 **tu enim**   C. explains why he had committed himself without consulting Atticus—he knew from the remark quoted that Atticus would approve. That remark gives a clue to the personality of Pontidia's candidate, here as elsewhere (114 (v. 21). 14 and probably, 97 (v. 4). 1) associated with the younger Servius (*illum a Servilia, ibid*.). He was not Dolabella, of whose engagement to Tullia C. writes in August *nihil minus putaram ego* (121 (VI. 6). 1), nor the only other named suitor, Ti. Claudius Nero; for the message which C. sent about Nero (*ibid*.) arrived after Tullia's betrothal to Dolabella, which took place about the end of May or beginning of June (cf. Caelius, *Fam*. VIII. 13. 1; C. heard of it early in August (121 (VI. 6). 1)); whereas the letter or letters which C. here says he wrote to Tullia and Terentia must have been sent in mid-February (between 114 (v. 21) and 115 (VI. 1)) and should therefore have arrived over a month before the *fiançailles* (cf. also 118 (VI. 4). 2). Besides, neither Dolabella nor Nero fits Atticus' remark about C.'s 'old gang'. *grex* as a colloquial term for a set of friends or acquaintances comes in Ter. *Eun*. 1084 *oro ut me in vostrum gregem | recipiatis*. Laelius apologizes for using it so in *Amic*. 69 *saepe enim excellentiae quaedam sunt, qualis erat Scipionis in nostro, ut ita dicam, grege*; cf. *Fam*. VII. 33. 1 *gregalibus illis, quibus te plaudente vigebamus, amissis*. The implication here is doubtless partly social: cf. *Verr*. II. 2. 174 *homine non nostri generis, non equestri loco profecto, sed nobilissimo*; *Mur*. 16 *qua re ego te* (sc. *Sulpicium*) *semper in nostrum numerum adgregare soleo . . .cum equitis Romani esse filius*. But there is also a likelihood that Pontidia's candidate came from Arpinum, the home of the pleader M. Pontidius mentioned in *Brut*. 246 (*municeps noster*). Writing in December 51 under the impression that Pontidia was not serious (114 (v. 21). 14), Atticus had come down in favour of Servius, but had added a word of regret that C. would not be 'going back to his own gang'. But after dispatching 114 (v. 21) C. must have had news, no doubt from Terentia, that Pontidia was *not* 'trifling' after all, so her protégé returned to favour.

4 **Memmiana**   Memmius was perhaps the name of the bearer: cf.

337 (XIII. 45). 1 *Diocharinae*. The letter may have been one from Terentia to say that Pontidia was 'trifling', which she had now corrected, thereby clearing the way for Pontidia's candidate.

6 **Saufeium** Cf. 8 (I. 3). 1 n. The conjectural name is virtually guaranteed by the rare praenomen *Appi*; for Pliny (*N.H.* VII. 183) mentions a *scriba* Ap. Saufeius (perhaps the same man), and a L. Saufeius Ap. f. occurs in an inscription (*C.I.L.* XIV. 2624). L. Saufeius crops up again in October (123 (VI. 9). 4), when he was starting for Rome from Athens, which at this time was probably his normal place of residence (cf. Nep. *Att.* 12. 3).

9 **Bursa** T. Munatius L. f. Plancus Bursa, brother of C.'s unfaithful friend L. Plancus. Titus, Tr. pl. 52 and a follower of Clodius (*simiolus*, *Fam.* VII. 2. 3), had apparently been a client of C.'s but became his particular *bête noire* (*ibid.*). At the end of his Tribunate he was prosecuted by C. *de vi* for his share in the riots following Clodius' death and condemned, in spite of strenuous efforts by Pompey on his behalf (*Fam.* VII. 2. 2 f., etc.); perhaps Saufeius had taken part in the trial. In 49 Bursa was brought back from exile by Caesar, after whose death he became an active supporter of Antony.

11, 1 **Furni** Cf. 95 (V. 2). 1 n. As Tribune he will have assured Atticus afresh of his readiness to block any extension of C.'s term unless a certain contingency, perhaps a Parthian attack in the summer, arose. I regard it as altogether improbable that *exceptio* (cf. 97 (V. 4). 3 n.) refers to a piece of legislation proposed or carried by Furnius.

2 **tempus** 'Time', but with the implication of 'circumstances', as e.g. in *Flacc.* 80 *si tempus aliquod gravius accidisset*.

5 **dissimulantem** Atticus may have written something like C.'s *eadem fere cogitantem aut bene dissimulantem* in 203 (X. 12). 3. Cf. 85 (IV. 9). 1 *ut loquebatur—et, opinor, usquequaque, de hoc* (sc. *Pompeio*) *cum dicemus, sit hoc quasi* 'καὶ τόδε Φωκυλίδου'.

sed *sed enim*, adduced by Quintilian (*Inst.* IX. 3. 14) as a Virgilian archaism (cf. *Thes.* V (ii). 573. 80), is unlikely to be genuine, all the more so as *enim* can easily be dismissed as a reflection from *te enim sequor*. Less probably, it represents another word, as *rerum* (Müller, comparing *Fam.* III. 12. 1 *rerum ordo*) or *mea* (T.–P.). Watt substitutes ἡ, assuming confusion between H and a common contraction of *enim*. But it is not C.'s habit to put in the article in such cases: cf. 201 (X. 10). 3 *dum est* ἀρχή; 204 (X. 12a). 4 *aut* ἀρετὴ *non est* διδακτόν; 238 (XII. 2). 2 *iam explicandum est* πρόβλημα; 390 (XV. 12). 2 κατηχήσει.

12, 2 **Isocrates** Cf. *de Orat.* III. 36; *Brut.* 204. Quintus, like Theopompus, needed the rein.

3 **Liberalibus** The festival of Liber and Libera on 17 March was the

usual day for a coming of age ceremony (Ov. *Fast.* III. 771 ff.; Marquardt, *Röm. Privatleben*, p. 122): cf. 113 (v. 20). 9.

5 **in amoribus** Cf. *Fam.* VII. 22.3 *est mihi, ut scis, in amoribus.*

13, 1 **Thermum, Silium** Governors of Asia and Bithynia. Like Thermus (cf. 106 (v. 13). 2 n.), P. Silius received a number of letters of recommendation from C. at this time (*Fam.* XIII. 47, 61–5), and is doubtless the friend of Atticus whose *horti* C. wished to purchase in 45. The family was senatorial and this Silius was probably ancestor of the consular Silii Nervae (cf. 272 (XII. 31). 1 n.). There is nothing to show that he himself had a cognomen.

2 **M. Nonium** Clearly (by process of elimination) governor of Macedonia. He is usually identified with M. Nonius Sufenas (cf. 90 (IV. 15). 4 n.), most recently by Miss L. R. Taylor (*Athenaeum*, 42 (1964), pp. 17 ff.); according to her, he is also the *struma Nonius* of Catull. 52 (*sella in curuli struma Nonius sedet*) and held the Praetorship in 55. A difficulty with which Miss Taylor does not deal is Sufenas' inclusion in 165 (VIII. 15). 3 of March 49 among a number of Pompeians in Italy holding *imperium*. In the context this must mean that he had been appointed to provincial office in 49, which is scarcely compatible with a governorship in 50. I therefore return to the view that Nonius Sufenas and *struma* (Struma?) Nonius are to be distinguished, and would identify this governor with the latter.

Scrofa Cf. 97 (v. 4). 2 n. His province was evidently insignificant, which rules out Macedonia and leaves Crete and Cyrene. He and Silius were back in Rome by the autumn (124 (VII. 1). 8), as was Thermus by the end of the year (173 (VII. 13*a*). 3).

3 **ceteri** Who are these? If Macedonia and Crete-Cyrene are assigned to Nonius and Scrofa, all the eastern provinces are catered for. There remain, apart from Caesar and Pompey together with their Legates, M. Cotta in Sardinia, C. Considius Longus in Africa, and an unknown in Sicily (cf. Broughton, p. 250). But obviously C. was thinking of his neighbours in the East. I therefore read *firmant* for the vulgate *infirmant*. *ceteri* = all those mentioned except Scrofa, whose post was too unimportant for him to count one way or the other.

4 πολίτευμα The policy of protecting the provincials from governmental rapine: cf. 21 (II. 1). 10. But it looks as though C. had some specific *actio* of Cato's in mind. He may well have been behind Pompey's five-year ordinance in 52, which had already been passed as a *senatus consultum* or *auctoritas* (cf. Dio, XL. 46. 2, 56. 1; Gelzer, *RE.* XXI. 2165. 60).

causam Concerning his tenure: cf. 110 (v. 17). 5.

5 **Amiano** Perhaps Atticus' runaway slave (cf. 108 (v. 15). 3) rather than a debtor. The name may well be corrupt (for *Amianto*?).

6 **Terenti** By the name, probably *not* the aforesaid slave, but some-

one else connected with the affair. Democritus seems to have been an agent, perhaps a freedman.

8 **tum. . .locutus sum**   Watt has rightly deserted the vulgate *tum cum Democrito tuo ⟨cum⟩ locutus sum* (Lambinus); cf. *Towards a Text*, pp. 26 f. Of Lehmann's alternative supplements *cum de ea re* is better than *cum de eo*, which would naturally be referred to Moeragenes (my former objection (*l.c.*) falls to the ground if Amianus is the fugitive).

9 **Rhosica vasa**   Expensive, gaily decorated pottery from Rhosus in Syria (Athen. 229c). The point of the jest is that earthenware as opposed to plate belonged to the simple manners of old: cf. *ibid.* and *Parad.* 11 *quid, a Numa Pompilio minusne gratas deis immortalibus capudines ac fictiles urnulas fuisse quam felicatas aliorum pateras arbitramur?* For Atticus' domestic economy see Nepos' life, 13. 5 ff. The same kind of joke is a favourite with reference to the wealthy Papirius Paetus (370 (XIV. 16). 1; *Fam.* IX. 20. 2, etc.).

13 **modo. . .canat**   Cf. 148 (VII. 24) *non dubito quin Gnaeus in fuga sit; modo effugiat.*

14, 1 **litteras**   Cf. 114 (V. 21). 2.

11 **erit ad sustentandum**   Perhaps most naturally taken as equivalent to *erit unde sustentem* (sc. *rem*), somewhat as in *post Red.* 30 *omnis erit aetas mihi ad eorum erga me merita praedicanda*: cf. Ter. *Andr.* 705 *dies mihi ut satis sit vereor | ad agendum*, also *de Orat.* II. 202 *quod tibi unum ad ignoscendum homines dabant. . .te pro homine pernecessario. . . dicere*, where *ad ignoscendum* = *propter quod tibi ignosci posset*. Reid's *id* for *ad* is not an improvement.

12 **suum. . .fore**   Cf. 261 (XII. 22). 3 *habe tuum negotium*; 347 (XIII. 49). 2 *habuit suum negotium Gallus.*

15, 1 **novi**   Sometimes understood as *nōvi*; but C. would surely have seen a copy of the edict.

exceptionem   Evidently a clause designed to leave the governor some latitude as to the enforcement of plainly inequitable contracts; commentators quote *Dig.* II. 14. 7. 7 *Pomponius. ait praetor: 'pacta conventa quae neque dolo malo neque adversus leges plebis scita. . .neque quo fraus cui eorum fiat facta erunt servabo'.* In Atticus' perhaps prejudiced opinion Bibulus' wording ranged him on the side of the provincials against the *publicani*.

4 **Q. Muci**   Cf. 110 (V. 17). 5 n.

8 **breve sqq.**   On the structure of C.'s edict see A. J. Marshall's article so named in *Am. Journ. Phil.* 85 (1964), pp. 185 ff. C., as he convincingly maintains, is not here describing his edict as it actually appeared but the classificatory method on which it was based, which 'may represent only a mental process preliminary to actual composition'. He points out that the words διαίρεσις and *genus* 'belong to the terminology of the Greek

dialectical method, i.e. the analysis into genera and species with the study of their governing principles'.

9 duobus generibus The first category, that of administrative law (*provinciale*), had to be published in the edict 'since it was neither invariable from year to year like the civil law content nor matched to any extent in other concurrently available law'. Law covered by the *edicta urbana* on the other hand C. included only in so far as he judged desirable, reproducing items of everyday concern for convenience of reference (this is his second category), but for the rest merely declaring that his decisions would be in conformity with the city edicts. The body of civil law which he did not include constituted a third category. Its omission, a novelty in provincial edicts as we gather, made C.'s edict shorter than normal.

12 sine edicto I.e. unless made easily available by inclusion in an edict published in the province.

13 possidendis Cf. Lenel, *Edictum Perpetuum*[3], p. 423, n. 2, cited by Watt (*l.c.* p. 379).

14 magistris faciendis, bonis vendendis Watt rightly discards the traditional *vendendis, magistris faciendis* (Lambinus) on the ground that this transposition 'destroys the natural order, since the appointment of the *magister* preceded the sale of the goods', comparing Lenel, *op. cit.* p. 425. His insertion of *bonis* is indeed a much more satisfactory solution. On *magistri bonorum* cf. 10 (I. 1). 3 n.

17 urbana Issued by the Praetors, Urbanus and Peregrinus.

itaque = *et ita.*

18 peregrinis iudicibus Larsen (*Cl. Phil.* 43 (1948), pp. 187 ff.) explains with reference to the widespread Hellenistic practice of choosing judges from other communities, *peregrinus* being simply the reverse of *civis*; cf. also F. de Visscher, *Les Édits d'Auguste découverts à Cyrène*, pp. 132 f. If C. had meant 'non-Roman', he would surely have written *Graecis* or *suis*. The main point was that under C.'s government cases between provincials could be tried according to their own system: cf. 116 (VI. 2). 4 *omnes suis legibus et iudiciis usae* αὐτονομίαν *adeptae revixerunt.*

20 nostri I.e. *Romani*: cf. 16 (I. 16). 4 *nostri iudices*. I follow Watt here (*l.c.* pp. 379 f.). *vestri* cannot = 'Epicureans' or 'Athenians' or 'Epirotes' because (*a*) any of these interpretations requires *tui* [or *vos*] and (*b*) the names are Roman, and mentioned to show that Roman judges could be as unworthy as 'Greek'. The former objection applies to Manutius' explanation 'qui Romae iudicant' (cf. 33 (II. 13). 2 *regnum vestrum*: that Atticus was not in Rome at this time hardly matters). Münzer took *vestri* to mean Romans in Cilicia (*RE*. VIIA. 1431. 67), which is just possible but far from plausible.

16, 2 τὸ παραδοξότατον This 'most surprising', or 'paradoxical', thing requires some introduction; we reach it after *itaque*. Cf. 218 (XI. 7). 3 n. (*tamen*).

3 **usuras** On tax arrears.

pactionibus Cf. 106 (V. 13). 1 n.

4 **Servilius** P. Servilius C. f. Vatia Isauricus, Cos. 78, Proconsul in Cilicia 78–74, where he won his triumphal cognomen. He was now in his eighties and lived until 44. *etiam* implies that he was an exceptionally good governor: cf. *Verr*. II. 3. 211.

5 **quam ante si solverint** Sc. *Graeci*. Such changes of subject are not uncommon when the context precludes mistake.

7 **si illa sqq.** *si* (variously 'emended') = *si quidem*, *illa* being anticipatory. Examples in K.–S. II, pp. 427 f. are hardly to the point, but cf. *Fam.* XI. 5. 1 *qua re hortatione tu quidem non eges, si ne in illa quidem re quae a te gesta est post hominum memoriam maxima hortatorem desiderasti.*

10 **scis reliqua** We do not know the rest, but something like πίστευε or πρόσεχε τὸν νοῦν seems to be implied: cf. 116 (VI. 2). 5 *itaque publicanis in oculis sumus*. 'gratis' inquis 'viris'. *sensimus*. μὴ γὰρ αὖ τοῖς...in 328 (XIII. 20). 4 can be explained along the same lines.

17, 1 statua Africani Metellus Scipio (cf. 10 (I. 1). 3 n.) had taken a statue of the younger Africanus (Cos. 147, Cens. 142) for one of his great-grandfather P. Scipio Nasica Sarapio (Cos. 138 and slayer of Ti. Gracchus), and in so doing had shown himself ignorant of the fact that the latter never held the Censorship. C. explains how. The *titulus* of this statue, the first of three here to be mentioned, contained nothing but Cos. after his name, i.e. it ran something like P. CORNELIUS P. F. SCIPIO COS., which could designate either Africanus or Sarapio. But another statue (*quae est ad* Πολυκλέους *Herculem*), obviously of the same man, was inscribed COS. CENS. Since Metellus thought the first statue was that of his own ancestor he must have made the same mistake about the second, despite the evidence of the inscription; hence he must have been unaware that CENS. could not apply to Sarapio. This blunder, C. proceeds, explains why in one of a group of ancestral statues set up by Metellus on the Capitol a likeness of Africanus bore Sarapio's name. He had thought when he saw it that a workman had mixed up the two, whereas the error was evidently Metellus' own.

The substitutions of *cos.* for *censor* (*cens.*) and of *cos. cens.* for *consul* (*cos.*) are indispensable, and the former is confirmed by T.–P.'s observation that a man would not ordinarily be described on his statue simply as 'Censor' (Watt's interpretation (*l.c.* p. 381, n. 2) of *nihil habuit aliud inscriptum nisi* '*censor*' as 'bears this very word "CENSOR"' is obviously unacceptable). Some misconceptions are to be avoided here. C. mentions three statues, not two. The first two were clearly old statues, and there is no reason to suppose that

Metellus put them in their places. The third was probably a copy which Metellus had caused to be made from the first.

What had all this to do with Atticus and C.? The most likely guess is that the matter had been raised by Metellus with Atticus *à propos* of a statement in the *de Republica* which implied that the first statue (*quae ab Opis parte postica in excelso est*) was a statue of Africanus (not Sarapio). But this statement is pretty certainly *not* Laelius' complaint, recorded by Macrobius (*Somn. Scip.* I. 4. 2) that no statue of Nasica (Sarapio) had been set up *in interfecti tyranni remunerationem*. For in order to confute that statement Metellus must needs show not merely that the statue near the temple of Ops represented Sarapio but that it had been put up between Ti. Gracchus' murder in 133 and the supposed date of the dialogue, 129. Obviously he had not attempted to do this. But it is quite conceivable that Laelius' remark arose out of a mention of Africanus' statue, and that this was what stirred up Metellus.

4 ab Opis parte postica   Cf. Liv. XXIII. 8. 8 *posticis aedium partibus.* The paradosis *posita* leaves *parte* without orientation. Cf. *Div.* I. 120 *ut. . . tum a dextra, tum a sinistra parte canant oscines*; *Nat. Deor.* II. 114 (*Aratea*) *Vincla videbis / quae retinent Pisces caudarum a parte locata*; Ov. *Met.* XV. 740 *laterumque a parte duorum*; *Phil.* VI. 12 *aspicite illam a sinistra equestrem statuam inauratam*; *Nat. Deor.* II. 143 *ab inferiore parte* et sim.

5 Πολυκλέους Herculem   Three statuaries called Polycles are on record, one in the fourth, the other two in the second century B.C.

8 inauratarum   In bronze, covered with gold leaf. There was one such of C. himself at Capua (*Pis.* 25). In 43 he proposed that a *statua equestris inaurata* of M. Lepidus should be set up *in rostro aut quo alio loco in foro vellet* (*Phil.* V. 41).

18, 1 nam   This does not *prove* that the foregoing refers to the *de Republica*. The thought could be: 'I say "disgraceful", even though I may myself have made a mistake about Flavius. For that was in a different class of error, if error it was.'

2 et tu. . .et nos   Correlative; neither Atticus nor C. was to be blamed. With *ut multa* understand *sunt*. Watt makes a more regular but less natural sentence by placing *et tu. . .sumus* in parenthesis.

4 quis enim sqq.   This story is recorded only here. 'Eupolis is continually turning up as a *corpus vile* in the Grammarians; and the sole consistent piece of information about him which emerges is the fact that he was drowned.. . . But the association of the author of the *Baptae* with drowning is suspicious, to say the least of it' (K. J. Maidment, *Cl. Quart.* 29 (1935), p. 10, n. 3).

7 Duris Samius   Fl. *c.* 300. He wrote among other things a historical work, usually cited under the title of Μακεδονικά, and an account of Agathocles.

in historia Or ἐν ἱστορίᾳ? Cf. 116 (VI. 2). 3 *etenim erat* ἱστορικώτατος.

8 quis Zaleucum sqq. Cf. *Leg.* II. 15, where Timaeus is said to have denied Zaleucus' existence: *sed sive fuit sive non fuit, nihil ad rem. loquimur quod traditum est.*

10 tuo familiari Cf. 27 (II. 7). 4 n.

19, 1 de Philotimo sqq. This is probably in part concerned with Milo's property, of which more in 118 (VI. 4). 3. But that aside, C. apparently had interests in the Chersonese to which Philotimus was attending: cf. 119 (VI. 5). 2.

3 Camillus Cf. 101 (V. 8). 3 n.

20, 4 num quid The veiled wording and the emphatic assurance that all is well suggest that C. had his brother in mind here; cf. 126 (VII. 3). 8 n., and contrast the uninhibited language about Mescinius Rufus in 117 (VI. 3). 1.

21, 1 M. Octavio Cf. 114 (V. 21). 5 n.

2 Caelius Cf. 101 (V. 8). 3 n. Though the topic of panthers for Caelius' games often crops up in his extant letters to C., the letter here mentioned and C.'s reply to it are lost. The austerity of the latter as C. describes it contrasts notably with his playful tone in *Fam.* II. 11. 2 of 4 April, where he tells Caelius that he is doing his best, but the animals are shy. We may suspect that he had not yet actually written to Caelius, and that when he came to do so his mood had relaxed. In that case this passage would be analogous to the account of his letter to Pompey in 151 (VIII. 1). 2 (see *ad loc.*).

3 et * * * a civitatibus *et de civitatibus* (Lambinus) is insufficiently specific, and Sjögren was probably right in preferring a supplement such as *et a civitatibus ⟨ut sibi pecuniam conciliarem⟩*. He refers to Q. *Fr.* I. 1. 26 on the *vectigal aedilicium* (subsidies decreed by provincial communities towards Roman games) from which Q. Cicero liberated Asia. One Roman nobleman complained that its abolition had robbed him of 200,000 sesterces. Watt suspects that the form *vectigaliorum*, cited by a grammarian as from a letter to Atticus, may belong here (⟨de vectigaliorum exactione⟩ *a civitatibus*; cf. *Fr. Epp.* p. 174).

4 ad alterum *alterum* is Caelius' request, not C.'s grievance.

6 erogari Sc. *a civitatibus*: cf. Q. *Fr. l.c. quanta tandem pecunia penderetur, si omnium nomine quicumque ludos facerent (quod erat iam institutum) erogaretur?*

8 cum alios accusasset Cf. *Brut.* 273. The prosecution of C. Antonius for malversation in Macedonia had been particularly notable; of that C.

had said in public six years previously *durissimis se ipse legibus iam obligavit. non enim potest qui hominem consularem. . .in iudicium vocarit ipse esse in re publica civis turbulentus* sqq. (*Cael.* 77 f.). For the sentiment cf. also *Verr.* II. 3. 1 ff.; Quint. *Inst.* XII. 7. 3 *creditique sunt etiam clari iuvenes obsidem rei publicae dare malorum civium accusationem.*

22, 1 **Lepta** Cf. 110 (v. 17). 2 n. *meque. . .posuit* seems to be a playful touch.

2 **filiola sqq.** If, as is likely, Attica was less than a year old, this is persiflage, no doubt reciprocal (see below).

4 **quod. . .vidit** So Watt, but without the further change of *mihi* to *me*, which the context requires. Attica's greetings are said to be a greater attention than Pilia's, not because they were sent to C. (*mihi*), but because she (unlike Pilia) had never seen C. (and therefore could not be expected to send affectionate messages). Besides, *mihi* (sc. *salutem adscripsit*) is both obscure and inelegant. Cf. 112 (v. 19). 2 *eamque quam numquam vidi tamen et amo et amabilem esse certo scio*, a remark which, coming as it did in the last letter Atticus had received from C. (§1), might well provoke some banter on his part (see above).

7 **iuris iurandi** The oath sworn by C. on the last day of his Consulship, *rem publicam atque hanc urbem mea unius opera esse salvam* (*Pis.* 6; cf. *Fam.* v. 2. 7). *suavem* and *quod non eram oblitus* shows that the reminder was explicit. Atticus may have ended his letter *d. prid. Kal. Ian., quo die clarissimum ius iurandum iurasti.*

8 **Magnus** Cf. 21 (II. 1). 6 *sibi enim bene gestae, mihi conservatae rei publicae dat testimonium* (sc. *Pompeius*).

9 **χρύσεα χαλκείων** *Il.* VI. 236, where Glaucus gets the worst of an exchange of armour with Diomedes.

23, 2 **proposuit** Cf. *Verr.* II. 2. 78 *fidem cum proposuisses venalem.* Lucceius did in fact part with his *Tusculanum* as well as some other property (*Fam.* v. 15. 2; 126 (VII. 3). 6). The point, as generally understood, is that 'these embarrassed Roman nobles' (none of them in fact *nobiles* except Lentulus, but all optimates) were tempted to sell themselves to Caesar. Caelius actually did change sides, but not (at least not only) for financial reasons (cf. 126 (VII. 3). 6 n.). More probably (without Atticus' letter we cannot be certain) C. is thinking simply of their reluctance to clear off their debts by selling their property: cf. *Catil.* II. 18 *tu agris, tu aedificiis. . copiosus sis, et dubites de possessione detrahere, adquirere ad fidem?. . .meo beneficio tabulae novae proferuntur, verum auctionariae; neque enim isti qui possessiones habent ulla ratione alia salvi esse possunt.*

3 **cum suo tibicine** This expression, however cryptic in the absence of a parallel, is not likely to be corrupt. The general sense suggested by the

context is 'if he really means it, and is not just talking idly'. Possibly *cum suo tibicine* (sc. *loquitur*) might mean just that. In Roman Comedy all lines except *senarii* were declaimed to a musical accompaniment by a *tibicen* (cf. W. Beare, *Roman Stage*, pp. 211 ff.). A lazy actor who did not trouble to get his lines across to the audience might be said to be 'talking to his accompanist', and the phrase might pass into currency for idle talkers who did not apply themselves to the business in hand. Perhaps a particular incident or story gave rise to it, as to Persius' *cum scrobe = clam* (I. 119).

4 **status**   Financial, evidently.

Lentulum   *nostrum* shows that Lentulus Spinther is meant: cf. 162 (VIII. 12). 6; 164 (VIII. 14). 3. Neither Atticus nor C. seems to have had much to do with Lentulus Crus, of whom C. had a poor opinion (cf. Appendix II, p. 315; Balbus (165A (VIII. 15A). 2 calls him *meum*, not *nostrum*).

praeter Tusculanum   Watt (*l.c.* p. 382) suggests that the name of another *praedium* has fallen out after *Tusculanum*, e.g. *Pompeianum*. That is more likely to be right than *omnia* (Lambinus) before *praeter*. As Watt points out, we find Lentulus Spinther still in possession of his *Puteolanum* in 178 (IX. 11). 1. Moreover, a man in his position would surely keep a house in Rome if he kept anything.

7 **est**   I.e. *verum est*: cf. Ter. *Phorm.* 508 *ipsum istuc mihi in hoc est.*

αἴδεσθεν κ.τ.λ.   *Il.* VII. 83; also, and more appositely, cited in 420 (XVI. 11). 6. The application here is inexact whichever way we understand the context (that, as I understand it, requires ὤκνησαν rather than δεῖσαν); but, as T.–P. say, 'it is quite a modern law that a quotation should exactly suit the thing to which it is applied'.

8 **Memmio**   He and Curio were cousins; cf. 30 (II. 12). 2 n.

9 **Sidicini**   Probably a cognomen like Calenus, Parmensis, etc., though Sidicinus could mean 'of Teanum Sidicinum'; cf. *Phil.* II. 107. Nothing further is known of this Egnatius or of his debt to C.

10 **Pinarium**   There is not enough evidence to sort out the contemporary Pinarii who crop up in various places. This man will hardly have been one of the brothers mentioned in Q. F . III. 1. 22, who, one would think, were too well known to C. to need a letter of recommendation. But a stray reference in 165 (VIII. 15). 1 may apply to him. The T. Pinarius who was recommended by C. to Cornificius in 43 (*Fam.* XII. 24. 3) is likely, despite Münzer's doubts (*RE.* XX. 1399. 26), to be the T. Pinarius of Q. F. *l.c.* The gens was of immemorial antiquity (cf. 82 (IV. 8a). 3 n.), but these people may have been merely clients.

25, 1 †genua vos sqq.   This passage has not remained a riddle for lack of clues. If, as editors think, Caesar owed the sum mentioned to Atticus and certain unnamed associates ('le groupe Atticus'), why is it expressed in

Attic talents instead of sesterces? In order to sustain their theory they have to invent an agent, perhaps freedman, of Atticus' called Herodes, whom they discover again in 406 (xv. 27). 3 (Watt, however, reads *Erotem*; cf. 207 (x. 15). 1 n.). And how should Atticus and his friends have 'squandered' (that is what *comedere* means in classical writing: cf. *Thes.* III. 1767. 25) money repaid by Caesar? All this is idle. *vos* = *Athenienses* (cf. 16 (I. 16). 8 *quem* ἀγῶνα *vos appellatis*). Herodes is in all likelihood the Athenian *littérateur* of 22 (II. 2). 2. If Münzer (*RE.* VIII. 920. 38) is correct in identifying the latter with the Strategus of *I.G.* II. 488, fr. b, he must have been a man of consequence in Athens. The obvious deduction is that Caesar had promised the money for some Athenian civic purpose, like Ap. Pulcher's πρόπυλον in the next paragraph. C. was reminded of it by his mention of Atticus' forthcoming visit to Athens.

The restoration of *vos* from the paradosis *genuarios* seems almost certain. Of what precedes all that can be said with fair confidence is that it introduced a question (see Watt, *Glotta*, 41 (1963), p. 141). The reading *iamne vos*, attributed by Bosius to the Tornesianus (as well as to two of his fictitious MSS), is satisfactory in itself, but I agree with Watt that Bosius probably took it from Lambinus' note, where it is ascribed (along with *Erotem* and another reading of no importance) to an unspecified MS. Bosius may have thought, as Watt supposes, that Lambinus meant the Tornesianus, or simply made a slip. I do not, however, see any manifest superiority, palaeographical or other, in *quem ad modum vos*, which Watt thinks much more probable. Perhaps *hocne verum est (verū ē)? vos* is no further afield than either. If *ho* dropped out, almost anything might have come out of *cneuerūēuos*.

2 **ut audio** From Vedius (see below).

4 **in Nemore** Caesar built a villa by Lake Nemi at great expense, but not entirely liking it, pulled it all down again; so Suetonius (*Iul.* 46), who adds that he did this while still poor and in debt (*tenuem adhuc et obaeratum*); but the poverty may have been a false inference from the debt. It is clear that he was heavily in debt to Pompey, who presumably feared that the more Caesar lavished in other directions the more energetically he would go ahead with his building in order to get it finished while he still had money to spend. If Suetonius is to be believed, Caesar must have destroyed the villa after his return to Italy in 49.

5 **P. Vedio** Probably to be identified with Augustus' luxurious friend P. Vedius Pollio, who fed slaves to his *muraenae* (Plin. *N.H.* IX. 77, etc.). Pollio died in 15 B.C. (Dio, LIV. 23. 1), and so could have been in his thirties or even forties in 50. See R. Syme, *Journ. Rom. Stud.* 51 (1961), pp. 23 ff.

6 **obviam venit** As C. was approaching Laodicea, ten days or so

before this letter was written. Vedius' ἀπάντησις will have been a mark of respect.

7 **equis**   As distinct from mules.

8 **legem**   Clearly Curio's *lex viaria* mentioned by Caelius, *Fam.* VIII. 6. 5 (cf. E. Weiss, *RE.* XII. 2323. 34). Probably it was dropped (Caelius, *Fam.* VIII. 11. 3 *ceteras suas abiecit actiones*).

centenos   Probably 100 sesterces per day (?) per slave beyond a permitted minimum.

11 **Pompeium Vindillum**   Perhaps a freedman of Pompey, who would in that case be his heir if he died childless and intestate (Buckland, *Text-book of Roman Law*, pp. 378 f.). Vindillus suggests a Celtic (Galatian?) origin: cf. W. Schulze, *Gesch. Lat. Eigennamen*, p. 22, n. 3.

13 **Magnum**   With adjectival value, as usual in C. (cf. 16 (I. 16). 11 n.), though here merely distinguishing Pompey the Great from Pompeius Vindillus.

C. Vennonius   A *negotiator* and a friend of C.'s (117 (VI. 3). 5). He was dead by 46 (*Fam.* XIII. 72. 2).

16 **sororis amici tui**   Junia, daughter of D. Silanus (Cos. 62) and Servilia, was half-sister to M. Brutus. She married M. Aemilius Lepidus, the future Triumvir. Hence the puns, *bruti* (cf. 368 (XIV. 14). 2 fin.) and *lepidi*. Twenty years later she was involved in her son's plot against Octavian, but her husband saved her from the consequences (App. *B.C.* IV. 50 ff.).

17 **uxoris**   *Iunia Lepidi* for *Iunia uxor Lepidi* is ordinary usage; but, as T.-P. say, *uxoris* is demanded by *sororis* preceding.

18 **παριστορῆσαι**   'Learn by the way': cf. L.-S.-J. p. 2097 and Watt, (*Mnem. l.c.* pp. 382 ff.).

26, 1 πρόπυλον   As Consul in 54 Ap. Pulcher had vowed to rebuild the old vestibule to the temple of the Goddesses at Eleusis (*C.I.L.* III, 547), one of several similar benefactions which Münzer (*RE.* III. 2855. 14) attributes to his 'Religiosität'. It was completed by two nephews after his death.

4 **ipsas**   The city itself, apart from or as well as its inhabitants: cf. 103 (V. 10). 5. *Verr.* II. 4. 3 *nam ipsa Messana. . .vacua atque nuda est*, where the city is contrasted with a private house, is hardly in point.

5 **falsas inscriptiones**   Editors compare Plut. *Ant.* 60 τοὺς Εὐμενοῦς καὶ Ἀττάλου κολοσσοὺς ἐπιγεγραμμένους Ἀντωνείους. Dio Chrysostom's *Rhodiaca* (*Orat.* XXXI) denounces the practice.

6 **mysteria**   Cf. 114 (V. 21). 14 n.

7 **post. . .quinto**   I.e. 20 February, reckoning inclusively from 18 January 52, with one intercalary month adding 23 days: cf. 106 (V. 13). 1 n. There is no apparent reason why the 'battle of Bovillae' should be called the battle of Leuctra other than that one side lost its general in both.

116 (VI. 2)

The letter was written before 7 May (§6), probably towards the end of April (see on §4 (*egi*) and §6 (*inambulabam*)).

1, 1 Philogenes Cf. 106 (v. 13). 2 n.

4 qua Cf. 188 (VIII. 9). 1 *qua autem est 'aliquid impertias temporis'.*

7 id consilium A divorce between Quintus and Pomponia: cf. 117. (VI. 3). 8.

ego autem A favourite collocation, as pointed out by Watt (*l.c.* p. 253). I regard this as a slight improvement on *de isto autem*. The main point is that the former vulgate *quod ad te scriptum est. . .id consilium probari. probari autem? de isto* sqq. has been proved wrong. When *autem* is so used in a question which repeats the writer's own word in order to correct it, the correction follows (in dialogue, when the speaker changes, this does not apply: cf. Ter. *Hec.* 100, *Eun.* 798). Normally the word or phrase to be substituted follows immediately, as in *Fam.* I. 9. 10 *inimicum meum—meum autem? immo vero legum, iudiciorum,. . .bonorum omnium*: see *Thes.* II. 1579. 57. Note that *autem* occurs three times in the next eight lines.

2, 3 lenivi *leniri* would make the point clearer—that Quintus' outbursts need not be taken too tragically. On his *mollitia naturae* cf. 17 (I. 17). 4.

4 militiave 'Service' rather than 'campaign' suits *peregrinatione* ('absence abroad'); and C. is not likely to be referring only to the campaigning months.

8 ac Misunderstood and therefore suspected by Wesenberg and others. The sense is 'It is not enough for me to promise to use my own influence (i.e. I must enlist others), *and*, in fact, the boy can do more than anyone'.

11 magnum Cf. 201 (x. 10). 6 *mirum est enim ingenium,*

12 multiplex Cf. 13 (I. 13). 4 *nihil simplex.* The younger Pliny makes the epithet a compliment: *amabam Pompeium Saturninum. . .laudabamque eius ingenium, etiam antequam scirem quam varium, quam flexibile, quam multiplex esset* (*Ep.* I. 16. 1).

quod. . .regendo Cf. 125 (VII. 2). 4 *in iis libris quos tu laudando animos mihi addidisti*; K.–S. I, p. 736. *quod ego ⟨in⟩ regendo* would be better than the vulgate ⟨*in*⟩ *quo ego regendo*, but the simple ablative, as with *exerceri* (cf. *Thes.* v (ii). 1370. 17), seems quite acceptable: cf. *Phil.* VI. 17 *partis honoribus eosdem in foro gessi labores quos petendis.*

3, 2 Peloponnesias sqq. This passage concerns two points raised by Atticus on a sentence in *Rep.* II. 8 *nam et ipsa Peloponnesus fere tota in mari est nec praeter Phliuntios ulli sunt quorum agri non contingant mare.*

omnis   All, that is, with the exception of Phlius.

4 **tabulis**   It would not appear that C. had consulted maps; he relied on Dicaearchus' verbal statement, but says *tabulis* for the sake of the amphibolia ('maps' and 'accounts'), which paves the way for the comparison between Dicaearchus and those distinguished 'Dicaearchean' men of business, Vestorius and Cluvius. *multis nominibus* and *crederemus* also play on business terms. Dicaearchus may however have produced maps in his geographical work, Γῆς Περίοδος; cf. F. Wehrli, *Die Schule des Aristoteles*, p. 48.

in Trophoniana Chaeronis narratione   The framework of Dicaearchus' work (probably a dialogue in three books: cf. 305 (XIII. 32). 2 n. (*tris eos libros*)) entitled εἰς Τροφωνίου Κατάβασις (or simply Κατάβασις for short) seems to have been an account by one Chaeron of a descent into the oracular cave of Trophonius at Lebadea. Its main topic is uncertain, possibly divination (cf. Wehrli, *op. cit.*, p. 47).

5 **maritima**   *tam secuti sunt* cannot stand. In C. *tam* = *tanto opere* only when followed by *quam* or in a negative clause. If there is an exception in 333 (XIII. 25). 3, it is one that proves the rule (see also 362 (XIV. 8). 1 n.).

7 **ἱστορικώτατος**   'Well-informed' or 'accurate', not 'learned in history'. Dicaearchus is not considered here as a historian.

8 **adcredens**   The compound verb is very rare in classical prose (once in Nepos, once in Columella). *ad* could easily be due to *admirabar* just preceding.

9 **de deo [cum] isto**   Watt suggests that *cum de isto* in most of the MSS is a repetition of *cum Dionysio* above, and reads *quod de Dicaearcho*. But we need something that brings out the connexion between the name of the author and Dicaearchia, the ancient name of Puteoli, where Vestorius and Cluvius lived. The best attempt for sense so far published is Purser's *de Chaerone isto Dicaearcheo*. But the reading of the Mediceus can be followed in the main, since nothing forbids us to suppose that the sentiment in question was put into the mouth of Zeus Trophonios himself.

11 **C. Vestorio**   Like Cluvius a business man of Puteoli. Note that he is here presented as Atticus' friend rather than C.'s. Most of the savour of the jest lies in the fact that he (and presumably Cluvius also) was an uncultivated fellow, *homo remotus a dialecticis* (366 (XIV. 12). 3: cf. 93 (IV. 19). 1 n.).

M. Cluvio   A wealthy banker, friend of Pompey and C.; his affairs are recommended to Thermus in a contemporary letter (*Fam.* XIII. 56). When he died in 45 he left C. a large part of his fortune.

12 **Lepreon**   In Triphylia, but a member of the Arcadian confederacy: cf. Paus. v. 5. 3 ἐθέλουσι μὲν δὴ οἱ Λεπρεᾶται μοῖρα εἶναι τῶν Ἀρκάδων, φαίνονται δὲ Ἠλείων κατήκοοι τὸ ἐξ ἀρχῆς ὄντες. Pliny (*N.H.* IV. 14, 20) distinguishes between Lepreon in Elis and *Lepreon Arcadiae*.

As for the other places, perhaps cited by Atticus as inland communities to refute C.'s statement, Aliphera in Cynuria is reckoned by Pliny (*ibid.* 22) as a separate community apart from Arcadia. Tenea was in Corinthian territory (cf. the proverb (Leutsch–Schneidewin, *Corp. Paroem. Gr.* I, p. 82 εὐδαίμων ὁ Κόρινθος, ἐγὼ δ'εἴην Τενεάτης), Tritia or Tritaea in Achaia (Herod. I. 145). All of them were ruled out of court by Dionysius as post-Homeric foundations.

16 **fac ut habeas**   None the less the Vatican palimpsest (5th–6th century) has *Phliuntios*.

4, 2 egi   Probably epistolary in view of §5 *fin.* The usual assumption that the assize was at an end, therefore that the letter belongs to early May, is unwarranted.

3 Ciliciae   Cilicia proper, beyond Taurus. C. had presumably held an assize there in December–January, since his objects in returning to Tarsus in June were military (cf. *Fam.* II. 13. 3). He says nothing about a Cilician assize in 117 (VI. 3). 3 or 118 (VI. 4). 1. It was a task for the winter months (107 (V. 14). 2).

7 generibus = *modis.*

9 nullum. . .ne terruncius quidem   A double echo of a letter written two to three months previously: cf. 114 (V. 21). 5, 7.

5, 4 sine ulla ignominia   Cf. Plut. *Cic.* 36 ἀνευρὼν δὲ πολλὰ τῶν δημοσίων κεκλεμμένα τάς τε πόλεις εὐπόρους ἐποίησε καὶ τοὺς ἀποτίνοντας οὐδὲν τούτου πλεῖον παθόντας ἐπιτίμους διεφύλαξεν.

suis umeris   I find nothing strange in this expression, bearing in mind that *pecunias* means, in effect, bags of coin. *suis umeris referre* is perfectly good Latin (cf. *Dom.* 40 *dicebas te tuis umeris me custodem urbis in urbem relaturum; post Red.* 39 *cum me. . .Italia cuncta paene suis umeris reportarit*), and the hyperbole, *suis umeris* for *sua sponte*, an agreeable touch. There is no need for textual change or for explanations like Bayet's 'l'image peut se référer à des jeux de scène comiques et à des attitudes d'esclaves (cf. par ex., Plaute, *Asin* 277, 657 s., 661. . .)'. In the absence of other evidence I would not interpret *suis viribus*, i.e. *suo Marte*, but Sesostris' inscription translated by Herodotus (II. 106) may be noted: ἐγὼ τήνδε τὴν χώρην ὤμοισι τοῖσι ἐμοῖσι ἐκτησάμην.

7 lustri   Cf. the contemporary letter to Caelius, *Fam.* II. 13. 3 *cum. . . publicanis etiam superioris lustri reliqua sine sociorum ulla querela conservaram.* *reliqua* is generally added here, with Wesenberg. I am inclined to think this unnecessary, like his alteration of *in pecuniae exactae* (sc. *capite*) to *in pecuniam exactam* in *Fam.* V. 20. 6 (cf. *Proc. Cam. Phil. Soc.* N.S. 5 (1958–9), p. 8). Cf. 125 (VII. 2). 7 *at hic idem Bibulo dierum* XX (sc. *supplicationem decrevit*).

8 **gratis. . .viris** Cf. 115 (VI. 1). 16 n. C. evidently blamed his old allies for their lukewarmness in 58.

nec imperita 'Knowledgeable'. C. was a merciful judge, but knew too much to be led by the ears: cf. 113 (v. 20). 1 *nihil lenius, nihil gravius*; 125 (VII. 2). 7 *iustitiae, clementiae.*

10 **provinciales** Cf. Tac. *Ann.* XV. 31. 1, where the King of Parthia asks on behalf of his brother *ne. . .complexu provincias obtinentium arceretur foribusve eorum adsisteret.* Pompey's accessibility in the East is eulogized in *Man.* 41, Q. Cicero's in Q. *Fr.* I. 1. 25 *facillimos esse aditus ad te, nullius inopiam ac solitudinem non modo illo populari accessu ac tribunali sed ne domo quidem et cubiculo esse exclusam tuo.*

nihil. . .domi Hence apparently Plutarch *l.c.* ἡ δ᾽οἰκία θυρωρὸν οὐκ εἶχεν, οὐδ᾽ αὐτὸς ὤφθη κατακείμενος ὑπ᾽ οὐδενός, ἀλλ᾽ ἔωθεν ἑστὼς ἢ περιπατῶν πρὸ τοῦ δωματίου τοὺς ἀσπαζομένους ἐδέξατο. Cf. Q. *Fr.* I. 1. 25 *facillimos esse aditus ad te. . .nullius inopiam. . .ne domo quidem et cubiculo esse exclusam tuo.*

11 **inambulabam** Epistolary = *inambulare soleo*; cf. 16 (I. 16). 11 fin. *auferebamus, nondum* below shows that all this was still going on.

6, 7 **constantia** At the Senate's meeting on 1 March Curio took the line that Caesar should not be recalled from Gaul unless Pompey gave up his command in Spain, and maintained it thereafter with his tribunician veto (cf. Münzer, *RE.* IIA. 870 f.). The result, as Caelius had prophesied (*Fam.* VIII. 5. 2), was that no new provincial governors were appointed.

7, 1 **tuum, immo nostrum** So four years later in *Brut.* 20 *ad Brutum tuum vel nostrum potius.* It is unnecessary to see (with How) a hint that Atticus had been over-zealous on Brutus' behalf.

6 **litteris** Cf. 114 (v. 21). 14 *Thermum. . .creberrimis litteris fulcio.* An ellipse would be exceptionally awkward here, where *litteris* is needed to balance *praesens.*

10 **centesimis sqq.** Cf. 115 (VI. 1). 5.

12 **quid tu** Some supplement is required (despite Watt, *l.c.* p. 383). There are other possibilities of course, as *tu ⟨quid ais⟩, qui ais.*

13 **cupere** A strong word. By Atticus' account Brutus was not only willing but anxious to make a sacrifice, if by that he could get the matter settled.

quaternas. . .syngrapha As T.-P. saw, an imaginary reply by Atticus to the question.

15 **omnino** With *audio*, not with *paenitere* ('il s'en repent bien').

18 **ea lex** *Auli lex* (Victorius, and editors until Bayet) is inappropriately jocular.

19 **ex ista syngrapha** Cf. 114 (v. 21). 11 f. The added preposition could

perhaps be dispensed with: cf. 120 (VI. 7). 2 *ut confectas rationes lege Iulia apud duas civitates possem relinquere.*

8, 2 tibi nescio   Perhaps *tibine* should be read; cf. 134 (VII. 11). 4.

Catoni   Cf. 115 (VI. 1). 7.

5 elegantiae   Cf. 113 (V. 20). 6 *moriar si quicquam fieri potest elegantius.* Commentators cite *Sull.* 79 *qui cum summa elegantia atque integritate vixistis.*

6 Ennius   *Ann.* 578 (Vahlen).

9 minus multi   Variously put at 74 (Liv. *Epit.* 95), 70 (App. *B.C.* 1.1. 16), and 30 or more (Flor. III. 20. 3).

10 tenera   At first sight an odd epithet for an island, but it makes excellent sense: Cyprus, being quite defenceless, was easily hurt. *tener* carries a range of appropriate associations—'soft', 'yielding', 'effeminate'. On the other hand *tenui* (Reid) is implausible; a tiny island like Lipara (*Verr.* II. 3. 85) might be called *tenuis*, but hardly the second largest in the eastern Mediterranean.

11 non fecissent autem?   Cf. §1 n.

15 cuius. . .cogito   Cf. Sen. *Ep.* 25. 5 *'sic fac' inquit 'omnia tamquam spectet Epicurus.' prodest sine dubio custodem sibi imposuisse et habere quem respicias, quem interesse cogitationibus tuis iudices.*

18 probamus   No need to substitute *probaramus* or *probabimus.* In writing to Atticus or to C. himself (cf. 115 (VI. 1). 7) Brutus may have expressed approval of C.'s rule, though wishing to make Scaptius an exception. But he clearly had not done so to C.'s knowledge when 115 (VI. 1) was written (cf. §6).

19 sumptu sqq.   'Nisi forte, quod equites potius alere vult Scaptius, id eo fit quod iam repente prodigus et sumptuosus factus est' (Schütz). Apparently Scaptius was ready to maintain the troopers at his own (i.e. Brutus') charges.

9, 1 volunt   Usually taken 'they will have it so', i.e. 'it's their own fault', like Caesar's *hoc voluerunt* after Pharsalia (Suet. *Iul.* 30). But this pretty well stultifies C.'s ironic *scio*; he would be deliberately misunderstanding the word he himself puts into Scaptius' mouth, evading its point—a most frigid device in such an imaginary dialogue, however effective in a real one. It might not surely be beyond Scaptius' effrontery to allege that the chief men in Salamis, or some of them, actually wanted to have the troopers brought in so as to get the business out of the way as soon as possible, or perhaps to save themselves the task of collecting the additional money.

4 statim   Actually about a week later, when C. reached Laodicea: cf. 115 (VI. 1). 6.

7 solvunt   'Are for paying', 'are ready to pay', a natural extension of the ordinary present for future (cf. K.–S. I, p. 119).

9 **eos libros**   *de Republica.* Cf. 117 (VI. 3). 3; 125 (VII. 2). 4; 126 (VII. 3). 2.

10 **nimis, nimis inquam**   *inquam* almost demands the second *nimis*: cf. *Thes.* VII. 1782 ff.

11 **atque** = καίτοι.

10, 1 **pro Appio**   Prosecuted *de maiestate* by Dolabella; cf. the contemporary letters to Caelius (*Fam.* II. 13. 2) and Appius himself (*ibid.* III. 10. 1, 5), also *Proc. Cam. Phil. Soc.* N.S. 5 (1958–9), pp. 6 f.

4 **C. Coelium**   C. Coelius L. f. Caldus, grandson of the Consul of 94, the last *novus homo* before C. to attain the office. He was sent out to succeed Mescinius Rufus, and did not arrive until late June or July; see C.'s letter to him (*Fam.* II. 19). The sentence is best taken as a question. In Epirus Atticus might not have heard this item.

5 **Pammenia**   Cf. 113 (V. 20). 10. If *sed* is retained, it would appear that Coelius was mixed up in the matter of Pammenes' house, which is on the face of it unlikely. Something may of course have fallen out of the text, e.g. *sed ⟨quid refert⟩?*

8 **Semproni Rufi**   Cf. 95 (V. 2). 2 n.

11 **Caeciliam**   Attica.

12 **salvebis a meo Cicerone**   The construction seems to be unique.

117 (VI. 3)

C. had planned to leave Laodicea on 7 May (116 (VI. 2). 6). This letter was written somewhere between Apamea (cf. §6) and Tarsus, where he arrived on 5 June (118 (VI. 4). 1).

1, 7 **πολλά κ.τ.λ.**   Provenance unknown. Bergk (*Lyr. Gr.*⁴ III, p. 693) suggests Archilochus only on the ground that C. often quotes him; but 'often' is an overstatement. T.–P. recall *Il.* I. 156 ἐπεὶ ἦ μάλα πολλὰ μεταξὺ | οὔρεά τε σκιόεν᾽ ιᾳ θάλασσά τε ἠχήεσσα.

9 **obrepit**   Cf. 119 (VI. 5). 3 *et mihi decessionis dies* λεληθότως *obrepebat.*

14 **discesserat**   For the second time. After having left earlier in the year *maximis suis rebus coactus* Pomptinus came back from Ephesus to Laodicea, allegedly for Ap. Pulcher's sake (*Fam.* III. 10. 3; cf. 114 (VI. 21). 9). *ex pacto et convento* is a legal phrase: cf. *Caec.* 51 *pacti et conventi formula,* 22 *ex conventu vim fieri oportebat.*

quaestorem   Mescinius Rufus: cf. 104 (V. 11). 4 n.; 118 (VI. 4). 1. *tagax* is a Lucilian word (1031 (Marx)), but it does not follow that C.'s appraisal is a fragment of a verse like *levis, libidinosus, vinosus, tagax* (Palmer). L. A. Thomson suggests that C.'s unfavourable estimate of Mescinius at this juncture was coloured by a desire to appoint the *nobilis* Coelius Caldus as his deputy (*Am. J. Phil.* 86 (1965), pp. 381 ff.).

2, 9 tua provincia   Epirus, facetiously speaking.

12 iam   Best taken with *si* = *si iam* (cf. *Thes.* VII. III. 28).

13 quid vellem   A good illustration of the difference between *quid* and *quod* after *habere*. *nec quod vellem habebam* would mean 'I have no satisfactory course open'.

3, 3 iis. . .dilaudas   Cf. 116 (VI. 2). 9 *eos libros quos tu dilaudas*.

5 contumelia   Cf. *ibid.* 5.

8 clausula   The rounding off of a period or colon, hence a conclusion, literary or practical.

4, 3 de Curione, de Paulo   In office both supported Caesar, contrary to what had been expected of them.

4 stante   Often of persons, as well as things, preserving their place and consequence: cf. 364 (XIV. 10). 2 *stantibus nobis*; *Fam.* VI. 6. 2 *qui illam* (sc. *rem publicam*) *cadere posse stante me non putarunt*, VII. 2. 3 *eorum auxilio qui me stante stare non poterant*; *Pis.* 16 *me stante et manente in urbis vigilia* et sim. *aut etiam sedente* is a semi-humorous adjunct, 'sitting' implying 'sitting still and looking on', rather as in 179 (IX. 12). 3 *stat urbs ista, praetores ius dicunt, aediles ludos parant. . .ego ipse sedeo*: cf. *Leg. Agr.* I. fr. 4 *castra denique Cn. Pompei sedente imperatore xviri vendent*; Liv. XXXI. 38. 8 *sedentem Romanum debellaturum credi poterat*; Hor. *Ep.* I. 17. 37 *sedit qui timuit ne non succederet*.

valeat modo   About this time Pompey fell dangerously ill at Naples.

6 formam. . .rei publicae   Cf. 19 (I. 19). 8 *nostrae. . .rationis ac vitae quasi quandam formam*; 135 (VII. 12). 6 *velim. . .formam mihi urbis exponas*; *Fam.* II. 8. 1 *ut ex tuis litteris cum formam rei publicae viderim quale aedificium futurum sit scire possim* (sim. III. 11. 4, XII. 23. 3). Otherwise *ibid.* VII. 3. 4 *si esset aliqua forma rei publicae* (sim. *ad Brut.* 23. 10); cf. *Tusc.* II. 36 *illi qui Graeciae formam rerum publicarum dederunt*; *Rep.* II. 22, V. 2.

8 accedam ad urbem   C. could not *enter* Rome proper without laying down his *imperium* and with it the prospect of a Triumph.

10 hospitem   Cf. 87 (IV. 13). 2 n.

5, 1 et quod paene praeterii   'Cette transition négligente semble ironique, les adjurations d'Atticus en faveur de Brutus devant être obsédantes' (Bayet). Rather perhaps C. wishes to suggest that he is a little tired of the subject.

2 numerabant   Cf. 116 (VI. 2). 7 *numerabantur nummi: noluit Scaptius*.

15 C. Vennonio   Cf. 115 (VI. 1). 25 n.

16 et quod   The expression would be more logical with *et* deleted or replaced by *id*. But Sjögren well compares Plaut. *Stich.* 3 *a nos. . .quarum viri hinc absunt,* | *quorumque nos negotiis. . .sollicitae. . .sumus semper*; Ter. *Hec.*

477 *sese esse indignam deputat matri meae | quae concedat cuiusque mores toleret sua modestia.*

18 †aut Scaptius Watt reads *aut Scaptius. . .fuit?* (sc. *quid poterit queri?* similarly T.–P. suggest *ut Scaptius. . .fuit?*). If this seems too awkward, as it does to me, there is no sure remedy; *Scaptio, at Scaptio, alteri e Scaptiis* have been tried. I suspect that *ut Scaptius* was a gloss on *is qui. . .noluit,* which ousted *alteri Scaptio* vel sim. in the text.

19 tribunatum Sc. *militum.* But in 115 (VI. 1). 4 it is a Prefecture C. says he promised. Probably one statement or the other is a μνημονικὸν ἁμάρτημα.

6, 1 Gavius Cf. 115 (VI. 1). 4.

3 canis Cf. *Verr.* II. 1. 126 *canibus suis quos circa se haberet.*

proficiscentem Apamea In August 51 (109 (V. 16). 2).

6 habuissem The ambiguity, whereby 'had as' shades off into 'looked on as', is hard to reproduce in English. Although C. does not choose to say so explicitly, it is quite evident that Gavius had accepted the Prefecture. For neither here nor in 115 (VI. 1). 4 is there any suggestion that he refused, as there would have been if that had been the fact; and even Gavius would not have had the impudence to demand *cibaria* if he had not supposed himself to hold the title. C. however appears to have considered the appointment as cancelled by the man's ill behaviour. It may not have been usual to grant *cibaria* to persons whose Prefectures were merely titular.

10 nuper As distinct from the previous summer. The word suggests that a few days at least, probably more, had elapsed since the incident.

11 Culleolum C. wrote two recommendatory letters (*Fam.* XIII. 41–2) to a Proconsul L. Culleolus, probably in 59 or a little earlier. This may or may not have been the same man—the official rank is no disproof. His *nomen gentile* may have been Cornelius (cf. *Div.* I. 4).

7, 4 qui esse debet Cf. 115 (VIII. 8). 2 *ille vir qui esse debuit.*

7 ἀκοινονόητον Cf. 115 (VI. 1). 7 n.

9 Granius Cf. 28 (II. 8). 1 n.

12 aut ad quem This puts the point more forcibly than *quid ad quem scribat,* which according to Nipperdey is what C. would have written if he had been going to write *quid* and not Nipperdey's conjecture *qui* (*Philol.* 3 (1848), p. 148).

8, 1 et certe Boot cites Cn. Matius *ap.* Gell. x. 24. 10 *ut recordor, et certe* and Ter. *Ad.* 648 *ut opinor, eas non nosse te, et certo scio.*

epistulam From *idem. . .quod ad me* (sc. *scripseras:* cf. 116 (VI. 2). 1) it may be inferred that the letter was from Statius and mentioned the possibility of a divorce.

2 de meo consilio On this notable admission cf. 104 (V. 11). 7 n.

9, 1 Hortensius filius   The younger Q. Hortensius Hortalus (I think with Syme (*Roman Revolution*, p. 63, n. 1) that Catull. 65. 2 is evidence for the cognomen) was on bad terms with his father (now probably on his death bed (*Fam.* VIII. 13. 2)), who was expected to disinherit him (Val. Max. v. 9. 2) but in fact did not do so (cf. 126 (VII. 3). 9 n.). In the Civil War he joined Caesar, who made him Praetor and governor of Macedonia. As such in 43 he placed himself under Brutus and obeyed his order to put to death Mark Antony's brother Gaius in reprisal for the proscriptions in Rome, for which he was himself executed after Philippi (Plut. *Brut.* 28; *Ant.* 22).

2 **gladiatoribus**   Lit. 'at the shows', as in *Fam.* x. 32. 3, etc.

3 **eiusdem patris causa**   To take no notice of Hortensius junior would be an insult which his father might resent as reflecting on the family. But to make a fuss of him would equally offend his father in the circumstances. C. steered a middle course.

7 **quem mehercule. . .diligo**   As Atticus well knew, this had not always been the case.

10, 1 Q. Celeris   Cf. 92 (IV. 18). 5 n. C. seems to have thought well of him as a speaker: cf. 191 (X. 1a) *Celer tuus disertus magis est quam sapiens.* The trial of M. Servilius, who was involved in proceedings *de repetundis* against Thermus' predecessor as governor of Asia, C. Claudius Pulcher, was complicated and notorious: see Caelius' account in *Fam.* VIII. 8. 2 f. (on which *Philol.* 105 (1961), p. 86). The result is unknown, but Servilius may be the republican Tribune of 43 (cf. *Phil.* IV. 16; *Fam.* XII. 7. 1), who served as Legate under Cassius and Brutus in 43–42. His praenomen indicates that he was one of the plebeian Servilii, perhaps related to Isauricus.

2 **si nihil. . .nihil fieri**   The vulgate was *si nihil, ⟨nihil⟩ fieri* (Bosius), now improved by Watt to *si nihil ⟨fit, nihil⟩ fieri.* But cf. 82 (IV. 8a). 4 *ubi nihil erit quod scribas, id ipsum scribito*; 194 (X. 3a). 1 *etiam si nihil erit, id ipsum ad me velim scribas*; 237 (XI. 24). 5 *sin, ut perspicio, nihil erit, scribas id ipsum*; 286 (XII. 44). 4 *tu mihi, etiam si nihil erit quod scribas. . .tamen id ipsum scribas velim, te nihil habuisse quod scriberes, dum modo ne his verbis. vel per tuum tabellarium* is commonly understood 'or even send a verbal message', as though Atticus was likely to send a courier of his own without a letter: cf. 111 (V. 18). 4 *mitte tamen ad nos de tuis aliquem tabellarium.*

4 **Piliae et filiae**   Cf. 122 (VI. 8). 5 *et Piliae tuae et filiae.* The jingle is probably deliberate; otherwise C. would have written something more affectionate, like *filiolae.* The quantity of the first syllable of *Pilius* is unknown.

118 (VI. 4)

After arriving at Tarsus on 5 June (§1) and staying we do not know exactly how long, C. marched away with his army to the River Pyramus (cf. *Fam.*

III. 11. 1) some fifty miles to the east. He had no doubt arrived there when he wrote the following letter of 26 June. This was written *en route* (§3).

1, 2 **latrocinia** An unintended commentary on the efficacy of the previous year's campaign.

4 **illud. . .difficillimum, relinquendus erat** Cf. K.–S. II, pp. 162 f., also 136 (VII. 13). 1 *hoc tamen profecit, dedit illi dolorem*; 327 (XIII. 21a). 4 *accedit, si quid hoc ad rem*, εὐγενέστερος *est etiam quam pater*; 414 (XVI. 6). 1 *illud satis opportune, duo sinus fuerunt* sqq.; *Fam.* XII. 22. 2 *illud profecto quoad potero, tuam famam et dignitatem tuebor*; *Verr.* II. 2. 47 *verum illud est praeclarum, Syracusani. . .reddebant,* 4. 113 *quae sunt omnia permagna, verum illud maximum, tanta religione obstricta tota provincia est* sqq.; *Arch.* 26 *neque enim est hoc dissimulandum. . .trahimur omnes studio laudis*; *Planc.* 88 *nihil dico amplius nisi illud, victoriae nostrae graves adversarios paratos. . .esse. . .videbam*; Nep. *Thras.* I. 1 *illud sine dubio, neminem huic praefero fide. . .in patriam amore.*

6 **de Coelio** Cf. 116 (VI. 2). 10 n.

audiebamus Cf. 1 (I. 5). 3 n.

9 **improbitas** We do not hear elsewhere of misbehaviour by the troops under C., though some of them had been mutinous before his arrival. But that is no sufficient reason to suspect the word.

2, 1 **quando** = *quando quidem*: cf. Madvig on *Fin.* V. 21.

3 **condicione** 'Match', as often. The letter to Terentia was probably the one referred to in 115 (VI. 1). 10, since Ti. Nero is not mentioned until 121 (VI. 6). 1.

4 **quod. . .meis** C.'s fear was needless. His official letter announcing his military successes had already resulted in the decree of a *supplicatio*: see Caelius' account in *Fam.* VIII. 11.

3, 2 **odorabere** Not, I think, 'you will scent my meaning', but 'you will smell out the matter', i.e. see what Philotimus has been up to: cf. τοῦτο δὴ περισκεψάμενος below and 119 (VI. 5). 2 *hoc tu indaga, ut soles.* C. often uses *odorari* thus.

ὁ ἀπελεύθερος Philotimus. Cf. 117 (VI. 3). 1.

4 τοῦ Κροτωνιάτου τυραννοκτόνου Milo, slayer of Clodius, whose namesake the athlete was a citizen of Croton.

δέδοικα δὴ μή τι—νοήσεις δήπου Watt has cleared away the darkness here, pointing out (*l.c.* p. 384) that 'the natural fear for Cicero to entertain was that Philotimus's malversations would be exposed; such exposure would cause embarrassment and unpleasantness for Cicero, since he had been involved in the plan by which Philotimus became one of the joint possessors of Milo's property'. For νοήσεις δήπου he compares οἶσθα ὃν λέγω above and 39 (II. 19). 5 *si obscure scribam, tu tamen intelleges.*

6 τὰ λοιπά Other transactions of C.'s in which Philotimus might be

concerned: cf. 119 (VI. 5). 3 *reliqua vide*; 124 (VII. 1). 9 *reliqua expediamus.*
7 **volent**   Cf. 39 (II. 19). 3 *litterae Capuam ad Pompeium volare dicebantur.*
9 **atque** = *atque adeo*: cf. *Tusc.* v. 45 *hebeti ingenio atque nullo* et sim.

119 (VI. 5)

1, 1 **quo. . .gaudeo**   Cf. 125 (VII. 2). 2 n. (*gaudeo*).

2, 2 **παρέδωκεν**   'Transferred', *delegavit*, so that Camillus would be the
nominal creditor instead of Philotimus—the real creditor was C. The word
is usually understood 'rendered an account of', without any warrant that I
know of.

μνῶν . . . ὀφείλημα   Possibly the sum referred to in 115 (VI. 1). 19
HS $\overline{XX}$DC. For the genitive cf. Andoc. *Myst.* 118 τὴν μὲν γὰρ φανερὰν
οὐσίαν οὐδὲ δυοῖν ταλάντοιν κατέλιπε; *Verr.* II. 2. 53 *hereditas HS
quingentorum milium* et sim. The vulgate μνῶν κδ', μη' would denote two
debts (*nomina*), one of 24 minae (= 2,400 drachmae or denarii = 9,600
sesterces), the other of twice that amount; the money was no doubt due to
Milo and hence to Philotimus as co-purchaser of his goods (cf. 120 (VI. 7).
1 *de nominibus Milonis*). But this requires ὀφειλήματα, which may of
course be right. ὀφειλημάτων Καμίλλῳ in some modern editions is un-
intelligible to me.

τῷ Καμίλλῳ   Cf. 101 (v. 8). 3 n.

ἑαυτόν   Still governed by παρέδωκεν. Philotimus transferred
himself as debtor (i.e. his debt) from C. to C.'s agent Camillus. So *delegare* is
used with a personal object (as *debitorem*).

3 **Χερρονησιτικῶν**   Cf. 115 (VI. 1). 19.

4 **κληρονομῆσαι**   The infinitive depends on a verb of saying implicit
in the context (this seems to be what Philotimus told Camillus).

χμ'   640 minae = HS 256,000. χμ', χμ' or χμ', ψμ'(Haywood, *Am.
Journ. Phil.* 54 (1933), p. 67) are supposed to denote two legacies, but I
hardly think C. would have so expressed himself.

5 **διευλυτῆσθαι**   Sc. ἔγραψεν ἐμοὶ ὁ Κάμιλλος? The verb is found
in papyri (see L.-S.-J.).

τοῦ δευτέρου μηνός   By the Roman reckoning, i.e. February.

6 **τὸν δὲ ἀπελεύθερον αὐτοῦ**   Whether of Milo or Camillus or
Philotimus himself is not clear. The name of Conon's father was Timotheus.

9 **ὅσας . . . δέδοικα**   Again I follow Watt, who suggests that δὲ
κλοπάς vel sim. has fallen out after ὅσας and rightly dismisses ὅσας (sc.
ἡμέρας) αὐτὸν ἠνέγκαμεν: 'ἡμέρας ὅσας is, in this context, an unnatural
expression for ὅσον χρόνον: the tense of δέδοικα is wrong (a past tense is
required); and there is no conceivable reason why Cicero should have been

afraid while Philotimus was with him. He was not afraid of Philotimus himself; what he was afraid of was the length to which Philotimus's malversations might already have gone (δέδοικα = "I tremble to think of")' (*l.c.* p. 385; cf. 118 (VI. 4). 3 n.).

12 αἰσχρὸν κ.τ.λ. *Il.* II. 298.

13 τὰ μὲν διδόμενα Sc. δέχου. Cf. Dodds on Plat. *Gorg.* 499 C. 'Beggars can't be choosers' comes to much the same thing. *meque obiurgavit* shows that Philotimus meant the proverb to apply to C., not to himself.

3, 1 reliqua Cf. 118 (VI. 4). 3 τὰ λοιπὰ ἐξασφάλισαι.

3 dies enim XXXIII This fixes the date of the letter.

5 maerore suo While in Syria Bibulus learned that two of his sons, *egregiae indolis*, had been killed by soldiers of Gabinius left in Egypt. Queen Cleopatra sent him the killers in chains, but he returned them at once with the comment that their punishment was a matter for the Senate (Val. Max. IV. 1. 15). A third son lived till 32 (271 (XII. 32). 2 n.).

6 quaestor Probably the Proquaestor Sallustius (see below) is meant; so Mescinius Rufus (Q. 51) is called Quaestor in letters of this year (117 (VI. 3). 1; 118 (VI. 4). 1), similarly Antony (131 (VII. 8). 5).

amici eius Some editors omit *eius* ('an *mandatu eius*?' Müller), for which Watt compares *Fam.* XIII. 21. 2 *domum eius. . .libertum eius.* Cf. also *Inv.* II. 117 *ex ceteris eius scriptis et ex factis, dictis, animo atque vita eius*; Nep. *Eum.* 13. 4 *ossaque eius in Cappadociam ad matrem atque uxorem liberosque eius deportanda curarunt*; Liv. III. 7. 2 *eorum. . .eorum.*

13 potius Sc. *quam de Parthis.* About three weeks later C. wrote to the Proquaestor Sallustius (probably not the historian) *ille* (sc. *Bibulus*) *autem, cum ad Thermum de Parthico bello scriberet, ad me litteram numquam misit, ad quem intellegebat eius belli periculum pertinere; tantum de auguratu fili sui scripsit ad me* (*Fam.* II. 17. 6).

15 Caldus C. had written to him urging haste (*Fam.* II. 19).

4, 2 iocari Cf. 98 (V. 5). 1 n.

120 (VI. 7)

Fears of a Parthian invasion in 50 proved liars. Instead of attacking Cilicia the Parthians withdrew beyond Euphrates (*Fam.* II. 17. 3), and C. himself returned to Tarsus, where we find him on 17 July (*ibid.* 1). It was probably from there that he wrote this letter, since it shows him intending to travel to Rhodes by way of Laodicea (cf. *Fam.* II. 19. 4), which in fact he did not do (§2 n.).

1, 2 currentem Cf. 102 (V. 9). 1 n.

3 etiam The context speaks strongly for this word (see App. Crit.).

267

6 **nihil est movendum** 'No action is to be taken.' Cf. Liv. XLII. 29. 9 *si penes Romanos victoria esset, sua quoque in eodem statu mansura esse, neque ultra quicquam movendum*; Curt. III. 1. 21 *satis gnarus cuncta in expedito fore si nihil ab eo moveretur*; Cels. III. 5. 5 *cum eo tempore fere pessimi sint qui aegrotant, verendum est ne si quid tunc moverimus fiat aliquid asperius*; Ov. Met. V. 44 *testatus. . .deos, ea se prohibente moveri, ex Pont.* II. 2. 56 *an nihil expediat tale movere vide.*

7 ἀφελῶς   As though *sans arrière pensée*: cf. 116 (VI. 1). 8.

8 **receperit**   Subjunctive because Atticus would say *expedi ut recepisti*.

9 **aut certe perspicies**   Cf. 119 (VI. 5). 3 *reliqua vide et quantum fieri potest perspice.*

2, 1 **Laodiceae**   C. gives the three principal stages on his journey home. In fact he travelled to Rhodes by sea and sent his *scriba* Tullius to Laodicea (*Fam.* V. 20. 1 f.).

2 **lege Iulia**   Cf. 103 (V. 10). 2 n.

duas   Laodicea and Apamea (*Fam.* V. 20. 2).

possim   The present is natural in this case: cf. 173 (IX. 4). 1 *sumpsi mihi quasdam tamquam* θέσεις. . .*ut et abducam animum a querelis et in eo ipso de quo agitur exercear.*

3 **Rhodum**   Sc. *ire*, as in 166 (VIII. 16). 2 *Arpinum cogitabam.* Cf. *Fam.* II. 17. 1 of about 17 July *commoraturum me nusquam sane arbitror: Rhodum Ciceronum causa puerorum accessurum puto, neque id tamen certum.* 'Cupiebat enim insulam et rei navalis gloria et artium operibus et eloquentiae studiis claram adulescentibus ostendere' (Boot). Posidonius (cf. 21 (II. 1). 2 n.) had probably died the previous year (cf. K. Reinhardt, *RE.* XXII. 563 f.).

4 **sed * * * plane volo**   A word or two seems to have dropped out here, perhaps *istuc*; cf. 131 (VII. 8). 4 *ante quam istuc venirem.*

7 **tardandum**   Intransitive, as in *ad Brut.* 26. 1.

10 **adulescente**   Cf. 113 (V. 20). 9. n.

121 (VI. 6)

C. had planned a journey by land from Tarsus to Laodicea, whence he might have turned south to reach a port near Rhodes. Instead he took ship to Side in Pamphylia, landing there on 3 August (*Fam.* III. 12. 4). At Side he received letters *a meis* (*ibid.*), including *Fam.* VIII. 13 from Caelius, which announced his daughter's engagement to Dolabella; and from Side he wrote *Fam.* II. 15 in reply to Caelius and *Fam.* III. 12 to Ap. Pulcher. This letter to Atticus was written about the same time. Apart from the topic of the engagement common to all three, the passages in the letters to Caelius (§4) and Atticus (§§3 f.) on Coelius Caldus' appointment are so closely parallel as to make their coincidence in time virtually certain. Schmidt (*Briefwechsel*, p. 91), followed by subsequent editors, erroneously concluded from the reference to Hortensius in §2 that this letter to Atticus was written from Rhodes; for in *Brut*. 1 C. says it was in Rhodes that he heard of Hortensius' death. But his words to Atticus do not imply the knowledge that this had already taken place; on the contrary *excrucior* suggests painful suspense rather than certainty—exactly what we should expect from a man who had just read Caelius' postscript (*Fam*. VIII. 13. 2), Q. *Hortensius, cum has litteras scripsi, animam agebat*. The opening suggests that C. was still in his own province, and it would be odd indeed if he had written from Rhodes without a word about the voyage or his reception there.

1, 2 **accusatoris** I.e. P. Cornelius P. f. Dolabella (cf. 116 (VI. 2). 10 n.), a young patrician; but Appian's statement (*B.C*. II. 129) that he was born in 69 is hardly credible. Caelius (*Fam*. VIII. 13. 1) speaks of his indiscretions as *aetate iam decussa*. In 51 he became a Quindecemvir, having already survived two prosecutions on capital charges in which he was defended by C. (*Fam*. III. 10. 5; cf. VI. 11. 1). He had now just divorced a wife (*Fam*. VIII. 6. 1), apparently elderly (cf. Quint. *Inst*. VI. 3. 73). Though a favourite of Caesar's it is hard to believe that he would have been given the Tribunate at 21 (becoming a plebeian for the purpose) or the Consulship at 25. C.'s professions of astonishment at the news of the engagement, settled, as he tells Appius (*Fam*. III. 12. 2), entirely without his knowledge, do not have to be disbelieved. Dolabella had indeed been under consideration as a *parti* for a long while, perhaps even before C. left Italy: see Caelius' paragraph on the subject in a letter of February 50 (*Fam*. VIII. 6. 2). Caelius there advises that if C. liked the idea he should give no sign until Appius' trial was over. We do not know that C. did like it; at any rate he seems to have taken the advice, and in a letter to Appius of April 50 (*Fam*. III. 10. 5) he disclaims any wish for such a connexion (hence now to Caelius, *Fam*. II. 15. 1 *quid si meam legas quam ego tum ex tuis litteris misi ad Appium?*, where *tum* refutes T.–P.'s view that *meam* is III. 12, not III. 10). He had given his wife and daughter *carte blanche*, so he tells Appius (*Fam*. III. 12. 2 *quibus ego ita mandaram ut, cum tam longe afuturus essem, ad me ne referrent; agerent quod probassent*). The result, coming when it did, may have surprised and disconcerted, even though it did not really displease him.

socer *In prospectu*, as a Consul-Designate can be called a Consul.

3 **crede mihi** Cf. 103 (V. 10). 1 n.

4 **Ti. Nerone** Ti. Claudius Ti. f. Nero, a patrician like Dolabella and young Ser. Sulpicius, had wished to prosecute Gabinius in 54 (*Q. Fr*. III. 1. 15, 2. 1). He was in Asia earlier this year, when C. gave him a character (*adulescentis nobilis, ingeniosi, abstinentis*) in a recommendatory letter to the

269

governor of Bithynia (*Fam.* XIII. 64). He served and held office under Caesar (Q. 48, Pontifex 46) and became Praetor in 42. Having taken the wrong side in the Perusine War he fled to Sicily with his wife Livia (later Augusta) and their baby son Tiberius, returning after the treaty of Misenum to Italy, where he died some years later.

8 **cetera** Cf. Caelius, *Fam.* VIII. 13. 1 *cetera porro, quibus adhuc ille sibi parum utilis fuit, et aetate iam sunt decussa et consuetudine atque auctoritate tua, pudore Tulliae, si qua restabunt, confido celeriter sublatum iri; non est enim pugnax in vitiis neque hebes ad id quod melius sit intellegendum* (cf. *ibid.* II. 15.2). In *Phil.* XI. 9 Dolabella is charged with delight in cruelty and unnatural lusts *a puero*: *et hic, di immortales, aliquando fuit meus! occulta enim erant vitia non inquirenti.*

ἐξακανθίζειν   Usually understood 'pick holes in'. But to pick out thorns from a man is a strange way of picking holes in him. Just as ἐξανθίζω means 'deck with flowers, paint in various colours' (L.–S.–J.) so ἐξακανθίζω means 'deck with thorns', i.e. 'paint in black colours' ('spinosa facere, exacuere' Corradus).

2, 1 πυροὺς εἰς δῆμον   This sounds like a cant phrase, as we might say *panem et circenses.* Atticus had evidently made a present of grain to Athens.

2 **libri** *de Republica.* The surviving parts contain nothing on this subject.

largitio. . .in civis Cf. *Mur.* 77 *nec candidatis ista benignitas adimenda est quae liberalitatem magis significat quam largitionem; de Orat.* II. 105 *ut possis liberalitatem ac benignitatem ab ambitu atque largitione seiungere.* The ethics of public benefactions are discussed in *Off.* II. 55 ff.

3 **de Academiae** προπύλῳ   Interpreters stand the passage on its head, imagining that Atticus had urged C. to build the porch. That stultifies *tamen.* In 115 (VI. 1). 26 C. is anxious to make the gesture, but doubts if Atticus will approve. Neither does *cum iam Appius de Eleusine non cogitet* mean that Appius had dropped *his* project, which in fact was under way, though it was not completed till after his death. Clearly Atticus, while not actually disapproving of C.'s idea, had recommended further consideration; but Appius, says C., is not *considering* but doing: cf. Cato, *R.R.* III. 1 *aedificare diu cogitare oportet; conserere cogitare non oportet, sed facere oportet;* Ter. *Eun.* 56 *proin tu, dum est tempus, etiam atque etiam cogita.* Corradus seems to have glimpsed the sense when he wrote 'potest esse iocus ex ambiguo'.

5 **de Hortensio** See introd. note above.

6 **familiariter vivere** Cf. *Amic.* 77 *nihil enim est turpius quam cum eo bellum gerere quocum familiariter vixeris.*

3, 1 **Coelium** Cf. *Fam.* II. 15. 4 to Caelius Rufus (a parallel passage throughout) *ego de provincia decedens quaestorem Coelium praeposui provinciae. 'puerum' inquis. at quaestorem, at nobilem adulescentem* sqq.

puerum   As Quaestor Coelius was presumably over thirty, so that 'boy' is a *façon de parler.*

2 **fortasse fatuum**   Atticus would not seem to have known Coelius personally any more than C. (cf. 116 (VI. 2). 10) before his arrival, so that *fatuum* sqq. may be regarded as (somewhat illogically) giving C.'s own impression of him on first acquaintance.

3 **fieri. . .aliter**   I do not think Watt's addition of *sed* before *fieri* is an improvement.

4 ἐπέχειν   A term expressing philosophic doubt: cf. Strabo, II. 1. 11 ὁ δ'ἐπέχων οὐδ' ἑτέρωσε ῥέπει. The contrast with ἀθέτησις in 123 (VI. 9). 3 suggests that it was used in literary criticism.

6 **traderem**   Cf. §4 *ego sorte datum offenderem? tradere* is possible no doubt.

8 **nam**   'Occupatory.' Pomptinus, Q. Cicero's equal in rank as *praetorius*, had left for Rome (*Fam.* II. 15. 4).

9 **nobili**   Cf. 117 (VI. 3). 1 n. (*quaestorem*). Thomson compares C.'s advice to Minucius Thermus in a similar situation not to pass over the *nobilis* L. Antonius (*Fam.* II. 18. 2).

tamen   Referring back to *illud non utile nobis, nam. . .ferrem* being parenthetic.

12 **incredibili felicitate**   This 'crowning mercy' of the Parthian withdrawal made a great impression on C.'s mind: cf. 124 (VII. 1). 2; 125 (VII. 2). 8; 150 (VII. 26). 3 n.; 161 (VIII. 11). 7.

13 **sermones**   Similarly to Caelius (*l.c.*) *dicerent iniqui non me plane post annum, ut senatus voluisset, de provincia decessisse, quoniam alterum me reliquissem; fortasse etiam illud adderent, senatum eos voluisse provinciis praeesse qui antea non praefuissent; fratrem meum triennium Asiae praefuisse.* To Caelius C. also says that Quintus would not have been willing to stay.

num   The challenging question (cf. *Cl. Quart.* N.S. 3 (1953), p. 125) is much more forcible than a negative statement.

4, 3 **quae fert vita hominum**   Cf. 329 (XIII. 22). 4 *sed vita fert.* This softens the implied criticism of Quintus (cf. 15 (I. 15). 1 n.). To Caelius Rufus C. is naturally less specific: *denique nunc sollicitus non sum; si fratrem reliquissem, omnia timerem.*

4 **non dimittebat**   I.e. *dimittere nolebat* (supposing he did stay): cf. 123 (VI. 9). 3.

6 **quod egerit**   Sc. *id actum habebo* (cf. Lehmann, *de Cic. ad Att.*, pp. 198 f.). Similarly 416 (XV. 13). 3 *Cloelium nihil arbitror malitiose; quamquam— sed quod egerit*; *Fam.* XVI. 23. 1 *Antonius de lege quod egerit*, 24. 2 *sed quod egerit.*

7 **Pompeius sqq.** So to Caelius: *postremo non tam mea sponte quam potentissimorum duorum exemplo, qui omnis Cassios Antoniosque complexi sunt, hominem adulescentem non tam allicere volui quam alienare nolui.* Q. Cassius and Mark Antony were of course *nobiles* like Coelius.

eo robore vir, iis radicibus 'Metaphora desumpta a quercu' (Boot). Cf. *Phil.* IV. 13 *virtus est una altissimis defixa radicibus, quae numquam vi ulla labefactari potest, numquam demoveri loco*; Symm. *Ep.* V. 54. 5 *quid restat, nisi ut aequitas vestra privatam petitionem nullis sustineri radicibus iudicet, cui sacrae reverentiae umbra praetexitur?* Persons like Pompey and Caesar, it might be thought, would have no need to bolster up their *gratia* in this way.

Q. Cassium Cf. 113 (V. 20). 8 n.

sine sorte Such choice *extra sortem* was a concession, probably a rare one, made by the Senate to particular governors: cf. Mommsen, *St.* II, p. 533.

8 **Antonium** M. Antonius M. f., the Triumvir. He was Quaestor in Gaul in 51, not (as Broughton) 52 (Hirt. *B.G.* VIII. 2. 1).

10 **senectuti** Old men should seek a quiet life and avoid making enemies: cf. 23 (II. 3). 4 *senectutis otium*; 367A (XIV. 17A). 3 (Antony) *quamquam tuam fortunam, Cicero, ab omni periculo abesse certum habeo, tamen arbitror malle te quietam senectutem et honorificam potius agere quam sollicitam*, et sim.

12 **sed librari tui** Editors whimsically suppose that the letter was dictated by C. himself to a secretary lent him by Atticus. But C. appears merely to be noticing that Atticus had used an amanuensis, probably Alexis (cf. 113 (V. 20). 9; 125 (VII. 2). 3; 426 (XVI. 15). 1). Atticus may well have coupled his ἐποχή with some complimentary phrases about Coelius; he seems to have been rather in favour of his appointment (cf. 123 (VI. 9). 3) in preference to that of Quintus. It is just possible however that he sent a special letter for C. to read to Coelius, in which case C. may imply that the composition as well as the writing was the clerk's.

13 **amicorum** Cf. 122 (VI. 8). 5; 124 (VII. 1). 7. One wonders who they were. Caelius' letters do not mention the subject of a Triumph except incidentally in *Fam.* VIII. 5. 1 of July 51. Cato alludes to the possibility very bleakly (*Fam.* XV. 5. 2). But the Senate, so C. told his family, clamoured for it in 49 (*Fam.* XVI. 11. 3).

14 **παλιγγενεσίαν** No doubt, as Manutius explains, with reference to C.'s return from exile: cf. 65 (III. 20). 1 n. (*diemque natalem*). He develops the theme much more fully in a letter to Cato written some months earlier (*Fam.* XV. 4. 13 f.), where he says that, whereas before his exile he had foregone a number of honours which he might easily have obtained, he had since been desirous of such things (*studui quam ornatissima senatus populique Romani de me iudicia intercedere*). In this desire he says there was *aliqua vis*

desideri ad sanandum vulnus iniuriae. παλιγγενεσίαν however rather suggests that, whereas between 63 and 58 his position was such that nothing could enhance it (cf. *Fam.* III. 7. 5 *ita et cepi et gessi maxima imperia ut mihi nihil neque ad honorem neque ad gloriam adquirendum putarem*), in 57 he had started as it were afresh.

122 (VI. 8)

C. may be supposed to have arrived in Rhodes about 10 August. How long he spent there we do not know, but from §4 it appears that the voyage from Rhodes to Ephesus had been delayed and that he had been held up in Ephesus for some time by unfavourable winds. He wrote this letter on 1 October, just before embarking for Athens (*ibid.*).

1, 2 Batonius Otherwise unknown. The name, found in inscriptions, derives from Bato(n): cf. W. Schulze, *Gesch. Lat. Eigennamen*, pp. 44, n. 5, 555. n. 2.

3 II This notation, though not common in the extant MSS is sufficiently attested · see Sjögren *ad loc.*

navigationis From Epirus to Italy.

4 opportunitate Piliae 'Quae tibi obviam progressa, opportune advenienti occurrerit' (Manutius). C. was similarly fortunate in November: cf. *Fam.* XVI. 9. 2 *hora IIII Brundisium venimus, eodemque tempore simul nobiscum in oppidum introiit Terentia.*

5 coniugio This does not prove that the wedding had already taken place: cf. *Philol.* 105 (1961), p. 88.

2, 1 meros So rightly Watt: cf. 77 (IV. 7). 1 *mera monstra*; 178 (IX. 11). 3 *mcras proscriptiones, meros Sullas* et sim. Müller, followed by Sjögren, etc., keeps *miros*, appealing to 116 (VI. 2). 5 *mira erant. . .furta Graecorum* and 415 (XVI. 7). 5 *gratias miras.* The corruption is naturally found elsewhere (cf. 124 (VII. 1). 9; *Thes.* VIII. 846. 42).

3 dimissurum Not 'disband' but 'relinquish'; cf. 130 (VII. 7). 6 *exercitum retinentis.* There was no question of *disbanding* the Gallic army. *tradere* in 132 (VII. 9). 2 and 3 expresses the same thing.

4 praetores designatos tris Excluding L. Manlius Torquatus (see on 161B (VIII. 11B). 1) we know seven out of the eight. No one could have expected Favonius to support Caesar, nor, to judge by the event, C. Coponius (nor Torquatus, if he is counted in). P. Rutilius Lupus and C. Sosius were reckoned as firm republicans at the outset, whatever they did later (cf. 167 (IX. 1). 2 n.). That leaves Caesar with M. Lepidus, A. Allienus, L. Roscius Fabatus (and possibly one unknown).

Cassium Quintus no doubt: cf. 113 (V. 20). 8 n. Since C. Cassius (the conspirator), who supported Pompey in the war, also was Tribune in 49, perhaps Q. should be added. Mark Antony and some other members of the College also supported Caesar, but Q. Cassius (cf. 130 (VII. 7). 4 n.) is specially mentioned because as Pompey's ex-Quaestor his attitude came as a surprise (cf. 126 (VII. 3). 5 n.). With *tribunum pl.* and *consulem* we can understand *designatum*.

5 **Lentulum** L. Cornelius P. f. Lentulus Crus, Clodius' chief prosecutor in 61. As Praetor in 58 he was regarded as a firm optimate and Ciceronian sympathizer (cf. *Q. Fr.* I. 2. 16; *Pis.* 77). According to Hirtius (*B.G.* VIII. 50. 4; cf. Suet. *Iul.* 29. 2) Caesar's enemies considered his election and that of his colleague C. Marcellus as a triumph for their party; and in fact he took a strongly anti-Caesarian line. Yet Caesar continued to have hopes of detaching him, through his protégé Cornelius Balbus (cf. 160 (VIII. 9a). 2; 161 (VIII. 11). 5; 165A (VIII. 15A). 2). He was heavily in debt (Caes. *B.C.* I. 4. 2; Vell. II. 49. 3: cf. 217 (XI. 6). 6), and in C.'s opinion both he and his colleague were as unstable as a feather or a leaf (165 (VIII. 15). 2). In 48 he landed in Egypt the day after Pompey and met a similar fate.

urbem relinquere With the notion of abandonment (more than merely 'leave'). Nevertheless I hardly think (as Gelzer, *RE.* XXI. 2177. 54) that Pompey was supposed at this stage to be contemplating an evacuation in the face of armed force such as actually took place in the following January. The fear surely was that Pompey might go to Spain, leaving Caesar master in Rome: cf. 104 (v. 11). 3 *nihil esse melius quam illud nusquam discedere*; 132 (VII. 9). 3 *eo consule Pompeio certum est esse in Hispania*. See also on 131 (VII. 8). 5.

3, 1 illo Calidius: see Appendix II. The mention of Lentulus reminded C. of Calidius' defeat, so that *sed heus tu* sqq. is better not printed as a separate paragraph.

4, 1 vehementissimi An easy and necessary correction. Corruption of *i* to *e* needs no explanation, but may here have been due to a mistake about the gender of *etesiae*.

detraxit As though from an unspecified fund of time in hand. *addidit* might have seemed more natural.

2 aphractus Rhodi *aphractus Rhodiorum* (cf. 202 (X. 11). 4) is the vulgate. But the singular is odd in view of *aphractis* below, and the meaning obscure. If C. refers to the voyage from Rhodes to Ephesus, how can the ship be said to have wasted a precise number of days in addition to (*etiam*) the winds? *Rhodi*, which is virtually the paradosis, leaves us to suppose with Schütz that one of C.'s ships arrived late in Rhodes or had to be refitted. But he certainly might have been more explanatory, unless something has dropped out.

3 **L. Tarquitio** Unknown. A C. Tarquitius P. f. was Quaestor in Spain in 81.

4 **aphractis** Dative 'of advantage'.

5 **tranquillitates** 'Calms', not 'fair weather'. These vessels 'were built for rowing, and therefore would travel fastest in smooth water; moreover C. considered them unsafe in a rough sea' (R. L. Dunbabin, *Cl. Rev.* 39 (1925), pp. 112 f.). Cf. 105 (v. 12). 1 n.

5, 1 **raudusculo Puteolano** Perhaps, as Manutius suggests, a small sum owing to (or by?) Vestorius.

4 **pedem...extulit** Cf. 152 (VIII. 2). 4 *pedem porta non extulit*; Suet. *Tib.* 38 *biennio continuo post adeptum imperium pedem porta* (the city gate) *non extulit.*

consul Something to define the time is indispensable. *cos.* is more explicit than *olim* and more likely to have fallen out than *in consulatu* (Müller).

6 αἰσχρὸν σιωπᾶν βαρβάρους δ'ἐᾶν λέγειν. From Euripides' *Philoctetes* (Nauck, fr. 796).

10 **Piliae...filiae** Cf. 117 (VI. 3). 10 n.

123 (VI. 9)

1, 1 **in Piraeea** Cf. 126 (VII. 3). 10. *Piraeum* was the usual form.

Acasto Cf. 124 (VII. 1). 1 *Acasto nostro.* He also brought a letter from Terentia (*Fam.* XIV. 5. 1). C. left him at Patrae to look after Tiro (*ibid.* XVI. 5. 2, 14. 2).

4 **quae...tuae** Cf. 121 (VI. 6). 3 *quas...tuas acceperam litteras*; 124 (VII. 1). 9 *rationibus quas ille meas tractat. quia* (Klotz) is usually read.

5 **ne multa** In fact C.'s account is oddly circumstantial. Presumably he wanted to impress Atticus with his concern.

ex eo quod ita scripseras Not 'from the style of writing'. C. might have *guessed* from the writing that Atticus was out of sorts, but could not have *learned* the facts.

11 **amavi** Cf. *Fam.* IX. 6. 1 *delectarunt me tuae litterae, in quibus primum amavi amorem tuum qui te ad scribendum incitavit*, XIII. 62. 1 *in Atili negotio te amavi*; 8 (I. 3). 2 n.

2, 1 **Turranio** Possibly the *homo* χρηστομαθής of 2 (I. 6). 2.

litteras Probably 119 (VI. 5).

2 τοῦ φυρατοῦ Cf. 118 (VI. 4). 3 and 119 (VI. 5). 1 πεφυρακέναι τὰς ψήφους; 124 (VII. 1). 9 *merus est* φυρατής. φιλοτιμία (cf. *ibid.* 1) may simply allude to the name; but Philotimus was prone to give himself airs above his station (cf. 174 (IX. 7). 6; 200 (X. 9). 1). The word is often used in a bad sense, 'ambition' or 'partisanship'.

αὐτίκα γάρ   'The adverb αὐτότατα is surely impossible. Even if it is replaced by αὐτότατος this is a very odd way of saying "per te ipsum" ' Watt, *l.c.* p. 386. His ingenious correction seems worth a place in the text. As he says, it eases the transition from one sentence to the other, which is otherwise abrupt.

4 **Precianam**   C. writes next day to Terentia *de hereditate Preciana, quae quidem mihi magno dolori est (valde enim illum amavi)—sed hoc velim cures, si auctio ante meum adventum fiet, ut Pomponius aut, si is minus poterit, Camillus nostrum negotium curet (Fam.* XIV. 5. 2). Nothing else is known about this Precius or Praecius, unless he is the person alluded to in *Fam.* VII. 8. 2 (July 54, to Trebatius) *quod scribis de illo Preciano iure consulto, ego te ei non desino commendare,* whose name was not necessarily Precianus; cf. also 176 (IX. 9). 4 n. *(egi. . .venale).* A dedicatory inscription at Arpinum records the names of Cilix, slave of Tullius, Tepa, slave of Precia, and Philotimus (*C.I.L.* X. 5678).

6 **nec me κενόν sqq.**   Cf. *Pis.* 57 *tamen erat angusti animi atque demissi iusti triumphi honorem dignitatemque contemnere. nam ut levitatis est inanem aucupari rumorem et omnis umbras etiam falsae gloriae consectari, sic est animi lucem splendoremque fugientis iustam gloriam, qui est fructus verae virtutis honestissimus, repudiare.*

7 ἄτυφον   Ordinarily a term of praise, the opposite of κενός. But we can say 'don't be modest' ('ne fais pas le modeste'), meaning 'don't be coy'. Suidas glosses ἀτυφία with ταπεινοφροσύνη. Or does C. mean 'phlegmatic, blasé?' Cf. τὸν τῦφον in 300 (XIII. 29). 1 and *Brut.* 282 *sine adrogantia gravis esse videbatur et sine segnitia verecundus.*

3, 1 **ex tuis litteris**   Not the letter brought by Acastus, but another received later from Xeno (124 (VII. 1). 1 fin.).

3 **litterarum**   The imperfects (*scribebas, monebas*) and ἐπιχρονία below show that C. had more than one letter in mind, but chiefly perhaps the one mentioned in 121 (VI. 6). 3 as received *multo ante.*

   erat   Cf. K.–S. II, p. 402 (*dubitatione dignum = dubitandum*).

4 **et talem fratrem**   'Volontairement ambigu' according to Bayet. There is no ambiguity, voluntary or involuntary. An allusion to Quintus' 'charactère dangereux' would be nonsensical here.

7 τοὐμὸν ὄνειρον ἐμοί   Callim. *Epigr.* 32. 2 (Pfeiffer); cf. Leutsch–Schneidewin, *Corp. Paroem. Gr.* II, p. 774.

4, 1 **tabellarios**   They carried 124 (VII. 1) and no doubt other letters to the persons included in *vos.* Acastus had brought letters from many friends (*Fam.* XIV. 5. 1).

5, 3 **censoribus**   Ap. Pulcher and L. Piso (Cos. 58) had been elected.

4 **signis, tabulis**   Appius was harrying art collectors among others:

cf. Caelius, *Fam.* VIII. 14. 4 *scis Appium censorem hic ostenta facere, de signis et tabulis, de agri modo, de aere alieno acerrime agere...?* According to Caelius his own house was made of glass: *et quam primum haec risum veni, legis Scantiniae iudicium apud Drusum fieri, Appium de tabulis et signis agere.*

dedi To Saufeius.

5 **legiones IIII** Sc. *ducturus erat.* An alarmist rumour like the later ones mentioned by Appian, *B.C.* II. 31; cf. 129 (VII. 6). 2 n. F. W. Sanford (*Nebraska Univ. Studies*, XI (1911), p. 4) suggests that it originated in the orders issued by Caesar to his legions at the end of his tour of Cisalpine Gaul in early September to assemble for the review at Nemetocenna (Hirtius, *B.G.* VIII. 52. 1).

6 **statio** Caesar often uses the word of military posts or pickets (*in statione esse*). A jest seems to be intended here; C. rather likes his 'station' behind the walls of the citadel in these dangerous times (*nunc*). Note that he was not staying with Aristus (cf. 103 (v. 10). 5 n.).

124 (VII. 1)

This is the letter promised in 123 (VI. 9). 4.

1, 4 **ambulant** An appropriate verb because, while properly meaning 'walk', it could be extended to travel generally—probably a colloquial use at this period (cf. 173 (IX. 4). 3; *Thes.* I. 1873. 68, 1874. 63). Philosophers would move without unseemly haste.

9 **cohorruisse** Probably a facetious touch, as T.-P. thought, in allusion to Atticus' fever. The reference to the legions comes at the end of 123 (VI. 9), but C. may have changed the order of topics for the sake of his joke. Cf. however 122 (VI. 8). 2 *horribilia.*

10 **quod** Relative. 'I shuddered because your letter reported' instead of 'I shuddered at what...' is not normal human speech. It is not absolutely necessary to supply (*in*) *eo*, though such ellipses of the antecedent are uncommon in classical writing, Varro excepted: cf. K.-S. II, p. 282. But *me* is unlikely to be sound. It is not needed (after *scis me*) any more than with the preceding infinitives; and if C. had meant it emphatically, to balance *tuo*, he would surely have written *ipsum*. How easily *autem* (*in*) *eo co-* would become *autem me co-* needs no demonstration.

11 **egi** *egisse* seems to be an assimilation in the common vein of copyists to the preceding perfect infinitives. These give facts of which C. had informed Atticus in his letter. But he had not informed Atticus of what he actually wrote in the letter; for that an indicative, like *exposui* below, is required. *et* too goes better with *egi*.

φιλοτιμία   Cf. 123 (VI. 9). 2 n.

14 **Xenone** Cf. 103. (v. 10). 5 n.

2, 4 **videre...videor** C. liked this combination: cf. K.–S. ii, p. 570.
10 **te auctore** Cf. Introd. p. 24, n. 8.
13 ἀλλ' ἐμὸν κ.τ.λ. *Od.* ix. 33 (ἔπειθεν—as elsewhere C. adapts his quotation). πατρίδος in the MSS appears to be an import from the margin, where a reminiscent copyist or reader had added the next words from the poem, ὡς οὐδὲν γλύκιον ἧς πατρίδος. Victorius and others would supply ὡς...ἧς before πατρίδος; but 'totius loci ratio illa verba reicit' (Boot).
17 **itaque** I.e. *et ita.* This is quite acceptable (cf. 374 (xiv. 20). 4, as now punctuated, *gratas fuisse meas litteras Bruto et Cassio gaudeo, itaque iis rescripsi*; K.–S. ii, p. 15).

3, 1 **nec...cum Pompeio...Caesare** 'Malaespina's transposition *cum Caesare sentienti...cum Pompeio* has been the vulgate for so long that it seems to have acquired squatter's rights in conservative eyes. It is a palaeographically violent change, neither necessary to the sense nor even, in my judgement, plausible intrinsically. Did Cicero ever quite envisage himself as *cum Caesare sentientem*, words which in this context can only refer to politics? Why not let him say that in cultivating Pompey *and* Caesar he had felt justified by two considerations?—(*a*) Pompey being fundamentally a good citizen, friendship with him would never entail disloyalty to the state. (*b*) Alliance with Pompey could not be combined with hostility to Caesar— they were too close to one another to allow of that. In other words, alliance with Pompey was a safe plan for a patriot, and the abandonment of enmity with Caesar its unavoidable corollary. It might be suggested that the second *Pompeio* is a gloss upon *eo*; but even that is unlikely, cf. Sjögren, *Comm. Tull.* pp. 160 f.' (*Towards a Text*, p. 29, followed (as elsewhere, tacitly) by Watt).

4, 3 **agentur** In the Senate.

ratio absentis The normal requirement that a candidate for a magistracy should apply in person for permission to stand could be waived by the Senate in special cases (cf. Mommsen, *St.* i, pp. 481 f.; J. P. V. D. Balsdon, *Journ. Rom. Stud.* 52 (1962), pp. 140 f.). A law dispensing Caesar had been passed in 52 on the proposal of the entire college of Tribunes. In the same year Pompey put through a law *de iure magistratuum* in which the obligation was reaffirmed in general, and then, after remonstrances from Caesar's friends, added a clause exempting persons who had already received dispensation. But the validity of the supplementary clause was open to dispute since Pompey's law had already been passed and its text deposited in the *aerarium* (cf. Mommsen, *St.* i, p. 504, n. 2). Balsdon, however, persuasively argues (*l.c.* p. 141) that this traditional account is a caricature of history derived from sources hostile to Pompey, it being 'obvious from the fact that Pompey's bill encountered no opposition from any of the ten tribunes that it never reached the people in a form in which it invalidated the special powers which Caesar had already received'. He further cites in translation Dio, XL. 56. 3, but in fact Dio's language supports the tradition (n.b. προσέγραψε. . . τῷ νόμῳ. . .διέφερε δ'οὐδὲν τοῦτο τοῦ μηδ' ἀρχὴν κεκωλῦσθαι).

4 **dimittat**   Cf. 122 (VI. 8). 2 n.

dic, M. Tulli   C. imagines himself in the Senate, called upon by the presiding magistrate to deliver his *sententia*. Cf. 126 (VII. 3). 5; 130 (VII. 7). 7.

6 **ubi. . .dexterae?**   Cf. *Verr.* II. 5. 104 *ubi fides, ubi exsecrationes, ubi dexterae complexusque?*; Sen. *Contr.* III. 8 *ubi hospitales invicem dexterae?* et sim. As Sjögren observed (*Comm. Tull.* p. 87), the unusual and alliterative epithet *densae* suggests a verse quotation (*ubi illáe sunt dénsae déxteráe?*). W. B. Sedgwick (*Mnem.* 4th Ser. 9 (1956), p. 236) compares Eur. *Med.* 496 φεῦ, δεξιὰ χείρ, ἧς σὺ πόλλ' ἐλαμβάνου (but his statement that C. himself normally has *dextra* is belied by MSS (cf. *Thes.* v (i). 917)). I would how-ever understand *densae* with certain early commentators not of the frequent reiteration of the pledges but of the hands 'tight-packed', i.e. tightly clasped. *tensae* would hardly do duty for *datae* or *iunctae*.

7 **hoc**   Sc. *ut ratio absentis haberetur.*

8 **Ravennae**   C. must have visited Caesar there in the winter of 53–52 (cf. *B.G.* VII. I. I), a fact not otherwise attested, and agreed to use his influence to ensure that Caelius Rufus, Tribune in 52, did not oppose the *privilegium*. Yet in 130 (VII. 7). 6 he says that he disapproved of it (cf. 142 (VII. 18). 2), and in *Phil.* II. 24 claims that he urged Pompey against it. Allowing this to be true we must suppose that he gave way in the end under strong pressure from Pompey (cf. 126 (VII. 3). 4 *cur tanto opere pugnatum est ut de eius absentis ratione habenda decem tribuni pl. ferrent?*; 153 (VIII. 3). 3 *idem etiam tertio consulatu, postquam esse defensor rei publicae coepit, contendit ut decem tribuni pl. errent ut absentis ratio haberetur.*

9 **divino**   Surely with a flavour of irony, even though C. did on the whole approve of Pompey's role in 52.

sensero   I.e. *censebo (sententiam dicam).*

αἰδέομαι   Cf. 25 (II. 5). 1.

10 **Πουλυδάμας κ.τ.λ.**   From Hector's speech (*Il.* XXII. 100); the original has ἀναθήσει.

11 **quis? tu ipse**   Cf. *Q. Fr.* II. 11. 3 'ne. . .Graios omnis convocet', per quos mecum in gratiam rediit, as interpreted in *Journ. Rom. Stud.* 45 (1955), p. 36.

5, 1 **plagam**   plăgam, lit. 'trap'.

3 **ipsum** Cf. *Fam.* XVI. 11. 2 *incidi in ipsam flammam civilis discordiae*; *de Orat.* I. 3 *incidimus in ipsam perturbationem disciplinae veteris.*

ut...dicat A much vexed phrase, convincingly explained by W. B. Sedgwick (*Mnem.* 4th Ser. 9 (1956), p. 256) as a proverbial saying, 'perhaps from an Atellane originally', like 'Fools rush in where angels fear to tread': cf. Ter. *Heaut.* 585 *Chreme, vin tu homini stulto mi auscultare?* For *ut* cf. *Rep.* I. 34 *ut etiam pro his dicam; Phil.* II. 12 *ut eum primum nominem* et sim. Note that if *dicat* were replaced by *ferat* or changed places with *sententiam* we should have a senarius.

9 **illa prima** The good behaviour of his staff: cf. 104 (v. 11). 5; 110 (v. 17). 2; 114 (v. 21). 5.

10 ἐπίτηκτα Lit. 'poured upon', i.e. gilded, not solid gold.

6, 3 annuo sumptu An official expense allowance; to be distinguished from the *vasarium*, of which the governor did not have to render any account (Mommsen, *St.* I, p. 296, n. 1).

6 **ut...invenirer** Egregiously misunderstood by T.-P. C. means, of course, that if he had done what his staff wanted he would have shown that his care for the finances of the provincial communities (cf. 116 (VI. 2). 4 f.) did not extend to those of Rome.

8 **et mea laus** *et* is correlative with *nec tamen.* C.'s conduct to his staff was balanced between a determination not to give way to their greed and a readiness to gratify them by courtesies and compliments—cold comfort, no doubt, from their standpoint.

9 **honorifice** Cf. 126 (VII. 3). 8 *meisque honorificentissimis erga se officiis.* Note that C. says nothing to except his brother from the indictment (cf. *ibid.* n. (*neminem*)).

10 **ut ait Thucydides** I. 97. 2 ἔγραψα δὲ αὐτὰ καὶ τὴν ἐκβολὴν τοῦ λόγου ἐποιησάμην διὰ τόδε κ.τ.λ. *non inutilis* is, I think, part of what is attributed to the historian, for although he does not use the words οὐκ ἀχρεῖον they are implied in his justification of the 'digression'. C. may not have remembered verbatim.

7, 1 tu...cogitabis Reverting to the subject introduced in §4.

2 **tueamur** 'Live up to': cf. 18 (I. 18). 6 n.; 347 (XIII. 49). 1n.; also *Catil.* III. 29 *ut ea quae gessi in consulatu privatus tuear atque ornem; Q. Fr.* I. 1. 30 f. *in his honoribus tuendis.* The usual translation 'keep' accords less well with C.'s usage. Moreover it was the reproach of bad faith and ingratitude towards Caesar that C. feared (cf. §4 ' "*ubi illae sunt densae dexterae?*" ') rather than the forfeiture of his good will.

benevolentiam As instanced in his kindness to Q. Cicero (cf. 93 (IV. 19). 2; *Q. Fr.* III. 6. 1 *ex optimi et potentissimi viri benevolentia*) and his loan to C. himself. Atticus however considered, and C. agreed, that Caesar might have been more generous: cf. 126 (VII. 3). 3.

ipso triumpho *ipso* because C. has already (§5) presented the Triumph as one possible way of avoiding political commitment, i.e. commitment against Caesar, so that from this point of view it comes under his first item. Now he asks Atticus to consider it in its own right, so to speak.

5 **qui non decrevit** Cato. The circumstances are known also from letters of Caelius (*Fam.* VIII. 11) and Cato himself (*ibid.* XV. 5). When the proposal for a *supplicatio* on account of C.'s successes in the Amanus came before the Senate at the end of April, Cato spoke in opposition, but at the same time proposed a decree commending C.'s administration in general. Hirrus (who had originally meant to speak at length) contented himself with expressing assent to Cato's proposal, and Favonius did likewise. Otherwise support for the *supplicatio* was unanimous and the motion passed without a division. *decrevit* is, as often, used loosely for the proposal of an individual Senator: cf. 73 (IV. 1). 6 n.

plus decrevit This is Cato's own contention in his letter (§2), *triumpho multo clarius est senatum iudicare potius mansuetudine et innocentia imperatoris provinciam quam vi militum aut benignitate deorum retentam atque conservatam esse; quod ego mea sententia censebam.* Less than six weeks later C. was looking at Cato's behaviour with very different eyes: cf. 125 (VII. 2). 7, a notable illustration of the way his judgements could vary according to mood and context.

7 **Hirrus** Cf. 89 (IV. 16). 5 n. He and Favonius simply said *M. Porcio* (or *M. Catoni*) *adsentior*; cf. 126 (VII. 3). 5.

scribendo adfuit No doubt as a conciliatory gesture. This shows that a Senator might witness a decree (cf. 19 (I. 19). 9 n.) which he had opposed in debate.

9 **triumphat** A curious choice of word in this context (cf. 125 (VII. 2). 7 *exsultat Catonis in me ingratissimi iniuria*).

8, 1 **coeperas** Sc. 'before the debate' or 'before you wrote'.

2 **Scrofam** Cf. 97 (V. 4). 2 n.

Silium Cf. 115 (VI. 1). 13 n. Evidently Scrofa and Silius were back in Rome by the summer of 50 (cf. Broughton, p. 251).

etiam antea. . .et iam So now Bayet and Watt (cf. *Towards a Text*, p. 29). Sjögren deletes *etiam* as a reflection of *et iam*, but it can quite well stand. C. says he had written to Scrofa and Silius even before he knew of Hirrus' moderate behaviour in the debate, implying that the purpose of his letters had been to ask them to mediate with Hirrus. Now, having learned of Hirrus' conduct and his conversation afterwards, he had written to Hirrus himself. There is no reason to understand a future (*scribam*) with *ad ipsum Hirrum*, as Sjögren prescribes.

3 **locutus enim sqq.**   Cf. Caelius, *Fam.* VIII. 11. 2 *renuntiatum nobis erat Hirrum diutius dicturum. prendimus eum; non modo non fecit sed, cum de hostiis ageretur et posset rem impedire si ut numeraretur postularet, tacuit; tantum Catoni adsensus est, qui ⟨de⟩ te locutus honorifice non decrerat supplicationes. commode* goes with *locutus erat*, not (as apparently Watt and others) with *potuisse*.

4 **tantum**   *tamen* spoils the sequence. Hirrus represented his support for Cato not as contrasting with his decision not to obstruct but rather as in itself a friendly, or at least not unfriendly, act. C., like Caelius (see above), wrote *tantum*. The MSS often confuse the contracted forms.

6 **litteras misisse**   Before the debate. Letters to Cato and both Consuls survive (*Fam.* XV. 4, 10, 13).

7 **verum**   In substance, if not quite literally.

Crassipedem   In 51 he was Silius' Quaestor in Bithynia, where C. wrote him a recommendatory letter (*Fam.* XIII. 9). Presumably his divorce from Tullia made C. reluctant to ask for his support, but they seem to have been on outwardly friendly terms in 49 (cf. 178 (IX. 11). 3).

9, 2 **illo**   Philotimus.

Lartidius   Perhaps a real or stage villain whose name had become a byword; several Lartidii are recorded in Augustus' time and afterwards. The notion that the name is a latinization of Λαερτιάδης can be given up, but an association is likely enough. For *Lartius* or *Lertius* = Λαέρτιος (Λάρτιος) cf. Neue–Wagener, *Formenlehre*[3], I, pp. 129 f., II. p. 43, also Quint. *Inst.* VI. 3. 96 *ut Cicero in Lartium, hominem callidum et versutum, cum is in quadam causa suspectus esset, 'nisi si qua Vlixes intervasit Lartius'* (sc. *versum posuit*).

3 ἀλλὰ τὰ μὲν κ.τ.λ.   *Il.* XVIII. 112, XIX. 65.

4 **quae**   Cf. *Pis.* 95 P. *Rutilio, quod specimen habuit haec civitas innocentiae*; Liv. XXX. 40. 3 *Verminem etiam, Syphacis filium, quae parva bene gestae rei accessio erat, devictum* et sim. It seems hardly possible to take *cura* (without epithet) as appositional (cf. 93 (IV. 19). 2 *ad summam laetitiam meam. . .magnus illius adventus cumulus accedet*; Ov. *Her.* XV. 71 *ultima tu nostris accedis causa querelis* et sim.).

5 **quicquid est**   Cf. 123 (VI. 9). 2 *quantulacumque est.*

7 **posset**   Impersonal: cf. Sjögren, *Comm. Tull.* pp. 165 f.

9 **hanc quoque. . .curam**   Anticipatory. Atticus is not likely to have written from Epirus or Athens about the Precius inheritance, which C. first mentions in his letter of 15 October (123 (VI. 9). 2). Nor can I follow Manutius and Watt (*l.c.* pp. 386 f.) in referring *curam* back to *sperati triumphi*. C. would hardly promise his own help in this (*in eo ego te adiuvabo*), and *quem ad modum experiamur* does not combine (see below). *quoque* rather suggests a

new topic. I think C. refers to Caesar's loan, which despite 94 (v. 1). 2, 97 (v. 4). 3, and 108 (v. 13). 3, had still not been repaid: cf. 126 (VIII. 3). 11.

10 **expediamur** Appropriately of extrication from financial obligation or embarrassment, as 370 (XIV. 16). 3 *nunc, mi Attice, me fac ut expedias*, 414 (XVI. 6). 3 *nomina mea, per deos, expedi exsolve*, ibid. *hoc quod satis debeo peto a te ut ante provideas planeque expedias*, 426 (XVI. 15). 6 *consenti in hac cura ubi sum, ut me expediam*. C. is thinking of his debt to Caesar (cf. 126 (VII. 3). 11; 131 (VII. 8). 5 fin.). Watt, taking *curam* as referring to *sperati triumphi* (see above), keeps *experiamur*. But the verb would be excessively odd (C. would have written *agamus*; *omnia experiar* in the next letter (§6) is quite incommensurate).

125 (VII. 2)

The Ciceros travelled west via Patrae, where Tiro was again left behind ill (2 November). A letter to him, written at the same time as this, gives the further stages of the journey (*Fam.* XVI. 9. 1): 'As you know, we left you on 2 November. We arrived at Leucas on the 6th, at Actium on the 7th, where we stayed over the 8th, on account of the weather. From Actium to Corcyra on the 9th, an excellent voyage. We stayed at Corcyra till the 15th, held up by bad weather. On the 16th we travelled 120 stades to Corcyra Harbour, near Cassiope, where winds held us up till the 22nd; many folk who were too impatient to wait were shipwrecked during that period. That evening we weighed anchor after dinner. Sailing through the night and the following day under a clear sky and the mildest of southerly breezes we gaily made our way to the Italian coast at Hydrus. Next day (i.e. 24 November) the same wind brought us to Brundisium at 2 o'clock of the afternoon.'

1, 1 **tua** Cf. 122 (VI. 8). 1. *laetatus sum felicitate navigationis tuae*. Not 'your proverbial luck' (cf. 93 (IV. 19). 1).

2 **lenissimus Onchesmites** Onchesmus (Santi Quaranta) was the port of Phoenice in north Epirus. It is possible that there really was a wind so called; the Aristotelian fragment *de Ventis* shows many winds thus locally named—Iapyx, Hellespontias, etc. But probably C. invented it.

3 **τῶν νεωτέρων** The *cantores Euphorionis* of *Tusc.* III. 45 (*poetae novi Orat.* 161), of whom only Catullus survives. The spondaic ending and the recondite *Onchesmites* are meant to be redolent of their style. It seems to me most improbable that 'the words of Cicero fell by chance into a spondaic hexameter'.

vendito Perhaps literally, and of course facetiously: a νεώτερος might put down money for so stylishly Alexandrine a verse: cf. Plin. *N.H* XXXV. 88 *famamque dispersit* (sc. *Apelles*) *se emere* (sc. *opera Protogeni*) *ut pro sui* *venderet.* More probably, 'puff', as in 320 (XIII. 12). 2 *Ligarianam praeclare vendidisti;* Hor. *Ep.* II. I. 74 *versus*. . .*unus et alter | iniuste totum ducit venditque poema;* Juv. VII. 135 *purpura vendit | causidicum; Har. Resp.* 46 *ut modo se his modo vendat illis. vendita* (Gronovius) is doubly needless, though quite possibly right.

2, 4 alteram. . .alteram   Cf. 154 (VII. 6). 5 and Cels. III. 3. 5 *at accessiones etiam modo singulae singulis diebus fiunt, modo binae pluresve concurrunt, ex quo saepe evenit ut cotidie plures accessiones remissionesque sint, sic tamen, ut unaquaeque alicui priori respondeat.*

Pamphilus   Probably a slave, perhaps a *tabellarius.*

8 Trebulano   Cf. 95 (V. 2). I n.

10 **gaudeo**   A better addition than the vulgate *quod si ita est,* ⟨*est*⟩ *quod* . . .*opto, idque* sqq. (Bosius): cf. 88 (IV. 14). I *si iam melius vales, vehementer gaudeo;* 119 (VI. 5). I *nunc quidem profecto Romae es, quo te, si ita est, salvum venisse gaudeo* et sim.

3, 2 quae quidem   This restrictive use of *qui quidem* is not common; cf. 77 (IV. 7). 2 n.

3 **Alexidis**   Cf. 113 (V. 20). 9.

4 **tuae**   *tuae litterae* can be defended: literally = 'what you write' rather than 'your handwriting', but the two meanings would here virtually coalesce. *littera* is what somebody writes in passages like Varro, *L.L.* VII. 2 *Aelii*. . .*interpretationem carminum Saliorum videbis et exili littera expeditam et praeterita obscura multa;* Ov. *Tr.* IV. I. 92 *tutaque iudicio littera nostra suo est, A.A.* I. 428 *littera* ('something in writing') *poscetur.* In Ov. *Her.* XVII. 144 *fungitur officio littera nostra tuo* and 266 *littera iam lasso pollice sistat opus* it is the act of writing. It is the style of handwriting *ibid.* XV. I (*Ep. Sapphus*) *ecquid, ut aspecta est studiosae littera dextrae, | protinus est oculis cognita nostra tuis?,* as in Juv. XIII. 138 *arguit ipsorum quos littera gemmaque princeps | sardonychum* and Fronto, *ad M. Caes.* IV. 2. 4 *Sota*. . .*et in charta puriore et volumine gratiore et littera festiviore quam antea fuerat videtur.* But these are only so many aspects of one main sense, 'writing', not to be too sharply distinguished. Manutius' simple deletion of *manum* gives a better point than Meutzner's *tuae, litteras non amabam quod indicabant* and better suits *indicare,* which suggests indirect revelation. But on the whole I prefer to follow Watt, since *litterae* could well have been added at the same time and for the same reason as *manum.* The deletion of both certainly makes a tidier sentence.

6 **adulescentem. . .probum**   The paradosis can be defended as in *Towards a Text,* p. 30, *ut nosti* taken as *qualem nosti.* But it is simpler to suppose that an epithet has fallen out, or rather more than one in view of *adde, si quid vis.* For *diligentem* cf. 120 (VI. 7). 2 *nihil enim illo adulescente castius, nihil diligentius.* Müller's punctuation *adulescentem, ut nosti (et adde, si*

quid vis), *probum* is against analogy, which shows that *probum* goes with *adde*: cf. Hor. *Sat.* II. 7. 39 *imbecillus, iners, si quid vis, adde popino* and many other examples in *Towards a Text, l.c.*

10 **M'. Curi** Cf. 126 (VII. 3). 12 and *Fam.* XVI. 5. 2 (to Tiro) *ego omnem spem tui diligenter curandi in Curio habeo* (also XVI. 4. 2, 9. 3, 11. 1). This friend of Atticus carried on business at Patrae (*Fam.* XIII. 17. 1, 50. 1), where he entertained C. on his homeward journey. Despite C.'s statement in a letter of recommendation (*Fam.* XIII. 17. 1) that his own friendship with Curius dated back to the latter's early days (*ut primum in forum venit*), the present passage shows that their closer acquaintance only started with this visit. Cf. Curius' own letter (*Fam.* VII. 29. 1) in 45 *sum enim* χρήσει μὲν *tuus,* κτήσει δὲ *Attici nostri*. Münzer identifies him with the Curius mentioned in a letter to Coelius Caldus of June 50 (*Fam.* II. 19. 2) as *consobrinus tuus, mihi, ut scis, maxime necessarius,* who had written to C. on Coelius' behalf, as had also another relative, C. Vergilius (Pr. 62). But apart from the difficulty of reconciling *maxime necessarius* with the wording here, this seems a surprising social milieu for a *negotiator*. C. stayed with him again during the Civil War (*Fam.* XIII. 17. 1) and wrote him three extant letters thereafter (*Fam.* VII. 28, 30, 31).

13 **αὐτόχθων.. .urbanitas** C. means that Curius' wit and manners had the authentic Roman flavour (not that he was 'one of nature's gentlemen'): cf. Lys. *Epitaph.* 43 γνησίαν δὲ καὶ αὐτόχθονα τοῖς ἐκ τῆς Ἀσίας βαρβάροις τὴν αὐτῶν ἀρετὴν ἐπεδείξαντο and C. to Curius himself (*Fam.* VII. 31. 2) *equidem vellem uti pedes haberent* (sc. *tuae res*), *ut aliquando redires. vides enim exaruisse iam veterem urbanitatem* sqq. Cf. also to Papirius Paetus (*Fam.* IX. 15. 2) *accedunt non Attici, sed salsiores quam illi Atticorum Romani veteres atque urbani sales. ego autem. . .mirifice capior facetiis, maxime nostratibus* sqq.

14 **trium** M. Cicero junior was still a minor. According to Ulpian (*Dig.* XXVIII. 1. 20 praef.) legatees might witness a will but not heirs, at any rate not the principal heir. But Gaius (II. 108; cf. Justinian, *Inst.* II. 10. 10 f.) states that even an heir could legally do so, though it was very inadvisable, and *Mil.* 48 furnishes an example.

cohortisque praetoriae On the *cohors amicorum praetoria*, consisting of friends and clients, see Mommsen, *Hermes*, 14 (1879), pp. 25 ff.; *Thes.* III. 1553. 18.

15 **palam** Witnesses to a will did not necessarily know the contents: cf. Buckland, *Text-Book of Roman Law*, p. 294.

libella.. .terruncio Fractions of the denarius, which originally contained ten asses or libellae, each of twelve unciae.

in Actio Corcyrae Not mentioned anywhere else. *in* shows that this Actium was a locality, not a town: contrast 92 (v. 9). 1; *Fam.* XVI. 6. 2.

16 **Alexio** Probably manager of Atticus' estate at Buthrotum; cf. 333 (XIII. 25). 3 n.

muneratus est With presents of food and drink: cf. 102 (v. 9). 1 n.

17 **Thyamim** The river which ran through Atticus' property. Its beauty is praised in *Leg.* II. 7, but C. probably means only that Quintus wanted to see his uncle's estate and that this was why the party stopped at Corcyra.

4, 1 filiola Cf. 112 (v. 19). 2 n.

2 στοργὴν τήν A necessary addition. The doctrine maintained by Stoics and others (cf. Madvig on *Fin.* III. 62) that the affection of parents for their offspring is 'natural' should have been rejected by Atticus as a good Epicurean (cf. Usener, *Epicurea*, pp. 318 ff.). The fact that he admitted it is among the indications that the philosophy of Epicurus was not his lodestar (cf. Introd. p. 8, n. 5).

etenim sqq. Cf. *Fin.* III. 62 *pertinere autem ad rem arbitrantur intellegi natura fieri ut liberi a parentibus amentur; a quo initio profectam communem humani generis societatem persequimur; Off.* I. 12 *eademque natura vi rationis hominem conciliat homini et ad orationis et ad vitae societatem, ingeneratque in primis praecipuum quendam amorem in eos qui procreati sunt.*

hoc Sjögren refers to Madvig on *Fin.* III. 21 *in eo collocatum. haec* impairs the sense. C. does not mean 'if affection towards children does not exist' (everyone admits that it does), but 'if this (i.e. the doctrine that such affection is "natural") is not true'.

4 Carneades Of Cyrene (214/13–129/8), head of the Academy and a polemist against philosophic, especially Stoic, dogma. Commentators have done their best to find indecency in his *bene eveniat!*, Causaubon suggesting that the original might have been τύχῃ ἀγαθῇ παιδοποιῶμεν (not surely a very shocking expression); but that would be mere flippancy, no answer to the Stoics. *spurce* need not however imply obscenity, any more than 'filthy' or for that matter 'obscene' in colloquial English: cf. 224 (XI. 13). 2 *spurcissime*; Plin. *N.H.* XXIX. 14 *nos quoque dictitant barbaros et spurcius nos quam alios* Ὀπικῶν *appellatione foedant; Dom.* 47 *hanc tibi legem Cloelius scripsit spurciorem lingua sua* et sim. Carneades' εὖ ἔστω was therefore probably just a cynical dismissal of the Stoic argument, about equivalent to 'tant pis'.

5 prudentius If *pudentius* (Hervagius) had been in the MSS, it would have been desirable to emend it. C. attacks the Epicureans for their stupidity (*non intellegunt*), not for their impudence.

Lucius noster Doubtless Saufeius (cf. 115 (VI. 1). 10 *Saufeium nostrum*; 123 (VI. 9). 4 *nostrum Saufeium*), who had recently been in C.'s company (*ibid.*), not L. Manlius Torquatus (cf. 92 (IV. 18). 3 n.).

Patron Cf. §5 below. But the MSS have *Patro* in *Fam.* XIII. 1. 3.

6 nec 'Rectius statuemus ante v. *quidquam* excidisse *nec* vel potius *numquam*' (Orelli). I should say '*numquam* vel potius *nec*', though *numquam quemquam* is probably right in *Fin.* III. 29.

8 intellegunt The subjunctive could stand as causal after *qui*, but it then becomes easier to misunderstand and mispunctuate the sentence, as Sjögren and Watt have done.

9 callido homine Cf. *Leg.* I. 41 *tum autem, qui non ipso honesto movemur ut boni viri simus sed utilitate aliqua atque fructu, callidi sumus, non boni.*

5, 2 Philoxeno Perhaps a slave or freedman of Q. Cicero's: cf. 313 (XIII. 8) n.

dedisses = *te dedisse scripseras.*

3 Pompei Atticus' letter must have arrived at Corcyra after 15 November since C. left the place on the 16th (see 125 (VII. 2), introd. note), so the conversation may have taken place about the beginning of the month.

5 integritatis As governor.

6, 2 Bibuli Cf. 122 (VI. 8). 5.

amplissima The word-order supports this easy correction (final *e* and *a* are often confused); cf. however Caes. *B.C.* III. 53. 5 *cohortemque postea duplici stipendio. . .militaribusque donis amplissime donavit.*

4 honori Probably a prospective Triumph rather than the *supplicatio* in view of *idem* below.

9 valebis I.e. in time to assist.

7, 1 raudusculo Numeriano Nothing is known of this business. Numerius is probably a *nomen gentile*, as in the case of the anti-Ciceronian Tribune of 57, Q. Numerius Rufus (cf. Statius, Vibius, Salvius).

quid egerit In his will; cf. 126 (VII. 3). 9 *Hortensi legata cognovi; nunc aveo scire* sqq. It is absurd to suppose that C. was longing to know what Hortensius had done about his own *supplicatio* in April. If Hortensius was well enough to attend the Senate he must have supported it (cf. 124 (VII. 1). 7 n.). As for C.'s triumphal aspirations, they had scarcely developed before Hortensius' death in June. Watt (*l.c.* p. 288) maintains that Hortensius the son is meant here and in 126 (VII. 3). 9, finding it difficult to believe that C., who had heard of Hortensius' death early in August, should not have learned the provisions of his will by 26 November. According to his view the information which C. wanted was what the younger Hortensius had done about paying his father's legacies. But it is far more natural to understand *Hortensi legata* as 'the legacies left by Hortensius (the father)' than as 'the legacies payable by Hortensius (the son)'. *quid egerit* need not imply total ignorance on C.'s part; he may well have heard that the will made Hortensius junior the heir and contained a number of legacies without knowing the full details.

2 **Cato quid agat** After *quid Hortensius egerit* the question obviously has to do with Hortensius or his estate; exactly what, we cannot say. The family links were remarkable. Hortensius had wanted to marry Cato's eldest daughter, already wedded to Bibulus (Plut. *Cat. Min.* 25). Instead, he took Cato's wife Marcia by amicable agreement. After Hortensius' death she reverted to her former husband. Perhaps this was the subject of C.'s curiosity—would Cato remarry Marcia?

qui. . .malevolus Wording as well as context suggests a change of topic. If *quid agat* had concerned C.'s Triumph, *qui* rather than *qui quidem* would have stood in the relative clause.

3 **iustitiae, clementiae** Cf. 116 (VI. 2). 5 n. (*nec imperita*).

6 **in me ingratissimi** The superlative at least and perhaps the whole phrase *Catonis. . .iniuria* was doubtless in Caesar's letter; for such hidden quotations cf. e.g. 171 (IX. 5). 1 *scelus accusans Pompei*; 190 (X. 4). 6 *de meo animo a suis rationibus alienissimo*; 344 (XIII. 41). 1 *de tua in illum iniuria*; 366 (XIV. 12). 1 *legem a dictatore comitiis latam*.

7 **dierum XX** Sc. *supplicationem decrevit*. If the number of days, which many have thought absurdly high, is correct, Bibulus was given parity with Caesar, who had twice been awarded a *supplicatio* of twenty days for his victories in Gaul (*B.G.* IV. 38. 5, VII. 90. 8)—a longer period than any previously voted (*Balb.* 61). Cato had strong personal and political reasons for favouring his son-in-law Bibulus, whose services may after all have seemed much more important to himself, to Cato, and to the Senate than they seemed to C. (cf. T. Frank, *Am. Journ. Phil.* 34 (1913), pp. 324 f.). Whether Bibulus could claim technical responsibility for Cassius' victory in 51, achieved about the time of his arrival in the province (cf. 113 (V. 20). 3 f.), may be doubtful. But he evidently took credit for the Parthian retreat in the following year, which C. himself regarded as a marvellous deliverance (cf. 121 (VI. 6). 3 n.). Even so Frank's suggestion that *DXX* came from *die* ⚼ *X* is worth attention. Even ten days would be a high honour, first accorded to Pompey in 63 (*Prov. Cons.* 27).

ignosce As a friend and admirer of Cato; cf. Introd. p. 7, n. 3.

8, 1 **iam. . .videbo** In fact this did not happen for over a month from the time of writing.

2 **Chrysippo** We gather that he and his unnamed fellow-delinquent were recently manumitted slaves in attendance on C.'s son. He is probably the man mentioned in connexion with the purchase of books for Q. Cicero's library in 54 (Q. *Fr.* III. 4. 5, 5. 6). But the Chrysippus of 212

(XI. 2). 3 and later letters will be Vettius Chrysippus the architect (cf. 24 (II. 4). 7 n.).

8 **Drusi**   Probably M. Livius Drusus, Cos. 112. Another of his judgements as Praetor Urbanus (there is no need to assume that the slave in the case was his own) is mentioned in *ad Her.* II. 19. *ut ferunt*, of course, applies to the whole story.

9 **eadem**   The same oath (to perform certain duties to his future *patronus*) that he had sworn before manumission as a condition thereof— Atticus is assumed to know the details. Cf. *Dig.* XL. 12. 44, where the jurist Venuleius is cited to the effect that doubt had formerly existed whether such an oath before manumission was legally binding upon a freedman. He himself thought not, holding that the purpose of the oath was to impose a moral obligation to repeat it after manumission, which done it would of course become binding. C. evidently regarded Drusus' ruling as implying that the act of manumission could be repudiated by a *patronus* in case of gross misconduct on the part of the beneficiary.

10 **nemo**   I.e. no legally qualified *adsertor libertatis* (cf. Buckland, *Text-Book of Roman Law*, p. 73). These two slaves seem to have been freed informally *inter amicos*, not by process of *vindicta*, and so did not possess *iusta libertas* (*ibid.* p. 77; cf. Suet. *Aug.* 40. 4; Tac. *Ann.* XIII. 27. 4).

ut videbitur   Atticus approved (128 (VII. 5). 3).

12 **uni**   Written *in suburbano* (126 (VII. 3). 6).

14 **Parthi faciunt**   Cf. 121 (VI. 6). 3 n.

15 **semivivum**   'Metu Parthorum paene exanimatum' (Schütz).

126 (VII. 3)

1, 1 **Aeculanum**   Aeclanum in inscriptions and itineraries, in Samnium on the Via Appia 15 miles east of Beneventum.

litteras   In answer, as appears, to 123 (VI. 9) and 124 (VII. 1). These will have been delayed by bad weather.

5 **te. . .negas**   Cf. 36 (II. 16). 3. This must have been in answer to C.'s rueful confession in 124 (VII. 1). 5 that he wished he had stayed in Cilicia after all. Atticus may be supposed to have written something like this: 'Yes, I think it *would* have been better for you to have stayed, holding as I do that Dicaearchus was wrong to advocate the active life (ὁ πρακτικὸς βίος) in preference to the contemplative (ὁ θεωρητικός). For in the present state of political ferment you will indeed find more to bother you in Rome than in Cilicia.' The usual interpretation, according to which ὁ πρακτικὸς βίος is represented by C.'s provincial office, makes Atticus approve its relinquishment. In that case he must be supposed to have missed the point of C.'s

admission, nor would C. have had any reason to defend his action as he proceeds to do. The whole sequence down to ἀμεταμέλητος *debet esse* shows that Atticus had taken the other line.

12 utile During the Parthian threat C. had thought of staying on as governor in the public interest, even though that meant infringing the terms of his appointment (121 (VI. 6). 3); still, nobody could blame him for not doing so, particularly as the threat had disappeared. By *utile* he may however mean 'expedient to myself'. Atticus' letter, to which *istius* seems to refer, would settle the doubt.

2, 1 quid si hoc melius? Cf. *Fam.* XIII. 47 *utamur igitur vulgari consolatione, 'quid si hoc melius?'*

saepe...ut in hoc ipso Cf. *Flacc.* 37 *equidem in minimis rebus saepe res magnas vidi, iudices, deprehendi ac teneri, ut in hoc Asclepiade*; *ad Her.* III. 21 *saepe rerum naturae gratia quaedam iure debetur, velut accidit in hac re*; *Cels.* praef. 45 *quod in plurimis contentionibus deprehendere licet sine ambitione verum scrutantibus, ut in hac ipsa re* et sim.

5 ubicumque essem Subjunctive because the clause is part of a hypothetical statement: cf. K.–S. II, p. 204.

9 sexto libro *de Republica.* The portrait of the ideal statesman was in the lost earlier part of Book VI.

quid...faciam? Cf. Plaut. *Pseud.* 78 *quid faciam tibi?*; Madvig on *Fin.* II. 79. The thought runs: 'Apart from the Triumph, I have conformed to the ideal. What more (in all other ways) could you ask of me? And even the Triumph I shall surrender, if I find I ought.'

12 sed Dismissive.

3, 1 nam 'Occupatory'.

quod putas sqq. Cf. 124 (VII. 1). 5.

4 adsentior The paradosis gives *adsentio* again in 176 (IX. 9). 1. Since C. certainly used the active form in the perfect he may have used it in the present too; but the examples are few and insecure: cf. Neue–Wagener, *Formenlehre*³, III, pp. 19 f.

6 nequaquam...fuisse Cf. Introd. p. 30, n. 9. Apart from his loan to C., Caesar had given Quintus a large sum (220 (XI. 9). 2 *etiam tantam illi pecuniam dedisse honoris mei causa*).

officiis Including support in the Senate for Caesar's position and claims in 56, defence of Vatinius and assistance in Caesar's building operations in 54, and intervention with Caelius Rufus in 53–52 (cf. 124 (VII. 1). 4 n. (*Ravennae*)).

7 causam We can only guess what Atticus' explanation was. He may have argued that Caesar knew C. too well to expect to buy his unlimited support.

8 †et eis   The text can hardly be right as it stands, and Wesenberg's clumsy supplement *quae de me acta sunt* (after *consentiunt*) is hardly the way to rectify it. It would be simpler to substitute *ea* for *eis*, taking the latter as a copyist's *Falschverbesserung*; but there are other possibilities (see App. Crit.).

quae...scribis   Again the nature of Caesar's dealings with his two Legates is conjectural, but it would seem that he was thought to have treated them less than handsomely (*acta* does not necessarily imply formal or public proceedings: cf. 103 (v. 10). 4; 145 (VII. 21). 3), perhaps in connexion with their joint and highly successful operations in west and south-west Gaul the previous year (Hirt. *B.G.* VIII. 27 ff.). If my suggestion as to Atticus' explanation of Caesar's motive in C.'s case is correct, it would follow that both were regarded as politically unreliable from Caesar's point of view. Certain data fit this picture though they do not establish it. In Fabius' case there is his friendship with Atticus (cf. 153 (VIII. 3). 7 *Fabium tuum*) and the rumour rife in February 49 that he had deserted Caesar's cause (*ibid.*); in Caninius', his close ties with Scribonius Libo and Caesar's choice of him as a peace negotiator (*B.C.* I. 26. 3).

Fabio   C. Fabius M. f. His cognomen, if he had one, is unknown, but it pretty certainly was not Maximus. Plebeian Fabii are quite numerous at this period. An ex-Praetor and governor of Asia, he had been active from 54 onwards as a Legate in Gaul. Despite the rumour of his defection above mentioned he served Caesar loyally and well against the Pompeian armies in Spain in early 49, but then disappears from view.

Caninioque   C. Caninius C. f. Rebilus, descended no doubt from a namesake, Praetor in 171, was prominent in the Gallic campaigns of 52 and 51. He continued to serve Caesar in the Civil Wars, as a negotiator in 49 (see above), then in Africa under Curio and in the campaigns of 46 and 45. In the last year Caesar named him Consul Suffectus for its one remaining day. Supposed evidence of a personal connexion with C. is fictitious (cf. 183 (IX. 15). 4 n. (*Trebatium*)).

10 custos urbis   Before fleeing Rome in 58 C. dedicated a statue of Minerva *custos Vrbis*, previously in his house, on the Capitol: cf. *Leg.* II. 42; *Fam.* XII. 25. 1. The inscription is unknown. It need not have been long or elaborate.

12 Vulcatium aut Servium   Cf. 160 (VIII. 9a). 1 and 177 (IX. 10). 7, where M'. Lepidus replaces Servius. In putting forward these two elder statesmen as examplars at this time Atticus was probably recommending the same policy as in 44 *ut nec duces simus nec agmen cogamus* (416 (xv. 13). 1): see Introd. p. 31, n. 2. On Ser. Sulpicius cf. 25 (II. 5). 2 n. L. Vulcatius Tullus, of senatorial but not noble family, became Consul in 66. After the republican débâcle in January, he like Servius took a non-committal line which came

to look more and more like collaboration with Caesar. Unlike Servius he did not subsequently join Pompey. No more in fact is heard of him after the beginning of April (cf. 190 (x. 1*a*). 2 n.) until 46, when he appears as deprecating Caesar's pardon of M. Marcellus (*Fam.* IV. 4. 4)— apparently a sycophantic gesture. C.'s argument here needs attention. There is really no need, he implies, for Atticus to make appeals to his patriotism. If the question were as simple as that, he would not merely range himself with moderate *boni* like Servius and Vulcatius (cf. 160 (VIII. 9*a*). 1 *minus multa dederant illi rei publicae pignora*), he would feel bound to take a leading, individual role. But it is not, for a reason which he proceeds to explain.

4, 5 illo modo Not through the Senate but by the consular lex Pompeia Licinia of 55. C. may also be thinking of the violence and irregularity with which the authors of the law were elected. Cf. 130 (VII. 7). **6 ita latum**; 132 (VII. 9). 4 *praeteriit tempus non legis sed libidinis tuae*.

pugnatum Cf. 124 (VII. 1). 4.

7 civi Cf. Neue–Wagener, *Formenlehre*[3], I, p. 338.

spes. . .sit Cf. 397 (XV. 20). 2 *vidi nostros tantum spei habere ad vivendum*; Liv. XLIII. 18. 10 *cum spei nihil ad resistendum esset* et sim. *vires* (E). . .*sint* (Klotz) or *vis*. . .*sit* (Gronovius: cf. Vell. II. 61. 1 *vis ad resistendum nulli aderat*) are not recommended by *viris* adjoining.

5, 2 ποῦ κ.τ.λ. Cf. Eur. *Troad.* 455 ποῦ σκάφος τὸ τοῦ στρατηγοῦ; Atticus followed by C. (unless the misquotation is C.'s only) cited the words inaccurately (putting Agamemnon and Menelaus in the same boat!) and without regard to their original context, simply as a way of saying 'Which is the side to join?'.

4 dic, M. Tulli Cf. 124 (VII. 1). 4 n.

Cn. Pompeio adsentior Cf. *ibid.* 8 *adsensum tantum esse Catoni*.

7 rem I am much tempted to read *rem p*(*ublicam*) with Watt: cf. *Fam.* XVI. 11. 3 *numquam maiore in periculo civitas fuit, numquam improbi cives habuerunt paratiorem ducem*; *post Red.* 4 *magno in periculo rem publicam futuram*; D. Brutus, *Fam.* X. 10. 1 *quae* (sc. *res publica*) *quanto sit in periculo*. . .*exponam*. But cf. *Sest.* 68 *res erat et causa nostra eo iam loci ut erigere oculos et vivere videretur*.

vos scilicet plura Cf. 416 (XV. 13). 2 *vos omnia prius*.

9 damnatos. . .ignominia adfectos Especially the victims of Pompey's courts in 52 and of Ap. Pulcher's recent 'partisan housecleaning' (Broughton).

11 valentis C. usually applies this term to political opponents: cf. *Philol.* 105 (1961), p. 85 on Caelius, *Fam.* VIII. 4. 2 †*Laelios*† *et Antonios et id genus valentis*.

12 Q. Cassio Cf. 122 (VI. 8). 2 n. It is very unlikely that C. refers to the

Pompeian Gaius rather than the Caesarian Quintus. Some prefer to delete the praenomen.

pluris   Genitive as in *Fam.* IX. 19. 2 *peto a te ne pluris esse balbos quam disertos putes*; *Sest.* 142 *quis Carthaginiensium pluris fuit Hannibale. . .?*; *Nat. Deor.* III. 26 *sit sane adrogantis pluris se putare quam mundum*; Plaut. *Asin.* 435 *neque esse servom in aedibus eri qui sit pluris quam ille est*; Nep. *Dat.* 5. 2 *quod illum unum pluris quam se omnes videbant*, *Epam.* 10. 4 *ex quo intellegi potest unum hominem pluris quam civitatem fuisse*; Hor. *Sat.* I. 6. 12 *Laevinum. . . unius assis | non umquam pretio pluris licuisse*; Ov. *Tr.* I. 9. 44 *nemo pluris emendus erat.* C. characteristically finds humour in the idea that the insolvents were 'worth more' (i.e. counted for more) than he had supposed. Of course *pluris* could be accusative plural (cf. *Div.* II. 5 *quos quidem pluris quam rebar esse cognovi*), in which case we have only a rather flat statement of fact.

13 causam. . .causa   Another piece of word-play. *causam* means a cause to fight for, *causa* a political 'movement'; cf. 55 (III. 10). 1 n.

14 hic omnia facere omnis   Cf. *Orat.* 4 *sed par est omnis omnia experiri . . .qui res magnas concupiverunt.* If C. had meant 'on our side' he would have written *hac* (Lehmann). But in fact most of the leading republicans were the reverse of pacific, though it was otherwise with the rank and file (cf. 128 (VII. 5). 4; 129 (VII. 6). 2). Nor would such a statement reinforce C.'s main contention that the situation was extremely dangerous. *hic* is therefore to be taken as 'here', i.e. in the part of Italy from which C. was writing (cf. *ibid.*). *omnia facere* perhaps means little more than *cupidissimos esse*; but the *municipales* could at least write to their friends in Rome.

17 Veientonem   Cf. 91 (IV. 17). 3 n.

19 declaravit   By his action. Cato did not *say* this (see below).

iis   I.e. people like C.: cf. *Catil.* III. 28 *cum praesertim neque in honore vestro neque in gloria virtutis quicquam videam altius quo mihi libeat ascendere.* With *non* Cato is supposed to have *said* that the only persons whom he did not envy were those whose dignity admitted of little or no augmentation (like Bibulus)—as though Cato would have confessed to all but universal *invidia* or C. have thought such a remark worth repeating some six months later. On intruded negatives see Müller, p. xxvi. T.-P.'s cherished fallacy (cf. Vol. III, p. 303, v. p. 5) that interference with a negative is a specially rash and violent act of criticism, i.e. that the probability of a conjecture has to do with the degree to which it changes the *sense* (or nonsense) of the paradosis, can still mislead the unwary (witness E. Badian, *Cl. Rev.* N.S. 11 (1961), p. 108). Here however *non* may possibly come from *nunc*, in allusion to Cato's actions on earlier occasions, such as Pomptinus' Triumph (cf. *Q. Fr.* III. 4. 6) in 54.

6, 2 et iis. . .et iis   The first was presumably the 'very eloquent' letter received at Brundisium, to which C. did not reply at the time (125 (VII. 2). 8), the second the one brought by Philotimus (§1).

in suburbano   No doubt Atticus' *rusticum praedium* near Nomentum (Nep. *Att.* 14. 3), called *Ficulense* in 273 (XII. 34). 1.

3 **ad privata venio**   The temptation to tamper with these words is obvious, but C. probably wrote them where they stand. Sjögren compares 19 (I. 19). 5; 113 (V. 21). 5; *Nat. Deor.* III. 16. Here we have the additional but not incredible oddity that having twice announced his change of topic C. still fails to change it. Purser's transposition (see App. Crit.) would be highly commendable if such dislocations were not so rare.

Caelio   Caelius Rufus, Curule Aedile this year, had joined Caesar. His *volte-face* had been foreshadowed in a letter to C. written in September (*Fam.* VIII. 14. 3), where he says that when it comes to civil war the stronger side is the better. In 48 he gave different reasons, at least as likely to be genuine—resentment against Ap. Pulcher and friendship with Curio (*Fam.* VIII. 17. 1). C. put it down to his own absence (*Brut.* 273 *nescio quo modo discessu meo discessit a sese*).

6 **vici**   Rows of town houses here (cf. §9).

Luccei   Cf. 115 (VI. 1). 23. Caelius' money presumably came from Caesar.

7, 1 †**mihi**   This pronoun has no business here that I can see.

4 **commentarium**   Probably an account of C.'s financial position drawn up before he left for the East.

5 **si praestaret**   The rendering 'if he paid' is nonsense. C. cannot mean and does not say that *even* if Philotimus paid the balance he would *still* owe as much or more than the total of his (C.'s) debts. *reliquum* ought to represent the whole outstanding sum due from Philotimus. Also the tenses do not fit; C. would have written *si praestabit* or *praestarit. . .debebit* or *si praestet. . . debeat. si praestaret* means 'if he were paying' (or 'making good': cf. *Rosc. Com.* 35 *Roscium, si quid communi nomine tetigit, confiteor praestare debere societati*), i.e. 'were ready to pay': cf. 116 (VI. 2). 9 *solvunt enim Salamini,* 'the Salaminians are willing to pay'. In fact, we gather, Philotimus was now querying the debt or part of it.

7 **non accusabimur**   Cf. *de Orat.* II. 245 *tum quaesitor properans 'modo breviter'. hic ille 'non accusabis: perpusillum rogabo'.*

9 **et amicorum. . .occupati**   Sjögren saw that the suppression of *et* is no answer here, but his *et amicorum ⟨et alienorum⟩* is unconvincing; we should expect *negotiis* rather than *multitudine* (a point against my earlier proposal (⟨*et in re publica*⟩ *et amicorum*), and it would not be C.'s way to say that he was kept busy by the number of his friends, i.e. by his legal work, etc. on their behalf, without also mentioning the cares of state: cf. *Fam.* IV. 6. 2

non amicorum negotiis, non rei publicae procuratione impediebantur cogitationes meae (cf. Sulpicius, *Fam.* IV. 5. 3 *in re publica, in amicorum negotiis*); *de Orat.* I. 3 *quantum mihi vel fraus inimicorum vel causae amicorum vel res publica tribuet oti*, 78 *nos. . .quos in foro, quos in ambitione, quos in re publica, quos in amicorum negotiis res ipsa ante confecit*, II. 24 *quando ages negotium publicum? quando amicorum?*; *Off.* II. 4 *quantum superfuerat amicorum et rei publicae temporibus*; Plin. *Ep.* III. 5. 19 *quem partim publica, partim amicorum officia distringunt*.

10 **ergo** This looks back to *non accusabimur posthac*. C. promises to pay more attention to his finances in future, and that will mean availing himself of Atticus' proffered assistance.

8, 1 de serpirastris Not to be taken too closely with *nihil est quod doleas*. Atticus will have written that C.'s staff seemed to need knee-splints to strengthen their moral legs, or something of the kind; cf. 124 (VII. 1). 5 f.

3 **minime** So Watt[1]: cf. *Amic.* 11 *nisi enim, quod ille minime putabat, immortalitatem optare vellet*. *neminem* (Aldus) is not even Latin. Neither C. nor any other classical author has *nemo* when he means *nihili* (*nullius pretii*). And why should C. make so much ado about a person whom Atticus held in contempt? Manutius' explanation 'quem minime omnium putas' gives the right sense, but cannot be extracted from *neminem*. *nemo* of the MSS (probably from *nemo* preceding) might be replaced by *non* or *nullus*, the latter likely to puzzle a copyist; but *minime* comes neatly after *magis*. As for the question of identity, Mescinius Rufus is impossible in view of 117 (VI. 3). 1 and 118 (VI. 4). 1; *he* had evidently not (in C.'s opinion) formed any self-denying resolutions, nor did he leave Cilicia in C.'s company (cf. 120 (VI. 7). 2). I have suggested brother Quintus as the only other of C.'s companions of sufficient importance to suit his language. A veiled reference in so delicate a context was only to be expected: cf. that to Quintus junior in 420 (XVI. 11). 8, who when in disgrace is apt to become *quidam* or *sororis tuae filius*. The absence of any saving clause in 124 (VII. 1). 6 may well have made

[1] The history of this conjecture is as follows: the gist of my note, discrediting the vulgate *neminem*, appeared in *Towards a Text*, pp. 31 ff. Mr Watt, who was good enough to read and comment on some of the notes in that volume before their publication (see its preface), agreed with this one, but suggested *minime* as an alternative to *nullus*. *minime* had in fact occurred to me, as it was almost bound to occur to anyone who read Manutius with the right sense in mind; but as I had omitted it in the draft sent to Mr Watt I attributed it to him (with his permission) in my published note. There presumably Bayet found it, and quoted it in his edition of 1964 without reference to the note which was its *raison d'être*. What is more remarkable, Mr Watt, who has made a point of referring conjectures quoted in his apparatus to the places of their original publication, preferred in this one instance merely to write *scripsi*.

Atticus wonder. In 47 Quintus senior is found complaining that in the previous year C. had not offered him any share in his Cilician savings (224 (XI. 13). 4).

9, 1 Curio   Cf. 125 (VII. 2). 3 n.

2 cognovi   The information will hardly have come in answer to C.'s question in 125 (VII. 2). 7. A letter dispatched from Brundisium on 25 November could scarcely bring a reply to Aeclanum by 6 December.

†**hominis**   If sound this word must refer to Hortensius the son, even though *Hortensi legata* means 'the legacies left by Hortensius (the father)'; cf. 125 (VII. 2). 7 n. But *quid hominis sit* would normally mean 'what sort of a fellow he is' (cf. *Thes.* VI. 2888. 58) and, as Watt remarks (*l.c.* p. 388), C. knew the answer to that question only too well. The substitution of *heredis* (*Towards a Text*, p. 32) has therefore something to commend it, though the contraction *hiḋs* would not be likely to appear in a literary text (cf. W. Clausen, *Cl. Phil.* 57 (1962), p. 184). Watt proposes *quid hominis ⟨in animo⟩ sit* (C. would surely have written *homini*).

3 portam Flumentanam   The entrance to the Velabrum from the Campus Martius; presumably Lucceius' *vici* were situated thereabouts. Hortensius evidently left property in Puteoli (cf. 95 (V. 2). 2 and archaeological evidence adduced by J. H. D'Arms, *Am. Journ. Phil.* 88 (1967), p. 196 *ff.*), where by coincidence C. came into a large estate five years later. The jest would be improved if Caelius came from Puteoli, as he did if the old conjecture *Puteolani* is right after all in *Cael.* 5.

10, 1 venio ad 'Piraeea'   Perhaps with a play on the literal sense. Atticus had taken C. to task for writing *in Piraeea cum exissem* in 123 (VI. 9). 1, maintaining that the preposition was incorrect because Piraeus was a town. C.'s defence is somewhat confused. Its main plank is that he had used the preposition in the belief, right or wrong, that Piraeus, as an Attic deme, was not a town but a locality—the error, if there was one, was factual, not grammatical. That would have been pertinent if Atticus had really taxed him with ignorance of the rule that Latin propositions of place and direction are not used with the names of towns. Obviously Atticus did not intend such an imputation; his objection must have been *de re*, though of course it may have been badly or ambiguously worded. When he read C.'s excuse 'if I have made a mistake it was in speaking of a place instead of a town', Atticus must have thought 'just so'. C. can however quote authorities to show that even on this ground he has Latin usage on his side.

3 omnes nostri   As C. himself in 89 (IV. 16). 3; 124 (VII. 1). 1 and Ser. Sulpicius in *Fam.* IV. 12. 1.

4 et tamen   I.e. 'I prefixed *in* not as with a town but as with a locality (and in that I may have been wrong); and yet. . .'. Watt reads *etiam*, holding that 'the various expedients to which the defenders of *et tamen* are compelled to resort. . .are quite unconvincing' (*l.c.* p. 389).

5 **Nicias Cous**   *Curtius Nicias haesit Cn. Pompeio et C. Memmio; sed cum codicillos Memmi ad Pompei uxorem de stupro pertulisset, proditus ab ea Pompeium offendit, domoque ei interdictum est.* So Suetonius, *Gramm.* 14, the only authority for Nicias' *nomen gentile*, unless he is the Curtius of 317 (XIII. 9). 1. The rest of Suetonius' notice, apart from mentioning a work on Lucilius, refers to his friendship with C., giving two citations from extant letters (*Fam.* IX. 10 and 265 (XII. 26). 2), the first of which presents Nicias as a textual critic—he has been conjecturally identified with a grammarian cited in Homeric scholia. Later he is found specially attached to Dolabella, who perhaps had introduced him to C. Clearly he was not a freedman but a native of Cos granted Roman citizenship. He has been identified with the tyrant of Cos in the Antonian period mentioned by Strabo (XIV. 2. 19) and attested by coins and inscriptions; but if 'Nicias the *grammaticus* and Nicias the tyrant are clearly one and the same person' (R. Syme, *Journ. Rom. Stud.* 51 (1961), p. 27), Suetonius' apparent unawareness of the fact is surprising. The name was a common one; at least three other contemporary owners of it are on record.

non rebatur   The archaic *noenu* appears in some texts after a suggestion of Lachmann's (on Lucr. III. 199). Watt (*l.c.* p. 389) suggests that the variants in the MSS may well have arisen from *non* misread as *nomen*, remarking that some of the early editions actually printed *nomen rebatur oppidi*.

6 **de re**   Orelli's objection that *de re* is used 'prorsus insolite pro *de ea re*' is beside the mark; no less so Watt's defence (*ibid.*). *re* is emphatic, the question of fact as opposed to grammar.

8 **Caecilium**   Cf. 16 (1. 16). 15 n.

9 **malus. . .auctor**   Cf. Gell. IV. 16. 8 *C. etiam Caesar, gravis auctor linguae Latinae.* Caecilius' bad reputation was shared by Pacuvius (*Brut.* 258 *Caecilium et Pacuvium male locutos videmus*).

10 **C. Laelio**   Cf. Ter. *Ad.* (prol.) 15 *nam quod isti dicunt malevoli hominis nobilis | hunc adiutare adsidueque una scribere, | quod illi maledictum vehemens esse existumant, | eam laudem hic ducit maximam.* Laelius speaks of Terence as his *familiaris* in *Amic.* 89. The two quotations are from the *Eunuchus* (539, 114); in the former the original has *in Piraeo*.

15 **grammaticus**   'There seems a mild play on words. . .for γράμματα can be used for commercial documents, e.g. St Luke XVI. 7, "bill" or "bond" ' (T.–P.). But it may be doubted whether γράμματα has any more specifically commercial application than 'document(s)' or 'paper(s)'.

persolveris   Normally 'discharge, pay'. Here *per-* seems to be intensive, 'solve thoroughly'. Perhaps, as commentators have thought, there is a deliberate play on the usual sense (*liberare* also is a business term: cf. 78 (IV. 4*a*). 2 n.); if so it is an awkward pleasantry.

11, 3 **digitum nusquam**   Sc. *discedere:* cf. 328 (XIII. 20). 4 *in omni sua vita quemque ⟨a⟩ recta conscientia traversum unguem non oportet discedere;* Otto, *Sprichwörter*, p. 356.

6 **Caelio**   C. did think of taking over a claim upon an unknown Caelius in 45, but Caelius the banker is a figment of commentators (cf. 306 (XII. 6). 1 n.). Obviously Caelius Rufus is meant here, though hardly in earnest; his new affluence (cf. §§6, 9) would make him a good 'touch'.

hoc   The ζήτημα aforesaid. The idea of borrowing from Caelius is more than half facetious, so that *tamen* amounts in effect to 'but seriously'.

8 **Tartessium. . .tuum**   I.e. Balbus, who looked after Caesar's financial affairs. Tartessus (Tarshish) lay somewhat to the west of the less ancient Gades, Balbus' native city. After its destruction by the Carthaginians at the end of the sixth century the two places were confused (cf. A. Schulten, *Camb. Anc. Hist.* VII, p. 775).

exeunti   Balbus was not a Senator.

iube. . .curare   Literally 'please give orders to pay': cf. 202 (X. 11). 2 *curari tamen ea tibi utique iubet;* 226 (XI. 15). 2 *quod superest velim videas ut curetur.* The object of *iube* (*argentarium?, dispensatorem?*) is left vague, naturally enough. But *curari* (Manutius) may well be right.

12, 2 **vel. . .vel**   Practically = *et. . .et* ('whether you look at his cleverness or. . .'). *humanitatis* implies consideration for others, 'good manners' in the widest sense: cf. 83 (IV. 6). 1. *satis* is very likely a case of dittography, though *satis ⟨est⟩* (cf. 312 (XIII. 5). 2 *quoniam ad Bruti adventum fore te nobiscum polliceris, satis est*) or *satis ⟨sit⟩* (cf. Ov. *Tr.* I. I. 55 *carmina nunc si non studiumque quod obfuit odi, / sit satis*) would serve, not to dwell on less plausible proposals (including Watt's ingenious ⟨*vel*⟩ *salis*).

reliqua   Cf. 121 (VI. 6). 1 n. (*cetera*).

3 †**aperierimus**   *aperuerimus* cannot be forced into any semblance of tolerable sense. Even if 'you know whom I revealed to you' could pass muster from that standpoint, *tibi* would be needed. As for renderings like 'you know what we discovered to be the real character of the other suitors', *aperire aliquem* might be just conceivable Latin (though *se aperire*, as in Ter. *Andr.* 632 *tum coacti necessario se aperiunt*, hardly proves it), but not *aperire aliquem talem. abiecerimus* (Boot) is the only conjecture of merit, but *praeterierimus* (*pter-*) would be preferable palaeographically.

4 **eum. . .egimus**   Cf. 115 (VI. 1). 10.

reum me facerent   They would have forced (or be forcing) C. to borrow money on their behalf; for *reus* = 'debtor' cf. 255 (XII. 17) *etsi reus locuples est.* The words could also be understood in the sense that C.

would have become surety for their loans: cf. Liv. IX. 9. 18 *Samnitibus sponsores nos sumus, rei satis locupletes in id quod nostrum est. . .corpora nostra et animos*; only then *ipsis. . .ferret* does not fit. Contrast *Mart.* X. 48. 23 *de prasino conviva meus venetoque loquatur, | nec faciant quemquam pocula nostra reum.* Normally of course *reum facere* = 'prosecute'.

5 **expensum. . .ferret**   Cf. *Phil.* VI. 15 *quis umquam in illo Iano inventus est qui L. Antonio mille nummum ferret expensum?*; *Thes.* V (ii). 1644 f.

7 **Tironis sqq.**   Cf. 125 (VII. 2). 3.

127 (VII. 4)

Probably from C.'s *Cumanum*. Caelius Rufus paid him a visit there about this time (*Fam.* II. 16. 3); sec on 130 (VII. 8). 5. Since Dionysius, who took the letter to Rome, arrived on 16 December (130 (VII. 7). 1), it was probably written about the 13th.

I, 3 **sanctum**   Cf. 115 (VI. 1). 12. There is nothing to be said for *sane* (ς).

5 **libertinum**   As Dionysius actually was; so perhaps *ut* (Bouhier) has fallen out after *ne*. *frugi* is an epithet often applied to freedmen and slaves (as in *Fam.* V. 6. 1, XIII. 70, etc.; cf. Plin. *Paneg.* 88. 2 *tu libertis summum quidem honorem, sed tamquam libertis habes, abundeque sufficere his credis si probi et frugi existimentur*), though not confined to them (cf. 82 (IV. 8a). 2 n. (*Fabio Lusco*); add 299 (XIII. 28). 4 *modestum et frugi*).

2, 1 **vidi**   At Capua, so Gelzer conjectures (*RE.* VIIA. 989. 59).

3 **monere**   The advice may not have been entirely disinterested, since Pompey clearly did not share C.'s anxiety for a peaceful settlement. In fact, C. did attend the Senate in January (cf. 178A (IX. 11A). 2 n.).

5 **in hoc officio**   I.e. *de triumpho*, contrasted with the following *de re publica*; so Watt (*l.c.* p. 390), who has rescued the conjecture *sermone eius* from undeserved neglect. As he says, no satisfactory sense, in this context can be extracted from *hoc officio sermonis*.

7 **nihil ad spem concordiae**   Cf. 61 (III. 16) *id quod attulerunt* (sc. *litterae*) *ad spem*; 205 (X. 13). 1 *si quid ad spem poteris* (sc. *scribere*); 266 (XI. 15). 1 *cui. . .neque ab his ipsis quicquam ad spem ostendatur*; Caes. *B.C.* II. 28. 3 *huc pauca ad spem largitionis addidit*; Liv. XXVI. 6. 15 *nihil ad eam spem agnoscentem.*

9 **venisse sqq.**   On the mixture of pronouns in this sentence cf. 21 (II. 1). 5 n. (*eos*).

Hirtium   A. Hirtius A. f. rose to notice under Caesar in Gaul, perhaps as chief of his secretariat. He held the Praetorship in 46, the Consulship in 43 until his death at Mutina. More politician than soldier, more man of letters and *bon viveur* than either, Hirtius was one of several in Caesar's inner circle with whom C. cultivated friendly relations which, on his side at least, did not go far beneath the surface. Nine books or more of their correspondence were extant in antiquity.

11 **de tota re** 'On the whole situation' (i.e. to discuss it): cf. 138 (VII. 14). 3 *de totaque re quid existimes.*

12 **ad Scipionem** Balbus, a protégé of Pompey as well as of Caesar, seems to have known Metellus Scipio well: cf. Caelius, *Fam.* VIII. 9. 5. Perhaps their talk was intended as a preliminary to a meeting between Hirtius and Pompey, who was evidently still in Rome (*ad se non accessisse*) on the 6th. He left the following day (cf. Bardt, *Hermes*, 45 (1910), p. 340).

13 τεκμηριῶδες Probably with reference to the use of τεκμήριον in Aristotelian logic, 'demonstrative proof, opposed to the fallible σημεῖον and εἰκός' (L.–S.–J.).

3, 2 alterum consulatum As elsewhere, C. assumes that if only Caesar were willing to lay down his command he could be certain of the Consulship in 48; evidently he did not regard Cato's threat of a prosecution as serious (cf. Introd. pp. 38 ff.).

3 **potentiam** The political influence which might more fairly have been attributed to Caesar's own qualities and achievements than to fortune.

4 **ruere** Cf. 34 (II. 14). 1 n.

5 **ad urbem** I.e. to the neighbourhood of Rome. C. could not enter the city boundary without laying down his *imperium* and so forfeiting his hopes of a Triumph.

128 (VII. 5)

This letter can only be dated in relation to those before and after.

1, 1 tuas Sc. *epistulas* (cf. 320 (XIII. 12). 1 n.), one of them in answer to 125 (VII. 2); cf. §3 *de Chrysippo.*

5 **date. . .valeatis** Such formulae assign a larger place to the invalid's own efforts than is now customary; cf. §5 fin. By a similar mode of thought good health, as evidence of care and temperance, was a recognized theme for praise (*ad Her.* III. 14; cf. Sen. *Ep.* 58. 29).

3, 1 Philogenes Cf. 106 (V. 13). 2. The business may be the money matter referred to in 129 (VII. 7). 2, where it appears that he had repaid a sum to C.'s account. In any case I suspect that *lusgenio* does not conceal the vulgate *Luscenio* (an unattested *nomen*), still less Corradus' arbitrary *Lucenio* (cf. Varro, *RR.* II. 5. 1), but a sum of money, perhaps HS C̄ (*centu*) or HS CCIƆƆ IƆƆ.

3 **in Arcanum** To join her husband.

Chrysippo Cf. 125 (VII. 2). 8.

4 **nihil**   Sc. *veniam. nihil*, like οὐδέν, sometimes replaces the ordinary negative for greater emphasis. The usage is chiefly colloquial: cf. K.–S. I, p. 818.

5 **τοῖς ἀπαντῶσιν**   Cf. 21 (II. 1). 5 n. (*itum obviam*).

7 **Pomptinum †summam**   *Pomptinam summam* could not mean 'the north part of the Pomptine marshes'. There was no such area as Pomptina, and C. must be naming a definite place. It is unlikely however that there was a place called *Pomptina summa* on the Appian Way, as M. Hofmann assumes (*RE*. Suppl. VIII. 1184. 5). *Pomptinum* is probably a villa and *summam* a corruption of the owner's name. In 53 C. had stopped at the *Pomptinum* of one M. Aemilius Philemon (*Fam.* VII. 18. 3). Less probably *Pomptinum* is C.'s Legate; hence Corradus' and Purser's conjectures (see App. Crit.).

Albanum   Sc. *petam*. Pompey had evidently invited C. to stay at the villa in his absence.

4, 1 ut putantur   Similar qualifications are common in the letters of this period: cf. *Fam.* XVI. 12. 2 *iis qui boni habentur*; 130 (VII. 7). 7 *quicumque dicentur boni*; 151 (VIII. 1). 3 *iis qui dicuntur esse boni*; 169 (IX. 2u). 3 *nec enim ferre potero sermones istorum, quicumque sunt; non sunt enim certe, ut appellantur, boni.* Even in 59 we have *eorum hominum qui appellantur boni* (36 (II. 16). 2). The reading is thus verified, as against *putatur, putavi,* or *putaram.*

3 **hoc iter Pompei**   On 7 December Pompey left Rome for Campania to take over the two 'Appian' legions (cf. 136 (VII. 13). 2 n.) there stationed and to raise new levies, as authorized by a commission from the Consul C. Marcellus (cf. Gelzer, *RE.* XXI. 2177). *cetera* as well as *iter* could be taken with *Pompei* (see on 207 (X. 17). 1 *vellem cetera eius*), but if C. had so intended he would probably have written *cum cetera Pompei tum hoc iter.*

6 **quid ad te scribam**   *quid* seems better kept (so also at the start of the next letter), since *deest = non habeo (reperio)*: cf. 129 (VII. 6). 1; K.–S. II, p. 500.

5, 1 iocari   Cf. 98 (V. 5). 1 n.

si hic sinat   'Si per Caesarem liceat' (Manutius). C. affects to regard Caesar as already omnipotent. So Nero after Vindex' revolt *iam se etiam prolaturum omnia in theatrum affirmavit, si per Vindicem liceret* (Suet. *Nero* 41. 2). To take *hic* as Pompey spoils the point.

3 **aluimus**   So 153 (VIII. 3). 3 *istum...ille aluit, auxit, armavit*; 158 (VIII. 8). 1 *aluerat Caesarem*; 390 (XV. 12). 2 *alendus est.* Cf. *ad Her.* IV. 48 *eum...alitis ad rei publicae perniciem.*

4 **de sententia tua**   Note the echo *senties...sententia.*

5 **nostrum negotium**   I.e. *triumphum.*

7 **diligentia**   See above (§1). So Atticus on his death-bed '*quantam*' inquit '*curam diligentiamque in valetudine mea tuenda hoc tempore adhibuerim,*

cum vos testes habeam, nihil necesse est pluribus verbis commemorare' (Nep. Att. 21. 5). C. is perfectly serious, though it is difficult to make him sound so in translation.

129 (VII. 6)

Written prior to receipt of Atticus' letter mentioned in 130 (VII. 7) 1, which was probably dispatched from Rome on the 17th.

1, 2 quod exspectem *quod* seems preferable to *quid* here, since *habeo* can hardly be taken as equivalent to *reperio (scio)*.

2, 3 opinione †valentior The paradosis cannot stand. An adversative particle is necessary to balance *quidem* and introduce the case for yielding to Caesar; and since *opinione valentior* (if sound) is clearly part of that case, *autem* cannot be that particle. Moreover *postulatio valens*, 'a demand backed by power', seems very dubious Latin. *violentior* (Koch) and *amentior* (Schmidt), with or without *atque* (Wesenberg) before *opinione*, give un- satisfactory sense. Caesar's claim to stand for the Consulship while retain- ing his command, or Curio's proposal (if regarded as emanating from Caesar) that he and Pompey should both give up their armies, might be impudent from C.'s point of view (and Pompey's; cf. 132 (VII. 9). 4) because it demanded a concession, however logical (cf. 130 (VII. 7). 6 init.), with the threat of force; but no one who had followed the manœuvres of the previous two years was likely to be surprised by the violence or insanity of such proposals. Lehmann's supplement *sed is qui postulat*, adopted by Watt, is less easy to dismiss, but I have no faith in it. True, in 126 (VII. 3). 5 C. expatiates on the amount of support for Caesar; but for the purpose of his argument here it is Caesar's actual strength that matters, not previous expectations, even if these did in fact fall short of the reality. And *postularet ...postulatio...postulat* seems too much of a good word. In 1960 I suggested a different approach. The public opinion which C. describes as favouring concession may have thought Caesar's claims not more but less exorbitant than might have been anticipated. Alarmist reports of his intentions had been current in Rome in the latter half of the year. Atticus had passed one on to C. (cf. 123 (VI. 9). 5) in September, and according to Appian (*B.C.* II. 31) a rumour that Caesar had crossed the Alps and was marching on the capital had spread temporary panic. Evidently it was widely expected that he might return to Rome after the fashion of Marius and Sulla. But now lovers of peace could tell themselves that Caesar was only asking what might easily have been granted to Pompey in 52. Perhaps then the answer is *opinione tamen lenior*. Caesar speaks of his own *postulata* as *lenissima* in *B.C.* I. 5. 5. C. of course would not have gone and does not go anything like so far; he merely says (if this reading is right) that people had expected something worse. Even that he might not have said but for the influence of the pacifist sentiment all around him.

4 autem Adding a further argument in favour of concession.

οὐ γὰρ κ.τ.λ. *Od.* XII. 209 (the original has οὐ μὲν δή; on ἔπει, ἔπι, ἔπει see Merry–Riddell *ad loc.*).

5 prorogabamus. . .ferebamus The two points on which C., as he claims in *Phil.* II. 24, urged Pompey not to fall in with Caesar's wishes; but cf. 124 (VII. 1). 4 n.

8 non idem With a play on the political (cf. 124 (VII. 1). 4 n. (*sensero*)) and ordinary meanings of *sentire*.

11 esse C. implies that he would publicly and powerfully advocate the policy of concession according to his real convictions, if only he were not muzzled by his sense of personal and peculiar obligation to Pompey. The vulgate *sed rursus hoc permagnum rei publicae malum est et quodam modo* sqq. defies rational interpretation. *hoc* has to be taken, not as any reader accustomed to good Latin would take it, in anticipation of the following accusative and infinitive (*me. . .dissidere*), but as 'the necessity imposed on the *boni* to "say ditto" to Pompey'—of which C. has said nothing. His mind is on his own position *vis-à-vis* Pompey and the public consequences it entailed.

12 me Bracketed by Boot. But cf. 282 (XII. 42). 1 n. (*ut*); 177 (IX. 10). 5 (Atticus) *ego quidem tibi non sim auctor, si Pompeius Italiam relinquit, te quoque profugere*; *Fam.* XI. 2. 3 (Brutus and Cassius) *cum de nobis certum sit nos quieturos*; Madvig on *Fin.* III. 10.

130 (VII. 7)

Atticus' letter (cf. §1), if dispatched on the 17th, probably arrived in Formiae in the afternoon or evening of the 18th. C. may be supposed to have replied next day.

1, 1 vir optimus Cf. 127 (VII. 4). 1 *plane virum bonum*. Atticus was not bound to repeat C.'s precise words.

3 litteras 127 (VII. 4).

4 putato If this is wrong, there is no knowing what is right. The available proposals are implausible or impossible (Purser's *at illud, puto, non adscribis* falls into the latter category—C. *knew* what Atticus had written, *tot verba*), with the exception of Bosius' *puta tu. puta*, 'for example', makes quite good sense—the point might have been put in a variety of ways; but this use is first found in Horace (cf. K.–S. II, p. 199; cf. however *Phil.* II. 15 *cui? neminem nominabo: putate tum Phormioni alicui, tum Gnathoni, tum etiam Ballioni*). If it is to be allowed to C., then surely *putato* in the same sense can be allowed too. Of the two imperative forms he preferred it (cf. Neue–Wagener, *Formenlehre*[3], III, pp. 222 f.), and *tu* is rather in the way.

5 et.. .adscripsisses Cf. 131 (VII. 8). 1 n.

2, 1 Philogenes In July 51 this freedman of Atticus had been concerned in the negotiation of a bill of exchange for C. at Ephesus (cf. 106 (V. 13). 2). It would seem that C. found he did not require the money and had let Philogenes employ it (himself charging interest or participating in the proceeds?) *quoad liceret*, i.e. presumably until C. returned to Italy. Philogenes had now repaid it, to C.'s account surely, not Atticus'. C. seems at first to have forgotten that Philogenes owed the money unless, as is not very likely, 128 (VII. 5). 3 refers to a different transaction.

3 menses XIIII C. left Ephesus on 1 October 50.

3, 1 Pomptinum Presumably he had been back for two or three months (cf. 117 (VI. 3). 1 n.). C. had evidently expected him to stay outside the *pomerium* until the day when he accompanied his own entry as Triumphator. *cupio valere* (not, I think, 'formule de congé, moins désinvolte que l'habituel *iubeo valere*' (Bayet)) could of course mean 'I hope that he is (keeps) well', but C. would hardly have referred to Pomptinus' health at all if he had not been sick: cf. *Fam.* VII. 4, to the invalid M. Marius, *te cum semper valere cupio tum certe dum hic sumus*, XVI. 1. 2, to Tiro, *hoc tibi... persuade nihil me malle quam te valere*. The anxiety conveyed by *vereor* relates to Pomptinus' health, if to anything specific, rather than to C.'s prospects of a Triumph.

3 compitalicius dies Cf. 23 (II. 3). 4 n.

5 λῆψις *accessio*. C. also uses the converse διάλειψις (*decessio*).

6 nescio A 'humane' prevarication: cf. 131 (VII. 8). 2 n.

commoveri In the way of ἀπάντησις, or even to visit C. at his residence outside Rome.

incommodo Cf. K.–S. I, p. 411.

4, 1 suos tribunos Antony, Q. Cassius, and others (cf. §6 *tot tribuni pl.*), probably including L. Marcius Philippus (Cos. Suff. 38) and one Rubrius (see Broughton, pp. 258 f.).

3 aequi boni facit Cf. Ter. *Heaut.* 787 *ceterum equidem istuc, Chreme, | aequi bonique facio*; Liv. XXXIV. 22. 13 *si vos nec cura.. .nec periculum movet... nos aequi bonique faciamus* et sim. (K.–S. I, p. 459).

5 consilio Probably with irony, of Pompey's private circle of intimates, such as Theophanes, Lucceius, and Scribonius Libo (cf. 167 (IX. 1). 3 *Luccei consilia et Theophanis persequamur*).

quod imperium habeam C.'s connexions with the island might have been another reason. In fact Cato was appointed (cf. 139 (VII. 15). 2 n.).

6 'Αβδηριτικόν Cf. 91 (IV. 17). 3 n. The reason, *quod imperium habeam*, was no reason at all.

nec populus iussit C.'s *imperium* was conferred by law (probably only his *lex curiata*) as well as senatorial decree: cf. 217 (XI. 6). 2 *lictoribus quos populus dedit*; *Fam.* XV. 14. 5 *hanc provinciam, quam et senatus et populus annuam esse voluit*, and other passages cited by P. J. Cuff, *Historia* 7 (1958), p. 465, n. 75.

8 **refert** Through Marcellus' commission (cf. 128 (VII. 5). 4 n.).

9 **mittit** The indicative is quite possible; cf. 116 (VI. 2). 9 n. (*solvunt*).

utar...videro 'Quae prima porta erit, ea in urbem ingrediar' (Manutius). For *utar* cf. *uti via* (39 (II. 19). 2 n.), *itinere* (*Verr.* II. 3. 219), *perfugio* (*Verr.* II. 1. 82, etc.), *mari* (166 (VIII. 16). 1) et sim.

10 **primam** 'Parallels' hardly establish a case for *primum*. In *Catil.* III. 15 *quod mihi primum post hanc urbem conditam togato contigit* the adverb is part of a phrase, 'for the first time since the foundation of Rome', which coheres with the verb rather than the pronoun. Similarly in *Off.* III. 11 *eos qui primum haec natura cohaerentia opinione distraxissent*; one can say 'those who for the first time separated things naturally cohering', but not 'the gate I shall see for the first time' meaning 'the first gate I see'. Ernesti was probably right to read *primam* in *Mil.* 93 *quam primum tetigero bene moratam et liberam civitatem, in ea conquiescam* and Bentley to read *primus* in *Tusc.* I. 38 *Pherecydes Syrius primum dixit animos hominum esse sempiternos*, though in the latter 'said for the first time' makes tolerable sense.

5, 2 satis bonorum Cf. 39 (II. 19). 4 n.

3 **facturus** *sensurus* would be satisfactory. Authority decides here.

5 **ordines bonorum et genera** *genera* is the more comprehensive word, *ordines* referring in practice to Senate and Knights.

7 **per quem sqq.** As a result of Curio's vetoes on the appointment of successors in Caesar's provinces no provincial governors were appointed in 50. A proposal by M. Marcellus (Cos. 51) in May that the Tribunes (apparently Curio was not alone) should be 'treated with' had been rejected by the Senate (Caelius, *Fam.* VIII. 13. 2).

sine imperio A province administered by a deputy, the governor being absent or his term having lapsed without appointment of a successor, was technically said to be *sine imperio* (Mommsen, *St.* I, p. 677, n. 3).

8 **agi** The Senate might instruct the Consuls to 'treat' with a recalcitrant Tribune to induce him to withdraw his veto: cf. *Phil.* II. 52. The threat of further action, of doubtful legality, lay in the background: cf. 132 (VII. 9). 2 n. (*circumscriptus*).

11 **amicissimi** 'Ob remissam tertiam vectigalium partem' (Corradus); but that was nine years ago, and it is to be supposed that Caesar had found means of cementing the alliance in the interval.

6, 1 transierit By the time Caesar made his *professio* as candidate for the Consulship of 48 (cf. 21 (II. 1) introd. note) his term of command would on any showing have expired. The perfect subjunctive need not imply that it had already expired when C. wrote, though this may in his view have been the case. An editor may be excused if he declines the *Rechtsfrage*, and leaves professional historians to decide whether P. J. Cuff's elaborate and strenuous argument in *Historia*, 7 (1958), pp. 445 ff. has at long last produced the answer. Cuff concludes that after 52 there were two different opinions about the terminal date of C.'s command (*legis dies*): according to one, Caesar's, it was 1 January 49 (though Caesar felt entitled in virtue of ordinary practice to a further six months); according to the other, that of the anti-Caesarians, including Pompey and C., it was 1 March 50.

3 autem   *enim* is explained as an emphatic particle ('Why then') and *annorum...placet?* as Atticus' imagined retort. I know of no evidence for such a use of *enim* in questions (that after interrogative particles is quite different: cf. 260 (XII. 21). I n.), and this question is plainly C.'s own. The five-year extension of command and the leave of candidature *in absentia* go together, as in 126 (VII. 3). 4 and elsewhere. As in other passages (190 (X. 1). 1; 409 (XVI. 1). 5; cf. 164 (VIII. 14). 3), there is not much to choose between *autem* and *etiam* as substitute, but *etiam* in the next sentence may count in favour of the former.

4 ita latum   Cf. 126 (VII. 3). 4 n. (*illo modo*). C. is probably thinking of the lex Vatinia as well as the Pompeia Licinia: cf. 132 (VII. 9). 4 n. (*a te ipso*).

placet igitur   I.e. 'If we *do* approve of these things, we shall have to approve of others even more outrageous—they all hang together'.

5 agrum Campanum   Cf. 36 (II. 16). 1 n.

6 Gaditanum a Mytilenaeo   I.e. Balbus by Theophanes (cf. 23 (II. 3) n.). Neither this nor the adoption of a patrician by a plebeian was in itself illegal or even objectionable, but the two particular cases could be regarded as flagrant abuses of the institution.

Labieni   T. Labienus, son of a Roman Knight of Cingulum in Picenum, came from Pompey's country and was perhaps throughout Pompey's man rather than Caesar's: see R. Syme's interesting if rather speculative account of him in *Journ. Rom. Stud.* 28 (1938), pp. 113 ff. But as Tribune in 63 he was already in association with Caesar, notably in the affair of C. Rabirius (cf. *ibid.* p. 118), and became his chief subordinate commander in Gaul (*legatus pro praetore* 58–49). Having deserted his general on the outbreak of war (134 (VII. 11). 1) he fought against him until his own death at Munda. On his wealth cf. Caes. *B.C.* I. 15. 2.

7 Mamurrae   Roman Knight of Formiae, praenomen unknown, *nomen gentile* possibly Vitruvius (cf. Münzer, *RE.* XIV. 966. 50; P. Thielscher (*ibid.* IXA. 432 ff.) identifies him with the author of the *de Architectura*!).

He had been Caesar's *praefectus fabrum* since 58, with previous service under him in Spain and under Pompey in the East. Catullus' lampoons (29 and 57) were celebrated (cf. Plin. *N.H.* XXXVI. 48; Suet. *Iul.* 73). He probably died in 45 (353 (XIII. 52). 1).

horti et Tusculanum   In 74 (IV. 2). 7 C. alludes to his own Tusculan villa as a *suburbanum*. The two words seem to have been to some extent interchangeable, though when they are distinguished, as in 152 (VIII. 2). 3 *non in suburbanis? non in hortis?*, *horti* may imply closer proximity to the town (usually Rome; but cf. 179 (IX. 11). 1; 338 (XIII. 46). 3). A property near Lanuvium is called *hortuli* in 176 (IX. 9). 4. The site of Balbus' *horti* was a gift from Pompey (181 (IX. 13*a*)).

9 **nunc sqq.**   With this list cf. 126 (VII. 3). 5.

legiones XI   So Flor. II. 13. 5. Plutarch (*Pomp.* 58) speaks of ten, Hirtius (*B.G.* VIII. 54. 4) mentions eight left in Gaul and one sent to Italy in 50, apart from the two detached for use against the Parthians (cf. 136 (VII. 13). 2 n.). Apparently Caesar replaced these latter by new levies (cf. Kubitschek, *RE.* XII. 1207. 27), unless C. forgot to deduct them.

10 **Transpadani**   Cf. 104 (V. 11). 2 n. Their complete enfranchisement was achieved by a law passed early in 49 (Broughton, p. 258).

12 **e lege**   The law of the Ten Tribunes of 52.

7, 3 **tamen servias**   Cf. 128 (VII. 5). 4 *ex victoria. . .certe tyrannus exsistet.*

acturus   Cf. 44 (II. 24). 3 n. (*ita actum*) and *Towards a Text*, p. 9.

6 **quid sit optimum**   Peace on any terms.

7 **nemini. . .locupletum**   C. might have been expected to add something like *si vicerint, tamen nos servituros*. As it stands his formulation could be answered: 'but the risk is worth while'. He had however already made the missing point (*si viceris, tamen servias*).

ventum sit   *est* would imply that war had already begun.

10 **ἐμπολιτεύομαί σοι**   Cf. 14 (I. 14). 4 n. (*auditori*).

13 **T. Pomponio**   Even in this supposedly formal context C. does not use Atticus' adoptive *nomen*; cf. 68 (III. 23). 1 n.

131 (VII. 8)

C. may be assumed to have written this account of his talk with Pompey on the same evening or the next morning.

1, 1 **de Dionysio**   Cf. 130 (VII. 7). 1. Presumably Atticus had replied that Dionysius was indeed grateful, but that it had not occurred to himself to mention it.

4 **aliter cum aliis**   Not 'because I heard that he used different language about us to others' (Winstedt).

2, 1 diem tuum   I.e. the (periodically recurrent) day of your fever. In his last letter (§3) C. had professed ignorance, no doubt because if he had written that according to his calculation Atticus would be free of fever on 3 January that would have sounded too much like asking him to make the journey. *pro re nata non incommode* adds another touch of *humanitas*. It could not, C. implies, be *really* convenient for Atticus to travel in his present state of health, only 'not inconvenient, relatively speaking'; i.e. the 3rd was a better day than another.

2 mihi   With *scripseras*.

3, 1 Liviae   Unknown, but probably of the noble Livii Drusi, perhaps a daughter of the Tribune.

2 mutare nomen   I.e. to enter the gens of the testatrix by adoption under her will: cf. Mommsen, *St.* III, p. 40, n. 7. Presumably Dolabella refused. His subsequent adoption into a plebeian family and his name Lentulus can hardly have any connexion with this passage (correct on this point *Cl. Quart.* N.S. 10 (1960), p. 258, n. 3).

πολιτικόν 'Social' would be a better translation than 'political', but for the allusion in the next letter (§2).

5 quasi   So with numerals, as Ter. *Heaut.* 145 *quasi talenta ad quindecim / coegi.*

4, 2 Lavernium   'Fortasse vicus qui a Dea Laverna nomen accepit' (Boot). Apart from a mention in *Fat.* fr. 5 the place is otherwise unknown. C. had apparently made an excursion from Formiae, perhaps to Minturnae, and was on his way back when he was overtaken by Pompey travelling in the same direction.

7 dimisso   Cf. 122 (VI. 8). 2 n.

10 retenturum   Pompey appears to have assumed that if Caesar gave up his claim to the Consulship for 48 the Senate would leave him in his command during 49—contingency no. 3 of C.'s scheme in 132 (VII. 9). 2. T.–P. comment: 'It is strange that Pompey should hold this idea. Caesar would then only stave off the evil day, and be absolutely at the mercy of his enemies in 48'—justly enough, if Cato's threat of prosecution had been taken seriously; but Caesar was in no such peril: cf. Introd. pp. 38 ff.

fureret   Cf. 138 (VII. 14). 1 *illum furoris. . .suppaenitet.*

12 ξυνὸς ᾽Ενυάλιος καί τε κτανέοντα κατέκτα (*Il.* XVIII. 309).

5 2 contionem   Such speeches were sometimes taken down and circulated: cf. 40 (II. 20). 4 n.

3 a toga pura   From his assumption of the *toga virilis*.

de damnatis   Those condemned in 52, especially under Pompey's retrospective bribery law: cf. 182 (IX. 14). 2.

terror armorum   Not quite equivalent to *belli terror* (cf. *Man.* 30;

Liv. XXXVIII. 42. 11): cf. Hirt. *B.G.* VIII. 52. 4 *si quem timor armorum Caesaris laederet*; Caes. *B.C.* I. 2. 6 *terrore praesentis exercitus*; *Sest.* 52 *nec armati exercitus terrorem opponet togatis*; *Dom.* 131 *absentis exercitus terrore et minis*; *Leg.* III. 25 *adiuncto terrore etiam militari.*

4 **si. . .venerit** I.e. *si consul factus erit.*

5 **quaestor eius** Antony had just taken office as Tribune. He had been Caesar's Quaestor, by special selection, in 51 (cf. 119 (VI. 6). 4 n.).

7 **ex illa. . .†movet** Cf. *de sententia moveri* (*Phil.* II. 52), *demovere* (*-ri*) (*Verr.* I. 52; *Sest.* 101). The best thing to do with *ī* (*in*) of M is to eject it. Sjögren leaves *movet* without expressed subject, understanding *ea res* vel sim. But what *res*? *moveo* would be the simplest correction; or *ni*(*hi*)*l* (Müller) may have dropped out. I am much inclined to take *relinquendae* with reference, not to the military evacuation which actually took place in January, but to Pompey's intention to leave for Spain if Caesar should become Consul; cf. 122 (VI. 8). 2 n. Pompey's expressions of confidence and contempt for Caesar's military power would have consorted strangely with a declared plan to abandon the capital in face of an attack. When this happened C. was profoundly shocked (133 (VII. 10), etc.). On the other hand it would seem from a letter to Caelius some four months later (*Fam.* II. 16. 3) that Ampius Balbus had spoken to C. of the possibility that Rome and even Italy might be evacuated, and that C. in turn had discussed it with Caelius Rufus when the latter visited him at Cumae about 12 December (these talks may have been reported to Atticus in a lost letter, between 127 (VII. 4) and 128 (VII. 5)); and hereafter *relinquere urbem* is regularly used of the evacuation. So perhaps it is best on the whole to adhere to the usual interpretation, leaving the textual question open.

132 (VII. 9)

The opening words show that this letter was dispatched the day after the last. 131 (VII. 8) is not likely to have been *dispatched* before 26 December, so that 132 (VII. 9) will have followed on the 27th, two days before C. left Formiae (128 (VII. 5). 3).

1, 3 **L. Quinctius** Unknown—surely not the 'popular' Tribune of 74 (cf. *Cluent.* 74 ff.).

4 **bustum Basili** Cf. Ascon. 50. 7 *via Appia est prope urbem monumentum Basili, qui locus latrociniis fuit perquam infamis, quod ex aliis quoque multis intellegi potest.*

2, 3 **sane** C. is evidently thinking of 130 (VII. 8). 3, where he used the same Greek phrase (except that πρόβλημα replaces σκέμμα) about the matter of Livia's will. *This* problem was πολιτικόν in a more immediate sense.

4 **cum sit necesse sqq.** Four of the contingencies introduced by *aut* (the first being subdivided into two) entail a peaceful end to the crisis, the fifth war. The contingency of war is then divided (*illum autem initium facere* sqq.) into three aspects: the timing of Caesar's attack, the pretext or pretexts put forward, and the tactics to be employed in resisting it. Each of these produce a pair of mutually exclusive possibilities and the second possibility in the second pair is itself subdivided into five. Diagrammatically C.'s analysis could be represented thus (P = peace, B = war):

$$
\begin{array}{ccccc}
\mathrm{P^1} & \mathrm{P^2} & \mathrm{P^3} & \mathrm{P^4} & \mathrm{B} \\
\mathrm{P^{1a}} \quad \mathrm{P^{1b}} & & \mathrm{B(1)} & \mathrm{B(2)} & \mathrm{B(3)} \\
& & \mathrm{B(1)^1 \; B(1)^2} & \mathrm{B(2)^1 \; B(2)^2} & \mathrm{B(3)^1 \; B(3)^2} \\
& & & \mathrm{B(2)^{2a} \; B(2)^{2b} \; B(2)^{2c} \; B(2)^{2d} \; B(2)^{2e}}
\end{array}
$$

(For simplicity's sake I ignore the prior subdivision of B(2)², *senatum impediens aut populum incitans*.) How's remark that 'the one contingency not mentioned is what actually happened' is hardly fair. What happened is pretty well represented by B(1)¹+B(2)²ᵇ (with an admixture of B(2)²ᵉ)+B(3)²)(though Caesar was not in fact 'cut off').

5 **vel per senatum vel per tribunos pl.** The Senate might refrain from superseding Caesar or the Caesarian Tribunes might gain the same result by their vetoes.

6 **ita consul fiat** No mention once again of the possibility of a successful prosecution.

8 **illo patiente** That was what Pompey expected (130 (VII. 8). 4).

10 **ob eam causam. . .habeatur** C. would have done better to strike out these words which anticipate B(2)¹ and ignore B(2)².

13 **comitiis** Not 'in the assembly'.

e lege Cf. 130 (VII. 7). 6 *aut habenda e lege ratio*.

16 **notatus** I see no reason to understand this otherwise than of the censorial *nota*. The Censors appointed in the summer were still in office. Appius had already threatened Curio with expulsion from the Senate, desisting only on representations from his colleague Piso and the Consul Paulus (Dio, XL. 63. 5).

17 **circumscriptus** The process of 'treating with' a Tribune to persuade him to withdraw his veto (cf. 129 (VII. 7). 5 n.) might be so described: cf. the treatment of Serranus in 74 (IV. 2). 4. The Caesarian Tribunes complained of *circumscriptio* in January 49 (Caes. *B.C.* I. 32. 6; *Phil.* II. 53: cf. *Mil.* 88).

sublatus The Senate could not deprive a magistrate of his office but

could and occasionally did suspend him from exercising it. The cases of
Metellus Nepos and Caesar in 62 are in point (cf. Mommsen, *St.* I, p. 262,
n. I, III, p. 1244, n. 2). The conspirator Lentulus Sura in 63 was forced to
abdicate his Praetorship. On the other hand in 100 Glaucia and Saturninus
were more or less officially done to death while still magistrates (though
possibly suspended) after the passage of the Senate's 'Final Decree' (cf.
Catil. III. 15), and in 133 Ti. Gracchus was slain by private enterprise.
sublatus would cover all such eventualities.

expulsus Expelled from Rome. Writing to Tiro in January 49
(*Fam.* XVI. II. 2) C. denies that Antony and Q. Cassius had been forcibly
expelled. *sit* should be omitted; a Tribune treated in any of the ways mentioned might take refuge with Caesar.

19 **aut tenenda sit urbs** Instead of continuing *aut teneri urbem* C.
changes the construction as though *cum* and not *cum sit necesse* had preceded.

20 **intercludendus** C. envisaged a plan of campaign by which Caesar
might be allowed to occupy Rome while the republicans in north Italy cut
him off from Gaul. Evacuation of Italy is outside the pale even of his theory,
and How is quite astray with his reference to 176 (IX. 9). 2—the Pompeian
fleet could not cut Caesar off *a reliquis copiis*.

3, 2 **omnino** Concessive, answered by *autem*.

3 **idque...miror** *facere* and *miror* are both best taken as genuine
presents. Caesar could at any time signify that he accepted this solution.
The rendering 'if he does not succeed in getting permission...I shall be
surprised if he does not take this course' is grammatically inadmissible and
contradictory of what follows (*hoc quo illum posse adduci negant*). *obtinet* need
not be altered to *obtineat* (Kayser) or taken as a case of indicative in oratio
obliqua, for *si* is virtually 'seeing that' (= *si quidem*).

4 **ut quidam putant** Cf. 160 (VIII. 9a). 1 *ut quidam putant*. Perhaps
putat should be read in view of *putat aliquis* and *ut idem dicit* below. Even if
the plural is sound, 'certain people' is merely an oblique way of saying 'a
certain person', i.e. Pompey.

6 **istuc** Cf. Neue-Wagener, *Formenlehre*[3], II, pp. 399 f.

sic 'sic' ⟨sci⟩o (Sternkopf) is rightly discarded by Watt. The text is
better off without *scio*, let alone ⟨dic⟩o (Tunstall) or ⟨mal⟩o (Koch).

8 **cedendum...volet** It is hard to decide whether these words are
supposed to proceed from Atticus or are the conclusion of C.'s reply to 'at
...exercitu'. In any case *vide* (= *patere*; not 'but imagine him...!')...
priore should be in quotation marks, as addressed by Atticus to 'somebody'.
quem does not = *qualem* here.

9 **inquit** Sc. *aliquis* (i.e. Pompey).

10 **quid nunc putas?** Sc. *valiturum* or *facturum*. Editors fail to see that

this belongs with the preceding words, in 'somebody's' mouth. *et...
Hispania* is a point making the same way added by C. *in propria persona*. In
the following words he *seems* fully to accept Pompey's thesis, and no doubt
it did make an impact upon him. But he is presenting a case rather than
expounding his own considered view, which remained pacific.

13 **iam a bonis**   *iam iam ⟨a⟩ bonis* vulg. But *iama* would easily become
iam iā.

4, 1 **igitur**   *tamen* might seem more logical, but cf. Reid on *Fin.* I. 4.

negant   'People say' makes good sense, better I think than Orelli's
negat.

2 **concedere...postulat**   Watt makes this a question. It certainly
represents Pompey's view rather than C.'s, who seems to have meant, even
if he did not write, *concedere illi, ut idem dicit, quod....*

3 **nam quid impudentius?**   In effect these are Pompey's words rather
than C.'s; he is putting Pompey's case (*ut idem dicit*). Yet cf. 141 (VII. 17). 2
praesertim cum impudentissime postulaverit; *Fam.* XVI. 11. 2 *erat adhuc impudens
qui exercitum et provinciam invito senatu teneret*.

tenuisti...praeteriit   C. (and Pompey) may have held that Caesar's
command had already legally expired: cf. 130 (VII. 7). 6 n. (*transierit*). But his
language here is perfectly explicable on Mommsen's view that the legal
terminus was 1 March 49. C. presents the argument in dramatic form and
would naturally use the time framework appropriate to it. In other words
the dialogue may be imagined as taking place at the crucial date when
Caesar could legally be asked to hand over. How else could C. have
managed without spoiling his effect? If he had written 'in a little over two
months' time you will have held...', historians would be the wiser; but
Atticus did not have to deduce the facts from C.'s tenses.

4 **a te ipso sqq.**   Cf. 125 (VII. 3). 4 n. (*illo modo*); 130 (VII. 7). 6 n.
(*ita latum*). C. seems to be thinking at least as much of 59 as of 55.

7 **habe meam...nostram**   With a play on the technical and ordinary
senses of *rationem alicuius habere*; for the latter cf. e.g. *de Orat* II. 17 *vel
dignitatis vel commodi rationem non habet*.

11 **temporibus**   Cf. 374 (XIV. 20). 4 *consilia temporum sunt, quae in horas
commutari vides*.

APPENDIX I

CICERO'S ITINERARY IN 51, ATHENS–TARSUS

The complex problems of Cicero's journey to Cilicia, more especially his movements between his departure from Laodicea on 3 August and his departure from Iconium a month later, were handled, I think once for all, by L. W. Hunter in a masterly article (*Journ. Rom. Stud.* 3 (1913), pp. 73–97). He arrived at the following table:

24 June	Arr. at Athens	16 August	Arr. Philomelium
6 July	Dep. from Athens	20 August	Dep. Philomelium
22 July	Arr. Ephesus	23 August	Arr. Iconium town
26 July	Dep. Ephesus	24 August	Dep. and Arr. Iconium
27 July	Arr. Tralles		camp
28 July	Dep. Tralles	1 September	Dep. Iconium town
31 July	Arr. Laodicea	2 September	Return Iconium town
3 August	Dep. Laodicea	3 September	Dep. Iconium town
5 August	Arr. Apamea		(second time)
9 August	Dep. Apamea	18 September	Arr. Cybistra
10 August	Arr. Synnada	22 September	Dep. Cybistra
14 August	Dep. Synnada	5 October	Arr. Tarsus

Distances between Ephesus and Iconium were reckoned by Hunter (p. 78, n. 2) as follows:

Ephesus to Tralles	32 (Roman) miles
Tralles to Laodicea	81 (Roman) miles
Laodicea to Apamea	70 (Roman) miles
Apamea to Synnada	50 (Roman) miles
Synnada to Philomelium	60 (Roman) miles
Philomelium to Iconium	91 (Roman) miles

I have made brief mention in the notes of the principal points, but for a detailed and consecutive presentation the article itself must be consulted.

APPENDIX II
CALIDIUS, NOT HIRRUS

112 (v. 19). 3   quod scribis libente te repulsam tulisse eum qui cum
(21 September 51) sororis tuae fili patruo certaret, magni amoris signum.
itaque me etiam admonuisti ut gauderem; nam mihi in
mentem non venerat. 'non credo' inquis. ut libet; sed
plane gaudeo, quoniam τὸ νεμεσᾶν interest τοῦ
φθονεῖν.

122 (vi. 8). 3   sed heus tu, num quid moleste fers de illo qui se
(1 October 50) solet anteferre patruo sororis tuae fili? at a quibus victus!

M. Calidius, of senatorial family and Praetor in 57, was one of the first orators of the time. Gabinius and Scaurus in 54 and Milo in 52 were among his clients (Q. Fr. III. 2. 1; Ascon. 20. 17, 34. 17). Caelius (Fam. VIII. 4. 1) mentions his failure as a candidate for the Consulship in 51 and a subsequent prosecution; he himself unsuccessfully prosecuted one of his successful rivals, C. Marcellus (Fam. VIII. 9. 2, 5). In 50 he seems to have tried and failed again. Caesar, whose side he took in 49, made him governor of Cisalpine Gaul, where shortly afterwards he died (Jerome, Chron. Euseb. II.1 37d). Cicero discusses his merits and weaknesses as a speaker at length in Brut. 274 ff.; despite lavish praise the final effect is far from flattering. The once accepted view that Calidius was an 'Atticist', or at any rate a forerunner of that mode, has been successfully discredited by A. E. Douglas (Cl. Q. N.S. 5 (1955), pp. 241 ff.); but, notwithstanding his support for Cicero's recall in 57 (post Red. 22), it is easy to suppose that there was no love lost between the two, and that, as here appears, Cicero resented his rivalry.

That Calidius is meant, and not C. Lucilius Hirrus (cf. 89 (IV. 16). 5 n.), an unsuccessful candidate for the Curule Aedileship this year, was perceived by L. Moll (De temporibus epistularum Tullianarum (Berlin, 1883), pp. 1 ff.), whom T.–P. and Constans followed. Münzer in RE. III. 1354. 7 agreed, but ibid. XIII. 1643. 66 went back to Hirrus; this, like the reading certavit in his citation, may have been no more than inadvertence. More recently W. S. Watt (Mnem. 4th S. 16 (1963), pp. 373 ff.) maintains the earlier view. Three considerations disprove it:

(a) As Watt agrees, both passages clearly refer to the same person, who is described as habitually claiming superiority to Cicero (qui se solet anteferre). The tense of certaret (Watt reads certarit) likewise implies habitual competition. Now, so far as is known, Hirrus competed with Cicero on only one occasion, for the Augurate in 53; and Watt's suggestion (p. 375) that Cicero had this occasion primarily in mind but nevertheless used solet 'by way of a facetious

314

hyperbole' seems to me wholly unconvincing (where would be the joke?). A rival orator on the other hand fits naturally into the picture.

(b) If Hirrus is meant, Cicero's language in the first passage would be gratuitously disingenuous. His letter of congratulation to Caelius (*Fam.* II. 9) on the latter's election as Aedile is a long shout of glee over Hirrus' discomfiture, to which he had obviously been looking forward.

(c) The dates. The wording in 112 (v. 19). 3 (*nam mihi in mentem non venerat*) shows that Cicero had already heard about the *repulsa* before he read Atticus' letter (a point missed by Watt, p. 374), and he certainly knew the result of the consular elections, which as usual took place in July (cf. 111 (v. 18). 3 *amicos consules habemus*); it may have come to him in Atticus' letter of 19 July to which he refers in 111 (v. 18). 1. But the aedilician *comitia* did not take place until August. Writing on 1 August Caelius says that he had been putting off a letter in the hope of being able to report them (*Fam.* VIII. 4. 3). The fact that he did write then shows that he was not expecting them in the next day or two (so Constans, IV, p. 15, n. 3). Caelius' next extant letter (see *ibid.* pp. 15 f.) is *Fam.* VIII. 9 of 2 September, in which he refers to the election as having taken place some time ago. Cicero's congratulatory letter to Caelius, *Fam.* II. 9 (not in reply to *Fam.* VIII. 9, which arrived subsequently or not at all (*Fam.* II. 10. 1)), was probably written between 7 and 13 October (so Constans, *ibid.* p. 14, n. 1), at any rate after Cicero had moved into Cilicia. He excuses himself for writing so belatedly on the ground that he had been cut off from all news: everything took a very long time to reach him because of the distance and the activities of brigands (*latrocinia*). Clearly then Atticus' letter, written no later than 3 August and probably early that day or on the previous evening, did not announce Hirrus' defeat, news of which probably did not reach Cicero until two or three weeks later than his reply.

Add that *at a quibus victus!* in 122 (VI. 8). 3 well suits the successful candidates for the Consulship of 49, C. Marcellus and Lentulus Crus, of whom Cicero entertained a poor opinion (cf. 145 (VII. 21). 1 *nihil in consulibus*; 165 (VIII. 15). 2 *nec me consules movent, qui ipsi pluma aut folio facilius moventur*).

It follows that in 112 (v. 19). 3 *certarat, certarit,* and *certasset* are to be rejected as limiting competition to a single occasion. In 1960 I proposed *certare⟨sole⟩t*, on the ground that the subjunctive *certaret* would imply that the facetious periphrasis *cum sororis tuae fili patruo* was in Atticus' letter, whereas both here and in 122 (VI. 8). 3 it is clearly (*pace* Watt, p. 375) a pseudo-modest evasion of the first person singular on Cicero's part. This remains a possibility; but I now think that Atticus may have written *repulsam tulit is qui tecum certabat* and C. have substituted his own periphrasis, even though the clause is oratio obliqua.

CONCORDANCE

This edition	Vulg.	Vulg.	This edition
94	V. 1	V. 1	94
95	V. 2	V. 2	95
96	V. 3	V. 3	96
97	V. 4	V. 4	97
98	V. 5	V. 5	98
99	V. 6	V. 6	99
100	V. 7	V. 7	100
101	V. 8	V. 8	101
102	V. 9	V. 9	102
103	V. 10	V. 10	103
104	V. 11	V. 11	104
105	V. 12	V. 12	105
106	V. 13	V. 13	106
107	V. 14	V. 14	107
108	V. 15	V. 15	108
109	V. 16	V. 16	109
110	V. 17	V. 17	110
111	V. 18	V. 18	111
112	V. 19	V. 19	112
113	V. 20	V. 20	113
114	V. 21	V. 21	114
115	VI. 1	VI. 1	115
116	VI. 2	VI. 2	116
117	VI. 3	VI. 3	117
118	VI. 4	VI. 4	118
119	VI. 5	VI. 5	119
120	VI. 7	VI. 6	121
121	VI. 6	VI. 7	120
122	VI. 8	VI. 8	122
123	VI. 9	VI. 9	123
124	VII. 1	VII. 1	124
125	VII. 2	VII. 2	125
126	VII. 3	VII. 3	126
127	VII. 4	VII. 4	127
128	VII. 5	VII. 5	128
129	VII. 6	VII. 6	129
130	VII. 7	VII. 7	130
131	VII. 8	VII. 8	131
132	VII. 9	VII. 9	132

GREECE AND THE
BALKANS

Scales

20 40 60 80 100 120 140 160

English miles

20 40 60 80 100 120 140 160

Roman miles

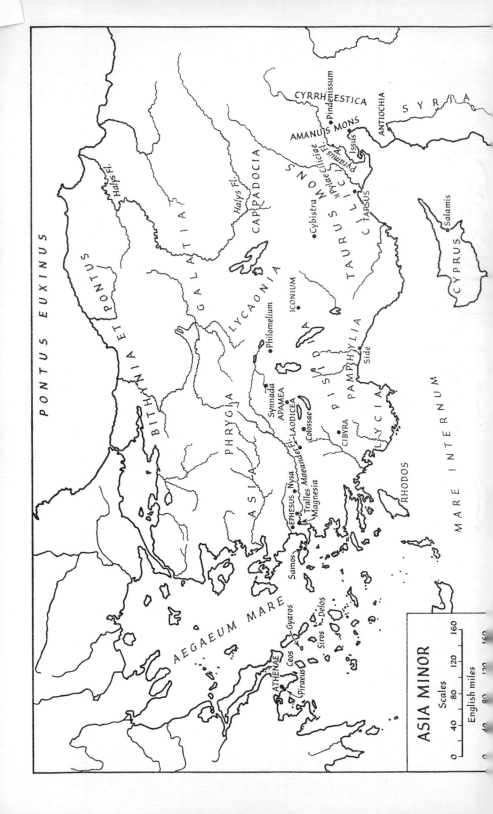

ADDENDA TO THE COMMENTARY

95 (v. 2)

2, 3 στρατηγήματι Mr Sandbach suggests that the paradosis *stragem alto* may represent an otherwise unattested diminutive στρατηγηματίῳ.

96 (v. 3)

3, 1 Lentulum Atticus' friend M. Laenius may well have been a relative of M. Laenius Flaccus, who had a house in Brundisium (*Fam.* XIV. 4. 2; cf. 113 (v. 20). 8 n. (*Laeni*)), so that if my suggestion *L(a)enium* is correct C. may have expected to meet him there.

97 (v. 4)

2, 2 senatus consultum For *populus* connoting the state-treasury cf. also *Fam.* V. 20. 5 *cum populus suum servaret*.

108 (v. 15)

1, 2 nihil clarius Cf. *Fam.* III. 11. 1 *nihil enim fuit clarius; Q. Fr.* III. 2. 7 *nihil hominum sermone foris clarius.* C. rarely uses *carus* ('beloved') except of persons or things easily personified (e.g. *res publica*). For the corruption cf. Hor. *Od.* I. 20. 5.

113 (v. 20)

5, 10 HS c̅x̅x̅ I should have mentioned that the figure of 8,000 sesterces in Hor. *Ep.* II. 2. 5 was a bargain offer.

123 (VI. 9)

2, 2 αὐτίκα γάρ For the paradosis αὐτότατα Mr Diggle suggests ἄγχιστα or αὐτόπτης. I might more safely have obelized here.

INDICES

To Commentary and Appendices only. References to Commentary are by letter (serial number of this edition), paragraph and line of lemma.
Further indices are planned to appear in a separate volume at the end of the series.

I. INDEX NOMINVM

Acastus, 123. 1. 1

Acilius Glabrio, M'. (cos. 67), 115. 4. 5

Actium Corcyrae, 125. 3. 15

Aelius Lamia, L., 101. 3. 7

Aelius Ligus, 97. 2. 6. *See also* Ligurinus Μῶμος

Aemilius Lepidus, M. (triumvir), 125. 25. 16

Aemilius Paulus, L. (cos. 50), 115. 7. 6

Africanus, *see* Cornelius Scipio

Alexio, 125. 3. 16

Alexis, 113. 9. 9, 11

Aliphera, 116. 3. 12

Amianus (?), 115. 13. 5

Andronicus, C., 108. 3. 10

Anneius, M. (legatus Ciceronis), 97. 2. 13

Annius Milo Papianus, T., 94. 2. 1; 101. 2. 4, 3. 7; 103. 4. 4

Annius Saturninus, 94. 2. 1

Antonius, M. (triumvir), 121. 4. 8

Apella (M. Fabii Galli libertus), 112. 1. 3

Appuleius, 104. 6. 3

Araus, 102. 1. 2

Arcanum, 94. 3. 9

Ariobarzanes (III), 111. 4. 5

Aristus (philosophus), 103. 5. 4

Artavasdes (rex), 113. 2. 5

Asinius Dento, 113. 4. 4

Atilius (eques), 94. 2. 3; 112. 1. 9

Attica, *see* Caecilia Attica

Balbus, *see* Cornelius Balbus

Basili bustum, 132. 1. 4

Batonius, 122. 1. 2

Bibulus, *see* Calpurnius Bibulus

Brutus, *see* Junius Brutus

Bursa, *see* Munatius Plancus Bursa

Caecilia Attica, 112. 2. 3; 115. 22. 4

Caecilius Metellus Scipio, Q. (cos. 52), 115. 17. 1; 127. 2. 12

'Caelius' (argentarius commenticius), 126. 11. 6

Caelius Rufus, M. (pr. 48), 101. 3. 7; 115. 21. 2, 8; 126. 6. 3, 11. 6

Caesar, *see* Julius Caesar

Calidius, M., 112. 3. 3, 6; pp. 314 f.

Calpurnius Bibulus, M. (cos. 59), 119. 3. 5, 13; 125. 7. 7

Camillus, C., 101. 3. 7

Caninius Rebilus, C. (cos. suff. 45), 126. 3. 8

Carneades, 125. 4. 4

Cassius Longinus, C. (tyrannicida), 111. 1. 6; 114. 2. 1

Cassius Longinus, Q. (tr. pl. 49), 113. 8. 8; 122. 2. 4; 126. 5. 12

Cato, *see* Porcius Cato

Celer, *see* Pilius Celer

Cestius, C. (?), 106. 1. 14

Chaerippus, 97. 2. 7, 10

Chrysippus. (Ciceronis libertus), 125. 8. 2

Cibyra, 114. 9. 2

Cilicia, 94, introd. note

Claudius Marcellus, M. (cos. 51), 97. 2. 1; 104. 2. 1

Claudius Nero, Ti. (pr. 42), 115. 10. 2; 121. 1. 4

Claudius Pulcher, Ap. (cos. 54), 113. 1. 14; 115. 2. 1, 2; 115. 26. 1; 116. 10. 1; 123. 2. 3, 5. 4

Cluvius, M., 116. 3. 11

Coelius Caldus, C. (q. 50), 116. 10. 4; 117. 1. 14; 121. 3. 1, 2; 121. 4. 12

Cornelius Balbus, L., 126. 11. 8; 127. 2. 12; 130. 6. 6

Cornelius Dolabella, P. (cos. 44), 97. 1. 8; 115. 10. 2; 121. 1. 2, 8; 131. 3. 2

Cornelius Lentulus Crus, L. (cos. 49), 115. 23. 4; 122. 2. 5

Cornelius Lentulus Spinther, P. (cos. 57), 96. 3. 1; 114. 4. 2; 115. 23. 4

Cornelius Scipio Aemilianus Africanus, P. (cos. 147), 115. 17. 1

Cornelius Scipio Nasica Sarapio, P. (cos. 138), 115. 17. 1

Crassipes, see Furius Crassipes

Culleolus, 117. 6. 11

Curius, M'., 125. 3. 10, 13

Curtius Nicias, 126. 10. 5

Deiotari (pater et filius), 110. 3. 1

Democritus (Attici libertus?), 115. 13. 6

Dicaearchia, 116. 3. 9

Dicaearchus, 116. 3. 4; 126. 1. 5

Dionysius, see Pomponius Dionysius

Dolabella, see Cornelius Dolabella

Drusus, see Livius Drusus

Duris (Samius), 115. 18. 7

Duronius, C., 101. 2. 4

Egnatius (Sidicinus), 115. 23. 9

Eleusis, 115. 26. 1

Eupolis (poëta), 115. 18. 4

Fabius, C. (Caesaris legatus), 126. 3. 8

Fabius Gallus, M., 112. 1. 3

Fausta (uxor Milonis), 101. 2. 9

Flumentana porta, 126. 9. 3

Funisulanus, 97. 1. 4

Furius Crassipes, 124. 8. 7

Furnius, C. (tr. pl. 50), 95. 1. 10; 115. 11. 1

Gavius, L., 117. 6. 6

Gavius Caepio, T., 113. 4. 5

Glabrio, see Acilius Glabrio

Helonius, 105. 2. 7

Herodes (Atheniensis), 115. 25. 1

'Herodes' (commenticius), 115. 25. 1

Hirrus, see Lucilius Hirrus

Hirtius, A. (cos. 43), 127. 2. 9

'Hister', 104. 6. 6

Hortensius Hortalus, Q. (cos. 69), 95. 2. 5; 105. 2. 1; 115. 8. 15; 117. 9. 1, 3, 7; 121, introd. note; 125. 7. 1

Hortensius Hortalus, Q. (superioris filius), 117. 9. 1, 3; 125. 7. 1; 126. 9 .1

Iconium, 113. 1. 14

Julius Caesar, C., 94. 2. 4; 115. 25. 1, 4; 123. 5. 5; 124. 3. 1, 4. 3, 8; 124. 7. 2, 9. 9; 126. 3. 6, 7, 8; 127. 3. 2; 129. 2. 3; 130. 5. 11; 131. 4. 10

Julius Caesar Strabo, C. (aed. cur. 90), 114, 13. 9

Junia (Lepidi uxor), 115. 25. 16

Junius Brutus, M. (Q. Servilius Caepio Brutus), 114. 10. 3; 115. 2. 2, 3. 2, 5. 1, 25. 16; 116. 7. 1

Junius Brutus Albinus, D., see Postumius

Labienus, T. (tr. pl. 63), 130. 6. 6

Laenius, M., 96. 3. 1; 113. 8. 4

Lamia, see Aelius Lamia

Lartidius, 124. 9. 2

Lavernium, 131. 4. 2

†Leius, 113. 8. 7

Lentulus, see Cornelius Lentulus

Lepidus, *see* Aemilius Lepidus
Lepreon, 116. 3. 12
Lepta, Q. (Paconius ?), 110. 2. 5
Licinius Crassus Mucianus, P. (cos. 131), 96. 2. 3
Ligurinus Μῶμος, 113. 6. 3
Ligus, *see* Aelius Ligus
Livia, 131. 3. 1
Livius Drusus, M. (cos. 112), 125. 8. 8
Lucceius, L. (M.f.), 114. 13. 7
Lucilius, Sex., 113. 4. 5
Lucilius Hirrus, C., 124. 8. 2, 3; pp. 314 f.
'Luscenius', 128. 3. 1

Magnus (Pompeius), 115. 25. 13
Mamurra, 130. 6. 7
Manlius Torquatus, A. (pr. 70), 94. 5. 5; 114. 10. 9
Marcellus, *see* Claudius Marcellus
Maso, *see* Papirius Maso
Matinius, P., 114. 10. 3
Memmiana epistula, 115. 10. 4
Menniana praedia, 94. 2. 3
Mescinius Rufus, L. (q. 51), 104. 4. 3; 117. 1. 14
Messalla, *see* Valerius Messalla
Metellus, *see* Caecilius Metellus
Milo, *see* Annius Milo
Minucius Thermus, Q., 106. 2. 1
Moeragenes, 108. 3. 3
Mucius Scaevola, Q. (Augur; cos. 117), 115. 4. 5
Mucius Scaevola, Q. (Pontifex; cos. 95), 110. 5. 6
Munatius Plancus Bursa, T. (tr. pl. 52), 115. 10. 9

Nemus, 115. 25. 4
Nero, *see* Claudius Nero
Nicanor, 96. 3. 2
Nicias, *see* Curtius Nicias
Nonius (Struma ?), M., 115. 13. 2
Nonius Sufenas, M., 115. 13. 2
Numerianum raudusculum, 125. 7. 1

Octavius, M. (aed. cur. 50), 114. 5. 2
Onchesmites (ventus), 125. 1. 2
Orodes (rex), 111. 1. 5

Pacorus, 111. 1. 5
Pammenes, 113. 10. 4; 116. 10. 5
Pamphilus, 125. 2. 4
Papirius (?) Maso, 97. 2. 6
Patro(n) (Epicureus), 104. 6. 4, 5; 125. 4. 5
Paulus, *see* Aemilius Paulus
Phemius, 113. 9. 11
Philippus (manceps ?), 105. 3. 6; 106. 3. 10
Philogenes, 106. 2. 3, 5; 128. 3. 1; 130. 2. 1
Philotimus (Terentiae libertus), 101. 2. 4; 115. 19. 1; 118. 3. 4; 123. 2. 2
Philoxenus (Q. Ciceronis libertus?), 125. 5. 2
Pilia, 104. 7. 3
Pilius Celer, Q., 117. 10. 1
Pinarius (incertum quis), 115. 23. 10
Pindenissum, 113, introd. note
Piraeus, 126. 10. 1
Plaetorianum incendium, 113. 8. 6
Plotius, A. (pr. 51), 108. 1. 6
Pompeius Magnus, Cn., 99. 1. 3; 100. 8; 108. 1. 7; 124. 3. 1, 4. 3; 131. 3. 7
Pompeius Vindillus, 125. 25. 11
Pomponius Dionysius, M., 131. 1. 1
'Pomptina summa', 128. 3. 7
Pomptinus, C. (pr. 63), 117. 1. 14; 130. 3. 1
Pontidiae filius (?), 97. 1. 8; 114. 14. 1; 115. 10. 2
Pontius, L., 95. 1. 2
Porcius Cato (Uticensis), M., 115. 13. 4; 124. 7. 5; 125. 7. 2, 7; 126. 5. 19
Postumia, 114. 9. 13
Postumius (D. Junius Brutus Albinus ?), 114. 9. 13
Preciana hereditas, 123. 2. 4

Puteolanum raudusculum, 122. 5. 1

Quinctius, L., 132. 1. 3

Rufio, *see* Sempronius Rufus

Sallustius (proquaestor 50), 119. 3. 6, 13
Sarapio, *see* Cornelius Scipio
Saufeius, Ap., 115. 10. 6
Saufeius, L., 115. 10. 6; 125. 4. 5
Scaevola, *see* Mucius Scaevola
Scaptius, M., 114. 10. 3 *et al.*; 116. 9. 1
Scaptius, M. ('qui in Cappadocia fuit'), 114. 10. 3; 115. 4. 7
Scrofa, *see* Tremellius Scrofa
Seius, M., 106. 2. 3. Cf. 113. 8. 7
Sempronius (Asellio?) Rufus, C., 95. 2. 2
Servilia (Bruti mater), 97. 1. 12
Servilius, M., 117. 10. 1
Servilius Vatia Isauricus, P. (cos. 78), 115. 16. 4
Sicinius, 97. 3. 1
Silius, P., 115. 13. 1; 124. 8. 2
Statius (Q. Ciceronis libertus), 117. 8. 1
Statius, Sex., 115. 6. 17
Sulpicius Rufus, Ser. (cos. 51), 126. 3. 12
Sulpicius Rufus, Ser. (superioris filius), 97. 1. 8, 13; 114. 14. 1; 115. 10. 2
Sybota, 102. 1. 2
Synnada (Synnas), 109. 2. 3; 114. 9. 3

Tarquitius, L., 122. 4. 3
Tartessius (*sc.* L. Cornelius Balbus), 126. 11. 8
Tenea, 116. 3. 12
Terentius, 115. 13. 6
†Thallumetus, 105. 2. 6

Theophanes, 130. 6. 6
Thermus, *see* Minucius Thermus
Thyamis (flumen), 125. 3. 17
Tiberius, *see* Volusius
Timotheus, 119. 2. 6
Tiro, *see* Tullius Tiro
Titinius, Q., 114. 5. 14
Torquatus, *see* Manlius Torquatus
Trebulanum, 95. 1. 2
Tremellius Scrafa, Cn., 97. 2. 11; 115. 13. 2; 124. 8. 2
Tritia, 116. 3. 12
Tullia, 97. 1. 7, 8; 115. 10. 2; 121. 1. 2; 122. 1. 5
Tullius, L. (legatus Ciceronis), 97. 2. 13
Tullius, M. (scriba), 97. 1. 5
Tullius Cicero, Q. (oratoris frater), 104. 7. 3; 114. 9. 10; 115. 20. 4; 123. 3. 4; 124. 6. 9; 126. 8. 3
Tullius Cicero, Q. (superioris filius), 113. 9. 2
Tullius Tiro, M., 113. 9. 11
Turranius, D. (?), 123. 2. 1

Valerius, P., 114. 14. 5
Valerius Messalla Rufus, M. (cos. 53), 105. 2. 1; 112. 1. 9
Vedius Pollio, P., 115. 25. 5
Vennonius, C., 115. 25. 13
Vestorius, C., 116. 3. 11
Vindillus, *see* Pompeius Vindillus
Volusius, Cn., 104. 4. 2
Volusius, Q., 114. 6. 2
Volusius (?), Ti., 114. 6. 2
Vulcatius Tullus, L. (cos. 66), 126. 3. 12

Xeno (Apollonidensis), 106. 2. 3
Xeno (Atheniensis), 103. 5. 5

Zaleucus, 115. 8. 8
Zoster, 105. 1. 3

INDICES

II. INDEX VERBORVM

A. *Latinorum*

ad senatum, 97. 2. 10. ad spem, 127. 2. 7
adcredere, 116. 3. 8
adde si quid vis, 125. 3. 6
adsentio(r), 126. 3. 4
adurere, 113. 8. 7
aequi boni facere, 130. 4. 3
agere, 97. 3. 8. quod egerit, 121. 4. 6
alius, 114. 12. 25
amavi, 123. 1. 11
ambulare, 124. 1. 4
aperire, 94. 2. 4; 126. 12. 3
atque (= atque adeo), 118. 3. 9
auctor, 126. 10. 9
auctoritas, 104. 3. 5
auferre, 97. 4. 3
autem, 116. 1. 7

barones (*sc.* Epicurei), 104. 6. 4
bene eveniat!, 125. 4. 4

caesa (inter caesa et porrecta), 111. 1. 12
campus, 108. 1. 4
canis, 117. 6. 3
captio, 97. 4. 2
casus, 115. 9. 4
causa, 126. 5. 13
circumscribere, 132. 2. 17
civi (*abl.*), 126. 4. 7
cogere, 114. 3. 9
cogitare, 121. 2. 3
commendare, 106. 2. 3
cottidie (= in dies singulos), 100. 1
crede mihi, 103. 1. 3
currens, 102. 1. 9

dein, 113. 1. 13
densae dexterae, 124. 4. 6
diecula, 114. 13. 10
dies tuus, 131. 2. 1

digitum nusquam, 126. 11. 3
dimittere, 122. 2. 3

efficere, 115. 3. 14
elegantia, 116. 8. 5
enim, 115. 11. 5; 130. 6. 3
Ephesius praetor, 106. 1. 8
esse ad, 115. 14. 11. esse in, 114. 7. 6
et (*redundant between relative clauses*), 117. 5. 16
etiam atque etiam vale, 113. 9. 13
exceptio, 97. 3. 2; 115. 15. 1
exhibere, 111. 4. 5
expedire, 124. 9. 10

faenus et impendium, 115. 4. 6
ferre, 121. 4. 3
forma, 117. 4. 6
fortunae (per fortunas!), 104. 1. 4
frugi, 127. 1. 5

gravis, 105. 2. 7; 113. 1. 16
grex, 115. 10. 2

hactenus (sed h-), 106. 1. 13, 5. 7
haerere (in visceribus) 115. 8. 2
honos, 114. 3. 2
horti, 130. 6. 7

iam (iam nosti), 105. 1. 6. si iam, 97. 1. 13. iam si, 117. 2. 2
impendium, *see* faenus
incendium, 113. 8. 6
ipse, 98. 2. 2; 115. 8. 6, 26. 1; 124. 7. 5
is (eius) 119. 3. 6.
itaque (= et ita) 115. 15. 17; 124. 2. 17
iubere (iussi valere), 95. 2. 9

liberalitas, 115. 2. 1
littera, 125. 3. 4
locus, 110. 5. 4
loreola, 113. 4. 2

maiora (*sc.* vero), 101. 3. 2
malum!, *see* quid, malum?
malus, 101. 2. 8
merus, 122. 2. 1
miratio, 97. 1. 11
movere, 120. 1. 6
multiplex, 116. 2. 12
munus, 102. 1. 2

-ne, 104. 1. 1
nihil, 128. 3. 4
nobilis, 113. 4. 4
nomen (bonum), 114. 12. 27
non modo . . . ne . . . quidem, 103.
    4. 5

pagina, 97. 4. 4
pedem porta efferre, 122. 5. 4
perducere, 114. 12. 15
persolvere, 126. 10. 15
Piraeea (*acc.*), 123. 1. 1
plane scio, 103. 3. 5
pluris esse, 126. 5. 12
populus, 97. 2. 2
posse (*impersonal*), 124. 9. 7
postdcus, 115. 17. 4
praestare, 102. 1. 12; 126. 7. 5
praetor (= στρατηγός), 104. 6. 9
primum (*adv.*), 130. 4. 10
probare, 114. 4. 10
proponere, 115. 23. 2
puer, 121. 3. 1
purus (toga pura), 113. 9. 2; 131. 5. 3
putato, 130. 1. 4

quaestor (= proquaestor), 119. 3. 6
quasi, 94. 4. 1; 131. 3. 5
quid (deest quid scribam), 128. 4. 6.
    Cf. 129. 1. 2. quid, malum?
    113. 1. 3. quid si hoc melius? 126.
    2. 1
quidem, 111. 4. 8. qui quidem,
    125. 3. 2
quisque (tricesimo quoque die),
    115. 3. 13

radices, 121. 4. 7
requirere, 115. 8. 7
reum facere, 126. 12. 4

Salaminorum, 114. 10. 2
salvere (ab aliquo), 116. 10. 12
sane scio, 103. 3. 5
II (= pridie) 122, 1. 3
sed (= et quidem), 106. 3. 8
si (= si quidem), 115. 16. 7; 132. 3. 3
splendidus, 113. 4. 5
spurce, 125. 4. 4
stare, 111. 2. 2; 117. 4. 4
statio, 123. 5. 6
sumere, 94. 3. 8

tam (= tanto opere), 116. 3. 5
tamen, 97. 2. 3; 110. 2. 1; 121. 3. 9;
    126. 10. 4
tanti (nihil est tanti), 101. 3. 2
tener, 116. 8. 10
terror armorum, 131. 5. 3
tibicen (cum suo tibicine), 115. 23. 3
tollere, 97. 2. 8
tottis, 103. 1. 3
tradere, 106. 2. 3
triduum, 100. 6; 109. 2. 3
tueri, 124. 7. 2
tum, 113. 10. 6

umeri, 116. 5. 4
uti, 130. 4. 9

valens, 126. 5. 11
vectigal, 115. 3. 17
vendere, 125. 1. 3
vestigia, 103. 1. 4
vultus, 94. 3. 14; 103. 3. 6

B. Graecorum

ἀκοινονοήτως, 115. 7. 9
ἄκρα Γυρέων, 105. 1. 8
†ανεзια, 104. 5. 10
ἄτυφος, 123. 2. 7
αὐτόχθων, 125. 3. 13

INDICES

ἀφαίρεσις, 115. 2. 7

βαθύτης, 115. 2. 1

γράμματα, 126. 10. 15

δυσεκλάλητος, 103. 3. 10

ἐγκέλευσμα, 115. 8. 1
ἐνδόμυχον, 97. 1. 7
ἐξακανθίζειν, 121. 1. 8
ἐπέχειν, 121. 3. 4
ἐπικεφάλιον, 109. 2. 4
ἔρδοι τις, 103. 3. 3

ἱστορικώτατος, 116. 3. 7

κενὰ τοῦ πολέμου, τά, 113. 3. 11
κέρας, 113. 9. 11

λῆψις/διάλειψις, 130. 3. 5

μετέωρος, 104. 6. 2
μηδὲν αὐτοῖς, 115. 16. 10

Μῶμος, 113. 6. 3

νεμεσᾶν, τό, 112. 3. 6

οἷαπερ ἡ δέσποινα, 104. 5. 5
οἰκονομία, 115. 1. 3

παλιγγενεσία, 121. 4. 14
παραδιδόναι, 119. 2. 2
παράπηγμα ἐνιαύσιον, 107. 1. 6
παριστορεῖν, 115. 25. 18
πρόσνευσις, 97. 2. 8
πύρους εἰς δῆμον, 121. 2. 1

τὰ μὲν διδόμενα, 119. 2. 13
τέθριππα, 114. 7. 12
τεκμηριώδης, 127. 2. 13

ὑπομνηματισμός, 104. 6. 8

φυρατής, 123. 2. 2

ὠνή, 109. 2. 5

III. INDEX RERVM

ablative, 107. 2. 3; III. 1. 5;
  113. 1. 10, 3. 12; 116. 2. 12
Academiae πρόπυλον, 121. 2. 3
actuariae, 102. 1. 6
amphibolia, 115. 25. 16; 116. 3. 4;
  126. 5. 12, 13; 132. 4. 7. Cf.
  126. 10. 15
aphracta, 104. 4. 3; 122. 4. 5
aposiopesis, 97. 1. 8, 2. 10
Archilochus, 117. 1. 7
asyndeton, 118. 1. 4
attraction (of mood), 97. 2. 13. (of
  case) 106. 3. 5; 124. 9. 4
auctoritas (senatus), 95. 3. 8

boni ('ut putantur'), 128. 4. 1

captives, sale of, 113. 4. 8

Cicero (Div. II. 49) 97. 1. 11.
  de Republica, 115. 8. 7, 15; 115. 17.
  1; 116. 3. 2, 16; 121. 2. 2; 126. 2. 9
clavus anni, 107. 1. 6
cohors praetoria, 125. 3. 14
corruptions (by assimilation), 124. 1.
  11; 126. 8. 3. (by dittography)
  126. 12. 2; (by words interpolated)
  124. 2. 13; 126. 5. 19. Cf. 115. 7.
  5. (by confusion of letters, etc.)
  106. 3. 5 (quam/cum); 122. 2. 1
  (merus/mirus); 124. 8. 4 (tantum/
  tamen); 125. 6. 2 (-e/-a)
Cyprus (privileges of), 114. 6. 5

dative, 94. 1. 1 (with testis)
Dicaearchus, Γῆς Περίοδος, 116. 3. 4.
  εἰς Τροφωνίου κατάβασις ibid.

dioecesis, 108. 3. 12

edictum (*Ciceronis provinciale*), 115. 15. 8, 9
ellipse (of noun), 116. 5. 7 (of pronoun), 124. 1. 10. (of verb) 94. 3. 8; 120. 2. 3; 126. 11. 3
Epicurei, 104. 6. 4. Cf. 125. 4. 2

fana (*praetorum in provinciis*), 114. 7. 12
fevers (quartan), 125. 2. 4
future, 102. 1. 12

gender, 98. 2. 6 (sum of money); 107. 1. 6 (*dies*)
genitive, 111. 1. 7 (appositive); 113. 2. 6 (*Cybistra Cappadociae*); 114. 7. 4. (variant forms of), 114. 2. 7

health (ancient view of), 128. 1. 5, 5. 7
Hercules Πολυκλέους, 115. 17. 5
hyperbaton, 100. 9; 104. 6. 10

imperator (title), 113. 3. 6
imperfect (indicative), 113. 1. 10; 121. 4. 4; 123. 3. 3
infinitive (with acc. after *videlicet*), 104. 7. 5. (with *illud*, etc.) 104. 3. 4
inscriptiones falsae (*statuarum*), 115. 26. 5
iudices peregrini, 115. 15. 17
iusiurandum (*Ciceronis consulis*) 115. 22. 7

jokes (ingredient of letters), 98. 1. 3

largitio in civis, 121. 2. 2
legiones (*Caesaris*), 130. 6. 9
lex Gabinia, 114. 12. 4
lex Iulia *de provinciis*, 103. 2. 3
lex Livia 104. 2. 1
lex Pompeia *de iure magistratuum*, 124. 4. 3

lex Pompeia Licinia, 126. 4. 5
lex viaria (Curionis), 115. 25. 8
Liberalia, 115. 12. 3

magistri bonorum, 115. 15. 14
Minerva *custos urbis*, 126. 3. 10
mysteria (*Romana*), 114. 14. 8

νεώτεροι, οἱ, 125. 1. 3

praefecti, 97. 3. 4; 104. 6. 1, 2. *praefectus fabrum*, 114. 6. 3
present (indicative), 116. 9. 7 (cf. 115. 7. 17)
provinciales aditus, 116. 5. 10
publicani, 116. 5. 8; 130. 5. 11

Quaestors (appointment *sine sorte*), 121. 4. 7

Rechtsfrage, 130. 6. 1; 132. 4. 3
Rhosica vasa, 115. 13. 9

satisdatio secundum mancipium, 94. 2. 3
scribae quaestorii, 97. 1. 5
Senate, 97. 2. 2 (grants to governors); 97. 2. 10 ('*consule!*' *aut* '*numera!*'); 111. 2. 10 (official dispatches); 124. 7. 7 (*scribendo adesse*). See *auctoritas*
slaves (manumission), 125. 8. 9, 10
statua Africani, 115. 17. 1
subjunctive (concessive in relative clause), 102. 1. 5. (after *etsi*), 104. 2. 1. (jussive, 2nd person), 105. 3. 3
sumptus annuus (*proconsulis*), 124. 6. 3
supplicatio, 125. 7. 7

Thucydides (III. 30. 4), 113. 3. 11
time, inclusive reckoning of, 101. 1. 3; 106. 1. 1; 109. 2. 3; 113. 2. 6, 3. 6; 115. 3. 13, 26. 7
Transpadani, 95. 3. 8; 104. 2. 1; 130. 6. 10

travel, speed of, 95. 1. 3; 100. 6; 112. 1. 3

Tribunes (veto), 114. 3. 6

vectigal aedilicium, 115. 21. 3

verses (accidental), 109. 2. 1. Cf.

125. 1. 3. (supposed citations), 117. 1. 14; 124. 4. 6. Cf. 124. 5. 3

Wills, witnessing of, 125. 3. 14, 15

Zeugma, 106. 3. 9